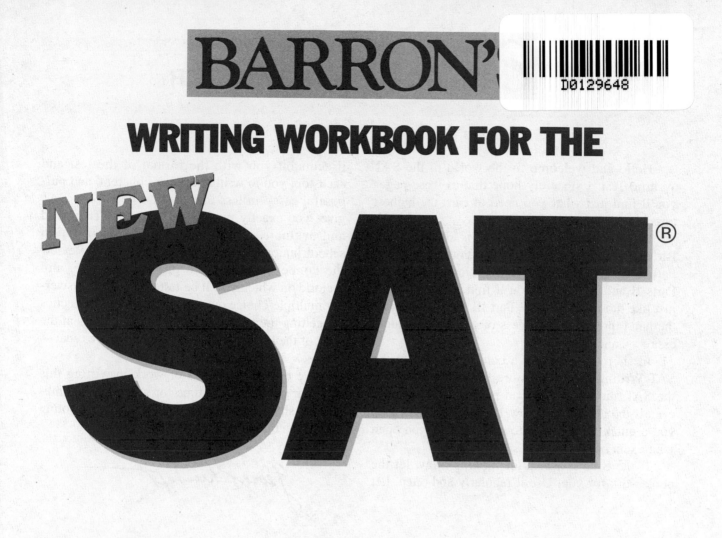

BARRON'S
WRITING WORKBOOK FOR THE
NEW SAT®

George Ehrenhaft, B.A., M.A., Ed.D.
Former Chairman of the English Department
Mamaroneck High School, Mamaroneck, NY

BARRON'S

GREETINGS FROM THE AUTHOR

Hello and welcome to the world of the SAT Writing Test. I sincerely hope that in these pages you'll find just what you need to earn the highest possible score on the exam.

If you're unsure what the test is all about, read Part I. If you need to brush up on grammar, turn to Part V. To fine-tune your test taking skills, go to Parts II and VI, where you'll find practice exams just like those on the SAT. Part III will take you by the hand through the process of writing a winning essay . . . and so on.

In short, my book is a complete guide to the SAT Writing Test. The more time you have until the SAT, the better you can prepare yourself. But even if the test is tomorrow, the book can still give you a quick fix on what to expect when you open your exam booklet.

If the SAT is weeks or months away, let the book work for you. Use it regularly and often. Let it acquaint you with the format of the test and accustom you to writing a clear, coherent, and purposeful essay in less than half an hour. (The SAT gives you exactly twenty-five minutes.) Then read and evaluate actual essays composed by high school juniors and seniors on SAT topics. Review the concepts of English grammar, usage, and rhetoric on which you'll be tested. Practice answering multiple-choice questions, using surefire tactics for getting them right. Take the practice tests at the back of the book, and watch your test scores soar—I hope.

I've done a mountain of work in writing this book for you. Now it's time for you to start climbing. So, shake a leg and best of luck! I'll be rooting for you on the sidelines.

George Ehrenhaft

© Copyright 2006 by Barron's Educational Series, Inc.

All inquiries should be addressed to:
Barron's Educational Series, Inc.
250 Wireless Boulevard
Hauppauge, New York 11788
http://www.barronseduc.com

Library of Congress Catalog Card No. 2005045389

ISBN 13: 978-0-7641-3221-6
ISBN 10: 0-7641-3221-0

Library of Congress Cataloging-in-Publication Data
Ehrenhaft, George.
    Writing workbook for the new SAT / George Ehrenhaft.
        p. cm.
    At head of title: Barron's.
    Includes index.
    ISBN 13: 978-0-7641-3221-6
    ISBN 10: 0-7641-3221-0
    1. Scholastic Assessment Test—Study guides. 2. English language—Composition and exercises—Examinations—Study guides. 3. Report writing—Examinations—Study guides. I. Title: Barron's writing workbook for the new SAT. II. Title.

LB2353.57.E37   2006
378.1′662—dc22   2005045389

PRINTED IN THE UNITED STATES OF AMERICA
9 8 7 6 5 4 3

CONTENTS

PART

THE BASICS: GETTING ACQUAINTED WITH THE WRITING TEST

Overview of the Writing Test
The Essay
Multiple-Choice Questions

From start to finish, the SAT lasts three hours and forty-five minutes. One hour is devoted to questions on writing. During the SAT's first twenty-five minutes, called Section 1, you will write an essay in response to a given topic. Later in the exam you'll find a second twenty-five minute section consisting of three types of multiple-choice questions that ask you to (1) correct poorly written sentences, (2) find grammar and usage errors in a set of sentences, and (3) revise an early draft of a given essay. Still later, you'll be given a third section that lasts ten minutes and contains several additional questions on correcting poorly written sentences. Together, the essay question and two sections of multiple-choice questions comprise the SAT Writing Test.

OVERVIEW OF THE WRITING TEST

Total Time	Content	Item Types	Score
60 minutes	Writing ability, grammar, usage, and word choice	An essay (25 minutes) and two multiple-choice sections (25 minutes and 10 minutes)	200–800

PURPOSE OF THE WRITING TEST

Asking you to write a short essay is a relatively accurate way for colleges to assess your potential for success in college courses that require writing. Your performance on the test also adds an important dimension to your college admissions profile. The essay tells admissions officials how well you write, especially how well you write under the pressure of time. Moreover, it provides colleges with useful information about

- **The depth of your thinking.** You reveal the depth of your thinking by responding perceptively to the topic, or question. Your response also shows whether you can devise a thesis, or main idea, and develop it insightfully.
- **Your ability to organize ideas.** You show your ability to organize ideas by arranging material according to a logical, sensible plan.
- **The way you express yourself.** You reveal your ability to express yourself by accurately and succinctly conveying your thoughts to the reader.

- **Your mastery of standard written English.** You demonstrate your use of standard written English by writing an essay relatively free of errors in grammar and usage

The multiple-choice questions deal with everyday problems in grammar, usage, style, word choice, and other basic elements of writing. Instead of asking you about obscure matters of grammar, the questions will ask you to identify common sentence errors and to improve sentences and paragraphs.

Colleges use the results of the SAT Writing Test as a criterion for admission. Some also use scores to determine academic placement. A high score may entitle you to waive a freshman composition course. A score that suggests deficiencies may place you in a remedial writing program to be completed either before classes begin or during the first semester. To understand just how your score will affect you, consult the literature of the colleges to which you are applying. Or, here's another idea: Bring up the use of SAT scores during your interview with a college admissions official.

HOW THE TEST IS SCORED

Your essay will be read by two experienced evaluators, most likely high school or college teachers trained to judge the overall quality and effectiveness of students' essays. Neither reader will know the grade that the other reader has given your essay. Nor will they know your name or the name of your school. Each reader will assign your essay a grade on a scale of 1 (low) to 6 (high). Your essay's subscore will be recorded as the sum of the two scores (2 to 12).

On the multiple-choice questions, you'll earn a point for each correct answer and lose a quarter of a point (0.25) for each wrong answer. An item left blank will neither add to nor take away from your score. A machine will score your responses to forty-nine questions and will report a subscore on a scale of 20 to 80.

Before scores are sent out, the College Board will convert the two subscores to the SAT scale of 200–800. (See page 39 for how this is done.) Your total for the Writing Test, along with your scores in math and critical reading, will be reported to you, to your guidance counselor, and to the admissions offices of the colleges you designate.

TO GUESS OR NOT TO GUESS

Subtracting credit for wrong answers on multiple-choice questions is meant to discourage blind guessing. If you haven't a clue about how to answer a question, leave it blank. If you can confidently eliminate one of the five choices, it probably pays to guess. The odds are one in four that you'll be right. These are not terrific odds, but suppose that on four questions you eliminate one wrong choice and you guess four times. If you guess right just once, you'll earn a point and lose three-quarters of a point, a net gain of one quarter. If you leave all four blank, you will gain nothing. Yes, it's a gamble because you could make four incorrect guesses, but the chances of losing every time are only one in four. And you could get lucky and hit two, three, or even four correct answers.

When a question gives you trouble, and you can't decide among, say, three choices, common wisdom says that you should go with your first impulse. Testing experts and psychologists agree that there's a better than average chance of success if you trust your intuition. However, there are no guarantees, and because the mind works in so many strange ways, relying on your initial choice may not always work for you.

Another piece of folk wisdom about guessing is that if one answer is longer than the others, that may be your best choice. That's not information you should depend on. In fact, since economy of expression is a virtue in writing, a shorter choice may more often be the best answer. The truth of the matter is that you can't depend on tricks or gimmicks on the SAT.

HOW TO PREPARE

By reading these words you've already begun preparing for the exam. Actually, you began years ago when you first wrote words on paper and a string of school teachers began hammering the basics of English grammar into your head.

But that was then. Now it's time to brush up on your grammar, become acquainted with the precise format of the test, and develop a number of useful tactics for writing the essay and answering the multiple-choice questions.

Once you have finished reading these introductory pages, take the diagnostic test in Part II. Afterwards, check your answers and identify the questions you missed. By doing so, you can tell not only how much studying you need to do but what material to study. If, say, you couldn't finish writing the essay in the allotted twenty-five minutes, you'd do well to read the pages of Part III that discuss planning and composing an essay. Or, if you missed a couple of multiple-choice questions related to pronoun choice or parallel structure, study the relevant pages in Part V, and do the practice exercises.

THE ESSAY

Writing an essay by hand in less than half an hour is a challenge. Even professional journalists, accustomed to working under the pressure of deadlines, would be hard-pressed to produce a good essay in twenty-five minutes. But take heart! The essay score is but one piece of data on your college application, and no one taking the SAT will have a nanosecond more than you to complete the assignment. If you've been a reasonably proficient essay writer in the past, be confident that you'll perform equally well on the SAT. In fact, you may do even better than usual because you're likely to be pumped up to do your best work.

When writing the SAT essay, you must condense into a few minutes all the steps that other writers, enjoying the luxury of time, might stretch into hours or even into days. Chances are you've done it before. An essay test in social studies, for example, may have required you to fill up a blank page quickly with all you knew about the Reign of Terror or causes of the Civil War. The numerous in-class essays you've produced over the years have no doubt trained you for the kind of instant essay asked of you on the SAT. In your classes, of course, success was based partly on how closely your ideas resembled those that the teacher had in mind. That's not true on the SAT. You can't cram for this essay the way you can for a test in physics or Spanish. Because you don't know the topic, you must quickly process your thoughts and get them onto paper. Ordinarily, an essay writer takes a long time to think about ideas and write them down. The verb *essay*, in fact, means to assess thoughtfully—not on the SAT, however. The time limit forces an almost instant response and limits leisurely reflection. If you manage to come up with one or more profound insights, more power to you, but keep in mind that the objective of an SAT essay is more mundane—to show colleges that you can organize your thoughts and express them clearly, interestingly, and correctly.

The answer you write in response to the question is not predetermined. What you need to know is already lodged inside you. The task you face on test day is to arrange your ideas and put them into readable form on paper. It is a measure of what you can do instead of what you know.

More precisely, the essay will measure your skill in elaborating a point of view on an issue. You must first think critically about the issue presented in the essay assignment, forming your own individual perspective on the topic. Then you must develop that point of view, supporting your ideas with appropriate evidence. An essay completed in twenty-five minutes is bound to be shorter than most essays required in high school or college courses. It won't be as polished as a piece written over a period of hours or days. But it represents what you can do during the initial phase of the writing process, and twenty-five minutes should give you enough time to prove that you have what it takes to write a respectable first draft.

The topic, called the *prompt*, consists of a quotation or a short passage followed by a question asking your opinion about the content of the quote or passage. Although no one can predict the subject of the prompt, you can be sure that the directions for writing the essay will always say something like:

Think carefully about the issue presented in the following excerpt and the assignment below:

The principle is this: each failure leads us closer to deeper knowledge, to greater creativity in understanding old data, to new lines of inquiry. Thomas Edison experienced 10,000 failures before he succeeded in perfecting the light bulb. When a friend of his remarked that 10,000 failures was a lot, Edison replied, "I didn't fail 10,000 times, I successfully eliminated 10,000 materials and combinations that didn't work."

Adapted from Myles Brand,
"Taking the Measure of Your Success"

Assignment: What is your view on the idea that it takes failure to achieve success? Plan and write an essay in which you develop your point of view on this issue. Support your position with reasoning and examples taken from your reading, studies, experience, or observations.

Adapted from

www.collegeboard.com/newsat/hs/writing/essay.html

Based on these instructions—read them two or three times, if necessary—you must write an essay explaining your position on the statement that "it takes failure to achieve success." An essay agreeing with the statement would argue that success, however you define it, comes about only as a result of failure and that success without failure does not qualify as true success. On the other hand, an essay that takes the opposite point of view would make the point that failure and success are unrelated. A third possibility, of course, is that success sometimes depends on failure and at other times doesn't.

What you say in the essay is completely up to you. There is no wrong or right answer. You won't be penalized for an unusual or unpopular point of view unless it is based on a faulty premise or pure fantasy. Once you've decided on your perspective, **present your case**. Concentrate on expressing your thoughts coherently and correctly. All parts of an essay should work together to make a single point. If the evidence you provide wanders from the main idea or raises additional issues that you don't have time to discuss, the effect of the essay will be diluted. Above all, you don't want readers to reach the end scratching their heads over the point of the essay.

Once you have decided on your position on the issue, **develop your thoughts** clearly and effectively. Developing your thoughts means nothing more than backing up your opinion with illustrative material, drawn from virtually any source you wish: from your **reading** inside or outside of school, from your **courses**, from **personal experience**, or from **observation**. In short, you may use facts, statistics, common sense, historical background—anything, really, to demonstrate that your opinion is grounded on something more solid than a feeling or a personal preference. Remember, the kind of writing expected on the SAT is rational discourse, not emotional blabbering.

The assignment urges you to **plan your essay** before you begin to write. For some people, that means using an outline; for others, just jotting a few notes on a piece of paper. Whether you prefer to write lists of ideas or just think about an approach before committing words to paper, on the SAT you must write an **essay**—not a play, not a poem, not a short story, not dialogue, not a fable, just an essay. Your essay need not follow a prescribed format, but you'll probably get the best results with a straightforward, no-nonsense approach consisting of some sort of introduction, a body of material that supports your main idea, and an appropriate conclusion. Variations are possible, but twenty-five minutes doesn't give you much time to be inventive.

The directions for writing the essay don't tell you how long it should be. That's because the number of words is up to you. Just remember that quantity counts less than quality. A single paragraph may not give you the chance to develop your ideas completely. Two paragraphs might do, but three or more suggest that you have the capacity to probe pretty deeply into the subject. Plan to write at least two or three paragraphs. Three, in fact, may be preferable to two, although that's a generalization that doesn't apply to every essay. (We'll talk more about that in Part III.) In the end, the number of paragraphs is less important than the substance of each paragraph. Even one paragraph can demonstrate that you are a first-rate writer.

A plain, natural writing style is probably best. Think of your readers as everyday folks who appreciate straight, plain, everyday language. Readers will be turned off by formal, pompous, or overblown prose. Elegant words have their place, of course, but use them sparingly to avoid sounding pretentious or foolish.

As SAT day draws near, review these suggestions for writing an essay. Knowing what to do ahead of time will add to your peace of mind and enable you to start work immediately when the proctor says, "Open your exam booklet and begin."

MULTIPLE-CHOICE QUESTIONS

Two separate sections of the SAT (25 minutes and 10 minutes) give you a total of forty-nine multiple-choice questions that deal with errors in grammar, usage, word choice (diction), and expression (idiom). There are three types of questions:

1. Improving Sentences (25 questions)
2. Identifying Sentence Errors (18 questions)
3. Improving Paragraphs (6 questions)

Of the three types, Identifying Sentence Errors are the briefest—rarely more than two or three lines. Most students answer them more quickly and easily than the others. The Improving Sentences questions take a bit longer because they require more reading, and the Improving Paragraphs questions take longer still because they relate to problems embedded in the text of an essay that you are given to read.

Yet, there's no need to rush through any of the questions. The test has been carefully calibrated to coincide with the time allotted, provided you work steadily.

THE ORDER OF QUESTIONS

Questions in the sentence-improvement and sentence-error sections are arranged more or less in order of difficulty Don't assume, however, question 7 will be harder than question 6, or 14 harder than 13. Because your mind works differently from everybody else's, you may often find later questions easier than earlier ones. If you come to a question that baffles you, don't agonize over it. Just go the next one, and go back later if time permits. Paragraph-improvement questions are arranged differently: They follow the progress of the passage. It makes sense to answer them in the order they are given, but don't be a slave to the order. You may find it useful, for example, to get specific questions out of the way before tackling questions dealing more generally with whole paragraphs or the complete essay.

IMPROVING SENTENCES QUESTIONS

In this section of the test you are asked to recognize errors in standard English as well as problems in style and expression. In each question, part of a sentence—or sometimes the whole sentence—is underlined. You are given five versions of the underlined words. Your task is to choose the best one. Because choice A always repeats the underlined segment of the original, select A only if you think no change is needed. In any case, never choose an alternative that substantially changes the meaning of the original sentence, even if its grammar and style are perfect.

Sample Questions

1. The custom <u>of awarding huge scholarships to college athletes have gotten out of hand</u>.
   (A) of awarding huge scholarships to college athletes have gotten out of hand
   (B) of huge scholarships awarded to college athletes has gotten out of hand
   (C) of awarding gigantically huge scholarships to student athletes attending college have gotten out of hand
   (D) is out of hand by which awards for college athletes are granted huge scholarships
   (E) of rewarding college athletes with huge scholarships are out of hand

Explanation: A basic rule of English grammar is that the subject of a sentence must agree in number with its verb. That is, a singular subject must have a singular verb, and a plural subject must be accompanied by a plural verb.

Choice B is the best answer because both the verb, *has*, and the subject, *custom*, are singular.

Choice A uses *have*, a plural verb that fails to agree with *custom*, a singular subject.

Choice C is an excessively wordy variation of choice A.

In choice D, both the subject, *custom*, and the verb, *is*, are singular, but the sentence contains an extremely awkward phrase, "out of hand by which."

Choice E uses *are*, a plural verb that fails to agree with the subject.

For more details on subject–verb agreement turn to Part V, page 152.

2. <u>Both of my cousins who live in San Francisco</u> speak both Chinese and Russian.

   (A) Both of my cousins who live in San Francisco
   (B) Both of my two cousins living in San Francisco
   (C) My two cousins, who lives in San Francisco
   (D) My two cousins in San Francisco
   (E) My two San Francisco cousins of mine

Explanation: Because sentences cluttered with unnecessary words are less effective than tightly written sentences, one of your tasks while answering Improving Sentences questions is to root out unnecessary and redundant words and phrases.

Choice D is the best answer because it is more concisely written than the other choices.

Choice A is grammatically correct, although it could be stylistically improved by eliminating the repetition of the word *both*.

Choice B also suffers from needless repetition but compounds the problem with the word *two*, a redundancy.

Choice C is more economical, but it contains a singular verb, *lives*, that disagrees with its plural subject, *cousins*.

Choice E contains a redundancy, *my* and *of mine*.

For more details on wordiness, turn to Part V, page 136.

How to Find Answers to Sentence Improvement Questions

- Read the entire sentence, paying close attention to its meaning.
- Be aware that errors may exist *only* in the underscored segment of the sentence.
- Try to *hear* the sentence in your head.
- Try to determine whether a problem exists.
- Search for wordiness and awkward expression in the underscored segment of the sentence.
- Read the choices, but ignore choice A, which is identical to the underscored segment of the original sentence.
- Eliminate all choices that contain obvious errors.
- Review the remaining choices for flaws in grammar and usage. (*See Part V for details about precisely what to look for.*)
- Eliminate any choice that changes the meaning of the sentence.
- If no change is needed, mark A on your answer sheet.

IDENTIFYING SENTENCE ERRORS

Identifying Sentence Errors questions come in the form of a sentence with portions of it underlined, as in the following examples:

1. <u>At the conclusion</u> of the ceremony, the new
         A

    members <u>sweared</u> that <u>they</u> would never
             B   C

    <u>reveal</u> the secret handshake. <u>No error</u>.
     D   E

2. <u>With the development</u> of antitoxins and
         A

    serums, <u>there</u> are hardly <u>no</u> cases of
           B   C

    smallpox or yellow fever <u>anywhere</u> in the
                           D

    world. <u>No error</u>
          E

Your job is to read each sentence carefully and identify the item that contains an error. Only one of the underlined parts in a sentence may contain an error, and no sentence contains more than one error. Sometimes a sentence may contain no error, in which case the correct answer will be E (<u>No error</u>).

Explanation: The correct answer to Question 1 is B because the past tense of the verb *swear* is *swore*. The verb *swear* doesn't adhere to the usual pattern of verbs—that is, creating the past tense by adding *-ed* to the present tense, as in *walk/walked* or *love/loved*. Rather, it follows a pattern of its own, just like other so-called irregular verbs, including *eat/eaten, ring/rung,* and *sleep/slept.*

Knowing about irregular verbs could have led you to the right answer. Yet, had you never heard about such verbs, you still might have been drawn to choice B by your innate sense of the way English sounds. In other words, your language "ear" may have told you that something was amiss. Nevertheless, even a good ear for language is not a reliable substitute for a thorough understanding of grammar and usage.

The correct answer to Question 2 is C because the underlined word is a double negative. Both *hardly* and *no* are negative words. Therefore, a phrase containing both words constitutes an error in standard usage.

To identify sentence errors on the SAT you don't need to know the technical terminology of grammar and usage, although it would help to study such basic concepts as the parts of speech, the structure of sentences, and verb tenses—all reviewed for you in Part V.

How to Find Answers to Identifying Sentence Errors Questions

- Read the whole sentence.
- Try to *hear* the sentence in your head.
- Focus your attention on awkward sounding words and phrases.
- Try to explain what the grammatical flaw might be. Review the remaining choices for flaws in grammar and usage. (*Likely errors are discussed fully in Part V.*)
- If all the underscored words are correct, mark E on your answer sheet.

The Improving Paragraphs section is the most comprehensive part of the test. It contains questions about many of the same principles of grammar and usage as the Improving Sentences section, but it raises additional issues related specifically to essay writing—style, organization, use of transitions, paragraph development, and topic sentences, among others. The questions are not meant to stump or trick you. Rather, they deal with aspects of writing familiar to any relatively experienced essay writer.

Questions are based on an unedited draft of a student's essay. Reading the essay, you'll probably notice that it falls short of perfection. Expect to answer one or two questions about problems of grammar and usage. The rest will pertain to improving the style and structure of the essay and expressing the meaning most effectively.

Sample Questions

The excerpt that follows is part of an essay written in response to the topic: *Preserving the Environment—Everybody's Job.*

[1] As people get older, quite obviously, the earth does too. [2] And with the process of the earth aging, we must keep recycling our waste products. [3] The idea of using things over and over again to conserve our natural resources is a brilliant one. [4] Those who don't do it should be criticized greatly.

[5] As we become more aware of the earth's limitations, we all say "Oh, I'd like to help." [6] Not everyone does, even though recycling is an effective place to start. [7] Taking cans and bottles back to the supermarket to be recycled is a clever idea. [8] It attracts anyone who wants the money (5 cents per can or bottle). [9] In addition, in almost every town there is a Recycling Center. [10] There are separate bins for paper, glass, and plastic. [11] This is a convenient service to those who support recycling. [12] It is so easy to drive a few blocks to a center to drop off what needs to be recycled. [13] This is just another simple example of how easy it really is to recycle and get involved. [14] Anyone who cannot see its sim-

plicity should be criticized for not doing their part to help make the world a better place.

[15] When I go to other people's houses and see glass bottles and jars mixed in with household garbage, I get disgusted and often say, "Why don't you recycle that glass instead of throwing it out?" [16] It angers me when they respond, "It's too much trouble." [17] Such people are ignorant and deserve to be taught a lesson about how wastefulness is slowly destroying the earth.

1. Considering the essay as a whole, which of the following best explains the main purpose of the second paragraph?

    (A) To explain the historical background of the topic
    (B) To provide a smooth transition between the first and third paragraphs
    (C) To define terms introduced in the first paragraph
    (D) To develop an idea presented in the first paragraph
    (E) To present a different point of view on the issue being discussed

Explanation: To answer this question, you must read the whole essay. You must also know something about how paragraphs function in an essay.

All the choices name legitimate uses of paragraphs, but only choice D applies to this essay because it develops by example an idea originating in the first paragraph—how easy it is to recycle. Choices A, C, and E can be quickly discarded. Choice B is a possibility because in a unified essay each paragraph, aside from the opening and closing paragraphs, in some way serves as a bridge between paragraphs. Because the second paragraph is the longest of the essay, however, its main function is probably more than transitional.

2. Which of the following sentences most effectively combines sentences 9, 10, and 11 (reproduced below) into a single sentence?

    [9] In addition, in almost every town there is a Recycling Center. [10] There are separate bins for paper, glass, and plastic. [11] This is a convenient service to those who support recycling.

    (A) Recycling centers offer recyclers convenience by providing separate bins for paper, glass, and plastic and by being located in almost every town.
    (B) Recycling centers, located in almost every town, provide convenient bins for separating paper, glass, and plastic.
    (C) Almost every town has a recycling center with separate bins for paper, glass, and plastic, and this is a convenience for recyclers.
    (D) Besides, people who recycle will find recycling centers in almost every town, providing convenient separation to recycle paper, glass, and plastic into bins.
    (E) For the convenience of recyclers in almost every town, paper, glass, and plastic are separated into provided bins at its recycling center.

Explanation: This question relates to sentence structure—in particular how the structure of a sentence helps to convey meaning. You probably know that in a series of short sentences each idea carries equal weight. But combining short sentences permits a writer to highlight the important ideas while de-emphasizing others. To answer this question, then, you must decide which idea expressed by the three sentences deserves to be given the greatest emphasis.

The three sentences in question come from a paragraph that discusses the ease and appeal of recycling. Because sentences 10 and 11 refer to the convenient arrangement of recycling bins, they are more important to the development of the paragraph than sentence 9, about the location of recycling centers.

Usually, the main point of a sentence is found in its main clause. Knowing that, read each of the choices. Choices A and C give equal weight to the location and convenience of recycling centers. Choice D stresses the location rather than the convenient arrangement of bins in recycling centers. Choice E not only alters the meaning but contains both an ambiguous pronoun reference ("its") and an awkward usage ("provided bins"). Therefore, choice B is the best answer. It highlights the facilities offered by recycling centers while diminishing the importance of their location.

How to Find Answers to Improving Paragraphs Questions

- Read the entire passage, paying attention to its main idea and to the writer's purpose.
- Ignore all errors except those raised by the multiple-choice questions.
- Carefully read each question and the five choices.
- Eliminate any choice that contains wordiness, repetition, and awkward expression. Also discard choices that contain flaws in grammar and usage. (*Which errors to look for is discussed fully in Part V.*)
- As you answer the questions, keep in mind the main idea of each paragraph and of the entire essay. (*For details on all aspects of essay writing, see Part III.*)

A WORD OF ENCOURAGEMENT

The multiple-choice sections of the SAT Writing Test pertain to matters of grammar, usage, and rhetoric typically taught in English classes. If your sense of grammar and usage is rusty, however, or if rhetoric is a mystery, take heart. This book, after all, is a thorough test-prep guide that explains virtually everything you need to know for the test and describes how you can earn a score to make you proud.

Are you ready to begin? If so, go to the next page and set aside an hour to complete the sample writing test. Good luck!

PART II

DRESS REHEARSAL:
A SAMPLE TEST

Sample Test
Answer Key
Performance Evaluation Chart
Conversion Table
Answer Explanations

By taking the sample test, you'll quickly become familiar with the length and format of the exam. You'll also begin to identify your strengths and weaknesses as a writer.

The SAT always begins with the essay question and then offers several sections of math and reading questions. The Writing Test resumes in Section 6 or 7 of the SAT with thirty-five multiple-choice questions and then, after still more math and reading questions, concludes with fourteen additional multiple-choice questions on writing. This sample test, therefore, differs from a real SAT because the three sections of writing questions follow one after the other.

Despite this difference, try to simulate actual test conditions as you administer this test to yourself. Here's how to do it:

- Set aside an uninterrupted hour.
- Use a timer, a watch, or a clock to time each section.
    Section 1: Essay Question—25 minutes
    Section 2: Multiple-Choice Questions—25 minutes
    Section 3: More Multiple-Choice Questions—10 minutes
- Work on only one section at a time.
- Don't skip ahead to the next section before the allotted time is up.
- Don't return to a previous section once it's over.
- Write the essay in pen or pencil on the blank pages provided in this book, or substitute your own paper no larger than 8½ × 11 inches, the size of an official SAT essay response sheet. (Computers may not be used on the SAT.)
- Mark your multiple-choice answers in pencil on the answer sheet provided.

When you've completed the test, check your answers with the Answer Key on page 37 and fill in the Performance Evaluation Chart. Your score on each section, along with your total score, will give you a profile of what you've done well and what you should study between now and SAT day. The chart will also tell you the types of questions you answered most successfully. Be sure to read the answer explanations for the questions you got wrong. On second thought, read all the explanations. You may pick up a pointer or two that will serve you well on future exams.

Although it's hard to assess your own essay objectively, don't shy away from trying. Let the essay cool for a while—maybe a day or more. Then, reread it with an open mind and a fresh pair of eyes. Rate your essay using the Self-Scoring Guide on pages 35–37. For a second opinion, find a trusted and informed friend—or maybe a teacher, counselor, or parent—to read, rate, and discuss your essay with you.

Finally, turn to page 39 to convert your raw scores into the SAT's 200–800 scaled score. Remember that your scaled score is only an approximation of what you might earn on an actual SAT Writing Test.

Are you ready to begin? Good luck!

SAMPLE TEST

Section 1
Essay

TIME—25 MINUTES

Directions: Plan and write an essay in response to the assigned topic. Use the essay as an opportunity to show how clearly and effectively you can express and develop ideas. Present your thoughts logically and precisely. Include specific evidence or examples to support your point of view. A plain, natural writing style is probably best. The number of words is up to you, but quantity is less important than quality. (*See Part III for tips on writing first-rate essays.*)

Limit your essay to two sides of the lined paper provided. You'll have enough space if you write on every line and avoid wide margins. Write or print legibly because handwriting that's hard or impossible to read will decrease your score.

BE SURE TO WRITE ONLY ON THE ASSIGNED TOPIC. AN ESSAY WRITTEN ON ANOTHER TOPIC WILL BE SCORED "ZERO."

If you finish in less than 25 minutes, check your work. Do not turn to another section of the test.

Think carefully about the following passage and the following assignment.

Whenever Social Studies teacher Karen Greene sits down to grade a stack of papers, she wonders what the grades really mean and whether they convey useful information about student learning to the students themselves, to parents, counselors, or even to colleges.

While most would agree that the general purpose of grading is to provide feedback on student performance, finding consensus on what criteria to use for grading is a different story. Should Karen reward high grades to a hard-working student with very low skills and limited achievement? Or should she risk discouraging the student by giving him the D that his work really warranted? What about grading a student capable of doing excellent work when she puts her mind to it but who rarely does the work? An F for lack of effort might prod her to work harder, but would it accurately reflect the real quality of her work?

Adapted from Lisa Birk, *Harvard Education Letter*, October 2004

Assignment: Should students who work very hard in a course earn very high grades, or should achievement rather than effort determine students' grades? Plan and write an essay in which you develop your point of view on this issue. Support your position with reasoning and examples taken from your observations, experience, studies, or reading.

Section 1

ESSAY
Time allowed: 25 minutes
Limit your essay to two pages. Do not skip lines. Write only inside the box.

Essay (continued)

End of essay.
Do not proceed to Section 2 until the allotted time for Section 1 has passed.

ANSWER SHEET FOR MULTIPLE-CHOICE QUESTIONS

Section 2
Improving Sentences

1. Ⓐ Ⓑ Ⓒ Ⓓ Ⓔ
2. Ⓐ Ⓑ Ⓒ Ⓓ Ⓔ
3. Ⓐ Ⓑ Ⓒ Ⓓ Ⓔ
4. Ⓐ Ⓑ Ⓒ Ⓓ Ⓔ
5. Ⓐ Ⓑ Ⓒ Ⓓ Ⓔ
6. Ⓐ Ⓑ Ⓒ Ⓓ Ⓔ
7. Ⓐ Ⓑ Ⓒ Ⓓ Ⓔ
8. Ⓐ Ⓑ Ⓒ Ⓓ Ⓔ
9. Ⓐ Ⓑ Ⓒ Ⓓ Ⓔ
10. Ⓐ Ⓑ Ⓒ Ⓓ Ⓔ
11. Ⓐ Ⓑ Ⓒ Ⓓ Ⓔ

Identifying
Sentence Errors

12. Ⓐ Ⓑ Ⓒ Ⓓ Ⓔ
13. Ⓐ Ⓑ Ⓒ Ⓓ Ⓔ
14. Ⓐ Ⓑ Ⓒ Ⓓ Ⓔ
15. Ⓐ Ⓑ Ⓒ Ⓓ Ⓔ
16. Ⓐ Ⓑ Ⓒ Ⓓ Ⓔ
17. Ⓐ Ⓑ Ⓒ Ⓓ Ⓔ
18. Ⓐ Ⓑ Ⓒ Ⓓ Ⓔ
19. Ⓐ Ⓑ Ⓒ Ⓓ Ⓔ
20. Ⓐ Ⓑ Ⓒ Ⓓ Ⓔ
21. Ⓐ Ⓑ Ⓒ Ⓓ Ⓔ
22. Ⓐ Ⓑ Ⓒ Ⓓ Ⓔ
23. Ⓐ Ⓑ Ⓒ Ⓓ Ⓔ
24. Ⓐ Ⓑ Ⓒ Ⓓ Ⓔ
25. Ⓐ Ⓑ Ⓒ Ⓓ Ⓔ
26. Ⓐ Ⓑ Ⓒ Ⓓ Ⓔ
27. Ⓐ Ⓑ Ⓒ Ⓓ Ⓔ
28. Ⓐ Ⓑ Ⓒ Ⓓ Ⓔ
29. Ⓐ Ⓑ Ⓒ Ⓓ Ⓔ

Improving Paragraphs

30. Ⓐ Ⓑ Ⓒ Ⓓ Ⓔ
31. Ⓐ Ⓑ Ⓒ Ⓓ Ⓔ
32. Ⓐ Ⓑ Ⓒ Ⓓ Ⓔ
33. Ⓐ Ⓑ Ⓒ Ⓓ Ⓔ
34. Ⓐ Ⓑ Ⓒ Ⓓ Ⓔ
35. Ⓐ Ⓑ Ⓒ Ⓓ Ⓔ

Section 3
Improving Sentences

1. Ⓐ Ⓑ Ⓒ Ⓓ Ⓔ
2. Ⓐ Ⓑ Ⓒ Ⓓ Ⓔ
3. Ⓐ Ⓑ Ⓒ Ⓓ Ⓔ
4. Ⓐ Ⓑ Ⓒ Ⓓ Ⓔ
5. Ⓐ Ⓑ Ⓒ Ⓓ Ⓔ
6. Ⓐ Ⓑ Ⓒ Ⓓ Ⓔ
7. Ⓐ Ⓑ Ⓒ Ⓓ Ⓔ
8. Ⓐ Ⓑ Ⓒ Ⓓ Ⓔ
9. Ⓐ Ⓑ Ⓒ Ⓓ Ⓔ
10. Ⓐ Ⓑ Ⓒ Ⓓ Ⓔ
11. Ⓐ Ⓑ Ⓒ Ⓓ Ⓔ
12. Ⓐ Ⓑ Ⓒ Ⓓ Ⓔ
13. Ⓐ Ⓑ Ⓒ Ⓓ Ⓔ
14. Ⓐ Ⓑ Ⓒ Ⓓ Ⓔ

Section 2
Multiple-Choice Questions

TIME—25 MINUTES

IMPROVING SENTENCES

Directions: The underlined sentences and sentence parts below may contain errors in standard English, including awkward or ambiguous expression, poor word choice (diction), incorrect sentence structure, or faulty grammar, usage, and punctuation. Read each sentence carefully and identify which of the five alternate versions most effectively and correctly expresses the meaning of the underlined material. Indicate your choice by filling in the corresponding space on the answer sheet. Choice A always repeats the original. Choose A if none of the other choices improves the original sentence.

EXAMPLE

My old Aunt Maud loves
to cook, and eating also.

(A) cook, and eating also
(B) cook and to eat
(C) cook, and to eat also
(D) cook and eat besides
(E) cook and, in addition, eat

ANSWER

Ⓐ ● Ⓒ Ⓓ Ⓔ

1. Inside Margaret Jackson's home were an art studio with a pottery kiln, high-tech stainless steel appliances, and there was a swimming pool lined with Italian marble.

   (A) there was a swimming pool lined with Italian marble
   (B) a swimming pool lined with Italian marble
   (C) lined with Italian marble was a swimming pool
   (D) the swimming pool was lined with Italian marble
   (E) a swimming pool with Italian marble was there

2. Mr. Rich was not the first math teacher to entertain and inspire his students, but he has been the first who turned math class into a party.

   (A) has been the first who turned
   (B) had been the first who turned
   (C) was the first having turned
   (D) was the first to turn
   (E) having been the first to turn

3. Our interscholastic athletic schedules were made <u>too recklessly, without sufficient planning behind it</u>.

    (A) too recklessly, without sufficient planning behind it

    (B) too reckless, without sufficient planning behind it

    (C) too recklessly, without sufficient planning behind them

    (D) too reckless, and there is not sufficient planning behind them

    (E) too recklessly, and there is not sufficient planning behind it

4. Many senior citizens are reluctant to go <u>online, it results from not knowing much about computers and being a bit scared of it</u>.

    (A) online, it results from not knowing much about computers and being a bit scared of it

    (B) online resulting from not knowing much about computers and being a bit scared of it

    (C) online for the reason being that they don't know much about computers and are a bit scared of them

    (D) online because of knowing little about computers and being scared of it

    (E) online because they know little about computers and are a bit scared of them

5. The program of extracurricular activities <u>were cut from the school budget in spite of them being regarded</u> as one of the most important aspects of high school.

    (A) were cut from the school budget in spite of them being regarded

    (B) was cut from the school budget in spite of them being regarded

    (C) was cut from the school budget in spite of their regard as being

    (D) were cut from the school budget in spite of regarding it

    (E) was cut from the school budget in spite of it being regarded

6. <u>Annie Oakley boasted that she could shoot better than any other cowboy at the rodeo; then she</u> proved it.

    (A) Annie Oakley boasted that she could shoot better than any other cowboy at the rodeo; then she

    (B) Annie Oakley boasted that she could shoot better than any cowboy at the rodeo; then she

    (C) Annie Oakley boasted that she could shoot better than any cowboy at the rodeo, therefore she

    (D) To boast that she could shoot better than any other cowboy at the rodeo, Annie Oakley

    (E) Boasting that she could shoot better than any other cowboy at the rodeo, Annie Oakley

7. <u>Residents of Chicago have just as much right to complain about the cold as Minneapolis, which</u> endures sub-freezing temperatures most of the winter.

    (A) Residents of Chicago have just as much right to complain about the cold as Minneapolis, which

    (B) Residents of Chicago have just as much right to complain about the cold as residents of Minneapolis, which

    (C) Residents of Chicago have equally the right to complain about the cold as residents of Minneapolis, which

    (D) Residents of Chicago, having the equal right to complain about the cold as Minneapolis, where the population

    (E) Residents of Chicago, rightfully complaining about the cold as the population of Minneapolis, where it

8. <u>When the baseball rulebook is followed too closely, they often spoil instead of enhancing the game</u>.

   (A) When the baseball rulebook is followed too closely, they often spoil instead of enhancing the game
   (B) When the baseball rulebook is followed too closely, it often spoils instead of enhancing the game
   (C) The baseball rulebook, if too closely followed, often spoils the game, not enhancing it
   (D) The baseball rulebook, if followed too closely, often spoils rather than enhances the game
   (E) If you follow too closely the baseball rulebook, it often spoils rather than enhances the game

9. At the airport passengers must pass through metal <u>detectors, but there are not frequent body searches of passengers</u>.

   (A) detectors, but there are not frequent body searches of passengers
   (B) detectors, and a bodily search of passengers is not frequent
   (C) detectors but are rarely subject to body searches
   (D) detectors, but the searching of their bodies is rare
   (E) detectors, but the search of bodies is rare among them

10. As modern astronomy increasingly employs sophisticated space telescopes, high-speed computers, years-long probes into outer space, <u>humankind's concept of the heavens has changed</u>.

   (A) humankind's concept of the heavens has changed
   (B) humankind's concept of the heavens have changed
   (C) there has been changes in humankind's concepts of the heavens
   (D) humankind have undergone a change in its concepts of the heavens
   (E) humankind has had changes in their concept of the heavens

11. The Broadway tradition of "musical comedy" has changed over the years because <u>of their stories and music exploring</u> serious themes, especially the consequences of war, tyranny, and dcath.

   (A) of their stories and music exploring
   (B) of their stories and music exploring their
   (C) its stories and music explore
   (D) its stories and music explores
   (E) of how it explores through stories and music

IDENTIFYING SENTENCE ERRORS

<u>Directions</u>: The underlined and lettered parts of each sentence below may contain an error in grammar, usage, word choice (diction), or expression (idiom). Read each sentence carefully and identify which item, if any, contains an error. Indicate your choice by filling in the corresponding space on the answer sheet. No sentence contains more than one error. Some sentences may contain no error. In that case, the correct choice will always be E (No error).

EXAMPLE

Jill went <u>speedily</u> to the <u>crest</u> of the
          A   B

hill in a <u>more</u> faster time <u>than</u> her
        C   D

friend, Jack. <u>No error</u>.
           E

ANSWER

Ⓐ Ⓑ ● Ⓓ Ⓔ

12. Although he left Texas <u>as</u> a small boy, Jim
                  A

returned <u>when</u> he was sixteen <u>and decides</u>
         B   C

that he'd <u>like to spend</u> the rest of his life
         D

there. <u>No error</u>.
      E

13. <u>Despite</u> the constant pressure of schoolwork
   A

and sports, Terry <u>has never been</u> more <u>happier</u>
              B   C

than <u>she is now</u>, in her senior year. <u>No error</u>.
     D   E

14. <u>At</u> the beginning of the play, <u>there is</u> two
   A   B

puzzling dilemmas that Medea must solve

if she is <u>going to survive</u> her ordeal.
C   D

<u>No error</u>.
   E

15. The common sentiment that hard work

<u>pays off</u> doesn't <u>necessarily</u> <u>apply to</u> a frail
   A   B   C

old man <u>which</u> has a heart condition and a
        D

long driveway to shovel after a snowstorm.

<u>No error</u>.
   E

16. Readers <u>can</u> easily draw a distinction
        A

between a so-called literary classic and

an escapist piece of pulp fiction by

considering <u>how many ideas</u> the books
          B

<u>give them</u> to think <u>about</u>. <u>No error</u>.
   C   D   E

17. Some symbols <u>acquire</u> a <u>multitude of meanings</u>,
          A   B

some <u>widely shared</u>, others personal, some
      C

contradictory, conflicted, <u>or</u> ambivalent.
                    D

<u>No error</u>.
   E

18. <u>Although</u> every road in the town is now
    A

    paved, there are <u>actually</u> some residents
                      B

    <u>who</u> <u>will prefer</u> that the dirt roads be preserved.
     C   D

    <u>No error</u>.
      E

19. The company <u>has begun</u> manufacturing
             A

    dishwasher soaps in bright colors because

    consumers respond to <u>this</u> <u>more eagerly</u> than
                 B   C

    <u>to dull, ordinary colors</u>. <u>No error</u>.
        D   E

20. The professor <u>explained that</u> the realistic
             A

    painter <u>is having to represent</u> reality, <u>while</u>
           B   C

    the impressionistic or abstract painter reveals

    a personal or emotional response <u>to reality</u>.
                          D

    <u>No error</u>.
      E

21. Many of the candidates, including the incumbent

    senator <u>herself</u>, <u>has opposed</u> the legislation
          A   B

    <u>that weakens</u> the ban <u>on snowmobiles</u> in
       C   D

    Yellowstone and other national parks. <u>No error</u>.
                                 E

22. <u>An</u> orientation program familiarizes new ninth
    A

    graders <u>with</u> the daily schedule, teaches them
          B

    the layout of the building, and <u>they have</u> the
                         C

    chance to practice going <u>from class to class</u>.
                         D

    <u>No error</u>.
      E

23. An examination of <u>the most reliable</u> current
                 A

    economic statistics <u>do not justify</u> <u>raising</u> the
                  B   C

    sales tax in the <u>foreseeable future</u>. <u>No error</u>.
                D   E

24. Saturday's game <u>demonstrated</u> <u>once more again</u>
                A   B

    why Paulie, one of the <u>league's finest</u> players,
                 C

    is being recruited <u>by many</u> colleges. <u>No error</u>.
              D   E

25. Since the early 1800s, the famous Hope

    Diamond <u>was</u> the most notorious gem
          A

    <u>in history</u>, leaving behind <u>a string of owners</u>
       B   C

    <u>who</u> have suffered one misfortune after
    D

    another. <u>No error</u>.
          E

26. <u>Because</u> the setting profoundly influences
    A

    the thoughts, emotions, and actions of the

    characters, a place can be as <u>significant for</u> a
                        B

    story as <u>any of</u> the people in <u>it</u>. <u>No error</u>.
          C   D   E

27. <u>Both</u> Jon Stewart and Conan O'Brien
    A

    <u>have become</u> <u>extremely</u> popular cable TV
       B   C

    comedians, but O'Brien has the <u>largest</u>
                          D

    number of fans. <u>No error</u>.
             E

28. During this past year, a rapport <u>has developed</u>
                                              A
    between my Spanish teacher <u>and I</u>; <u>in fact,</u>
                                    B   C
    I now call <u>her by</u> her first name, Louise.
                    D
    <u>No error.</u>
       E

29. <u>For</u> decades, scientists analyzed masses of
      A
    public-health statistics <u>before</u> <u>they</u> found a
                                  B   C
    high correlation <u>between</u> heavy smoking and
                           D
    the incidence of lung cancer. <u>No error.</u>
                                       E

IMPROVING PARAGRAPHS

<u>Directions</u>: The passage below is the draft of a student's essay. Some parts of the passage need improvement. Read the passage and answer the questions that follow. The questions are about revisions that might improve all or part of the passage's organization, development, sentence structure, or choice of words. Choose the answer that best follows the requirements of standard written English.

Questions 30–35 refer to the following passage.

[1] No student of American history can avoid having learned about a great technological feat, the building of the transcontinental railroad in the middle of the nineteenth century. [2] Though the Pacific Ocean could be reached by traveling overland in wagons or by sea via South America, many dreamed of a time when the East would join the West, linked by a transcontinental railroad. [3] In 1869, the dream became a reality. [4] It was a great physical achievement. [5] In accomplishing this great feat of engineering, the workers were exploited, and many of them died.

[6] Chinese immigrants were the backbone of the workforce. [7] They performed unskilled labor and also the highly specialized and dangerous jobs as well. [8] The workers were exploited ruthlessly. [9] Methods were unsafe and cost lives. [10] Baskets holding a single person were lowered down the side of a mountain, and the worker inside would place dynamite into the mountain's crevasse, light it, and try to make it back up. [11] If they were not pulled fast enough, or the rope broke, they fell to their deaths. [12] An estimated 1200 Chinese perished just so.

[13] With the help of the U.S. government, which contributed millions of dollars' worth of public land and funds for construction, the project was run by a group of four well-to-do but corrupt businessmen from California. [14] They used fraud to build their own personal fortunes, and their greed ran rampant.

30. Which of the following is the best way to deal with sentence 1 (reproduced below)?

    No student of American history can avoid having learned about a great technological feat, the building of the transcontinental railroad in the middle of the nineteenth century.

    (A) Make no changes.
    (B) Switch its position in the essay with that of sentence 2.
    (C) Change "having learned" to "learning."
    (D) Relocate "in the middle of the nineteenth century" between "history" and "can."
    (E) Delete the comma and insert "which was."

31. In context, which of the following is the best way to revise the underlined words in order to combine sentences 4 and 5?

It was a great physical achievement. In accomplishing this great feat of engineering, the workers were exploited and many of them died.

(A) It was a great physical achievement, in accomplishing this great feat of engineering

(B) The fact is that

(C) But students don't learn that this great physical feat of engineering came at a large price because

(D) As a result, historians say that this great achievement meant that

(E) Although building the railroad was a great physical achievement,

32. Which of the following ideas is the best to add to sentence 9 in order to link it to sentence 8?

(A) Consequently,

(B) Because laborers were pushed to complete the work as quickly as possible,

(C) On the other hand,

(D) With regard to taking advantage of the Chinese laborers,

(E) A good example of exploitation is that

33. Which of the following best describes the relationship between sentences 9 and 10?

(A) Sentence 10 provides material that illustrates the statement made in sentence 9.

(B) Sentence 10 proves the validity of the point made in sentence 9.

(C) Sentence 10 introduces sources of information that confirms the truth of sentence 9.

(D) Sentence 10 offers an alternative point of view about the point made in sentence 9.

(E) Sentence 10 restates opinions expressed in sentence 9.

34. Which of the following would be the best sentence to insert before sentence 13 to introduce the last paragraph?

(A) Building the railroad was such an expensive undertaking that no private individual of that era could afford to finance the whole thing.

(B) Paying for the construction of the railroad left the federal government with a mountain of debt.

(C) One set of construction crews started building from the east to the west, while another began in the west and built eastward.

(D) The building of the railroad was indeed an American milestone.

(E) The Pacific Railroad Act, a document rushed through Congress, was grossly over-generous in its benefits to the builders.

35. What material is the most appropriate to add immediately after sentence 14?

(A) How the four business tycoons happened to meet and form a partnership

(B) The facts that convinced the four men to build the railroad

(C) Reasons why shoddy construction methods were used

(D) Details about unethical business practices during the construction of the railroad

(E) An account of how the eastbound and westbound tracks met in Utah in 1869

End of Section 2.
Do not return to Section 1. Do not proceed to Section 3 until the allotted time for Section 2 has passed.

Section 3
Multiple-Choice Questions

TIME—10 MINUTES

IMPROVING SENTENCES

Directions: The underlined sentences and sentence parts below may contain errors in standard English, including awkward or ambiguous expression, poor word choice (diction), incorrect sentence structure, or faulty grammar, usage, and punctuation. Read each sentence carefully and identify which of the five alternate versions most effectively and correctly expresses the meaning of the underlined material. Indicate your choice by filling in the corresponding space on the answer sheet. Choice A always repeats the original. Choose A if none of the other choices improves the original sentence.

1. Tony showed three college acceptance letters to his counselor, he said that NYU was definitely his first choice.

   (A) Tony showed three college acceptance letters to his counselor, he
   (B) Three college acceptance letters, which were shown to his counselor by Tony, who
   (C) Three college acceptance letters were shown by Tony to his counselor, then he
   (D) After showing three college acceptance letters to his counselor, Tony
   (E) Tony, having shown three college acceptance letters to his counselor, he

2. Before going on the senior class trip, a parental permission slip must be filled out for each student.

   (A) a parental permission slip must be filled out for each student
   (B) a student must have their parental permission slips filled out
   (C) their parents must fill out a permission slip for each student
   (D) a student must have a parental permission slip filled out
   (E) permission for each student must be filled out by their parents

3. Despite being called "reality" television, the program about the plane crash in the Rockies seemed about as real as a cow jumping over the moon.

   (A) Despite being called "reality" television
   (B) Although its being "reality" television
   (C) It was called "reality" television
   (D) Because it was called "reality" television
   (E) Calling it "reality" television

4. To think that only money motivates people to choose a career in professional athletics is wrong because in sports many people do it to find personal satisfaction.

   (A) wrong because in sports many people do it to find personal satisfaction.
   (B) wrong because sports would have had an effect on find personal satisfaction
   (C) wrong, and the reason is because of the finding of personal satisfaction from a career in sports
   (D) wrong, because many athletes find personal satisfaction out of sports
   (E) wrong because many athletes find personal satisfaction in their sport

5. At the beginning of Joseph Conrad's story "Gaspar Ruiz," a soldier has been falsely accused of cowardice under fire, desertion of his post, and <u>he gave military secrets to the enemy</u>.

   (A) he gave military secrets to the enemy
   (B) giving military secrets to the enemy
   (C) gives military secrets to the enemy
   (D) military secrets were given to the enemy
   (E) the enemy received military secrets from him

6. Essential for doing business or just staying in touch with family and friends, <u>cell phones, they are increasingly popular</u>.

   (A) cell phones, they are increasingly popular
   (B) their popularity is growing
   (C) thcy havc become more popular
   (D) cell phones are increasingly popular
   (E) cell phones, they have grown more popular

7. <u>Although whales can grow</u> bigger than houses, they have ears so small that you can't clean them out with an ordinary Q-tip.

   (A) Although whales can grow
   (B) Whereas whales can grow
   (C) Despitc a whale growing
   (D) While a whale's size can grow
   (E) Since a whale can grow

8. <u>When you read at a very fast rate, your eyes often skip words, and your mind grasps the meaning nevertheless</u>.

   (A) When you read at a very fast rate, your eyes often skip words, and your mind grasps the meaning nevertheless
   (B) When you read at a very fast rate, your eyes often skip words, your mind nevertheless grasps the meaning
   (C) Because you read at a very fast rate, your eyes often skip words, and your mind grasps the meaning nevertheless
   (D) When you read at a very fast rate, your eyes often skip words, but your mind grasps the meaning nevertheless
   (E) Reading at a very fast rate, words are skipped by your eyes even when your mind grasps the meaning

9. <u>The author, guiding the reader through Emma's most intimate dreams and fantasies, accurately</u> portraying the plight of many middle-class women in France in the 1850s.

   (A) The author, guiding the reader through Emma's most intimate dreams and fantasies, accurately
   (B) The reader is guided through Emma's most intimate dreams and fantasies by accurately
   (C) The reader, guided through Emma's most intimate dreams and fantasies by the author who is accurately
   (D) The author, who guides the reader through Emma's most intimate dreams and fantasies, accurately
   (E) The author guides the reader through Emma's most intimate dreams and fantasies, accurately

10. The custom of naming ships after dead war heroes has been practiced <u>through many countries in honoring their</u> military personnel.

    (A) through many countries in honoring their
    (B) through many countries to honor its
    (C) in many countries; it is to honor its
    (D) by many countries to honor their
    (E) by many a country to honor their

11. In 2004, the cost of a gallon of gas increased <u>considerably, while continuing to grow</u> in 2005.

    (A) considerably, while continuing to grow
    (B) considerably, and it continued to increase
    (C) considerably, with continuing growth
    (D) considerably, it continued growing
    (E) considerably, continuing increasing

12. <u>The Black Death of the 14th century, possibly the world's deadliest epidemic, whose origin is thought to be central China</u>.

    (A) The Black Death of the 14th century, possibly the world's deadliest epidemic, whose origin is thought to be central China

    (B) The Black Death of the 14th century, possibly the world's deadliest epidemic, its origin is thought to be central China

    (C) Possibly the world's deadliest epidemic, the origin of the Black Death of the 14th century is thought to be central China

    (D) The origin of the Black Death of the 14th century, possibly the world's deadliest epidemic, is thought to be central China

    (E) The 14th century's Black Death is thought to have its origin in central China, was possibly the world's deadliest epidemic

13. Many problems among the faculty developed after Mr. Atkins took over as principal of the <u>school; these problems diminished both the reputation and the performance of the school</u>.

    (A) school; these problems diminished both the reputation and the performance of the school

    (B) school, they both diminished the reputation and performance of the school

    (C) school, which both diminished its reputation as well as diminished its performance

    (D) school; these problems diminished its reputation and performance

    (E) school, and they diminished its reputation as well as performance

14. Drive-in restaurants that serve fatty food can be found along almost every main highway in the <u>country, this explaining why</u> so many Americans are overweight.

    (A) country, this explaining why
    (B) country, this is why
    (C) country; this fact explains why
    (D) country; this fact explaining the reason why
    (E) country, and explains why

End of Section 3.
Do not return to Sections 1 or 2.

END OF WRITING TEST.

ANSWER KEY

SECTION 1—THE ESSAY

Before scoring your essay, review the unedited text of the following six essays written by other students in response to the same topic. Rate each one on a scale of 6 (high) to 1 (low), and write a comment about your impressions in the spaces provided. (Give a 0 to any essay not on the assigned topic.) Then compare your comments with those of two SAT evaluators. Finally, after rereading and scoring your own essay using the Self-Scoring Guide, find an informed and impartial reader to give your essay a second evaluation.

The original essays were written by hand, but these have been typed *exactly* as written.

Jan's Essay

Students should earn grades which reflect their achievement. There are many students who work hard, yet do not receive high grades. However, if they are unable to retain the knowledge they have been taught, then they should receive the grade they deserve. If the system were to change and every student who tried hard received a high grade, how would we differentiate between those who are truly gifted and those who merely make an effort? This is especially important in high school and college, where intelligence matters a lot. I, for one, would not want to go to a dentist or a doctor who got good grades in dental or medical school because they tried hard. I would want the best there is to take care of me.

In younger years of schooling, on the other hand, effort should be given some credit, but as junior high approaches, students should be divided by ability. This division should be made apparent within their grades.

The system of high grades for achievement should apply in every academic subject.

When electives are involved, a different process could be used. If someone is not artistic or athletic, but tries hard, they should be awarded a grade for effort. However, their artistic and athletic classmates should be awarded a grade for ability. If we were to change this efficient system, the determination of placement of all students would be disrupted.

Your impressions: _____

_____

_____

_____

_____ Score: _____

Comment to Jan: *Your essay addresses the topic directly with a concise and forceful opening statement: "Students should earn grades which reflect their achievement." Yet, you avoid being dogmatic about it by thoughtfully considering the use of different grading criteria at different stages of education. Especially in the first paragraph you back up your opinions with interesting and specific supporting material. Your reference to doctors and dentists is particularly apt. Throughout the essay you maintain a consistent point of view and organize your ideas logically. Sentences are varied and generally well-structured. Some imprecise* *language and awkward wording (e.g., "younger years of schooling," "the determination of placement") plus an enigmatic concluding sentence take away from the overall quality of the piece.*

Each reader gave the essay a score of 5, for a total score of 10.

Philippe's Essay

I feel that the issue here and where I stand depends on a lot. For example, I think it depends on what kind of student you are what kind of classes you are in and if you're an all around prepared student. Your grade realy depends on what kind of person you are. If your lazy and take everything as a joke. Never hand in work. Late a lot. Fail tests, then that's the grade you deserve.

If you re all around prepared student and you really try hard you should give someone high grades. I have had this experience in high school I have tried hard but have not achieved a lot though my effort. In Math Class I had in 9th Grade but I didn't do so good so Summer School here I come. I did better on it. I think that during summer school I set a goal for myself and the teacher helped me. That's why I did good I think if people set a goal for themselves they would try even in any subject.

Your impressions: _____

_____

_____

_____

_____ Score: _____

Comment to Philippe: The error-filled usage and confusing presentation of ideas suggest that you have severe problems with basic English expression. Your writing suggests that English may be your second language. Including a personal anecdote about your math class supports your point of view and indicates that you have learned a worthwhile writing technique that should serve you well on future essays. Numerous problems in the essay point to a need for remedial work in writing before you attend college.

Each reader gave the essay a score of 1, for a total score of 2.

Johnny's Essay

Ever since there were schools there has been controversy over grades, because grades in school in some ways determine the course of your life. Which is more important, achievement or effort? In which situations is one more important than the other?

I believe that a student who works very hard in a very difficult course, but doesn't quite make it into the 90 range, should be rewarded for their effort. On the other hand, a student who is naturally gifted in the area of the hard course and achieves say a 95 test average with little or no work, should remain with their test grades for their final average.

As must be evident to any one, a child in elementary school should be graded differently than a student at Harvard Law. Effort should be regarded as the basis for grading of a very young student, because grades K-6 are crucial ycars when children must be shown the importance of effort. Students at Harvard Law are different. They should be graded with emphasis on achievement rather than effort, because trying hard doesn't matter if when they go out into the real law world, their effort is not irrelevant. If they don't win the case, no one cares about how hard they worked.

It is ridiculous to expect that we can use the same basis for everyone in the educational world. Everyone is an individual and should be treated like one.

Your impressions: _____

_____

_____

_____

_____ Score: _____

Comment to Johnny: *You open your essay with an unnecessarily broad and pointless generalization about grades. Then you ask a couple of questions that suggest you are still searching for an idea to write about. The second paragraph, which might have served as a respectable opening paragraph, is more direct. It contains a strong topic sentence, but its development could be clearer and more economical. The remainder of the essay consists of vivid examples to support your main idea. Sentences are varied and occasionally highly effective. In the third paragraph the terse statement "Students at Harvard Law are different" contrasts nicely with the longer, more diffuse sentences that precede and follow it. The concluding idea, however, is not totally justified by the content of your essay. Overall, though, the essay attests to a measure of your promise as a writer.*

Each reader gave the essay a score of 4, for a total score of 8.

Gavin's Essay

The majority of students work their butts off in school. I believe they deserve high grades for their effort. If a student does'nt work hard and does'nt make an effort I believe that student deserves a low grade. If they like a certain subject they tend to make an effort and do well in the class. This type of student deserves a high grade. If the subject is disliked, the student still should strive and make an effort. They could have an attitude problem. If this student does badly, even if they try their best, I believe they deserve a high grade anyway.

If a student is behind in their educational careers, it does not make any difference. If this type of student tries hard they should receive a high grade. People who don't work hard normally get low grades anyway. Grades are not very important for this type of student. All they want is to graduate. They don't go to college. They are usually at the bottom of the class academicly, studying is the last thing they do. If they apply for a job, their employers won't ask to see their transcript All they want to know about the student is if they passed and got a diploma.

Your impressions: _____

_____

_____

_____

_____ Score: _____

Comment to Gavin: *Your essay, which focuses on the issue of grades and effort, takes into account the different needs of certain types of students. Although it's not always easy to follow your train of thought, you have clearly attempted to develop some of your ideas about grades and effort. Expression is awkward, however, and the repeated use of sentences beginning with "If" suggests a limited awareness of sentence variety. In a few places, the essay suffers from incoherence, and throughout it demonstrates little mastery of basic English usage, especially in the proper use of pronouns.*

Each reader gave the essay a score of 3, for a total score of 6.

Tad's Essay

I believe that in the ideal educational system students should be rewarded with high grades for their effort. No necessarily for their achievement. I believe that a system such as one based on effort would decrease the motivation for cheating. However, a system based entirely on effort might allow for an illiterate child who tries very hard to read to get excellent marks however never learn to read. A common analogy might be a player on a team. Some players try hard, but they shouldn't earn a starting position and cause the team to lose just for that. Realizing this discrepancy, I feel that if a "reward by effort" system was to be instituted, then students would still be required to maintain appropriate grades on exams in each subject. These exams would allow for regular "checks" on what a student's actual understanding of the "concepts at hand" were. Without appropriate grades on these "understanding exams" a student would not be allowed to advance through the educational process. On the aspect of lessening the motive to cheat, this "reward by effort" system could have great advantages. Because ones effort, not achievement, would be rewarded, a student would have to display their own effort in their work, but more importantly, in the classroom. It would be really very difficult to copy someone else's effort during a student's "lunch period."

Your impressions: _____

_____

_____

_____

_____ Score: _____

Comment to Tad: Your essay starts well and contains some interesting, although awkwardly worded, ideas about grades and effort. The examples you present to support your view are not altogether clear or effective. Toward the end of the essay, the point is lost in a puzzling array of quotation marks and a hard-to-follow structure. Had you written more than one paragraph, the meaning of the essay might have been more transparent.

Each reader gave the essay a score of 3, for a total score of 6.

Tiffany's Essay

Education today has turned into a race for the highest numbers. It doesn't matter how hard you work or how much you learn. What is important is the number that appears the top of the paper. In my opinion, this is the wrong way to look at education.

If grades only reflected achievement, there would be almost no point in going to school because almost every student would take the easiest courses, or they would cheat, or find some other way—any way that works—to get that good grade. Meanwhile, they would learn nothing. On the other hand, if students know that a good grade will come only after they put effort into their classes, not only will they work harder, but they would also learn something. In such cases, students will determine to put all they can into their studies. The easy way out will not pave the way to a high quality transcript.

Therefore, grades should indicate neither achievement nor effort alone but a combination of the two criteria. Of all the courses I have taken in high school the one that means the most is Russian History and Literature. In that course the teacher spelled out just what it takes to earn top grades. He expected that in a high-powered elective course with an academically bright population most of us students would earn 90. But if we aimed for the high or mid 90s, we'd have to "go the extra mile." We'd have to do more than just do the homework and participate in class. We'd have to show initiative in other ways, too, by keeping informed of the current events in Russia, for example, or viewing Russian films and reading extra books about Russian society and culture. Some students complained that they didn't have time to do work for extra credit and that it was unfair to be penalized for lack of time, and that a grade should only be for achievement. The teacher insisted, however, that a grade should reflect the whole learning experience, not just how a student did on a particular test. He claimed that intelligent people have a responsibility to exert even greater effort than other people. As they say, "A mind is a terrible thing to waste."

Your impressions: _____

_____

_____

_____

_____ Score: _____

Comment to Tiffany: *This is a well-reasoned argument for learning. Your opening is strong and appealing, and you've supported your point of view with clear observations and a compelling illustration taken from your own experience in school. Not only is the essay well organized, it consists of a coherent progression of ideas that demonstrate a high degree of competency in expressing yourself in writing.*

Each reader gave the essay a score of 6, for a total score of 12.

SELF-SCORING GUIDE

Using this guide, rate yourself in each of these six categories. Enter your scores in the spaces provided, and calculate the average of the six ratings to determine your final score. On the SAT itself, two readers will score your essay on a scale of 6 (high) to 1 (low), or *zero* if the essay fails to respond to the assignment. The score will be reported to you as the sum of the two ratings, from 12 (best) to 2 (worst). Because it's difficult to read your own essay with objectivity, you might improve the validity of your score by asking an informed friend or teacher to serve as a second reader. Or better, recruit two different readers to evaluate your essay.

Remember, too, that SAT essays are judged in relation to other essays written on the same topic. Therefore, this scoring guide may not yield a totally accurate prediction of the score you can expect on the exam.

Overall Impression

6 Consistently outstanding in clarity and competence; very insightful; few, if any, errors

5 Reasonably consistent in clarity and competence; occasional errors or lapses in quality; contains some insight

4 Adequate competence; some lapses in quality; fairly clear and with evidence of insight

3 Generally inadequate but demonstrates potential competence; contains some confusing aspects

2 Seriously limited; significant weaknesses in quality; generally unclear or incoherent

1 Demonstrates fundamental incompetence; contains serious flaws; significantly undeveloped or confusing

Score ☐

Development of Point of View

6   Fully developed with clear and appropriate supporting material; demonstrates high level of critical thinking

5   Generally well developed with appropriate examples, reasons, and other evidence to support a main idea; demonstrates strong critical thinking

4   Partly develops a main idea with relatively appropriate examples and reasons; shows some evidence of critical thinking

3   Weak development of main idea and little evidence of critical thinking; barely appropriate examples or other supporting material

2   Lacks a focus on a main idea; weak critical thinking; inappropriate or insufficient evidence

1   Fails to articulate a viable point of view; provides virtually no evidence of understanding the prompt

Score ☐

Organization of Ideas

6   Extremely well organized and focused on a main idea; supporting evidence presented in an effective, logical sequence

5   Generally well organized and reasonably focused on a main idea; mostly coherent and logical presentation of supporting material

4   Reasonably organized; shows some evidence of thoughtful sequence and progression of ideas

3   Limited organization and vague focus on main idea; contains some confusion in the sequence of ideas

2   Barely recognizable organization; little coherence; serious problems with sequence of ideas

1   No discernable organization; incoherent sequence of ideas

Score ☐

Language and Word Choice

6   Highly effective and skillful use of language; varied, appropriate, and accurate vocabulary

5   Demonstrates competence in use of language; appropriate and correct vocabulary

4   Adequate but inconsistent use of effective language; conventional but mostly correct use of vocabulary

3   Some minor errors in expression; generally weak or limited vocabulary; occasionally inappropriate word choice

2   Frequent errors in expression; very limited vocabulary; incorrect word choice interferes with meaning

1   Seriously deficient in use of language; meaning obscured by word choice

Score ☐

Sentence Structure

6	Varied and engaging sentence structure
5	Sufficiently varied sentence structure
4	Some sentence variation
3	Little sentence variation; minor sentence errors
2	Frequent sentence errors
1	Severe sentence errors; meaning obscured

Score ☐

Grammar, Usage, and Mechanics

6	Virtually or entirely error-free
5	Contains some minor errors
4	Some minor errors; one or two major errors
3	Accumulated minor and major errors
2	Contains frequent major errors that interfere with meaning
1	Contains severe errors that obscure meaning

Score ☐

<u>For rating yourself</u>

Total of six scores _____

Divide total by 6 to get score: _____ (A)

(A) + (B) = ESSAY SUBSCORE _____
                              (0–12)

<u>For a second opinion</u>

Total of six scores _____

Divide total by 6 to get score: _____ (B)

ANSWERS TO MULTIPLE-CHOICE QUESTIONS

Section 2

1. **B**	11. **C**	21. **B**	31. **E**
2. **D**	12. **C**	22. **C**	32. **B**
3. **C**	13. **C**	23. **B**	33. **A**
4. **E**	14. **B**	24. **B**	34. **A**
5. **E**	15. **D**	25. **A**	35. **D**
6. **B**	16. **E**	26. **B**	
7. **B**	17. **E**	27. **D**	
8. **D**	18. **D**	28. **B**	
9. **C**	19. **B**	29. **E**	
10. **A**	20. **B**	30. **C**	

Section 3

1. **D**	11. **B**
2. **D**	12. **D**
3. **A**	13. **A**
4. **E**	14. **C**
5. **B**	
6. **D**	
7. **A**	
8. **D**	
9. **E**	
10. **D**	

PERFORMANCE EVALUATION CHART

I. Self-rating Chart

Section 2

Improving Sentences, questions 1–11   Number correct _____

Identifying Sentence Errors, questions 12–29   Number correct _____

Improving Paragraphs, questions 30–35   Number correct _____

Section 3

Improving Sentences, questions 1-14   Number correct _____

Subtotal _____ (A)

Wrong answers (Do not count unanswered questions.)

Section 2   Number wrong _____

Section 3   Number wrong _____   Subtotal _____ (B)

Subtract ¼ point (0.25) from (B) for each wrong answer   _____ (C)

(A) minus (C) = _____ (D)

Round (D) to the nearest whole number for your MULTIPLE-CHOICE RAW SCORE   _____

ESSAY SUBSCORE   _____

CONVERSION TABLE

This table will give you an approximation of what your score would be if this practice test had been an actual SAT Writing Test. The essay counts for roughly 30% of the final score; the multiple-choice questions, for roughly 70%.

For example, if your Multiple-Choice Raw Score was 35 and your Essay Subscore was 6, the table indicates that your final score on the test would be approximately half-way between 500 and 710, or 600.

Multiple-Choice Raw Score	Essay Subscore						
	0	2	4	6	8	10	12
40–49	520–690	530–720	550–740	580–770	620–800	650–800	680–800
30–39	430–630	450–660	470–680	500–710	530–740	560–770	590–800
20–29	360–540	370–570	390–590	420–620	460–650	490–690	520–710
10–19	270–460	280–490	300–510	330–540	370–580	400–610	430–630
0–9	200–380	200–410	210–430	240–450	270–490	300–520	330–560
–12––1	200–280	200–310	200–330	200–350	240–390	270–420	300–450

ANSWER EXPLANATIONS

SECTION 2—IMPROVING SENTENCES

Note: Although some choices contain multiple errors, only one or two major errors are explained for each incorrect choice. Page numbers refer to relevant material for study or review.

1. **B**   Choice A violates the parallelism of the series of phrases.
Choice B is the best answer. It expresses the third item in the list of home furnishings as a noun phrase parallel in form to *a pottery kiln* and *high-tech stainless steel appliances*.
Choice C, by inverting the usual word order, is awkwardly expressed.
Choices D and E violate the parallelism of the series of phrases.
(See *Faulty parallelism*, page 146, and *Awkwardness*, page 137.)

2. **D**   Choices A, B, and E incorrectly shift the verb tense from the past tense to other tenses.
Choice C is in the past tense, but it also contains the clumsy and pointless phrase *having turned*.
Choice D is the best answer. It maintains a verb tense consistent with the rest of the sentence.
(See *Shifts in verb tense*, page 148.)

3. **C**   Choice A uses the singular pronoun *it* to refer to the plural antecedent *schedules*.
Choice B uses an adjective, *reckless*, instead of the adverb *recklessly*.
Choice C is the best answer.
Choice D, like B, uses an adjective where an adverb is needed and also includes the clumsily worded construction *and there is not*.
Choice E is clumsily expressed and, like A, uses a singular instead of a plural pronoun.
(See *Pronoun–antecedent agreement,* page 159, and *Faulty diction,* page 168.)

4. **E**   Choice A contains a comma splice. It also uses the singular pronoun *it* to refer to the plural noun *computers*.
Choice B includes an awkward construction, *resulting from not knowing*, and uses a singular pronoun *it* to refer to the plural noun *computers*.
Choice C is excessively wordy. Also, the construction *for the reason being that* is not expressed in standard English.
Choice D uses the singular pronoun *it* to refer to the plural noun *computers*.
Choice E is the best answer.
(See *Pronoun–antcedent agreement*, page 157, and *Comma splices*, page 142.)

5. **E**   Choice A uses a plural verb, *were*, with a singular subject, *program*.
Choice B uses the objective case pronoun, *them*, instead of the possessive pronoun, *their*.
Choice C uses a plural pronoun, *their*, to refer to a singular noun, *program*. It also includes the awkward and meaningless construction, *their regard as being*.
Choice D includes an awkward phrase, *of regarding it*. The sentence also fails to say who regards the program as an important aspect of high school
Choice E is the best answer.
(See *Subject–verb agreement*, page 152, and *Faulty pronoun case*, page 157.)

6. **B**   Choice A includes a comparison that uses the word *other*, indicating that Annie Oakley is a cowboy, an unlikely identity for someone named Annie.
Choice B is the best answer.
Choice C contains a comma splice.
Choice D shifts the structure of the sentence and makes little sense.
Choice E has the same problem as A.
(See *Incomplete comparisons*, page 174, and *Comma splice*, page 142.)

7. **B**   Choice A illogically compares residents of Chicago to the city of Minneapolis.
Choice B is the best answer.
Choice C correctly makes the intended comparison but includes a clumsy construction, *have equally the right*.
Choice D illogically compares residents of Chicago to the city of Minneapolis.
Choice E is a sentence fragment.
(See *Faulty comparisons*, page 163, and *Sentence fragments*, page 139.)

8. **D**   Choice A is unsatisfactory because the pronoun *they* fails to refer to any specific noun or other pronoun.
Choice B is unsatisfactory because the verbs *spoils* and *enhancing* are in different tenses.
Choice C is similar to B; the tense of the two verbs should be the same.
Choice D is the best answer.
Choice E is unsatisfactory because the word order in the first clause is nonstandard.
(See *Faulty pronoun reference*, page 162, *Shifts in verb tense*, page 148, and *Faulty idiom*, page 138.)

9. **C**   Choice A is unsatisfactory because the shift in grammatical subject from *passengers* to *searches* leads to the awkward usage *but there are not frequent*.
Choice B contains a subordination problem. The sentence would be more effectively expressed if one clause were subordinated to the other.
Choice C is the best answer.
Choice D shifts the subject from *passengers* in the first clause to *searching* in the second clause. This shift leads to the awkward usage *the searching of their bodies*.
Choice E violates standard English idiom.
(See *Shift in grammatical subject*, page 148, and *Faulty idiom*, page 138.)

10. **A**   Choice A is the best answer.
Choice B uses the plural verb *have changed* with a singular subject, *concept*. Use *has changed*.
Choice C uses the singular verb *has been* with a plural subject, *changes*. Use *have been*.
Choice D uses the plural verb *have undergone* with a singular subject *humankind*. Use *has undergone*.
Choice E uses the plural pronoun *their* to refer to a singular antecedent, *humankind*. Use *its* instead of *their*.
(See *Subject–verb agreement*, page 152, and *Pronoun–antecedent agreement*, page 159.)

11. **C**   Choice A contains a pronoun *their*, which fails to refer to any specific noun or other pronoun.
Choice B twice uses the pronoun *their*. Neither refers to any specific noun or other pronoun.
Choice C is the best answer. The pronoun *its* refers to *tradition*.
Choice D makes a noun–verb error by pairing a singular verb *explores* with two nouns, *stories and music*.
Choice E violates standard English idiom.
(See *Faulty pronoun reference*, page 161, and *Faulty idiom*, page 138.)

SECTION 2—IDENTIFYING SENTENCE ERRORS

12. **C**   Faulty verb tense. The present tense should not be used to describe an event that took place in the past. Use *decided*. (page 156)

13. **C**   Faulty comparison. When using *more* in making a comparison, use the positive form of the adjective as in *more happy*. (page 163)

14. **B**   Subject–verb agreement. The plural noun *dilemmas* requires a plural verb. Use *are*. (page 152)

15. **D**   Faulty diction. When referring to a person, use the pronoun *who* rather than *which*. (page 168)

16. **E**   No error.

17. **E**   No error.

18. **D**   Faulty verb tense. The past perfect tense should be used to express action completed prior to some other event or action. Use *had preferred* instead of *will prefer*. (page 180)

19. **B**   Faulty pronoun reference. The singular pronoun *this* fails to refer to any specific noun or other pronoun. (page 178)

20. **B**   Faulty parallelism. Verbs in a series should be in parallel form. Use *represents*. (page 173)

21. **B**   Noun–verb agreement. The plural noun *Many* requires a plural verb. Use *have opposed* instead of *has opposed*. (page 176)

22. **C**   Faulty parallelism. Verbs in a series should be in parallel form. Use *gives them* or an equivalent verb in the present tense. (page 173)

23. **B**   Noun–verb agreement. The singular noun *examination* requires a singular verb. Use *does* instead of *do*. (page 176)

24. **B**   Wordiness. Use either *once more* or *again*, but not both, because they are redundant. (page 171)

25. **A**   Faulty verb tense. Use *has been* (present perfect) to refer to action that occurred in the past and is still in progress. (page 180)

26. **B**   Faulty idiom. In standard English usage, the idiom is *significant to*. Use *to* in place of *for*. (page 166)

27. **D**   Faulty comparison. A double comparison is created by adding *-er* to the adjective. Use *larger* instead of *largest*. (page 163)

28. **B**   Faulty pronoun case. Pronouns in a phrase beginning with a preposition (*between*) must be in the objective case. Use *me* instead of *I*. (page 179)

29. **E**   No error.

SECTION 2—IMPROVING PARAGRAPHS

30. **C**   The writer has used "having learned," a form of the verb used to express action completed before another action. (For example, *Having learned about the impending hurricane, the residents evacuated their homes*.) In sentence 1, however, the writer intended to say that all students of American history have learned and continue to learn about the building of the transcontinental railroad. Therefore, a different form of the verb is a better choice.
Choice A is an unsatisfactory answer because the sentence uses an incorrect verb form.
Choice B suggests that sentence 2 would serve as a better opening sentence of the essay. But because sentence 1 is more general, it is a more effective introduction.
Choice C is the best answer.
Choice D alters the intended meaning by improperly placing the focus of the sentence on students who studied American history long ago.
Choice E improperly deletes the comma and adds needless words to the sentence.

31. **E**   Although sentences 4 and 5 are grammatical, they are wordy. The phrase "accomplishing this great feat of engineering" needlessly echoes the idea expressed by "great physical achievement." By combining the sentences, one of the repetitive phrases can be eliminated, thereby making the sentence more concise.
Choice A contains a comma splice. Two independent sentences may not be joined by a comma. Either a semicolon or a period and capital letter should be used.
Choice B is unsatisfactory because it eliminates one of the essay's important ideas—that the railroad was a technological marvel.
Choices C and D are unsatisfactory not only because they add irrelevant ideas to the essay, but they also create irrelevant links between the exploitation of the workers and other matters.
Choice E is the best answer. It reduces the number of words, eliminates the repetition, and adds interest to the sentence by alluding to the fascinating contrast between the colossal achievement of building the railroad and its horrendous cost.

32. **B**   Although sentences 8 and 9 are grammatically correct, to develop the essay more fully and to improve its coherence the relationship between the two sentences should be tighter. A transitional word or phrase is needed to explain the reason for unsafe conditions.
Choices A and C are common and often useful transitions, but neither is appropriate in this context.
Choice B is the best answer. It provides an idea that clearly links the information contained in the two sentences.
Choice D introduces an awkwardly expressed idea suggesting improperly that only the Chinese workers were exploited.
Choice E not only creates repetition but it mars the essay's objectivity. Whether a piece of evidence is good or not should be left for the reader to decide. Writers shouldn't editorialize on the quality of their examples.

33. **A** Good writers take pains to write specifically. The vagueness of the phrase "unsafe and cost lives" in sentence 9 might well leave readers wondering about what perils of railroad work the writer had in mind.

Choice A is the best answer. Along with sentence 11, it vividly details one of the perils faced by workers on the railroad.

Choice B overstates the function of sentence 10 because the writer offers no real "proof" that the methods were unsafe.

Choices C, D, and E fail to describe accurately how sentence 10 supports or develops sentence 9.

34. **A** The short last paragraph of the essay lacks a main idea. The two sentences contained in the paragraph refer to two different matters: (1) the government's role in paying for the railroad's construction, and (2) the character of the men who ran the operation. What the paragraph needs is a topic sentence that somehow unifies these disparate concerns.

Choice A is the best answer. It provides a reason for the government's financial participation in the project, and it alludes to the fact that the railroad's construction was basically a private enterprise.

Choice B is an unsatisfactory topic sentence for this paragraph. It is better suited for a paragraph on the debt incurred by the government to pay for the railroad.

Choices C, D, and E refer to matters related to the building of the railroad, but none of them focuses directly on the contents of sentences 13 and 14.

35. **D** Sentence 14 leaves the reader hanging. It asserts that greed drove the businessmen to engage in fraud but provides none of the gory details. To be convincing, the paragraph needs to be developed with specific evidence and examples.

Choices A, B, and E are related to the topic of the entire essay but have nothing to do with the issues raised in the last paragraph.

Choice C may be a tempting answer because it suggests vaguely that the men condoned shoddy construction methods in order to save money, but that is a detail better left for later in the paragraph. First, the paragraph should focus more generally on the men's unethical business dealings.

Choice D is the best answer. It correctly describes the material that should follow sentence 14.

SECTION 3—IMPROVING SENTENCES

1. **D** Choice A is unsatisfactory because it joins two independent clauses with a comma. Therefore, it is a comma splice.

Choice B is a sentence fragment. It has a subject, *letters*, but it lacks a verb.

Choice C is written in the passive voice and also contains a comma splice.

Choice D is the best answer.

Choice E contains two clauses with no grammatical relation to each other.

(See *Comma splice*, page 142, *Sentence fragments*, page 139, and *Mismatched sentence parts*, page 143.)

2. **D**   Choice A contains a dangling modifier; the clause that begins *Before going* should modify *student* instead of *parental permission slip*.
Choice B uses a plural pronoun, *their*, to refer to a singular antecedent, *student*.
Choice C uses a pronoun, *their*, that lacks a specific reference to a noun or other pronoun.
Choice D is the best answer.
Choice E contains a dangling modifier; the clause that begins *Before going* should modify *student* instead of *permission*.
(See *Dangling modifiers*, page 151, and *Faulty pronoun reference*, page 161.)

3. **A**   Choice A is the best answer.
Choice B contains the awkwardly worded construction *Although its being*.
Choice C creates a sentence containing a comma splice.
Choice D includes *because*, an illogical word choice in the context of the sentence.
Choice E contains a faulty modifier; the phrase that begins *Calling it* lacks an appropriate noun or pronoun to modify.
(See *Comma splices*, page 142, and *Misplaced modifier*, page 151.)

4. **E**   Choice A contains a pronoun, *it*, that lacks a reference to a specific noun or other pronoun.
Choice B shifts the verb from the present to the past perfect tense.
Choice C is excessively wordy.
Choice D contains an error in idiom. In context, *satisfaction out of sports* is nonstandard English. Use *satisfaction in*.
Choice E is the best answer.
(See *Faulty pronoun reference*, page 161, and *Faulty idiom*, page 138.)

5. **B**   Choice A violates the parallelism of a series. The first two accusations are stated as nouns—*cowardice* and *desertion*. The third should also be stated as a noun.
Choice B is the best answer.
Choice C violates the parallelism of a series. See A.
Choice D violates the parallelism of a series. See A.
Choice E violates the parallelism of a series. See A.
(See *Faulty parallelism*, page 146.)

6. **D**   Choice A incorrectly switches the grammatical subject from *cell phones* to *they*.
Choice B uses a pronoun, *their*, that fails to refer to a specific noun or other pronoun.
Choice C uses a pronoun, *they*, that fails to refer to a specific noun or other pronoun.
Choice D is the best answer.
Choice E incorrectly switches the grammatical subject from *cell phones* to *they*.
(See *Shifts in grammatical subject*, page 148, and *Faulty pronoun reference*, page 161.)

7. **A**   Choice A is the best answer.
Choice B misuses the word *whereas*, which means *in view of the fact that*.
Choice C contains the singular antecedent *whale* that disagrees with its plural pronoun *they*.
Choice D contains faulty expression. It is the whale itself, not its size, that grows.
Choice E sets up a faulty cause-and-effect relationship. The size of a whale's ear is not caused by the creature's overall dimensions.
(See *Faulty word choice*, page 138, and *Awkwardness*, page 137.)

8. **D**   Choice A, although grammatically correct, ineffectively uses the conjunction *and* to link its two independent clauses.
Choice B contains a comma splice.
Choice C illogically uses the conjunction *and* to link its two independent clauses.
Choice D is the best answer. The conjunction *but* effectively sets up a contrast between the sentence's two independent clauses.
Choice E contains a dangling modifier; the clause that begins *Reading at* should modify *your eyes* or *your mind* instead of *words*.
(See *Faulty coordination*, page 145, *Comma splice*, page 142, and *Dangling modifiers*, page 151.)

9. **E**   Choice A is a sentence fragment; it lacks a main verb to go with *author*, the grammatical subject. The *–ing* form of a verb (e.g., *portraying*) cannot serve as the main verb without a helping verb, as in *is portraying* or *had been portraying*.
Choice B contains mismatched sentence parts. It is the author, not the reader, who portrays the plight of women.
Choice C is a sentence fragment; it lacks a main verb to go with *reader*, the grammatical subject. See A.
Choice D is a sentence fragment; it lacks a main verb to go with *author*, the grammatical subject.
Choice E is the best answer.
(See *Sentence fragments*, page 139, and *Misplaced modifiers*, page 151.)

10. **D**   Choice A contains an error in English idiom. In context the phrase *through many countries* is nonstandard.
Choice B uses the singular pronoun *its* to refer to the plural noun *countries*.
Choice C uses the singular pronoun *its* to refer to the plural noun *countries*.
Choice D is the best choice.
Choice E contains the plural pronoun *their* to refer to the singular noun *country*.
(See *Awkwardness*, page 137, and *Pronoun–antecedent agreement*, page 159.)

11. **B**   Choice A contains a confusing sequence. The use of *while* suggests that 2004 and 2005 occurred at the same time.
Choice B is the best answer.
Choice C contains *with continuing growth*, a construction grammatically unrelated to the main clause of the sentence.
Choice D contains a comma splice.
Choice E is expressed in awkward, nonstandard language.
(See *Faulty subordination*, page 145, *Mismatched sentence parts*, page 143, and *Comma splices*, page 142.)

12. **D**   Choice A is a sentence fragment. Its grammatical subject, *The Black Death*, lacks a verb.
Choice B contains a clause (*its origin is thought . . .*) that is grammatically unrelated to the previous part of the sentence.
Choice C contains a misplaced modifier. The phrase beginning *Possibly the world's* should modify *Black Death* instead of *origin*.
Choice D is the best answer.
Choice E contains *was possibly the world's . . .* , a construction grammatically unrelated to the rest of the sentence.
(See *Sentence fragments*, page 139, *Comma splices*, page 142, *Misplaced modifiers*, page 151, and *Mixed construction*, page 147.)

13. **A**   Choice A is the best answer.
Choice B contains a misplaced modifier. *Both* should modify *reputation and performance* instead of *diminished*.
Choice C is wordy. The word *both* and the phrase *as well as* are redundant.
Choice D contains the pronoun *its*, which refers ambiguously to both *faculty* and *school*.
Choice E contains a problem in subordination. The sentence would be more effectively expressed if one clause were subordinated to the other.
(See *Faulty parallelism*, page 146, *Wordiness*, page 136, *Faulty pronoun reference*, page 161, and *Faulty coordination*, page 145.)

14. **C**   Choice A uses an awkward phrase, *this explaining*.
Choice B is a comma splice.
Choice C is the best answer.
Choice D contains a sentence fragment.
Choice E contains a nonsensical construction: The subject *restaurants* is unrelated to the verb *explains*.
(See *Awkwardness*, page 137, *Comma splice*, page 142, *Sentence fragments,* page 139, and *Mismatched sentence parts*, page 143.)

PART III

HOW TO WRITE AN ESSAY IN TWENTY-FIVE MINUTES

Don't be misled by the title of this chapter. It's a come-on, not a promise. For one thing, writing an essay in twenty-five minutes may be a contradiction in terms. An essay is basically the product of an author's thinking. It expresses a point of view arrived at after reflection, analysis, or interpretation of a subject or issue. When given the topic less than half an hour before the paper is due, you can't expect to pore over the assignment. If you think too deeply, before you know it, you'll have run out of time.

Another reason that the heading is illusory is that you don't learn to write very well by reading about how to do it. You learn to write by writing, by messing around with ideas and words, by experimenting, by practicing, and by doing what seasoned practitioners do when they face a sheet of blank paper or an empty computer screen: They write!

THE ESSAY-WRITING PROCESS

The next several pages will acquaint you with what expert writers think about as they practice their craft. In addition, as you learn what works and what to avoid, you'll become more attuned to some of the basic principles of good writing. Because you won't have time to invent a process when you write your SAT essay, it pays to have one in mind ahead of time. In preparation for the test, try out various processes while writing practice essays. Then develop the one that enables you to work most rapidly and efficiently while producing the best results. In effect, make a plan for what to do during each stage of the writing process.

The first stage, often called *pre-writing*, consists of everything that needs to be done before you actually start writing. During the second stage, *composing*, you choose the words and form the sentences that express your thoughts. And during the final stage, *revising and proofreading*, you polish and refine the text of your essay word by word, making it clear, correct, and graceful. The truth is that these three stages overlap and blend indiscriminately. Writers compose, revise, and proofread simultaneously, they jot down sentences during pre-writing, and even late in the process may weave new ideas into their text. In fact, no stage really ends until the final period of the last sentence is put in place—or until your proctor at the SAT test site calls "Time!"

No book can tell you just how much time to devote to each step in the process. What works for you may be different from what works for others. But the three best ways for anybody to prepare are (1) to practice, (2) to practice, and (3) to practice some more.

Pick sample essay topics found on pages 129–130. Following the instructions for SAT essays, write an essay a day for several days in a row, or until you get the feel of twenty-five minutes' writing time. Pace yourself. Keep a record of how much time you spend thinking about the topic, how many minutes you devote to composing the essay, and how long it takes you to proofread and edit. As you practice, adjust the following plan until you get the timing that suits you best and produces the results you want:

Pre-writing: 4–5 minutes
    Reading and analyzing the prompt
    Picking and narrowing the topic
    Choosing a main idea
    Gathering and arranging supporting ideas
Composing the essay: 15-18 minutes
    Introducing the thesis
    Developing paragraphs
    Choosing the best words for meaning and effect
    Structuring sentences effectively
    Writing a conclusion
Editing and proofreading: 4–5 minutes
    Editing for clarity and coherence
    Editing to create interest
    Checking for standard usage and mechanical errors, including spelling, punctuation, and capitalization

To make every second count, don't waste time inventing an essay title (your essay doesn't need one). Don't count words, and don't expect to recopy your first draft. Because readers understand that SAT essays are first drafts, feel free to cross out, insert words using carets (^), and move blocks of text—as though you were cutting and pasting—with neatly drawn arrows. If necessary, number the sentences to make clear the order in which they are to be read. You won't be penalized for a sloppy-looking paper. Just make sure that the essay is readable.

Because of the time limit, don't plan to write a long essay. Essays of more than 400 words are unnecessary. It doesn't take even that many words to demonstrate your writing ability. In fact, less can be more, for a shorter essay of, say, 250 to 300 words can focus sharply on a limited subject. It can also be written more quickly, leaving time for revising and polishing your work. But don't be satisfied with an abbreviated one-paragraph essay that could suggest empty-headedness. Just keep in mind that quantity counts less than quality.

PRE-WRITING: GETTING SET TO WRITE

READING AND ANALYZING THE TOPIC CAREFULLY

At the risk of stating the obvious, begin by reading the assigned essay topic, or prompt, very carefully. Read it twice or three times, or until you are certain what is being asked of you.

SAT essay prompts usually begin with a quotation or a short passage meant to draw you into an issue. Their intention is to provoke thought and suggest an idea or two to discuss in your essay. When writing your essay, you may wish to refer to the quotation or passage, but it's not a necessity. Weave it into your essay if you wish, but only if it's appropriate and advantageous to do so.

The prompt may not turn you on right away, but once you begin to think about it, you may begin bursting with good ideas. Consider your essay as a kind of contract or agreement between you and readers who'll be spending time with your words and want something that will engage their minds and hearts. As the writer, you are being challenged to write something so riveting that readers will resist the temptation of moving their eyes off of the page or letting their minds wander. In a way, writing an essay is a lot like giving a gift to a friend. You think about what they'd like, you try to please, you choose carefully, and you present the gift as stylishly as you can. And if all goes well, you get a reward for your efforts.

Practice in Analyzing Topics

Read the following pair of typical SAT essay topics carefully. Underline the key words that define the task to be performed. Then, in the blank spaces, write the steps that you would take to respond to the topic.

Topic A

Think carefully about the issue presented in the following statement and the assignment below.

> Failure should be our teacher, not our undertaker. Failure is delay, not defeat. It is a temporary detour, not a dead end. Failure is something we can avoid only by saying nothing, doing nothing, and being nothing.
> Denis Waitley, *Seeds of Greatness*

Assignment: Is failure a temporary setback resulting from inaction or indifference? Plan and write an essay in which you explain and develop your view on this issue. Support your position with reasoning and evidence drawn from your reading, studies, experience, or observation.

Required task:

_____

_____

_____

Explanation: Do you agree with Denis Waitley's definition of failure—that failure is a temporary condition that stems from apathy and indifference? Or do you think that failure is like an unavoidable chronic disease over which we have no real control? Or do you stand somewhere between those two extremes?

The essay you are asked to write should discuss your opinion. The position you take is less crucial than your ability to support your ideas with specific examples from your knowledge, background, or observation. Examples may come from books, from your studies, from personal experience, or from what you know about the lives of others.

An interesting and readable response to the question might be based on your own life. If you agree with the prompt, you might write about a failure you experienced in school, in a personal relationship, or in a task that you once undertook. Briefly describe the failure and explain its cause. Did it stem from your own apathy or inaction? Explain how your lack of success led to temporary setback from which you may have learned a valuable lesson.

On the other hand, through no fault of your own, you may have experienced a failure with life-altering consequences. In that case, your essay might show that the prompt is seriously flawed and shortsighted.

Obviously, there are at least two sides to the issue. Whatever your position, however, be sure to include more than one example. Single examples rarely make convincing arguments.

Topic B

Think carefully about the issue presented in the following quotation and the assignment below.

> Ask yourself whether you are happy, and you cease to be.
>
> John Stuart Mill (1806–1873)

Assignment: Does the need to question or evaluate your happiness mean that you are not as happy as you think? Plan and write an essay in which you state and develop your point of view on this issue. Support your position with evidence drawn from your reading, studies, experience, or observation.

Required task:

_____

_____

_____

_____

Explanation: What you write depends largely on your interpretation of the word *happiness*. If you take it to mean a state of blissful well-being and unexamined contentment, then you might agree with the prompt. Questioning your own happiness may indeed lead you to the startling discovery that you are less happy than you thought. Such an event may call to mind the fate of Adam and Eve. Once they tasted of the Tree of Knowledge, they lost their paradise forever. But if you think of happiness as a complex emotion requiring scrutiny from time to time, then your essay would take issue with the prompt. Think of Socrates' famous saying, "The unexamined life is not worth living."

Or you might take another, more circumspect, point of view. You may believe that absolute statements about happiness are foolish because happiness comes in many forms. Happiness experienced over a lifetime, for instance, differs greatly from short-lived merriment at a party on Friday night.

NARROWING THE TOPIC MERCILESSLY

A well-focused essay on a limited topic is always preferable to an essay that tries to cover too much ground in just a few paragraphs. That's why narrowing the topic is one of the crucial steps in planning your SAT essay. The sharper your focus, the better.

If you are a fast writer, you might scribble 350 well-chosen words onto the page in twenty-five minutes. (That's about the number of words on a double-spaced typed page using 12-point type.) If the topic is too broad, at best you are likely to state a few obvious generalities, resort to hackneyed ideas, and maybe even throw the bull a little bit. In short, your essay would be too vague, too superficial, and too empty of substance to demonstrate how deeply you can really think. On the other hand, if you've narrowed the topic sufficiently, you stand a far better chance of saying something sensible, scintillating, meaningful, provocative, and interesting. And never doubt that an interesting essay won't work on your behalf.

It's impossible to predict the topic you'll be asked to write on, but because it must accommodate a multiethnic, multicultural, and multitalented mass of test takers, it is bound to be extremely broad. Your first task, therefore, is to think small—to reduce the topic to a size snug enough to fit into a short essay.

It may be useful to construct a ladder of abstraction. That is, start at the top with the most general word or phrase suggested by the topic, such as *democracy, generosity, the human condition, politics,* or *acts of kindness.* As you descend the ladder, make each rung increasingly specific. Stop when you reach the level that provides you with a topic sufficiently narrow for a short essay. Consider these examples:

Topic 1

Let's say the prompt asks about common misunderstandings caused by faulty communication between people. Call the topic *Communications.*

Communications	*Highest level of abstraction*
Functions of communication	*Way too broad for a short essay*
Communications technology	*Still too broad*
Communications media	*Still too broad*
Electronic and digital communications	*Better, but still too broad*
The widespread use of cell phones	*Getting there, but still very broad*
Use of cell phones in public places	*Close, but not there yet*
Annoying aspects of cell-phone use in public	*An acceptable topic*
An unpleasant encounter with a cell-phone user in the school library	*Definitely a topic for a short essay*

Topic 2: Athletics

Athletes	*Highest level of abstraction*
Professional athletics	*Far too broad*
Baseball players	*Still too broad*
Players vs. owners	*Still very broad*
Salary negotiations	*Still rather broad for a short essay*
Why some players seem overpaid	*A reasonable topic*
How wealth affected X, a rich, young ballplayer	*A concise topic for a short essay*

Topic 3: Democracy

Democracy	*Highest level of abstraction*
Democracy in conflict with dictatorship	*Extremely broad for a short essay*
Individual rights vs. government control	*Still too broad*
The right to print opinions without censorship	*Very broad, but getting closer*
The right to print a scandalous story in a school newspaper.	*Possible topic for a short essay*
What happened to Pamela when *The Lantern* published a story about incompetent teachers	*Distinct possibility for an essay*

On the SAT, lack of time will prevent you from writing out a five- or six-step ladder of abstraction. Therefore, practice ahead of time, and by test day you may be able to jump mentally from the highest rung to the lowest without writing a word.

Some writers find that a more efficient way to narrow a topic is to begin writing. If the essay strikes them as dull or disappointing after a few sentences, they may realize that their topic was too vague, too broad, too boring (and if the writer is bored, imagine what the essay will do to prospective readers). Because they've written themselves into a cul-de-sac, they must grit their teeth, turn to another topic, and start again. Time restraints on the SAT won't give you more than one chance to start over. That minute you devote to narrowing the topic, therefore, may prove to be the most important sixty seconds of the exam.

Practice in Narrowing Topics

To reduce each of the following topics to a level of specificity appropriate for a short essay, build ladders of abstraction. Keep descending until you have a truly concise topic.

Celebrations   *Calamities*
Virtues of hard work   *The nature of beauty*
Catastrophic success   *Obsolescence*
Red tape   *Leisure*
Change vs. permanence   *Fear of the unknown*

CHOOSING A MAIN IDEA

Once you've narrowed the topic, it's time to decide what to say about the topic. That is, you need to devise an idea that will become the purpose, or point, of the essay. An essay shouldn't simply be "about," say, hard work, heroism, beauty, or any other topic. What counts in an essay is the statement you make about hard work, heroism, or beauty—in short, its main idea. Essays may be written with beautiful words, contain profound thoughts, and make readers laugh or weep. But without a main idea, an essay remains just words in search of a meaning. You don't want readers coming to the end of your essay scratching their heads and asking, "Huh? What's the point?"

Every bit of your essay from start to finish should contribute to its main idea, or thesis. Any material that wanders from the main idea should be discarded. It not only wastes words but detracts from the impact of your essay. Naturally, the main idea of your essay will depend on your response to the particular issue presented by the prompt. It will be a statement of your opinion.

Let's say the issue relates to the fundamental rights of high school students. So, you think about the issue and narrow the topic by focusing on high school dress codes. Your main idea might be any of the following:

1. Yes, a high schools may implement a dress code without violating a student's basic rights.
2. No, a high school should not be permitted to violate its students' rights by instituting a dress code.
3. High schools should be allowed to impose dress codes but only on students under age 16.
4. High school dress codes not only destroy students' rights but also imply that students lack good judgment.
5. Dress codes improve a school's environment, thereby enhancing students' rights to a good education.
6. A strict dress code teaches students about living in a repressive society.
7. A strict dress code encourages students to appreciate the rights that they will someday enjoy as citizens in a free society.

Using one of these main ideas as its starting point, the essay would then discuss the validity of your opinion.

Another SAT question may ask you to address an issue related to teenage drivers. Let's say, for instance, you are asked to write about seat belt laws that require everyone in a car—driver and all passengers front and back—to buckle up. Your main point might be that seat belt laws infringe on a driver's freedom of choice. Or the essay's point might be that safety laws supercede a person's right to choose whether to wear a seat belt. Or you might use the essay to prove that driving without seat belts is not a real issue because to do so is dangerous and stupid.

Choosing a Main Idea for Your SAT Essay

Topic: The prompt gives you an issue to write about.

Main Idea: The main idea is a statement of your opinion on the issue.

Purpose: The essay gives you an opportunity to develop support for your opinion using reasoning and examples taken from your reading, studies, experience, or observation.

If possible, choose a main idea that matters to you personally. SAT readers won't find fault with opinions with which they disagree. If you give your readers only what you think they might want, you're being dishonest, posing as someone you are not. Likewise, because you don't want to sound pompous or pretentious, avoid picking a main idea solely to show off intellectual superiority or political correctness. An essay that is truthful and comes from the heart will serve you best.

At the same time, however, steer clear of main ideas that are clichés and platitudes. Consider your readers. As they plod through scores of SAT essays on the same topic, they'll appreciate and reward those that contain fresh ideas. Try, therefore, to devise a main idea that will set you apart from other students. Not that your main idea should be off the wall. Creativity helps but it's not essential. You'll never be penalized for a clearly written, sober essay that demonstrates insightful thinking and beliefs.

Chances are that the SAT will give you a question to which you can respond without too much difficulty. But what if you don't care a fig for writing about it. What then? Is it possible to write an engaging essay on a topic that makes you yawn? The answer is yes, mainly because you have no choice. Doing so may annoy you or grate on your conscience, but don't raise a stink about it. Instead, accept the challenge, and create the illusion that you care deeply about the issue. Show your resilience—a quality that college admissions officials value and admire. Regardless of the topic, psyche yourself to write the essay of your life.

Practice in Choosing a Main Idea

Respond to each of the following prompts by writing three or more sentences that could serve as main ideas for an essay.

1. "Whether you think you can, or that you can't, you are usually right."

Henry Ford, 1863–1947

Assignment: Does attitude determine success and failure in an endeavor? Plan and write an essay that develops and supports your views on this issue.

A. _____

B. _____

C. _____

2. There's an old proverb, "Spare the rod and spoil the child."

Assignment: Which is a more effective means in teaching children to behave in a certain way—to promise rewards or to instill a fear of punishment?

A. _____

B. _____

C. _____

3. Advertisements for the New York State Lottery say "All you need is a dollar and a dream," a slogan that encourages the fantasy that a big win will solve all of life's problems. Yet, many lottery winners have suffered unexpected negative consequences. Their dreams have often turned into nightmares, and their lives are worse than they were before.

Assignment: Can the realization of a dream be disastrous? Plan and write an essay that develops and supports your views on this issue.

A. _____

B. _____

C. _____

4. "There is nothing like returning to a place that remains unchanged to find the ways in which you yourself have altered."

Nelson Mandela, *A Long Walk to Freedom*

Assignment: Do we need to understand our past in order to understand ourselves? Plan and write an essay that develops and supports your views on this issue.

A. _____

B. _____

C. _____

5. "Destiny is not a matter of chance. It is a matter of choice. It is not a thing to be waited for, it is a thing to be achieved."

William Jennings Bryan (1860–1925)

Assignment: Do you think that a destiny achieved by the decisions and choices you have made is preferable to a destiny that comes from chance or luck? Plan and write an essay that develops and supports your views on this issue.

A. _____

B. _____

C. _____

Suggested answers are on page 105.

GATHERING AND ARRANGING IDEAS PURPOSEFULLY

Unless you are blessed with a digital mind that instantly processes information and draws insightful conclusions, spend a few moments gathering and arranging specific ideas, arguments, anecdotes, examples—whatever you can think of to support and develop your essay's main idea. List your thoughts on paper—just a word or two for each idea. These jottings can be the working outline of your essay. Then draw circles around key words, connect related ideas with arrows, or just underline the thoughts you'll definitely use in your essay.

No single technique for gathering ideas excels any other, provided it helps you identify what you're going to write. While you plan, one idea may trigger a flood of others. Maybe you'll end up with more brilliant ideas than you can use. (Everyone should have such a problem!) Your task then would be to pick out and develop only the best of the best.

With materials assembled, decide what should come first, second, third. The best order is the clearest, the order your reader can follow with the least effort. But, just as a highway map may show several routes from one place to another, there is no single way to get from the beginning to the end of an essay. The route you plan depends on the purpose of the trip.

Each purpose will have its own best order. In storytelling, the events are usually placed in the sequence in which they occur. To explain a childhood memory or define an abstract term takes another organization. An essay that compares and contrasts two books or two people may deal with each subject separately or discuss the features of each point by point. No plan is superior to another provided there's a valid reason for using it.

The plan that fails is the aimless one, the one in which ideas are presented solely according to how they popped into your head. To guard against aimlessness, rank your ideas in order of importance. Then work toward your best point, not away from it. Giving away your *piece de resistance* at the start is self-defeating. Therefore, if you've come up with, say, three good ideas to support your thesis, save the strongest for last. Launch the essay with your second best, and sandwich your least favorite between the other two. A solid opening draws readers into the essay and creates that all-important first impression, but a memorable ending is even more important. Coming last, it is what readers have fresh in their minds when they assign the essay a grade.

The following guideline won't apply to every essay, but a body consisting of three sections is just about right. Why three? Mainly because three is a number that works. Three pieces of solid evidence in support of your main idea creates the impression that you know what you're talking about. One is insufficient, and two only slightly better. But three indicates thoughtfulness. Psychologically, three also creates a sense of rhetorical wholeness, like "blood, sweat, and tears," and "of the people, by the people, and for the people."

It shouldn't be hard to divide a main idea into three secondary ideas. A narrative essay, for instance, breaks naturally into a beginning, middle, and end. A process is likely to have at least three steps. In an essay of comparison and contrast, you should be able to find at least three similarities and differences to write about. And a similar division into thirds applies to an essay of argumentation—the kind expected on the SAT.

Each of three ideas may not demand an equal amount of emphasis, however. You might dispose of the weakest idea in just a couple of sentences, while each of the others requires a whole paragraph. But whatever you emphasize, be sure that each idea is separate and distinct. That is, the third idea mustn't simply rehash the first or second disguised as something new.

The Formula

The five-paragraph essay formula is a simple, all-purpose plan for arranging ideas into a clear, easy-to-follow order. It's a technique you can rely on any time you need to set ideas in order. Its greatest virtue is clarity. Each part has its place and purpose.

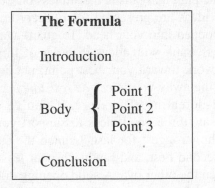

You needn't follow the formula slavishly. The truth is that seasoned writers rarely follow the formula to the letter. In fact, professionally written essays rarely adhere to this five-paragraph arrangement. Yet, many essay writers, even those who take a circuitous path between the beginning and end, use some version of it. Their *introduction* tells readers what they plan to say. The *body* says it, and the *conclusion* tells readers what they've been told. Because every essay is different, however, the steps contain endless, often surprising, variations.

Practice in Gathering and Arranging Ideas

For the following essay topics, write three different and distinct ideas that could be used to support each one. Think of each idea as the main point of a paragraph. Then rank them in order of importance.

A. Topic: The advantages (or disadvantages) of owning an SUV

1. _____

_____

2. _____

_____

3. _____

_____

B. Topic: The pros (or cons) of state lotteries

1. _____

_____

2. _____

_____

3. _____

_____

C. Topic: For (or against) an honor code in your school

1. _____

_____

2. _____

_____

3. _____

_____

D. Topic: Agree (or disagree): "There never was a good war, or a bad peace."

Benjamin Franklin

1. _____

_____

2. _____

_____

3. _____

_____

Answers are on page 106.

COMPOSING: PUTTING WORDS ON PAPER

WRITING A GRIPPING INTRODUCTION

Introductions let readers know what they're in for. But avoid making a formal announcement of your plan, as in:

> This discussion will show the significance of television as an influence on the learning of children from age 3 to 12. Distinctions will be made between early childhood (age 3–7) and middle childhood (8–12).

Such an intro may be useful in a section or chapter of a textbook but in a short essay it's out of place. Rather, just state your point. The reader will recognize the topic soon enough, even without a separate statement of your intention.

Jill B began her essay on the rights of high school students this way:

> On Monday morning, October 20th, I arrived in school to find every locker door in my corridor standing ajar. Over the weekend, school officials had searched through students' lockers for drugs and alcohol. I believe that this illegal action was a violation of both my civil rights and the civil rights of every other student in the school.

This opening sets the essay's boundaries. Because she can't cover all there is to say about students' rights in one or two pages, Jill focuses on one issue raised by her personal experience on a particular Monday morning.

Good SAT essays often begin with something simple and relatively brief that will grab and hold the readers' interest. Jill's opening is effective because it tells an informative anecdote that leads directly to her essay's main idea—that locker searches violate students' civil rights.

Here is the opening of Tom M's essay on the topic of drug and alcohol abuse:

> Drugs and alcohol are a problem for many young people in today's society. Many teenagers smoke pot or do other drugs. Many more participate in underage drinking. Society is working on the problem but has not found an effective solution.

That introduction should make you yawn. Why? Because nothing in that four-sentence paragraph says anything that you don't already know. In a word, it's dull. Not only that, the topic being introduced is far too broad for a short essay.

Compare it to this one:

> When sixth-graders get drunk and 13-year-olds smoke pot every Friday night, society's got a problem. And it's a problem that won't go away until someone figures out how to get kids to just say NO!

This introduction uses a compelling image of young children out of control. It provokes curiosity, leaving readers hungry to know more about the problem of abuse and how it can be solved.

Here is another example of a dull opening:

> Photography is one of the most popular hobbies in the world.

No reader except maybe an avid photographer would be moved to continue reading the essay. A more lively opening evokes a different response:

> I took my camera and twelve packs of fresh film on Spring Break, but when I came home ten of them were still unopened.

Aha! That's a sentence that leaves readers wondering what happened during Spring Break. It implies that the writer is about to tell a story that explains why he took so few photos.

Here's one more example:

> *Dull:* Most predictions that George Orwell made in his novel of the future, *1984*, did not happen.
> *Sharp:* Why did the brilliant author George Orwell goof?

The first opening, written as a nondescript statement of fact, won't interest anyone unfamiliar with *1984*, but the second one, a pithy question, is more powerful. It's intriguing that Orwell, a great intellectual author, had "goofed." The very idea entices readers to find out what happened.

By now the message should be clear: Openings should not only reveal the subject matter and main idea of the essay but also compel readers to go on to the next paragraph.

As you write practice essays, try using the following five common techniques, each illustrated with an example from an essay by a high school student.

1. Start with brief account of an incident—real or invented:

> By lunch period, Megan, a senior at Brookdale High School, had already traded e-mail messages with her brother in college, with her dad at work, and with a friend who was absent from school that day. Although every form of communication has drawbacks, e-

mail, like nothing since the invention of the telephone, has opened up the world to teenagers.
> Lisa N

With one sentence, Lisa has whetted her readers' curiosity about what comes next. Her list of e-mail messages suggests that the essay will be about the effects of staying in touch via e-mail or about some other aspect of communication.

2. State a provocative idea in an ordinary way or an ordinary idea in a provocative way. Either one will ignite reader interest.

> As any football hero will tell you, on the field brains count for more than brawn.
> Ollie G

This unusual idea may cause readers to question Ollie's sanity or maybe to analyze their own images of football players. Either way, Ollie has aroused his readers' interest with a provocative idea that presumably will be explained in the rest of the essay.

3. Use a quotation—not necessarily a famous one—from Shakespeare, a popular song, or your grandmother. Whatever the source, its sentiment must relate to the essay's topic.

> "You can take people out of the country but you can't take the country out of the people."
> Gary F

With this opening, Gary accomplishes a great deal. He gives a clever new twist to a common adage and with a few words has introduced his main idea—the futility of changing people's basic characteristics or core values.

4. Refute a commonly held assumption or define a word in a new and surprising way.

> Even though she's never written a rhyme or verse, my boss at Safeway is just as much a poet as Shelley or Keats.
> Rebecca V

Rebecca hints at a new and perhaps unusual definition of the word "poet." How can someone who has written neither rhymes nor verses can be called a poet? That the label "poet" applies to her boss is intriguing because most poets don't work as supermarket managers. In short, this intro quickens our interest in reading the rest of the essay.

5. Ask an interesting question or two that you will answer in your essay.

> Why are stories of crime so
> fascinating?
>
> Doug T

Doug's opening has wide appeal because most of us read the police blotter in the newspaper, tune to news channels that hype crime stories, talk about the latest murder, or watch *Law and Order* on the tube. In other words, Doug's essay invites us to explore our fascination with crime, both real and fictional.

An effective introduction always helps to draw readers into an essay, but you needn't feel obligated to contrive a super-catchy opening. A direct, clearly worded statement of the essay's main idea could serve just as well. Because there's no time to dawdle during the twenty-five minutes allotted for the essay, a plain statement conveying the topic and main idea of your essay may be all you need. For example, here are three ordinary openings written in response to the following prompt:

> Love your children with all your hearts, love them enough to discipline them before it is too late . . . . Praise them for important things, even if you have to stretch them a bit. Praise them a lot. They live on it like bread and butter and they need it more than bread and butter.
>
> Lavina Christensen Fugal,
> Mother of the Year, 1955

Assignment: Is it a good idea to praise children even when they don't really deserve it?

1. The statement that children should be praised, "even if you have to stretch them a bit" makes good sense for at least three reasons.

2. Is it a good idea to praise children even when they don't really deserve it? I don't think so. Sometimes it may be useful, but there are several circumstances when undeserved praise can hurt more than it can help.

3. Because praise is vital in the life of a child as well as in the lives of adults, I completely agree with Lavina Christensen Fugal.

None of these openings will win a prize for originality, but they all do the job—introducing the topic and stating the essay's main idea. Openings 1 and 2 also suggest a plan for the essay. The first essay is likely to discuss three reasons for agreeing with the prompt. The second will show how children can sometimes be helped and sometimes be hurt by undeserved praise.

Another virtue of these sample openings is that they are short. Long-winded openings can work against you on the SAT. An opening that comprises, say, more than a quarter of your essay reflects poorly on your sense of proportion.

If you can't think of an adequate opening right away, don't put off writing the body of the essay. A good idea may strike you at any time. In fact, many writers, needing time to warm up, begin with material they fully expect to delete. Once they hit their stride, they figure out the point of their essays and work on openings sure to hook their readers. As you practice, you might try a similar tactic. Delete your first paragraph unless it contains ideas you can't live without.

Practice in Writing an Appealing Opening

Here is a list of general essay topics. Try to write an appealing opening for each.

1. The courage of one's convictions

2. Deadlines

    _____

    _____

    _____

    _____

    _____

3. "Keep it! You may need it someday."

    _____

    _____

    _____

    _____

    _____

4. The wrong time in the wrong place

    _____

    _____

    _____

    _____

    _____

5. Responsibility

    _____

    _____

    _____

    _____

    _____

Suggested answers are on page 106.

BUILDING AN ESSAY WITH PARAGRAPHS

The inventor of the paragraph devised a simple way to steer readers through a piece of writing. Each new paragraph alerts readers to get ready for a shift of some kind, just as your car's directional blinker tells other drivers that you're about to turn.

Yet, not every new paragraph signals a drastic change. The writer may simply want to nudge the discussion ahead to the next step. Some paragraphs spring directly from those that preceded them. The paragraph you are now reading, for instance, is linked to the one before by the connecting word *Yet*. The connection was meant to alert you to a change in thought, but it was also intended to remind you that the two paragraphs are related. Abrupt starts may be useful from time to time to keep readers on their toes. But good writers avoid a string of sudden turns that can transform surprise into confusion.

In an essay, paragraphs usually play a primary role and one or more secondary roles. An *introductory paragraph*, for instance, launches the essay and makes the intent of the essay clear to the reader. The *concluding paragraph* leaves the reader with a thought to remember and provides a sense of closure. The majority of paragraphs, however, are *developmental*. They carry forward the main point of the essay by performing any number of functions, among them:

- Adding new ideas to the preceding discussion
- Continuing or explaining in more detail an idea presented earlier
- Reiterating a previously stated idea
- Citing an example of a previously stated idea
- Evaluating an opinion stated earlier
- Refuting previously stated ideas
- Providing a new or contrasting point of view
- Describing the relationship between ideas presented earlier
- Providing background material
- Raising a hypothetical or rhetorical question about the topic

Whatever its functions, a paragraph should contribute to the essay's overall growth. A paragraph that fails to amplify the main idea of the essay should be revised or deleted. Similarly, any idea within a paragraph that doesn't contribute to the development of the paragraph's topic needs to be changed or eliminated.

Topic and Supporting Sentences

Whether readers skim your paragraphs or slog doggedly through every word, they need to find sentences now and then that, like landmarks, help them to know where they are. Such guiding sentences differ from others because they define the paragraph's main topic; hence the name *topic sentence*.

Most, but not all, paragraphs contain topic sentences. The topic of some paragraphs is so obvious that to state it would be redundant. Then, too, groups of paragraphs can be so closely knit that one topic sentence states the most important idea for all of them.

Topic sentences come in a variety of forms. What they all have in common is their helpfulness. Consider them landmarks. To drive from your home to school, for example, you turn left at Blockbuster, take a half right under the railroad trestle, and a left at the gas station. Each landmark tells you where to turn. Similarly, in a piece of writing, a topic sentence often marks a turning point that tells readers the direction they'll be going for a while.

Most topic sentences come first in a paragraph, but they can be located anywhere. And some paragraphs don't even need a topic sentence. Instead, the main idea can be strongly implied by an accumulation of details and ideas. For instance, a description of a fast-food restaurant might detail the crowd, the noise, the overflowing garbage cans, the smell of cooking oil, the lines of people, the crumb-strewn formica tables, and so on. A reader would certainly get the picture. To state explicitly "It was a busy day at Burger King" would serve no purpose.

Practice in Developing Topic Sentences

Part A

Directions: The following paragraphs have been taken from longer essays. Underline the topic sentence in each. Some paragraphs may have an implied topic sentence.

1. [1] My family has moved so often I sometimes feel like a gypsy. [2] The first time we moved I was only four years old, and it didn't bother me. [3] It seemed as though we just got settled, though, when my father announced a new transfer—to California, where I got to start school and where we stayed for three years. [4] But then we heard it was time to move on, and we settled in Minnesota. [5] Just as I began to make friends and get used to the Midwest, the company sent us to Georgia. [6] From there it was two years in England and a year in Washington, D.C. [7] We've been in Massachusetts for almost six months now, and my main problem is answering *that* question, "Where are you from?"

2. [1] Another difficulty is that a person with a police record may have a hard time getting or renewing a driver's license. [2] A conviction for a felony can prevent a person from being able to enter a profession such as medicine, law, or teaching. [3] It can also make it difficult to get a responsible position in business or industry. [4] Special hearings are required before an ex-convict can hold a government job.

3. [1] Music blasts from twenty boom boxes. [2] Children screech while splashing their friends at the edge of the sea. [3] Teenagers throw frisbees at each other. [4] The waves rush up the sand, gurgle a bit, stop, and retreat. [5] A single-engine plane, trailing a long sign—EAT PIZZA AT SAL'S—buzzes overhead. [6] A vendor shouts, "Hey, cold drinks here, getcha cold drinks." [7] During the summer the beach is a noisy place.

4. [1] Clothing designers create new styles every year. [2] Therefore, consumers rush out and buy the new styles and cast away last year's designs even before the clothes are worn out. [3] Forgotten styles hang in closets gathering dust. [4] They'll never be worn again. [5] People fall in love with new cars and sell their old models long before they are obsolete. [6] Just for the sake of flashy style and shiny good looks, they scrimp and save their money or go deeply into debt. [7] And for what? [8] Just to look good. [9] All the money goes into the pockets of the manufacturers. [10] If people would get in the habit of buying goods only when they need replacement, waste would become an exception in America instead of a way of life.

5. [1] Perhaps it's true that "all the world's a stage," as Shakespeare said, because I have noticed that I act one way with one group of people and another way with a different group. [2] With one person I may act like a little kid. [3] I may act very shy or silly. [4] It's as though I can't control what I'm doing. [5] The circumstances just make me act that way. [6] Then, at another time with different people, I am the life of the party. [7] I won't stop talking, and people think I am about 20 years old. [8] I feel that I can pretend so realistically that I sometimes convince myself that I really am what I'm pretending to be. [9] That's a very scary thought.

6. [1] During these years, my family has had about sixty foster children come into our house to live. [2] We have had children from all backgrounds, races, and religions. [3] Each child brought to our door brings a different tale of misfortune. [4] These stories have gradually grown worse over the years. [5] When we first started, the parents of the child usually wanted him or her but were temporarily unable or unprepared to care for their son or daughter. [6] Now, it is not unusual for the mother to be sixteen years old, a drug addict, or a convict. [7] Most of the time the mother is a combination of those. [8] Right now, we have two children living with us. [9] Three of their four parents are in jail, and one of the fathers is unknown. [10] Truly, as time goes on, caring for foster children has become more challenging.

7. [1] True totalitarianism champions the idea that everyone should be subservient to the state. [2] All personal goals and desires should be thrown aside unless they coincide with the common good of society. [3] Freedom for the individual is sacrificed so that the level of freedom for all can be raised. [4] With this philosophy, drastic improvements may be made in a relatively short time. [5] Almost by edict from the head of the society, education and literacy rates can be improved, and unemployment and crime rates may decrease.

8. [1] During adolescence the most obvious change that occurs is physical. [2] Childlike boys and girls suddenly blossom into young men and women. [3] Besides undergoing physical changes, though, this period is usually the time when personal values are explored and molded. [4] Decisions need to be made about what is important and what is not. [5] A struggle takes place within the mind of every adolescent to form a moral and intellectual code that determines the quality of the lives they will have in both the immediate and long-range future.

9. [1] The story by Stephen Crane raises the question whether a soldier who runs away from inevitable death in battle must be considered less of a man than one who stays and dies. [2] To answer the question, one must first define "man." [3] Consider the stereotypical options. [4] There is the Arnold Schwarzenegger type who solves all of life's problems with physical strength and advanced weapons. [5] Then there is the Howard Roark type, a character from *The Fountainhead*, who climbs to the top by using his brilliant mind and integrity. [6] Finally, there is the Willy Loman type, a character in *Death of a Salesman*, who struggles his whole life pursuing an illusion. [7] At the end, he realizes that he has fought a hopeless battle, but at least he has fought.

10. [1] In World War II, the United States dropped two atomic bombs, one on Hiroshima and one on Nagasaki, in order to defeat the Japanese. [2] American history textbooks justify the bombings as something that needed to be done in order to prevent even more deaths during a longer war. [3] Our history books also say that the death toll was about 50,000, while the Japanese claim the bombs took almost twice that many lives. [4] If the United States had lost the war, then the bombings would have been thought to be criminal actions. [5] But since we won, the judgment of history is that the end justifies the means. [6] In fact, throughout history, the war crimes of the victors have repeatedly been justified.

Answers are on page 107.

Part B

Directions: Topic sentences have been deleted from the following paragraphs. After reading each paragraph, write an appropriate topic sentence in the space provided. Omit a topic sentence if none is needed.

1. _____

_____

My mother's nature is very outgoing, emotional, and impulsive. She enjoys dancing, going to parties, being with lots of people, and spending money freely. My father, on the other hand, is quiet, reserved, and controlled. He looks at things logically and practically, not giving in to his emotions. He feels more comfortable with only one or two friends, if any, and is content reading a book or going on a solitary walk for recreation.

2. _____

_____

This was especially true in track and field. As other countries learned American techniques of training, however, their runners improved. Now athletes from all over the world win as many as or even more medals than American track and field athletes.

3. _____

_____

One example of a self-destructive monopoly was the auto industry. In order to maintain their grip on the domestic market, Chrysler, General Motors, and Ford squelched the competition. Inventions that might have helped them in the long run were ignored. Automobiles were changed very little from year to year. Millions of dollars more were budgeted for advertising than for improving either the cars themselves or the process of building them.

4. _____

_____

An angry crowd thrust its way into the palace courtyard. Hundreds of people wielding sticks and knives and pastry rollers screamed at the figure who emerged on the balcony. "We need bread," they shouted, "we need bread!" The aristocratic figure above straightened her perfumed hair, wrapped her ermine shawl more tightly around her shoulders, and with a lift of her chin, turned and muttered to one of her ladies in waiting, "Let them eat cake."

5. _____

_____

From the first page to the last, I couldn't put it down. The author must have lived with the family in the book because she describes the members in lifelike detail. She tells what they ate, how they felt about religion, housing, politics, and sex. By the end, you know them as though they were your own brothers and sisters.

6. _____

_____

One day I was smoking in the boys' bathroom when a teacher walked in. He took me down to the principal's office, where I was given a three-day suspension. My mom grounded me for a month, and I didn't get the loan my dad had promised me to buy my friend's used car.

7. _____

_____

Probably the most important part of this new life is learning to get along with your roommates, the people you see most often. Finding the perfect roommate may be impossible. The person should be a nonsmoker and have similar interests to mine. She (it must be a *she*) should be considerate, courteous, generous, thoughtful, studious when I want to study, fun-loving when I want to party, respectful of privacy and personal property, and finally, she should have a great sense of humor. In a nutshell, she should be like me.

8. _____

_____

In childhood I never hesitated to take chances, to jump over wide cracks in the rocks. Sometimes I made it across with no problems; at other times I was not so lucky. I scraped my knees, bled a little, but came back daring to try again. But now that I'm older, I increasingly find myself shying away, afraid to fail, fearful of getting hurt. I live a style of life in which being in control and on top of things is paramount, where being the best and being perfect is what I yearn for. I am afraid to make mistakes, afraid to bleed, and afraid of being powerless. I take fewer chances.

9. _____

_____

He knew that he grew irritable more frequently. Why shouldn't he, when nurses spoke to him as though he was seven years old, pronouncing their words deliberately and slowly. They must have thought he was hard of hearing or didn't understand. They constantly forced medicine on him and did everything for him as though he was incapable of helping himself. Sometimes he grew angry about the way he was ignored after he asked for something. His words were nothing to them, just as he was nothing.

10. _____

_____

They did not have written language, but by 1000 A.D., they had built preplanned apartment houses four and five stories high. The foot-thick walls of oven-baked adobe brick, plastered over smoothly with clay, kept the occupants warm in winter and cool in summer. But by far their greatest architectural achieve-

ment was the intricate system of canals and reservoirs that irrigated their fields and brought water for miles across the desert directly into their homes.

Suggested answers are on page 107.

Part C

Directions: What follows is a three-paragraph excerpt from the journal of a visitor to the South Pole. In the blank spaces, write a topic sentence that is suitable for each paragraph.

Antarctic Adventure

_____

_____ .

Bellies flattened on the snow, they pant and claw their way across miles and miles of frozen landscape. On downhills, they have to be braked and kept under control by winding ropes around the runners of the sleds. After a day's run, the dogs eat supper and sleep soundly. The next morning, they bark and yip cheerfully, as though to shame their weary masters.

_____

_____ .

The scale is unreal, almost as if it were a landscape from another planet. Away from the coast, no life exists, and therefore, no bacteria, no disease, no pests, no human interference. It is antiseptic and can only be compared with life under the ocean or in space.

_____

_____ .

Although snow offers shelter, insulation, drink, building material, and a highway, its friendliness is a dangerous illusion. Ice blocks and sinister piles of snow tell a tale of avalanches tumbling regularly from the mountains all around. A person on skis could suddenly disappear in a cavern of deep, glistening powder. On foot, sunk to the hips in snow, you might cover less than a mile before dropping from exhaustion. Sudden snow squalls will blind you, cause you to lose your bearings and balance, trapping you hopelessly inside a drift that may ultimately be your burial mound.

Suggested answers are on page 107.

Part D

Directions: Print out or photocopy an essay you've written recently. On one copy underline all the topic sentences. Let a friend do the same on the second copy. Then compare your answers. If you agree, you can be pretty sure that your topic sentences are doing what they are supposed to do.

Paragraph Development

Like an essay, a paragraph should have a discernible organization. Ideas can be arranged from general to specific, or vice versa. Chronological and spatial arrangements make sense for narrative and descriptive paragraphs. In a cause-and-effect paragraph, logic dictates that the cause precedes the effect, but the opposite may sometimes be preferable. As always, clarity and intent should govern the sequence of ideas.

In general, a paragraph of only one or two sentences may be too scanty. Most of the time, thorough development of an idea calls for several sentences. Journalists, however, often write paragraphs consisting of one or two sentences. But the bulk of contemporary nonfiction consists of paragraphs of four to eight sentences.

In a coherent paragraph each sentence has its place and purpose. Disjointed paragraphs, on the other hand, consist of sentences arranged in random order. Or they contain ideas vaguely related or irrelevant to the main idea. Meaning serves as the primary glue that holds a coherent paragraph together, but transitional words and phrases such as *for example, also, but,* and *on the other hand* also help. In the following paragraph, notice how the italicized words and phrases tie sentences to each other.

[1] Tom Joad, the protagonist of John Steinbeck's *Grapes of Wrath,* faces a dilemma after his release on parole from an Oklahoma state penitentiary. [2] *Five years earlier, he* had killed a man in a fight when the man accosted him with a knife. [3] *Although* he claimed self-defense at his trial, Tom was found guilty. [4] *Upon his release,* he intends to follow the provisions of his parole, including the requirement to remain inside the state of Oklahoma. [5] When he finally catches up with his family, *however,* they are en route to California. [6] *Consequently,* he must decide whether to obey the law or help his family start a new life in the West.

Sentence 1 expresses the paragraph's most general idea and serves as the topic sentence. The pronoun *he* throughout the passage ties every other sentence to *Tom Joad,* the subject of the topic sentence. *Five years earlier,* in sentence 2, explains what had occurred before the events in the first sentence. In sentence 3, *although* signals that a new but contrasting idea is on the way. *Upon his release,* in sentence 4, adds still another link to the topic sentence. The word *however* in sentence 5 refers to the dilemma alluded to in sentence 1 and explained in sentences 2–5. And in sentence 6, *Consequently* introduces the precise nature of Tom's dilemma. Because of these linking elements, the six sentences cannot be arranged in any other way without destroying the paragraph's coherence.

Practice in Developing Paragraphs

Directions: The sentences in each of the following groups make up a coherent paragraph. They are not in order, however. Rearrange sentences logically. In the blank spaces, write the number that represents the position of each sentence in the paragraph.

1. ____ a. A particular worker, for example, may lack the skill to do a certain job.
   ____ b. Another important variable is inclement weather, which can set a project back for days on end.
   ____ c. In spite of the best laid plans and preparation, building projects sometimes work out badly.
   ____ d. The main reason is that the foreman can't always predict what the workers will do.
   ____ e. Then, the project can't proceed until another worker is found.

2. ____ a. They also tend toward an unhealthy lifestyle, according to a study of 374 college undergraduates at Carleton University.

   ____ b. Here is some bad news for students who put off studying.

   ____ c. In addition, student procrastinators are more likely to eat poorly, smoke more, and sleep less than students who keep up with their schoolwork.

   ____ d. Their overall college experience, as a result, is far less satisfying than the experience of students who do their homework promptly.

   ____ e. Procrastinators get more cold and flu symptoms and have more digestive problems than their punctual classmates.

3. ____ a. One popular place is the Web site *dailyjolt.com.*

   ____ b. But like so many other things, the Internet has given the board an electronic spin.

   ____ c. Now students can post their notices online.

   ____ d. The ride board on which students post notices to give or receive rides has been a campus tradition for generations

   ____ e. The site was founded in 1998 by an Amherst student who thought that sites about his college were "cheesy" and lacked the information that his classmates most wanted.

4. ____ a. In addition, a college official can often tell from an essay whether the applicant is eligible for a particular kind of scholarship or other type of financial aid.

   ____ b. At some colleges the essay counts heavily in admissions decisions and is used to place students in the proper academic programs.

   ____ c. College admissions officials read application essays with great care.

   ____ d. One reason is that the essays help colleges see each applicant more clearly and personally.

   ____ e. For example, an essay may explain why a bright student earned mediocre grades in high school.

5. ____ a. Soon thereafter, some colleges began to ask applicants whether they received professional help in completing their application essays.

   ____ b. They also found that teachers, counselors, and other adults were giving more than casual lessons in essay writing.

   ____ c. Wondering what caused the change, admissions officials soon discovered that many high schools had made instruction in writing an application essay a part of the curriculum

   ____ d. In recent years, students from certain parts of the country started sending in polished college application essays in large numbers.

   ____ e. For up to $150 an hour, some "consultants" were all but composing essays for anxious students.

Answers are on page 107. For additional practice in arranging sentences, turn to Part V, page 192.

Practice in Identifying Paragraph Unity and Coherence

Directions: The following paragraphs may suffer from either lack of unity, lack of coherence, or both. Identify the problem in each, and write a comment that offers an effective remedy. Some paragraphs may not need revision.

1. [1] *Lord of the Flies* is about a group of English schoolboys stranded on a remote island after an airplane crash. [2] When they arrive, they divide into groups. [3] There are groups at this high school, too. [4] On the island, Piggy is the leader of the group consisting of the most intelligent and rational boys. [5] He is a thinker, but he gets killed by another group, the savages, led by Jack. [6] A third group on the island is led by Ralph, who wants law and order and a set of rules. [7] The different groups in the novel are amazingly similar to groups in this school, known as the nerds, the jocks, and the preps.

Comment: _____

_____

2. [1] Under the present law, doing illegal drugs can have serious consequences for young people. [2] They may find their education interrupted and the future put in doubt by having a police record. [3] An arrest or conviction for a felony can complicate their lives and plans. [4] A police record causes embarrassment to a person's family. [5] Parents like to brag about their children's accomplishments. [6] Can you imagine a mother who would be proud of her daughter's experience in the courts and in prison?

Comment: _____

_____

3. [1] Today there is general agreement that we are experiencing unprecedented change. [2] Established institutions are crumbling. [3] The majority of people no longer live in traditional families that consist of two natural parents and their children. [4] Old moralities are being questioned. [5] The United States has an increasingly diverse population. [6] At an early age, ghetto children may learn the thrills offered by drugs, crime, and gang warfare. [7] Children at all social and economic levels learn to expect that lying, cheating, and stealing are rampant in business, politics, and almost every other endeavor. [8] Even the church is not exempt from corruption.

Comment: _____

_____

4. [1] Rival political parties make elections meaningful by allowing voters to choose among candidates with contrasting views and interests. [2] Most parties try to unite divided interests within their ranks in order to appeal to the widest number of voters. [3] In the United States and Great Britain, a two-party system has long been effective in uniting various interests. [4] In dictatorships, criticism of the party in power may be regarded as treason. [5] Often, only a single, controlling party is permitted to exist. [6] Elections mean little in such countries, for the people have no real choice among the candidates. [7] Nor do they have the freedom to openly criticize their government.

Comment: _____

_____

5. [1] Department stores, unless they are like general stores that still function is some small towns, usually hire employees by the hundreds for different jobs. [2] A large number of workers engage in buying, pricing, and selling merchandise. [3] A sales staff promotes sales by advertising and by designing attractive displays of goods to be sold. [4] In recent years, mail-order buying on the Internet has forced many department stores to go out of business. [5] In addition, the store's comptroller handles financial affairs, such as billing, credit, and payroll. [6] The personnel department hires employees and deals with employment problems.

Comment: _____

_____

6. [1] The porpoise, or bottlenose dolphin, is one of the most intelligent animals. [2] It can imitate the sounds of human speech and communicate with its fellow porpoises using barks, clicks, and whistles. [3] Scientists rate their intelligence between that of the chimpanzee, long held as the most intelligent nonhuman animal, and the dog. [4] Porpoises can be trained to leap high in the air, jump through hoops, catch a ball, fetch a stick, and even to participate in underwater work by serving as messengers between divers and surface ships.

Comment: _____

_____

7. [1] *Robinson Crusoe* is a memorable adventure story about a man marooned on a desert island and was written by the British author Daniel Defoe. [2] Defoe was born in London in 1660 and started writing only after he went bankrupt in a business career. [3] He wrote about politics, religion, economics, and geogra-

phy in addition to writing poetry and novels. [4] Today, he is best known for *Robinson Crusoe*, which is but a tiny fraction of his work.

Comment: _____

_____

8. [1] Aristotle made valuable contributions to the study of logic. [2] Plato, the teacher of Aristotle and Socrates' star pupil, believed that understanding the nature of perfect forms such as the circle and the square leads to understanding of ideal forms in all areas of life. [3] Socrates fought the Sophists all his life because he believed in truth, and the Sophists denied the existence of truth. [4] They said that everything was relative, including knowledge and morality. [5] The period of ancient philosophy reached its climax in Greece in 600–500 B.C.

Comment: _____

_____

9. [1] The American pioneers made simple farm implements and household tools. [2] They made pitchforks, for example, by attaching long handles to deer antlers. [3] Brooms were made by fastening together ten or twenty small tree branches. [4] They whittled wooden spoons, bowls, platters, and used gourds and the horns of sheep and other animals for drinking cups. [5] They made graters by punching holes into a piece of sheet iron. [6] Then they would rub kernels of corn across the jagged surface to make cornmeal.

Comment: _____

_____

10. [1] You can't find Potter's Field on a map. [2] It is not a real place. [3] Rather, it is the name given to any plot of land reserved for the burial of unidentified and destitute people. [4] The name was first used in the New Testament of the Bible. [5] After Judas betrayed Christ for thirty pieces of silver, the priests used the money to buy "the potter's field to bury strangers in." [6] Today, in many urban areas, potter's fields have disappeared. [7] Land is too valuable to use for burying unknown and unclaimed corpses. [8] For a fraction of the cost, bodies are cremated and ashes thrown into common graves.

Comment: _____

_____

Answers are on pages 107–108.

Transitions

Consider your readers as tourists in a foreign land and your essay as a journey they take from one place to another. Because you can't expect strangers to find their own way, you must lead them. As their guide, you must tell them where they are going (the introduction) and remind them of the progress they're making (the body of the essay).

In long essays, readers need more reminders than in short ones. To keep readers well informed, you needn't repeat what you've already written but rather plant key ideas, slightly rephrased, as milestone along the way. (The sentence you just read contains just such a marker. The phrase "To keep readers well informed" cues you to keep in mind the topic of this paragraph—helping readers find their way.) By regularly alluding to the main idea of paragraphs, you'll keep readers focused and hold their attention from start to finish.

You can help readers along, too, by choosing words that set up relationships between one thought and the next. This can be done with such words as *this*, which actually ties the sentence you are now reading to the previous one. The word *too* in the first sentence of this paragraph serves the same function; it acts as a link between this paragraph and the one before. Fortunately, the English language is brimming with transitional words and phrases for tying sentences and ideas together.

What follows is a collection of common transitional words and phrases grouped according to their customary use. With a bit of thought, you could probably add to the list.

When you **ADD** ideas: *moreover, in addition, further, besides, also, and then, then too, again, next, secondly, equally important*

When you make a **CONTRAST**: *however, conversely, in contrast, on the other hand, on the contrary, but, nevertheless, and yet, still, even so*

When you **COMPARE** or draw a **PARALLEL**: *similarly, likewise, in comparison, in like manner, at the same time, in the same vein*

When you cite an **EXAMPLE**: *for example, for instance, as when, as illustrated by*

When you show **RESULTS**: *as a result, in consequence, consequently, accordingly, therefore, thus, hence*

When you **REINFORCE** an idea: *indeed, in fact, as a matter of fact, to be sure, of course, in any event, by all means*

When you express **SEQUENCE** or the passing of **TIME**: *soon after, then, previously, not long after, meanwhile, in the meantime, later, simultaneously, at the same time, immediately, next, at length, thereafter*

When you show **PLACES**: *here, nearby, at this spot, near at hand, in proximity, on the opposite side, across from, adjacent to, underneath*

When you **CONCLUDE**: *finally, in short, in other words, in a word, to sum up, in conclusion, in the end, when all is said and done*

You don't need a specific transitional word or phrase to bind every sentence to another. Ideas themselves can create strong links. Notice in the following paired sentences that underlined words in the second sentences echo an idea expressed in the first.

[1] As a kind of universal language, music unites people from age eight to eighty. [2] <u>No matter how old they are</u>, people can lose themselves in melodies, rhythms, tempos, and endless varieties of sound.

[1] At the heart of *Romeo and Juliet* is a long-standing feud between the Capulets and the Montagues. [2] <u>As enemies</u>, the two families always fight in the streets of Verona.

[1] To drive nails into very hard wood without bending them, first dip the points into grease or soap. [2] <u>You can accomplish the same end</u> by moistening the points of the nails in your mouth or in a can of water.

One of your goals on the SAT is to assure readers a smooth trip through your essay. Without your help—that is, unless you deliberately tie sentences together with transitions— readers may find themselves lurching from one idea to another. Before long, they'll give up or get lost like travelers on an unmarked road. Even though not every sentence needs a specific transition, three or four successive sentences without a link of some kind can leave readers wondering whether the trip through your essay is worth taking.

Practice in Using Transitions

<u>Directions</u>: Use as many transitions as you can while writing paragraphs on the following suggested topics.

1. Write a paragraph on how to do something— drive a car from home to school, pull a practical joke, avoid doing homework, burn a CD, get on the good side of a teacher, give your cat/dog a bath. Use as many SEQUENCE/TIME transitions as possible, but don't overdo it.

2. Write a paragraph detailing a cause and its effect: the cause and effect of good teaching, of a new fad, of stress in high school students, of taking risks, of lying, of a close friendship. Use as many RESULT transitions as you can, but don't go overboard.

3. Write a paragraph that compares and contrasts one of the following: the way people respond to pressure, groups in your school, two athletes, then and now, boredom and laziness, two books, a friend who turned into an enemy, an enemy who became a friend. Use as many COMPARISON/ CONTRAST transitions as you can, but don't get carried away.

4. Write a paragraph in which you argue for or against an issue—electronic eavesdropping, school dress codes, educational vouchers, privileges for senior citizens, censoring the Internet, dieting, restrictions on smoking. Use as many ADDITION transitions as you can, but only where they make sense.

Sample answers are on page 108.

USING PLAIN AND PRECISE LANGUAGE

The SAT Writing Test is not a place to show off your vocabulary. To write clearly, use plain words. Use an elegant word only when it's the best and only word that expresses what you want to say. Why? Because an elegant word used merely to use an elegant word is bombastic. . . er . . . big-sounding and artificial. Besides, simple ideas dressed up in ornate words often obscure meaning. Or worse, they make writers sound phony if not foolish. For instance, under ordinary circumstances you'd never utter the words, "Let's go to our domiciles" at the end of a day at school. Nor would you call your teachers *pedagogues* or your dog a *canine*. Yet, the following overblown sentence appeared in a student's essay:

> Although my history pedagogue insisted that I labor in my domicile immediately upon arrival, I was obliged to air my canine before commencing.

How much clearer and more direct it would have been to write:

> I had to walk the dog before starting my history homework.

Fortunately, English is loaded with simple words that can express the most profound ideas. A sign that says STOP! conveys its message more clearly than CEASE AND DESIST. When a dentist pokes at your teeth, it *hurts*, even if dentists call it "experiencing discomfort." Simple doesn't necessarily mean short, however. It's true that plain words tend to be the short ones, but not always. The word *fid* is short, but it's not plain unless you are a sailor, in which case you'd know that a fid supports the mast on your boat or is an instrument used to pry open a tight knot in your lines. On the other hand, *spontaneously* is five syllables long. Yet it is a plain and simple word because of its frequent use.

Simple ideas dressed up in ornate words not only obscure meaning but make writers sound pretentious:

Fancy: The more I recalled her degradation of me, the more inexorable I became.
Plain: The more I thought of her insults, the more determined I grew.

Fancy: Lester has a proclivity toward prevarication.
Plain: Lester is a liar.

Fancy: The coterie of harriers gleaned the salience of synergy in competitive racing engagements.
Plain: The runners learned that teamwork pays off in races.

Ernest Hemingway called a writer's greatest gift a "built-in, shock-proof crap detector." Hemingway's own detector worked well. He produced about the leanest, plainest writing in the English language—not that you should try to emulate Hemingway. (That's already been done by countless imitators.) But an efficient crap detector of your own will encourage you to choose words only because they express exactly what you mean.

Euphemisms

Of course, there are occasions when the plainest words won't do. When you wish to soften or mitigate painful, unsavory, or objectionable truths, our language has innumerable euphemisms. For example, there are scores of euphemisms for the verb *to die* (*pass away, pass on, be deceased, rest, expire, meet one's maker*, and so on), for *bathroom* (*restroom, ladies'/men's room, W.C., lounge*), and for *drunk*, *vomiting*, and everything else that might upset a prissy sensibility. Pussyfooting with words has its place. We do it all the time, but in your essay writing, resort to euphemisms only when you have a valid reason for doing so.

Don't interpret this admonition to use plain words as carte blanche to use current, everyday slang or street talk in your SAT essay. Spoken language, which brims with colorful words and expressions like *chill, pig out, dissed*, and *bummed* has its place, but its place is not your SAT essay unless you definitely need current lingo to create an effect that you can't produce another way. If you insist on writing like a hipster, that's fine, but don't use quotation marks to draw attention to the fact that you can't think of standard or more original words. If, to make a point, you overload your essay with slang, be sure to demonstrate your mastery of standard English in at least part of the piece. After all, colleges want to know that you can write good, standard prose.

For the SAT, a plain, conversational style will always be appropriate. The language should sound like you. In formal essays, custom requires you to remove yourself from stage center and focus on the subject matter. But SAT essays encourage more casual responses in which references to yourself are perfectly acceptable. It's not essential to use the first-person singular pronoun, but using *I* is often preferable to using the more impersonal *one*, as in "When *one* is writing an SAT essay, *one* sometimes writes funny," or *you*, as in "Sometimes *you* feel like a dope," or by avoiding pronouns altogether. But an essay that expresses the writer's personal opinion will sound most natural when cast in first-person singular.

The point is, don't be phony! SAT essay readers are old hands at spotting pretense in students' writing. Let your genuine voice ring out, although the way you speak is not necessarily the way you should write. Spoken language is often vague, clumsy, repetitive, confused, and wordy. Consider writing as the everyday speech of someone who speaks exceedingly well—grammatically correct and free of pop expressions and clichés. Think of it as the kind of mature speech expected of you in serious conversation, say, with a panel of parents concerned about your school's curriculum. Or maybe even the way this paragraph sounds. You could do a lot worse!

Precise Language

Precise words are memorable, but hazy, hard-to-grasp words fade quickly away. Tell your garage mechanic vaguely, "This car is broken," and he'll ask for more information. Say precisely "My car won't

start in freezing weather," and he'll raise the engine hood and go to work. If a patient in the E.R. says, "I feel pain," a surgeon might at least like to know exactly where it hurts before pulling out her scalpels. In other words, precise language is more informative, more functional, and thus more desirable.

In the first draft of an essay, Jeff S used the following to illustrate what happened on a day he'd like to forget:

> It was an awful day outside. Everything was going wrong. I felt terrible. Things weren't going well in school. I got a below-par grade on a paper, and I was sure that I had failed my science quiz. I also had lots of things to do at home and no time to do them. My mother was in a bad mood, too. She yelled at me for all kinds of things. Then Penny called, and we got into a disagreement. I had trouble with my DVD player, and I couldn't pay for repairs. I went to bed early, hoping that tomorrow would be better.

Reviewing this paragraph a few days later, Jeff realized the writing begged for more precise language. Yes, the day had been dreadful, but his account needed details to prove it. The next draft took care of that:

> On a cold and rainy November day, my life was as miserable as the weather. I felt chills all day, and my throat was sore. In school I got a D on a history paper about the Bubonic Plague, and I was sure that I had failed the chemistry quiz. The homework was piling up: two lab reports, more than 150 pages to read in *Wuthering Heights*, a chapter in the history text, and about a hundred new vocabulary words in Spanish. I didn't have time or energy to do it all, especially when my mother started to pick at me about my messy room and the thank you letters I'm supposed to write to my grandparents. Just as she was reminding me that my SAT registration was overdue, Penny called to say that she couldn't come for Thanksgiving after all, so we argued about loyalty and trust and keeping promises. When I tried to watch *Lord of the Rings* again, the DVD player kept skipping scenes. The repairman said he would charge $100 just to look at the damn thing, but I don't have that kind of money. By 9:00 P.M. I was in bed, hoping that tomorrow would be better.

In this version Jeff included many precise details that vividly illustrate the wretchedness of that miserable day. Not every paragraph of every essay calls for such detail. But an essay consisting solely of abstractions will leave readers at sea.

Surely, vague, shadowy words are easier to think of. But they often cover up a lack of clear and rigorous thinking. For example, it's easy to pass judgment on a book by calling it "good" or "interesting." But what readers should be told is precisely why you think so. How simple to call someone an "old man" without bothering to show the reader a "stooped white-haired gentleman shuffling along the sidewalk." A student who calls her teacher "ugly" sends a different image of ugliness to each reader. But if the teacher is a "shifty-eyed tyrant who spits when she talks," then say it. Or if the teacher's personality is ugly, show her ill-temper, arrogance, and cruelty as she curses her hapless students.

Good writers understand that their words must appeal to a reader's senses. To write precisely is to write with pictures, sounds, and actions that are as vivid on paper as they are in reality. Exact words leave distinct marks; abstract ones, blurry impressions. As the following pairs of sentences illustrate, precise writers turn hazy notions into vivid images:

Hazy: Skiing is a fun sport. The mountains are pretty, and it takes skill.

Precise: On the ski slope, I marvel at the snow-decked pines and brilliant sky and thrill to the challenge of weaving gracefully down steep mountains.

Hazy: Rather violently, Carolyn expressed her anger at the other team's player.

Precise: Carolyn snarled, "Get out of my face" as she punched the Tigers' goalie in the nose.

Hazy: My parents were happy when I got accepted in college.

Precise: The letter thrilled my parents. Their worried looks suddenly disappeared, they stopped nagging me about homework, and because the question had been answered, they never again asked what would become of me.

Clearly, the precisely worded sentences are richer than the hazy ones. But they are also much longer. In fact, it's not always desirable or necessary to define every abstraction with precise details. Each time you mention *dinner*, for instance, you don't have to recite the menu. When you use an abstract word in an essay, ask yourself what is more important—to give readers a more detailed account of your idea or to push on to other, more important, matters. Context determines how abstract your essay should be. Just remember that nobody likes reading essays that fail to deal concretely with anything.

Practice in Using Precise Wording

<u>Directions</u>: The next ten sentences desperately need more precise wording. Please provide the verbal antidote to their vagueness.

1. The barn was old and run-down.

    _____

    _____

2. She did not take it lightly when the accusation was leveled against her.

    _____

    _____

3. Winning the overwhelming approval of the people gave the candidate great satisfaction.

    _____

    _____

4. She tried diligently to study, but one could see that it made no difference.

    _____

    _____

5. The atmosphere at the graduation party was intense.

    _____

    _____

6. One must do many things to earn a place on the roster of an athletic team.

_____

_____

7. It's rewarding to visit places where customs are different because unusual customs are always interesting.

_____

_____

8. She met with little success during her high school career.

_____

_____

9. The family was very poor.

_____

_____

10. In a perilous situation, Rod showed that he was brave.

_____

_____

Answers are on pages 108–109.

Fresh Language and Surprises

Dull language has three main qualities: (1) boring, (2) boring, and (3) boring. So, do your SAT readers a favor by giving them a verbal surprise. After reading hundreds of predictable essays on the same topic, readers will do cartwheels for something fresh and new. (Ha! SAT readers doing cartwheels— that's kind of a surprise, isn't it?) It takes courage and imagination to use fresh language, but here's a guarantee: A verbal surprise may not turn SAT readers into acrobats, but it will unquestionably give your essay a boost.

What is a verbal surprise? Nothing more than an interesting image or choice of words. That doesn't mean use odd words like *twit* or *fop*. Even ordinary words, used deftly, can dazzle readers. Moreover they'll sound more natural. For example:

Ordinary: I was ten before I saw my first pigeon.
Surprising: I was ten before I met my first pigeon.

Because we don't normally "meet" pigeons, the unanticipated change from *saw* to *met* is mildly surprising.

Ordinary: The shark bit the swimmers.
Surprising: The shark dined on the swimmers.

Changing the verb makes a common sentence surprising because *dined* suggests gentility and good manners, qualities that most sharks lack.

Ordinary: The gunshot frightened the pigeons, which flew away.
Surprising: The gunshot filled the sky with frightened pigeons.

The ordinary sentence states literally that the sound of the gunshot scared the pigeons. In the revision, the shot becomes a vital force with the power to fill the sky. Both the pigeons and the sentence have sprung to life.

Words can also surprise readers by suggesting certain sounds. The word *bombard*, for instance, has a heavy explosive sound. *Yawn* has a wide-open sound that can be stretched out indefinitely. *Slogging* is slow, just like the action it names, and *choke* sticks in your throat. *Murmuring streams* evokes the sound of—what else?

Readers find unexpected pleasure, too, from the repetition of sounds—both consonants and vowels, as in *the dark, dank day smelled of death; the machine sucked up sewage from the swamp;* and *the cold wind moaned over the ocean waves.* The appeal of such repetition is evidenced by the countless clichés that crowd our everyday speech and (regrettably) our writing, such as *footloose and fancy free*, *sink or swim*, and *blast from the past*. In short, an occasional treat for the ears will go far to captivate your readers. But don't repeat sounds too often because they might call attention to themselves and pull the reader away from the meaning of your words.

Surprise with Comparisons

English is filled with wonderful words to describe virtually anything. Yet, occasionally emotions and experiences seem almost beyond words. At such times, you can depend on figures of speech such as metaphors and similes to make meaning clear. How, for instance, do you show the weird look the bus driver gave you this afternoon, or what a city street sounds like at six o'clock on a summer morning? What about the feel of clean sheets, the taste of a stale Coke, the smell of a new car, a fear, a frustration?

A uniquely expressed comparison can catch elusive details and fleeting sensations. That bus driver, for instance may have looked at you "as though your were road-kill." The summer morning may have sounded "like an orchestra tuning up to play," and the bed sheets may have felt "like a drink of cold spring water on a sultry August afternoon."

In addition, comparisons are economical. They require fewer words than you might otherwise need to state an idea. To describe elderly men fishing from a pier, for instance, you might mention their creased faces, the folds of papery skin at their throats, the pale and cracked lips, and the white stubble on their chins. But if all those details were superfluous, you could simply compare the men to wooden slats on a weathered fence. Instantly your reader will see the resemblance: Gray men lined up on the pier like boards on a weather-beaten fence.

The limited vocabulary of young children keeps them from expressing all they want to say. By nature, therefore, they make up comparisons: "Daddy, when my foot goes to sleep it feels like ginger ale." "Mommy, this ice cream tastes like chocolate sunshine." As people grow older, they often lose this knack of making colorful comparisons and have to relearn it. But when you start consciously to seek comparisons, you'll find them sprouting like weeds in a garden—that is, everywhere.

Similes (Tim wrestles *like* a tiger) and metaphors (Tim *is* a tiger) point out likenesses between something familiar (tiger) and something unfamiliar (how Tim wrestles). To convey meaning, one side of a comparison must always be common and recognizable. Therefore, comparing the cry of the Arctic tern to the song of a tree toad won't enlighten a reader familiar with neither water birds nor tree toads. Because you can expect readers to know the sound of a fiddle, however, a more revealing comparison is *The cry of the Arctic tern sounds like a fiddler searching for a c-sharp.*

Make your comparisons fresh and original. Don't rely on old stand-bys such as "life is like a box of chocolates," or "like a bat out of hell," or "dead as a doornail." Our language is littered with countless comparisons that once may have been vibrant and fresh but have wilted from overuse. The fact is that every familiar combination of words, such as "I could care less" or "you've got to be kidding" or "what a bummer," was once new, cool, even poetic. But repetition has turned them into clichés.

Let clichés rest in the cliché graveyard. Don't drag them out for your SAT essay. That is an admonition easier to say that to follow because clichés crowd our conversations, swamp our airwaves, and deluge the media. Like the air we breathe (a cliché), we hardly notice them. In an essay, however, especially one that it supposed to demonstrate your unique cast of mind, you must avoid clichés like the plague. "Like the plague," in fact, is one you should avoid, along with other secondhand phrases and expressions like *the bottom line; on the ground; how does that sit with you; touch base with; there has been a sea-change in . . . ; off the top of my head; at the end of the day; a point well taken; two sides of the same coin; getting psyched; double-edged sword; go off the deep end; life on the edge; life in the fast lane; for openers; think outside the box; flipped out; a full plate; get a life; get real; super; chief honcho; the big cheese; so amazing; that's cool; the whole enchillada; no way, José,* and would you believe, *would you believe*? (This list of clichés is far from complete. No doubt you could add many more.)

On the SAT you won't be penalized for an essay lacking inventive and scintillating expressions, but you'll pay a price if your writing is overrun with clichés. Get into the habit, then, of purging all trite phrases from your writing vocabulary. *Half the battle*, as they say, is knowing a cliché when you meet one. The other half—expelling them—is still to be fought and won.

Practice in Writing Comparisons

Part A

Directions: Untold numbers of comparisons are waiting to be born. Because you see the world differently from everyone else, you can invent memorable comparisons that no one—not Shakespeare, not Milton, not Whitman, nor any other immortal—ever thought of. Write an original comparison for each of the qualities listed below. Avoid clichés.

1. as comfortable as

   _____

2. as tough as

   _____

3. as gorgeous as

   _____

4. as silly as

   _____

5. as serious as

   _____

6. as perfect as

   _____

7. as wild as

   _____

8. as unpredictable as

   _____

9. as impetuous as

   _____

10. as reliable as

    _____

Answers are on page 109.

Part B

Directions: Try your hand at writing an extended comparison, in which you expand upon a single metaphor or simile. If you can't think of one, try one of these:

> In what ways is life like a river? A carousel? A hero's journey?

> How does school resemble a zoo? A shopping mall? An airport?

> How is music like a clearing in the woods? A chapel? A painting?

_____

_____

_____

_____

_____

_____

_____

(Add paper, if necessary)

VARYING SENTENCE STRUCTURE

When writing an essay, it's easy to fall into a rut by using the same sentence structure over and over and over. But readers prefer a variety of sentences.

Variety for its own sake is hardly preferable to assembly-line writing—writing in which every sentence follows the same pattern. But variety that clarifies meaning or gives emphasis to selected ideas is something else. For one thing, it adds life to your prose.

English sentences are structured in three ways: **simple, compound,** and **complex.**

Simple: Terry fell asleep in math class.

The sentence is **simple** because it contains one grammatical subject (*Terry*) and one verb (*fell*). It also states a single main idea.

Compound: The competition is stiff, but it won't keep Mark from winning.

The sentence is **compound** because it is made up of two simple sentences joined by the coordinating conjunction *but*. Other coordinating conjunctions used in compound sentences are *and, yet, or, for, nor,* and *so,* as in:

The competition is stiff, *and* Mark is worried about winning.

Mark is worried about winning, *for* he has a bad cold.

Notice that the structure of each of these compound sentences gives roughly equal emphasis to its two main ideas.

Complex: Although he has a bad cold, Mark will win.

The sentence is **complex** because it is made up of two parts—a simple sentence (*Mark will win*) and a clause (*Although he has a bad cold*) that is not a complete sentence in itself but depends on the simple sentence for its meaning. Because the clause begins with a subordinating conjunction (*Although*), it is called a **subordinate clause**. Subordinate clauses contain ideas related to the complete sentence (called the **independent**, or **main**, clause), but they are usually less important. Other common subordinating conjunctions include *because, after, before, though, unless, until, whenever,* and *while*.

Not every simple, compound, and complex sentence is structured in the way just described. In fact, variations abound because English is a remarkably flexible language that can be shaped in countless ways, as you'll see next.

Most simple sentences start with the grammatical subject followed by the verb, as in:

Cats (subject) *fall* (verb) asleep in about three seconds.

They (subject) *sleep* (verb) best after eating and cleaning themselves.

I (subject) *wish* (verb) to be a cat in my next life.

A string of sentences with this subject–verb pattern resembles the prose in a grade-school primer—a style that just won't do on an SAT essay. To be sure that you write in a more mature and engaging way, analyze one of your recent essays. Do several sentences begin with grammatical subjects? If so, try shifting the subject elsewhere. Try leading off with a prepositional phrase, or with an adverb, adjective, or some other grammatical unit.

The following pairs of sentences show how a subject can be shifted from its customary position:

Before the shift: Ms. Bennett is one of the most popular teachers in the school.

After the shift: In this school, Ms. Bennett is one of the most popular teachers.

After a prepositional phrase was added, the subject (*Ms. Bennett*) has been moved further along in the sentence.

Before: She taught the novel *Giants in the Earth* to our eleventh-grade English class with enthusiasm.

After: Enthusiastically, she taught the novel *Giants in the Earth* to our eleventh-grade English class.

Obviously, the revised sentence begins with an adverb.

Before: Students were less excited about the book than she was.

After: Yet, students were less excited about the book than she was.

Well, here the subject (*students*) is stated after an opening connective.

Before: I loved the book, although it turned out to be an intolerable drag for most of my classmates.

After: Although the book turned out to be an intolerable drag for most of my classmates, I loved it.

After introducing the sentence with a dependent clause, the writer names the subject, *I*, and then adds the rest of the sentence.

Before: Ms. Bennett pushed the class to find symbolic meaning in various scenes to make the book more meaningful.

After: To make the book more meaningful, Ms. Bennett pushed the class to find symbolic meaning in various scenes.

To revise this sentence the writer begins with a verbal, in this case "to make," the infinitive form of the verb. (Verbals look and feel much like verbs but serve a different function. Verbals, though, come from verbs, hence their name and their resemblance.)

Before: I read the book in two days, hoping that it would never end.

After: Hoping that it would never end, I read the book in two days.

Aiming to diversify sentence openings, the writer starts this sentence with another kind of verbal, known as a **participle**. The *-ing* ending often indicates that a word is a participle.

Before: I was awed by the tenacity of the characters and absorbed by every soul-stirring syllable of the story.

After: Awed by the tenacity of the characters, I was absorbed by every soul-stirring syllable of the story.

Determined to try something different, the writer begins the sentence with an adjective that happens to sound like a verb because of its *-ed* ending.

Still another variation to try now and then is the sentence constructed from matched ideas set in juxtaposition. President Kennedy used such a sentence to memorable effect in his inaugural speech:

"Ask not what your country can do for you, ask what you can do for your country."

The power of such sentences lies in the balance of parallel clauses. Each clause could stand alone, but together they express the idea more vigorously. Another example:

It wasn't that the spirit of the pioneers caught my imagination, it was my imagination that caught the pioneer spirit.

Emphasis can also come from a reversal of customary word order. Out of context a sentence in which the predicate precedes the subject may seem awkward. But in the right spot an inverted sentence can leave an indelible mark. "Dull the book is not" packs more wallop than "The book is not dull" or "The book is exciting." In the right context, "Perilous was the climb to the top of the cliff" sounds more ominous than "The climb to the top of the cliff was perilous." Inverted sentences should be used sparingly, however. More than once in an essay diminishes the vigor of each occurrence and may sound silly.

No rule of thumb says that a certain percentage of sentences in an essay ought to be different from the usual subject–verb structure. It really depends on the purpose and style of the essay. But if you find yourself repeating the same sentence pattern, restructure some of your sentences. Your readers are bound to reward you for the effort.

Sentence Types

Our language offers a rich menu of sentence types. Declarative sentences predominate in most essay writing. (Just to refresh your memory, a **declarative sentence**, such as the one you are now reading, simply makes a statement.) But other types of sentences can create all sorts of fascinating effects. Take interrogative sentences, for example. (Do you remember that **interrogative sentences** ask questions?) An interrogative sentence appropriately placed in an essay consisting of declarative sentences can change the pace and rhythm of the prose, underscore an idea, and promote the reader's involvement.

Don't forget about imperative sentences (Keep in mind that **imperative sentences** make requests or give commands) and exclamatory sentences (What strong emotion an **exclamatory sentence** can express!).

Furthermore, you can write sentences interrupted at some point by a dash—although some editors and teachers claim that it's not proper to do so in formal prose. Direct and indirect quotations are useful, and on occasion you can drive home a point with a single emphatic word. Excellent!

There's peril, however, in scrambling sentence types for no other reason than to scramble sentence types, for you may end up with a mess on your hands. Be guided by what expresses your ideas most clearly and seems varied enough to interest your readers.

Repetition of Ideas

Repetition can be annoying, but adroitly used, it adds clout to an idea. When your sweetheart says, "I love you. I love you very much," the repetition intensifies the sentiment. If a coach admonishes his team, "OK, guys, knock it off. I said knock it off," you know he really means it.

The following paragraph may suggest that the writer has a one-track mind:

> In the fall Bethany will be going to college. She is psyched to get out of high school. She is psyched to break away from her small town and live in a big city. She is psyched for meeting new people from all over the country and the world, and she is psyched to get started on a program of studies that she expects will prepare her for law school. But first, she is psyched to take the SAT.

Every sentence but the first uses the same subject–verb combination. Yet, the overall effect is anything but monotonous. What's memorable is not repetition, but relentlessness. Repeating the verb *psyched* five times emphasizes Bethany's frame of mind. The point could not have been made as emphatically using a different verb in each sentence.

Or take this passage written by an incorrigible bagel freak.

> My taste for bagels knows no bounds. I stop at the bagel shop on my way to school each morning and grab an onion bagel and coffee. Lunch consists of an olive bagel and a couple of veggie bagels smeared with cream cheese. At snack time I'm not picky. Any style bagel will do, but I hate to have dinner without a buttered poppy-seed bagel. Before bed I wash down a plain toasted bagel with a glass of milk, and in case I have insomnia, I stash two or three garlic bagels on my nightstand for a tasty middle-of the-night pick-me-up.

The writer virtually beats you over the head with bagels. But the repetition won't allow you to forget the point—that the writer has eyes not for pizza, not for burritos, not for onion rings, but only for bagels.

A word of caution: Restatements of a word or phrase can sometimes be distracting. Therefore, stay alert for accidental repetition:

> In a corner of the room stood a clock. The clock said four o'clock.

> Columbus made three ocean voyages. The voyages took him across the Atlantic Ocean.

Combining such sentences will keep you from ending one sentence and starting the next one with the same words:

> The clock in the corner of the room said four.

> Columbus made three voyages across the Atlantic.

Sentences can also be marred by words or sounds that draw attention to themselves:

> Maybe some people don't have as much freedom as others; but the freedom they do have is given to them for free. Therefore, freedom is proof enough that the best things in life are free.

> The members of the assembly remembered that November was just around the corner.

These writers failed to listen to the sound of their words. Had they read their sentences aloud, they may have noticed that voices were stuck in a groove. In fact, reading your words aloud allows you to step back and examine word sounds. (Hold it! Those two words—*aloud* and *allows*—sound jarring and should not be permitted to stand side by side.) Hearing your written words spoken, you're more are apt to notice unwanted repetition. Whenever possible, let each of your practice essays cool for a while. Then enlist a friend to read it aloud. Hearing it in another's voice lends objectivity to the process of self-evaluation.

Short and Long Sentences

Another technique for fending off monotony in an essay is to vary the length of sentences. Long sentences (like this one) demand greater effort from readers because, while stepping from one part of the sentence to the next, they must keep track of more words, modifiers, phrases (not to speak of parenthetical asides), and clauses, without losing the writer's main thought, which may be buried amid any number of secondary, or less important, thoughts, while short sentences are usually easier to grasp. A brief sentence can make a point sharply because all its words concentrate on a single point. Take, for example, the last sentence in this passage:

> For three days, my parents and I sat in our S.U.V. and drove from college to college to college in search of the perfect place for me to spend the next four years. For seventy-two hours we lived as one person, sharing thoughts and dreams, stating opinions about each campus we visited, taking guided tours, interviewing students and admissions officials, asking directions a hundred times, eating together in town after town, and even sleeping in the same motel rooms. But mostly, we fought.

A terse closing sentence following a windy, forty-six-word sentence produces a mild jolt. Indeed, its purpose is to startle the reader. The technique is easily mastered but should be used sparingly. Overuse dilutes its impact.

A series of short sentences can be as tiresome as a succession of long ones. A balance works best. If you have strung together four or five sentences of equal length, try to re-format them. Here, to illustrate, is an overweight sentence that needs a complete makeover:

> In the 1870s, the archaeologist Heinrich Schliemann dug in the correct spot and discovered not only one ancient city of Troy, but nine of them, one lying on top of the other, since every few centuries a new city had been built upon the ruins of the old, causing Schliemann to dig right past the layer containing the ruins of the famous city of the Trojan Horse without realizing he had done so, a mistake not corrected until almost fifty years later by Carl Ble-

gen of the University of Cincinnati, by which time, unfortunately, it was too late for Schliemann because he had been dead for forty years.

The sentence is perfectly grammatical, but it carries a big 108-word load. Cut it down to size. Break it into pieces, rearrange it, add verbs, drop an idea or two, change the emphasis, and delete words. When you're done, the restyled sentence might sound something like this:

> In the 1870s, the archaeologist Heinrich Schliemann dug in the correct spot and discovered not only one ancient city of Troy, but nine of them, one lying on top of the other. He figured out that every few centuries a new city had been built upon the ruins of the old. Without realizing it, he had dug right past the layer he was seeking, the layer containing the ruins of the famous city of the Trojan Horse. His mistake was corrected fifty years later by Carl Blegen of the University of Cincinnati. By then, however, it was too late for Schliemann. He had been dead for forty years.

Likewise, a string of four or five equally long (or short) sentences can be combined to create a more balanced and varied paragraph. Here, for instance, is a paragraph, also about an ancient city, made up of short, choppy sentences:

> Pompeii was an ancient city. It belonged to the Roman Empire. It was near the base of Mount Vesuvius. In 79 A.D., the volcano on Vesuvius erupted. Tons of hot, wet ash fell on Pompeii. In less than a day, the city was buried. It just vanished. More than seventeen centuries later, an Italian peasant found Pompeii. His discovery was accidental. He was digging in a field. His shovel struck the top of a wall. That was two hundred years ago. Pompeii is still being excavated two hundred years later. About two-thirds of the city has been unearthed. It must have been a beautiful city.

With repetition eliminated and some ideas subordinated to others, here is what you get:

The ancient Roman city of Pompeii lay near the base of Mt. Vesuvius. In 79 A.D., Vesuvius erupted, burying the city with tons of hot, wet ash. In less than a day, the city vanished. More than seventeen centuries later, an Italian peasant digging in a field with a shovel accidentally struck the top of a wall. He had found Pompeii. Today, two hundred years later, the city is still being unearthed. The excavation reveals that Pompeii must have been a beautiful city.

For more details and practice in sentence combining, turn to Part V, page 189.

Varying Sentences—A Summary

Use a variety of sentence types: simple, compound, and complex.

Create variety by starting sentences with a

Prepositional phrase: *From the start, In the first place, At the outset*

Adverbs and adverbial phrases: *Originally, At first, Initially*

Dependent clauses: *When you start with this, Because the opening is*

Conjunctions: *And, But, Not only, Either, So, Yet*

Adjectives and adjective phrases: *Fresh from, Introduced with, Headed by*

Verbal infinitives: *To launch, To take the first step, To get going*

Participles: *Leading off, Starting up, Commencing with*

Inversions: *Unique is the writer who embarks . . .*

Balance long and short sentences.
Combine series of very short sentences.
Dismember very long sentences.

Practice in Varying Sentences

<u>Directions</u>: The following passages need greater balance. Divide some of the long sentences and combine some of the short ones. Try to preserve the original meaning of each passage.

1. Mr. Finn is the teacher. He's a good teacher. He runs the class like a dictatorship, however. He has no use for "democracy." He knows nothing about freedom. He announced his rules on the first day. He doesn't allow talking. He forbids gum chewing. He won't permit the wearing of hats. At the bell, he locks the classroom door. After-school detention is a consequence of lateness to class. His homework is compulsory. A girl once came without homework. Mr. Finn lowered the boom. The girl turned colors and almost wept. No one dares to come unprepared to class.

2. I have taken numerous science classes. In science classes we mostly talked about experiments. We didn't do experiments. The equipment was too costly. We had to make do with obsolete equipment. Scientific theories were taught. The theories were not practiced in labs. They were not demonstrated. The science department needs $1 million. With a million dollars it could give students a better education in science.

3. By dumping garbage, sewage, and other haz-ardous waste products into the sea, many nations are polluting the world's oceans, and in doing so are making beaches and swimming dangerous, poisoning fish with toxic materials that end up in fish, lobsters, clams, and other sea life that we humans eat, causing the toxins to enter our bodies.

_____

_____

_____

_____

4. The earth has experienced a sharp increase in natural disasters, from about 100 per year in the 1960s to five times that number in the early part of the twenty-first century, the reason being not that earthquakes, droughts, huge storms, and floods are happening more fre-quently and with greater intensity but that the population of the world has increased and peo-ple in greater numbers now occupy areas that are prone to natural disasters, such as flood plains, coastal lands, and cities built on subter-ranean fault lines. The planet has not changed. Humans have.

_____

_____

_____

5. The American Dream is a popular concept in American life. It has different meanings for different people. It commonly means finding a good job. It also means getting married. Dreams also consist of having a couple of kids and owning a home. The home has a white picket fence and a two-car garage. Some people think that such a dream is shallow. They say that the dream should also include a good education, friends, a feeling of well-being, good health, and above all, the blessings of lib-erty. By that they mean freedom of speech and freedom of religion. The dream must also have the freedom to choose to be part of an untradi-tional family made up of same-sex partners or any other combination of adults and children.

_____

_____

_____

Suggested answers are on pages 109–110.

ENDING YOUR ESSAY

Because it comes last, the final sentences of your essay should be written with care. Don't resort to that old stand-by, a summary ending. When an essay is short to begin with, it's insulting to review for readers what is evident on the page in front of them. Readers are intelligent people. Trust them to remember what your essay says.

An effective conclusion should fit the style and mood of the essay and spring naturally from its contents. A good essay can easily be spoiled by a grating conclusion. A serious essay, for example, shouldn't end with a joke. Also stay away from endings that are too common or cutesy, such as: *that's it; so long for now; happy reading; well, I can't think of anything else; sorry, I've run out of time; good-bye and God bless you.* Such trite end-ings say in effect that you and your imagination have run out of gas.

A short ending is preferable to none at all. A carefully written ending leaves readers satisfied that they have arrived somewhere and may sway them to judge your essay more favorably than oth-erwise. There are no guarantees, of course, but readers are bound to be touched by a memento of your thinking, your sense of humor, or your vision.

Even an ordinary thought, uniquely expressed, will leave an agreeable afterglow.

Here are some common techniques for writing conclusions:

1. Have a little fun; try to put a smile on your reader's face.

    Topic: *King of the World*, a biography of Mohammed Ali
    Purpose of the essay: To criticize David Remnick's biography of Ali. The writer ends with an apt metaphor that reiterates the essay's main idea.
    Conclusion: With this book, Remnick has dealt Ali's admirers a cruel blow below the belt.

    Topic: Growing old
    Purpose of the essay: To show that old people can still act young. The essay concludes with an anecdote about an elderly gray-haired man of about seventy on a crowded city bus.
    Conclusion: He carried bundles of packages and almost fell down as the bus lurched to a stop. At one point a young, gum-chewing woman stood up and pointed to the unoccupied seat. "Here, Pops, take this."

    He looked at her in amazement. "Cool it, girlie," he said, "I still run marathons," and he stood all the way to his stop.

2. End with an apt quotation drawn from the essay itself, from the SAT prompt, or from another source.

    Topic: Surviving high school
    Purpose of the essay: To describe an incident in which the writer found herself in need of a safe haven.
    Conclusion: At that point I knew by instinct, "This is the place."

    Topic: Computer glitches
    Purpose of the essay: To show that, because many consumers are uninformed, they waste lots of money when purchasing personal computers.
    Conclusion: To paraphrase an old saying, "What you don't know can hurt you."

3. Finish by clearly restating your essay's main point but using new words. If appropriate, add a short tag line, a brief sentence that creates a dramatic effect.

    Topic: Discrimination
    Purpose of the essay: To criticize the male chauvinism that exists in the school administration.
    Conclusion: As long as positions of authority are given to sexists, women must be prepared to fight against gender abuse in this institution.

    Topic: Modern communication
    Purpose of the essay: To explain the value and importance of e-mail to teenagers. The writer concludes with a popular e-mail symbol.
    Conclusion: A day without e-mail is a day I should have stayed in bed **:-(**

4. Bring your readers up to date or project them into the future. Say something about the months or years ahead.

    Topic: Vandalism in school
    Purpose of the essay: To condemn the daily carnage of smashed windows, graffiti, and broken ceiling tiles. The essay ends with a few questions about the future.
    Conclusion: How long can this go on? How can we turn away meekly? How much longer can we let the vandals make us their victims?

    Topic: Helping others
    Purpose of the essay: To explain why it is imperative to rid the world of the scourge of AIDS.
    Conclusion: When the history of the twenty-first century is written, let us hope that AIDS will have gone the way of the dinosaurs.

So, what happens if you can't think of a satisfactory ending or time is called before you finish? For one thing, don't despair. Although an effective conclusion adds luster to an essay, don't feel obliged to provide one at all costs. SAT readers will know how well you write long before reaching your essay's last sentence. Be confident that a good but incomplete piece of writing will be graded according to what you've done well, not what you haven't done at all.

Practice in Writing Conclusions

<u>Directions</u>: Try your hand at writing an appealing ending for each of the essays described here.

1. *Topic:* Language taboos

    Our society prohibits or frowns on the use of certain categories of words. In recent years, however, changes have made many language taboos obsolete. After citing several examples, the writer wonders about language usage in the future.

    _____

    _____

    _____

2. *Topic:* The value of school sports

    The writer, in comparing athletics in school to life, makes the point that in both endeavors you need to develop a winning strategy.

    _____

    _____

    _____

    _____

3. *Topic:* High school vs. junior high

    The point of the essay is that while high school is not perfect, it is far better than junior high, where students are treated like inmates, not like human beings.

    _____

    _____

    _____

    _____

Suggested answers are on page 110.

EDITING AND PROOFREADING: THE FINAL TOUCHES

Once you've ended your essay, spend whatever time is left editing and proofreading. You can't do a complete makeover, but you can do a great deal to improve communication between you and your readers.

> The following pages are meant to be a guide to editing your SAT essay. But keep in mind that the material will help you answer the multiple-choice questions later in the exam, especially the Identifying Sentence Errors questions.

EDITING FOR CLARITY

Check your essay for clarity by asking yourself whether a reader could misconstrue anything you've written. Penny T wrote her essay about missing teenagers—those kids whose faces are often printed on milk cartons. One of her sentences read "The last thing parents should do is talk to their kids." Coming to that sentence, a reader might well wonder whether Penny means that parents should talk to their kids as a last resort, or, that in a list of what parents ought to do, the final step is talking to their kids.

Later in the essay Penny wrote, "Ellen told her friend Debbie that she had made a serious mistake by running away from home." Penny certainly understood what she intended to say, but a reader can't tell whether Ellen took a dim view of Debbie's actions or whether Ellen herself had second thoughts about her own flight. Granted, these sentences have been quoted out of context, but the point remains: What may seem perfectly clear to a writer may send a puzzling message to the reader.

That's why you should work hard to arrange your words in the clearest order. Watch for grammatical perils that interfere with meaning, especially (1) misplaced modifiers, (2) dangling participles, and (3) lack of parallelism—all discussed in the pages that follow.

Misplaced Modifiers

Modifiers are words, phrases, and clauses that tell something about or limit the meaning of a particular word or statement. For example:

> The bedroom had a *broken* window.

The adjective *broken* is a modifier because it tells something about the condition of the *window*. In other words, *broken* "modifies" *window*.

> Jessica bought a mouse *that was guaranteed to work with her computer.*

The clause *that was guaranteed to work with her computer* is a modifier because it tells something about the mouse. It modifies the noun *mouse*.

Modifiers must be placed so that they modify the correct words:

> Mike only loves Sharon.

Here *only* modifies the verb *loves*. The modifier is appropriate if Mike feels nothing but love for Sharon—no admiration, no awe, no respect, nor any other emotion. If, however, Mike has but one love, and she is Sharon, then *only* is misplaced. Properly placed, *only* should come either before or after *Sharon*:

> Mike loves *only* Sharon. or Mike loves Sharon *only*.

Another example:

> Naomi decided *when she had finished the essay* to watch TV.

In this sentence, *when she had finished the essay* is the modifier. But it is hard to tell whether it modifies *decided* or *watch*. If it modifies *decided*, Naomi finished her essay and then made a decision to watch TV. If it modifies *watch*, Naomi worked on her essay and decided at some point that she would watch TV when she had completed the work.

> When she had finished the essay, Naomi decided to watch TV.

> While writing an essay Naomi decided to watch TV when she had finished.

Now the meaning of both sentences is unambiguous.

Obviously, misplaced modifiers can cloud a writer's intentions. To avoid the problem, place modifiers as close as possible to the words they modify:

> *Misplaced*: Philip donated his old car to a charity *that no longer ran well*.

The modifier *that no longer ran well* is too far from *car*, the word it modifies.

> *Clear*: Philip donated his old car *that no longer ran well* to a charity.
> *Misplaced*: The bowling alley lends out shoes to its customers *of all sizes*.

The modifier *of all sizes* should be closer to *shoes*, the word it modifies.

> *Clear*: The bowling alley lends out shoes *of all sizes* to its customers.

Dangling Modifiers

In a sentence words must fit together like pieces of a jigsaw puzzle. Sometimes, a misplaced word looks as though it fits, but it fails to say what the writer intended.

> (1) While running to English class, the bell rang.
>
> (2) Working full time, the summer passed quickly.
>
> (3) When only eight years old, my father warned me about smoking.

The ludicrous meaning of these sentences may not strike you immediately, but look again. Do you see that these sentences describe a surreal world in which bells run to class, summers hold full-time jobs, and youthful fathers dispense advice? The problem is that these sentences try to mate two groups of words that can't go together. The parts are mismatched. After the comma in sentence 1, you expect to find out who is running, but you are not told. Likewise, after the commas in sentences 2 and 3, you are not told who was working and who is only eight years old. In short, you're left dangling. Hence, the label **dangling modifier** has been given to this type of construction. To correct the error, add the noun or pronoun to be modified, as in:

> While the boys were running to English class, the bell rang.
>
> Because Charlotte worked full-time, her summer flew by.
>
> When I was eight, my father warned me about smoking.

Re-writing the whole sentence is often the best cure for a dangling modifier, as in:

> *Dangling*: Still sound asleep at noon, my mother thought I might be sick.
>
> *Clear*: My mother thought I might be sick because I was still sound asleep at noon.

> *Dangling*: While talking on the phone, the stew burned in the pot.
>
> *Clear*: While I talked on the phone, the stew burned in the pot.

Practice in Identifying Misplaced and Dangling Modifiers

Directions: Revise the following sentences that contain a misplaced or dangling modifier. Some sentences may be corrected by shifting the placement of one or more words. Others need more substantial revision.

1. After completing the chemistry homework, that pizza tasted great.

   _____

2. Sound asleep in the hammock, Denise discovered her boyfriend.

   _____

3. Used all night to illuminate the steps, I needed new batteries for the flashlight.

   _____

4. Driving down the mountain road, a rock hit my windshield and smashed it.

   _____

5. Stopping to rest after a long hike, a grizzly bear stood in front of me.

   _____

6. After a quick breakfast, the school bus picked me up.

   _____

7. A report was submitted about the bank robbery by the police.

   _____

8. At the age of ten, Sasha's family emigrated from Russia.

   _____

9. A bone was given to the dog we didn't want.

10. Left alone in the house, every sound terrified the child.

Answers are on page 110.

Parallelism

A lack of parallelism in phrases and clauses is not just bad form but can be a source of confusion. Sound parallel structure, in contrast, keeps equivalent ideas in the same grammatical form. Take, for example, a sentence that lists the characteristics of a restaurant in which to have a family birthday party:

> We are looking for a place that is private, plenty of space, has a friendly staff, and that people like to look at.

The sentence makes some sense, of course, but it's awkward because the four qualities of a desirable restaurant are not expressed in parallel form. Instead, they are a mix of an adjective, a phrase, and two clauses. One way to fix the problem is to use only adjectives, as in:

> We are looking for a place that is private, spacious, friendly, and attractive.

Or use a series of nouns each preceded by an adjective:

> We are looking for a place with total privacy, ample space, a friendly staff, and attractive surroundings.

When you arrange the pieces of a sentence in parallel form, the writing becomes clearer and stronger. It also puts you in the company of some of the world's greatest stylists. Abraham Lincoln, for example, used parallelism at Gettysburg: "We cannot dedicate, we cannot consecrate, we cannot hallow this ground." And later, "that government of the people, by the people, and for the people shall not perish from the earth."

John F. Kennedy used parallelism in his inaugural speech: "Let every nation know, whether it wishes us good or ill, that we shall pay any price, bear any burden, meet any hardship, support any friend, oppose any foe to assure the survival and the success of liberty."

Like Lincoln and Kennedy, good writers everywhere know and apply the following principles of parallel construction.

1. Parallel ideas in a series should be expressed in the same grammatical form. Each idea should be equally important to the meaning and structure of the sentence. Use conjunctions such as *and, but, for, or, yet, so*, and *nor* to join parallel ideas.

> *Faulty*:   Hazel's parents objected that she played loud music and to the late hours she kept.
>
> *Parallel*:   Hazel's parents objected to the loud music she played and to the late hours she kept.

The parallel ideas consist of prepositional phrases followed by a pronoun (*she*) and verbs in the past tense (*played, kept*).

2. When used to compare or contrast, parallel ideas should be grammatical equivalents. In a comparison, for example, an idea expressed in a phrase must be paired with another idea also expressed in a phrase. An idea stated in a clause must be paired with another idea stated in a clause, and so forth.

> *Faulty*:   They are worried more about public opinion than for what the effect of the proposal may be.

The prepositional phrase *about public opinion* may not be paired with the clause *what the effect of the proposal may be*.

> *Parallel*:   They are worried more about public opinion than about the effect of the proposal.

3. Parallel ideas can also be expressed with pairs of words such as *either/or, neither/nor, whether/or, both/and*, and *not only/but also*. But keep both words close to the parallel ideas.

> *Poor*: I *either* plan to invite my aunt *or* my uncle to go shopping with me.

The signal word *either* is too far removed from the parallel phrases, *my aunt or my uncle*. Its placement misleads the reader into thinking that the verb *plan* is one of the parallel ideas.

> *Proper*: I plan to invite *either* my aunt *or* my uncle to go shopping with me.

4. When articles, prepositions, and conjunctions appear before the first in a series of parallel items, they may have to be repeated before the others in the series.

> *Unclear*: Our mechanic did a better job on my car than his.

Did two mechanics work on the same car or did one mechanic work on two different cars? To clear up the ambiguity, repeat the preposition *on*, as in:

> *Clear*: Our mechanic did a better job on my car than *on* his.

Sometimes repeating both a preposition and an article is necessary:

> *Unclear*: Before signing the contract, Tiffany spoke with the president and treasurer of the company.

Did Tiffany speak with one person or with two? Repeating *with the* helps to clarify the meaning:

> *Clear*: Before signing the contract, Tiffany spoke with the president and *with the* treasurer of the company.

5. Parallel ideas should be logical equivalents.

> *Absurd*: Terry is six feet tall, kind, and a Texan.

Physical features, traits of character, and place of origin are not logically coordinated.

> *Less absurd*: Terry, a six-foot Texan, is kind.

It is still not terribly logical, but at least the revision emphasizes only one of Terry's qualities—his kindness.

> *Absurd*: On Sunday, Meredith not only painted her toenails but got married.

This sentence is grammatically flawless, but unless it was written to get a laugh, it is ludicrous. Regardless of what you may have been told, painting toenails and getting married are not equivalents.

> *Less absurd*: Before her wedding on Sunday, Meredith painted her toenails. or On Sunday, after painting her toenails, Meredith got married.

Subordinating one of the ideas restores the logic, however weird.

Practice in Identifying Parallel Structure

<u>Directions</u>: Look for faulty parallelism in the following sentences. Write a correct version of the offending word or phrase in the space provided. Some sentences may be correct.

1. Mr. Phillips is funny, interesting, and inspires his classes to learn history.

_____

2. The talk-show host not only was accused of being a bigot but also too stupid to continue working at the station.

_____

3. Since Jenny started taking AP Math, she has worked harder and fewer parties.

_____

4. Her job consisted mostly of writing and typing letters, reports, and various types of phone calls.

_____

5. Mike likes to go to bed early and getting up early to do his work.

_____

6. Our cat Sylvia was short-haired, affectionate, intelligent, and disappeared for days at a time.

_____

7. Maggie hasn't yet decided whether to be an art historian or commercial art.

_____

8. The audience at the graduation ceremony both felt pride and satisfaction when the announcement was made.

_____

9. The police officer walked into the courtyard, got caught in a crossfire, and was shot in the chest.

_____

10. Either way, Nat expects to move to the country because he loves nature and live simply because he has little money.

_____

11. The kids had not only scattered their books all over the bus but also the sidewalk.

_____

12. His ideal house would be in a good location, with land around it, and with a view.

_____

13. Joan's pencil was broken, yellow, and came from this box.

_____

14. His training in design would help him to know how to furnish the house simply and decorating would be simple, too.

_____

15. The landlady told him that he could not have a microwave in his room and showers after 11:00 o'clock.

_____

16. Hearing no car horns and buses and to be miles from friends may cause him to become bored and restless.

_____

17. Either the mouse will find a quick way into the attic or will gnaw at the siding for days.

_____

18. City living is exciting, convenient, and provides plenty of entertainment.

_____

19. After winning the lottery, he'll have an apartment in town, a house in the country, and find a job in the suburbs.

_____

20. I think that Adam has the ability to win his match, defeat Tom in the sectionals, and he'll emerge eventually as the best high school wrestler in the state.

_____

Answers are on pages 110–111.

EDITING FOR INTEREST

Your essay will be read by people—real people. Most of them are teachers who know that essays can be lively, scintillating, and a joy to read. Like any readers, they will be put off by writing that is dull. Therefore, one of your goals on the SAT essay is to inject life into your prose by

- Using *active* instead of *passive* verbs
- Writing *active* instead of *passive* sentences
- Omitting needless words
- *Showing* instead of *telling*

Using Active Verbs

Active verbs differ from being verbs. Because **active verbs** describe or show movement, they excel all other words in pumping life into your prose. What's more, they help you write more concisely.

Being verbs, in contrast, have almost no life in them. Their lifelessness is apparent in the common forms of the verb *to be*:

is	*are*	*was*
were	*am*	*has been*
had been	*have been*	*will be*

Used in a sentence, each being verb joins a subject to a predicate. In fact, a being verb functions much like an equal sign in an equation: "Five minus two *is* three" ($5 - 2 = 3$), or "Samantha *was* happy" (Samantha = happy), or "Your SAT scores are going up" (That = good news!). Because being verbs (and equal signs) show little life, use them sparingly.

To check whether you rely too heavily on being verbs, check a few of your most recent essays. If more than, say, one out of four sentences uses a form of *to be* as the main verb, try the following revision techniques.

Substitute a new active verb for the being verb:

Being verb: It *is* not easy for most students to write immortal essays.
Active verb: Most students *struggle* to write immortal essays.

Extract an active verb from a noun in the sentence:

Being verb: Monica *was* the winner of the essay contest.
Active verb: Monica *won* the essay contest.

Extract an active verb from an adjective:

Being verb: My afternoon at the ballgame *was* enjoyable.
Active verb: I *enjoyed* my afternoon at the ballgame.

As you delete being verbs, you may observe that some sentences resist change. When that happens, try turning subjects into verbs and verbs into nouns. Try also to eliminate unnecessary phrases. A full-scale revision will often result in sentences that bear little resemblance to the original. At the same time, your verb-swapping efforts may root out excess words and improve your essay's readability.

You may notice, however, that some nouns limit your options for using active verbs. For instance, you are pretty well stuck with a form of *to be* in any sentence that begins with *The reason*:

The reason that you should practice writing essays _____ . . .

What verb other than *is* can be used to fill the blank? Very few. There are few verb options, too, when the subject of the sentence is *thought, concept, idea, issue, way, cause*, and several other abstract nouns. The same applies to sentences that begin with "There," as in: "*There* is no way for you to do poorly on the SAT essay," and often for sentences that begin with "It," as in "*It* is a foregone conclusion that you'll do well."

In contrast, nouns that stand for specific places, people, events, and objects invite the use of active verbs. When a sentence contains a subject that can do something—a person, for example—you can never run out of verb choices.

As a bonus, concrete, easy-to-define nouns, when substituted for abstractions, tend to tighten and energize sentences:

Abstract subject:	The *cause* of Sharon's worry was her lack of tuition money.
Definite subject:	*Sharon* worried about her lack of tuition money.
Abstract subject:	The *issue* behind the strike was the workers' demand for higher wages.
Definite subject:	The *workers* struck for higher wages.

Being verbs are not the only verbs that sap the life out of sentences. They share that distinction with several other verbs, including forms of *to have, to come, to go, to make, to move*, and *to get*—verbs with so many different uses that they creep into sentences virtually unnoticed. *Webster's International Dictionary* lists sixteen different meanings for the verb *get* and a dozen more for *make* and *move*. It's true that we can hardly do without these verbs, but use them only if you can swear that no other words will do. Otherwise, trade them in for more vivid verbs, as in:

Dull:	The line to the box office *moved* very slowly.
Livelier:	The line *crept* (*crawled, inched, poked*) to the box office.

Note that by using a more animated verb, you eliminate the need for "very slowly," which has suddenly become redundant.

Dull:	The police officer *gave* drivers permission to turn left on red.
Livelier:	The police officer *permitted* drivers to turn left on red.

Note that this revision has created not just a more active sentence but one that contains fewer words—always a stylistic plus.

Practice in Using Active Verbs

Directions: Replace the weak, lifeless verbs in these sentences with stronger, active ones.

1. Shock was the feeling of most American people from the attack of 9/11.

   _____

2. In New York City, there were nearly three thousand people killed.

   _____

3. Afterwards, there was a controversy over who was to blame for America's vulnerability to terrorism.

   _____

4. There was an effort made to strengthen homeland security.

   _____

5. Many people were willing to give up some of their rights in order to be secure.

   _____

6. The issue of how much freedom to give up for the sake of security is difficult to resolve.

   _____

7. The war in Afghanistan was a significant event that was a result of 9/11.

   _____

8. Sweatshirts and baggy pants was our manner of dress whenever we went out.

   _____

9. There was quite a lot of commotion because of there being an all-American high school basketball player playing in the game.

_____

10. It is obvious that there should be more emphasis on math and science for the average college-bound student.

_____

Answers are on page 111.

Active and Passive Sentences

Active sentences strengthen prose; passive sentences weaken it. In an **active sentence** the person or thing performing an action is usually mentioned early in a sentence so that readers know right away who or what you are talking about. In some contexts, though, the actor is unknown or irrelevant. That's when a **passive sentence**—a sentence structured in the *passive voice*—is more appropriate. For example:

> *Passive*: The curtain was raised at 8:30 sharp.
> *Active*: At 8:30 sharp, a stagehand (or Maryanne, the production assistant) raised the curtain.

In the passive version, curtain time is the important fact. Who pulled the rope or pushed the button is immaterial.

Transforming a passive sentence to an active one takes a bit of editing:

> Six weeks were spent preparing for the spring carnival.

This sentence needs revision because it fails to tell who performed the action—that is, who prepared for the carnival. The following revision clears up the uncertainty:

> Six weeks were spent preparing for the spring carnival by the cheerleaders.

This version contains more information than the original, but it still emphasizes the action instead of who performed the action. To make the transformation complete, say something like

> The cheerleaders prepared for the spring carnival for six weeks.

In the active voice, this sentence gives the performers of the action top billing.

Why is the active voice preferable? It is mainly because most events in life don't just occur by themselves. Somebody does something; a person or thing *acts*. After all, burgers don't just get eaten; people cook and devour them. Marriages don't just happen; couples deliberately go out and marry each other. Goals don't score, salmon don't get caught, wallets don't get lost all by themselves. People do these things.

Good essay writers, taking advantage of readers' natural curiosity about others, strive to make the performer of the action the grammatical subject of their sentences:

> *Passive*: The award was presented to Carrie by the town Rotary Club.
> *Active*: The town Rotary Club presented an award to Carrie.

> *Passive*: Annapolis was attended by my brother, my cousin, and three of my uncles.
> *Active*: My brother, my cousin, and three uncles went to Annapolis.

As you prepare for the SAT, examine your essays for passive sentences. Change them to active sentences unless you have a very good reason not to.

Practice in Revising Passive Sentences

<u>Directions</u>: Please re-write the following sentences, putting each in active voice.

1. The backyard was covered by dead leaves.

_____

2. The crisis in the Middle East was discussed by us.

_____

3. Friday's quiz was failed because I had been at a play rehearsal every night that week.

_____

4. Portland was flown to at the start of our week-long vacation in Oregon.

_____

5. The great white whale was pursued by Captain Ahab and his crew.

_____

6. The newspaper is fetched by Fido every morning.

_____

7. The decision to go to war was made by the president and his advisors.

_____

8. Dinner was taken out by more than twenty customers on Friday night.

_____

9. Five of Shakespeare's plays were seen by our group in three days.

_____

10. Normally, the brain is called on by the body before you do something physical.

_____

Answers are on page 111.

Omitting Needless Words

Never use two words when one will do. Tell your readers quickly and directly what you have to say. Brevity works best. Cut out needless words. Readers value economy.

Stop! Have you noticed that the previous paragraph disregards the very advice it dispenses? Do you see repetition and redundancy? Couldn't the point have been made more briefly and succinctly?

Hold it, again! Look at that last phrase, *briefly and succinctly*. Aha! Another redundancy. The author should have used one, but not both, adverbs.

Here's a word to the wise:

You should work through all of the sentences you write by examining each one and crossing out all the words you don't definitely need.

In truth, that's twenty-four words to the wise—probably more than are needed.

Go through every sentence you write and cross out unnecessary words.

That's better—eleven words of free advice, but still too many. The sentence could be trimmed still further:

Cut unnecessary words out of every sentence.

This seven-word model is less than a third of the original twenty-four word clunker. But it can be pared even more:

Omit needless words.

Your sentences, like muscles, should be firm and tight. In lean writing, every word counts. To trim fat, wring your sentences through this four-step word trimmer:

1. Look for repetition. Then combine sentences.

> *Fat*:   Elena took Jesse to the movies. Jesse is Elena's brother. (10 words)
>
> *Trimmed*:   Elena took her brother Jesse to the movies. (8 words)

Granted, cutting ten words to eight is not much. But consider that it's a 20% reduction, and in a 500-word essay, a 20% reduction amounts to 100 words, the equivalent of a whole paragraph.

> *Fat*:   When Maria was sixteen years of age she accepted a position at Wilkens' Fabrics. In this position she learned about fabrics and about how to handle customers. (27)
>
> *Trimmed*:   At sixteen years old, Maria accepted a position at Wilkens' Fabrics, where she learned about fabrics and handling customers. (19)
>
> *Re-trimmed*:   Working at Wilkens' Fabrics at age sixteen, Maria learned to handle both fabrics and customers. (15)

2. Look for telltale words like *which, who, that, thing, all*. They often signify the presence of fat.

> *Fat*:   Edison was a man who was obsessed by the wonders of electricity. (12)
>
> *Trimmed*:   The wonders of electricity obsessed Edison. (6)

Changing the grammatical subject and replacing *was* with an active verb halved the word count.

> *Fat*:   What he most wanted was that the terrorists would release the hostages. (12)
>
> *Trimmed*:   He most wanted the terrorists to release the hostages. (9)

3. Hunt for phrases that add words but no meaning, such as *the fact that, due to the fact that, at this point in time, at the present time*, and comparable usages.

> *Fat*:   Hamlet returned home as a result of his father's death. (10)
>
> *Trimmed*:   Hamlet returned home because his father died. (7).

> *Fat*:   The troops were in danger due the fact that mines had been planted in the field. (16)
>
> *Trimmed*:   The mine field endangered the troops. (6)

Other Fat Phrases	Trimmed
what I mean is	I mean
on account of, as a result of	because
in the final analysis	finally
few and far between	few
each and every one	each
this is a subject that	this subject
ten in number	ten
at the age of six years old	at age six
most unique	unique
true fact	fact
biography of her life	biography
in regard to, with regard to, in relation to, with respect to	about

A rich vocabulary can also help turn flabby sentences into tight ones:

> *Fat*:   Use a tool with a sharp point that pokes holes in leather. (12)
>
> *Trimmed*:   Use an awl. (3)

> *Fat*:   Sometimes his grandfather had a cheerful and dynamic personality, but at other times he withdrew into himself and became angry and depressed. (22)
>
> *Trimmed*:   His grandfather suffered from bipolar disorder. (6)

4. Search for redundancies. Innumerable words are wasted on reiteration of what has already been stated, on repeating the obvious, on restating ideas, on saying the same thing again and again and over and over, driving readers to the brink of madness.

> **Fat:**   A cloud of black soot rose up to the sky. (10)

Soot, by definition, is black, and rising clouds can only go up.

> **Trimmed:**   A cloud of soot rose to the sky. (8)
> **Fat:**   He had a smile on his face. (7)

Where else but on a face would a smile appear?

> **Trimmed:**   He wore a smile. (4)
> **Fat:**   After carefully scrutinizing the X-ray, the doctor seemed fully engrossed in her own train of thought. (16)

Scrutinize means "to study carefully," and *engrossed* means "to think fully." Also, *her own train of thought* is nonsensical because no one can think others' thoughts.

> **Trimmed:**   After scrutinizing the X-ray, the doctor seemed engrossed in thought. (10)

After you have pared your sentences to the bone, re-read what remains and discard still more by tracking down little words like *the, a, an, up, down, its,* and *and.* Even though it may hurt to take out what you worked hard to put in, don't whine. Just grit your teeth and do it!

Practice in Trimming Needless Words

Part A

Directions: Tighten these sentences, but preserve their meaning.

1. The author, a man named Peter Jenkins, wrote a book with the title *A Walk Across America*, about walking across America, which he accomplished after walking twenty-five miles a day in order to prepare for his walk across America.

_____

_____

2. There is no reason for the chairperson of the committee, who is Carolyn Welles, to take offense at my suggestion, which is aimed at trying to make the meetings more productive and useful to the entire student body at large.

_____

_____

3. Molly was elected to be the editor of the yearbook in spite of the fact that her grades in writing in English courses are really not very good at all.

_____

_____

4. Some kinds of criticism are good, but other kinds of criticism do more harm than good. Harmful criticism is criticism that tears a person down instead of helping the person overcome or deal with a problem.

_____

_____

5. Every American should have a good knowledge of our country, and the best way to gain a good knowledge and familiarity with the United States is to visit and see places of historic interest and significance to our country.

_____

_____

Part B

<u>Directions</u>: This wordy paragraph appeared in an essay that advocated gaining weight. Please trim its fat.

Such weight-gaining ideas can be used to good advantage by each and every man, woman, and child who is interested in adding pounds of weight to his or her body. They are the latest, most up-to-date set of procedures available anywhere. Owing to the fact that health experts and authorities believe that it is better to be underweight than it is to be overweight, ideas for putting on weight are generally thought to be jokes not taken seriously, which is the reason why such ideas are kept under wraps and not publicized very widely or broadly. Yet, there are many people of all kinds who need to gain weight for a variety of diverse reasons. Here is a quotation that Slim Snyder, who is a graduate of Stanford University, stated during a speech he gave at a meeting of people gathered together at a health conference recently: "Lean people are victims of discrimination, just as obese people are."

_____

_____

_____

_____

_____

_____

_____

_____

Answers are on page 111. For additional practice in eliminating wordiness, turn to Part V, page 136.

Showing vs. Telling

Remember the principle that a picture is worth a thousand words? Whether that's true is arguable, but the point is not. Words help readers _see_. Therefore, _show_ more than you _tell_! Instead of describing your uncle as "absent-minded," _show_ him stepping into his morning shower dressed in his p.j.'s. Rather than telling the reader that your room is "a mess," _show_ the pile of wrinkled clothes in the corner and the books and Snickers wrappers scattered on the floor next to your unmade futon. The same principle applies to smells: "Her breath was foul with the stench of stale whiskey." To sounds: "the growl of a chain saw in the distance." To touch: "the feel of cool linen bed sheets." And to tastes: "a cold, sweet drink of spring water on a scorching summer day." In short, showing recreates experience for the reader, ultimately making the prose more interesting.

Telling:	I was happy after my meeting with Mr. Blair.
Showing:	I bolted from Mr. Blair's office, bounded down the steps four at a time, and shouted into the wind, "Hurray, I did it."
Telling:	My teacher, Mr. Franks, doesn't care to hear that I don't have the time to do math homework after school.
Showing:	When I explained to Mr. Franks that I'm kept from math homework by driving my brother Timmy to piano lessons or karate, by yearbook meetings on Tuesdays, by Peer Leaders and Students Against Driving Drunk, by French tutoring, and by a part-time job at the florist, he muttered, "That's _your_ problem."

No one expects you to load all your essays with a profusion of striking images that *show* instead of *tell*. The fact is that writers struggle for years to perfect the technique. Moreover, too much detail can be as unproductive as too little. A balance is best. No one can tell you exactly how to achieve that balance. You need time to get the feel of it, like riding a bike or doing a back flip. The context, as well as your judgment of a reader's need to know, should determine how detailed you need to be. To develop the knack, study a written passage that you admire. Pick out both details and broad statements. For practice, use the passage as a model for writing a paragraph of your own.

Practice in Showing Instead of Telling

<u>Directions</u>: Revise the prose of the telling samples into showing examples.

1. Telling: Mike is very tall.

   Showing: _____

   _____

2. Telling: After she won, she experienced a wonderful and unique feeling that made her want to win again.

   Showing: _____

   _____

3. Telling: The store was a quaint old place.

   Showing: _____

   _____

4. Telling: It smelled just the way a beach is supposed to smell.

   Showing: _____

   _____

5. Telling: The class is out of control.

   Showing: _____

   _____

6. Telling: Pioneers had a hard time.

   Showing: _____

   _____

7. Telling: The cabin was really run down.

   Showing: _____

   _____

8. Telling: The air pollution was sickening.

   Showing: _____

9. Telling: The speech stirred the crowd.

   Showing: _____

   _____

10. Telling: Mary Jane's mother is obsessed by cleanliness.

    Showing: _____

    _____

Answers are on page 111–112.

CHECKING FOR STANDARD USAGE AND MECHANICS

Practice these guidelines to minimize writing errors:

- Write correct sentences
- Use correct verbs
- Use adjectives and adverbs correctly
- Choose correct pronouns
- Correct punctuation and capitalization

Write Correct Sentences

Time won't permit you to analyze meticulously every sentence in your SAT essay. But if you habitually scrutinize the sentences in your practice essays and in other work you do for school, you'll soon purge from your writing such errors as **fragments**, (incomplete sentences), **run-ons**, which consist of two or more improperly joined sentences, and **comma splices**, formed when a comma separates two complete sentences.

To avoid these common errors, always look for the noun or pronoun that functions as the grammatical subject of the sentence and for the verb that it goes with. Every sentence states its subject except one that gives commands or makes requests (Make it snappy! Sit! Please hurry up.), in which case the subject is understood to be the addressee—you, the dog, a slowpoke . . . whomever.

For more details and practice in writing correct sentences, turn to Part V, page 139.

Use Correct Verbs

Of all the parts of speech, verbs are the most apt to be used incorrectly. As you edit your SAT essay, therefore, ask yourself the following three questions:

1. Do all nouns and pronouns agree in number with their verbs?
2. Is every verb in the correct tense?
3. Is every verb in the correct form?

Learn to answer these questions accurately by studying the following sections of Part V: Noun-verb agreement, page 152; proper use of verb tenses, page 156; and correct form of verbs, page 156.

Use Adjectives and Adverbs Correctly

Errors sometimes occur when an adjective is used where an adverb is required. The reverse—using an adverb in place of an adjective—occurs less often. Check your essay for the proper use of adjectives and adverbs.

For details and practice in adjective/adverb use, turn to Part V, page 168.

Choose Correct Pronouns

Skim your essay for pronoun errors, which turn up most often when pronouns are paired, as in *he and I* and *me and them*. If you can't depend on your sense of what sounds right and wrong, keep in mind that most common pronouns fall into two groups:

Group 1: *I, he, she, they, we, you*
Group 2: *me, him, her, them, us, you*

The pronouns in the first group are **nominative case** pronouns and are used in grammatical subjects and predicate nominatives. The second group—**objective case** pronouns—are used everywhere else. Because pairs must come from the same case, problems arise when pronouns from different cases show up in the same phrase, as "*Him* and *I* went to the movies." Any time you need a pair of pronouns, and you know that one of them is correct, pick the other from the same group. If you don't know either pronoun, here's a handy rule of thumb to follow: Substitute *I* or *me* for one of them. If *I* seems to fit, choose pronouns from Group 1; if *me* fits better, use Group 2.

For more details and a practice exercise in choosing the case of pronouns, turn to Part V, page 157.

As you review your essay, check the reference of all pronouns. That is, be sure also that every pronoun refers clearly to its antecedent—usually a noun or another pronoun. Confusion comes when no clear tie exists, especially when a pronoun seems to refer to more than one antecedent:

The librarian told Sarah that it was *her* responsibility to shelve the books.

Because the pronoun *her* may refer to either the librarian or to Sarah, the sentence needs revision:

> The librarian told Sarah that one of her responsibilities as a library clerk was to shelve books.

Also watch for implied references, which often involve the pronouns *it, they*, and *you*, but even more frequently, the relative pronouns *which, that*, and *this*.

Finally, don't use pronouns to refer to possessives, as in:

> In Eminem's latest hit, he stumbles over several words.

The pronoun *he* obviously refers to Eminem, but the word *Eminem* doesn't appear in the sentence. Because the possessive noun *Eminem's* is not a grammatical equivalent to *Eminem*, the revised sentence should be:

> In his latest hit, Eminem stumbles over several words.

For more details and an exercise in pronoun reference, turn to Part V, page 161.

Stay alert also for shifts in pronoun person within individual sentences, within paragraphs, and within the whole essay. Keep in mind that a sentence or a passage cast in the second person (*you*), for example, should usually remain so from start to finish. Likewise, a sentence or passage written in the first or third person should stay that way throughout.

For more details and an exercise in pronoun person, turn to Part V, page 159.

Finally, take a look at the agreement between all the pronouns and their antecedents. Do they agree in gender, number, and person? Problems frequently occur with words like *everyone, anyone*, and *nobody*—singular words that should usually be followed by singular pronouns. Sometimes such words are meant as plurals, however, and should be followed by plural pronouns.

For more details and an exercise in pronoun-antecedent agreement, turn to Part V, page 159.

Correct Punctuation and Capitalization

Because error-free essays tend to earn higher scores, it pays to review your essay for proper punctuation and use of capital letters.

Correct Punctuation

A few basic rules cover 90% of everyday punctuation. The hardest thing about the rules is knowing where and when to apply them.

Apostrophes. Apostrophes are used in only three places:

1. In **contractions** such as *won't, it's, could've*, and *where's*. Apostrophes mark places where letters have been omitted.
2. In **plurals** of letters, signs, or numbers, as in *A's* and *B's*, the *1960's*, and *10's* and *20's, although* many experts simplify matters by writing *1960s, Ps and Qs*, and so forth.
3. In **possessive nouns** such as the *student's class* and *women's room* and in indefinite pronouns such as *anybody's guess*. When the noun is plural and ends in *s*, put the apostrophe after the *s*, as in *leaves' color* and *horses' stable*. Some possessive forms use both an apostrophe and *of*, as in *a friend of the family's;* some others that specify time, space, value, or quantity also require apostrophes, as in an *hour's time, a dollar's worth, at my wit's end.*

Commas. Commas divide sentences into parts, clarify meaning, and prevent confusion.

1. Use a comma to signal a **pause**, as in:

   No pause: After brushing his teeth gleamed.
   Pause: After brushing, his teeth gleamed.

   Commas are needed after some introductory words and in forms of address:

   Well, you can open it whenever it's convenient.
   The letter will be waiting for you at home, *Jimmy*.

2. Commas set off words that **interrupt the flow** of a sentence, as in:

   Carolyn, *regrettably*, was omitted from the roster.
   Jennie, *on the other hand*, was included.

Commas separate information not essential to the meaning of the sentence:

The lost hikers, *who had come from New Jersey*, found shelter in a cave.

The three bikers, *whose map of the course was out of date*, arrived two hours later.

Commas set off **appositives**:

Samantha, *the defense counsel*, entered the courtroom.

The judge, *Mr. Peterson*, presided at the trial.

3. Commas separate the clauses of a **compound sentence**:

The competition is stiff, but it won't keep Miriam from winning.

Pete had better call my mother, or I'll be in big trouble.

4. Commas separate items in a **series**:

Rosie's car needs *new tires, a battery, a muffler, and an oil change*.

It was a wonder that Marv could sit through the *long, boring, infantile, and ridiculous* lecture.

Some writers prefer to skip the comma before the last item in a series, but just in case clarity may suffer, it can't hurt to put it in.

5. Commas separate parts of **addresses, dates, and place names**:

Who lives at 627 West 115th Street, New York, NY?

Richard was born on May 27, 1990, the same day as Irene.

Dave has lived in Madison, Wisconsin; Seattle, Washington; and Eugene, Oregon.

Note that, because each item in the last example already contains a comma, semicolons help to avoid confusion.

6. Commas separate quotations from attributions in **dialogue**.

John said, "Close the window."

"I want it open," protested Ben.

Semicolons. Semicolons may be used between closely related sentences, in effect, shortening the pause that would naturally occur between two separate sentences:

Mother was worried; her daughters never stay out this late.

The momentum was building; she couldn't be stopped now.

A caution: Because semicolons function like periods, use them only between independent clauses or in a series in which one or more items contains a comma, as in:

On his trek, Norwood met Allen, a carpenter from Maine; Dr. Jones, a pediatrician from St. Louis; Jonathan, an airline pilot; and me, of course.

Quotation Marks. Quotation marks usually surround direct quotations, as in:

Rita said to Bob, "I'm nuts about you."

Quotation marks also enclose the titles of poems, stories, chapter headings, essays, magazine articles, and other short works. Don't use them for longer works. Novels, plays, films, and magazine titles should be underlined in handwritten essays and italicized when they appear in print.

Avoid calling attention to clichés, trite expressions, or slang terms by using quotation marks. Rewrite instead, using fresh, original language.

Finally, quotation marks may enclose words that express the silent thoughts of a character, as in:

Carlos glanced at his watch. "I'm going to be late," he thought.

Periods and commas are placed inside close-quotation marks. Question marks and exclamation points go outside the quotation mark unless they are part of the quote itself.

"When will the seminar start?" asked Regis.

Do you understand the meaning of the concept "The end justifies the means"?

Practice in Using Punctuation

Part A. Possessives

Directions: Check your mastery of possessives by writing the correct possessive form of the italicized word in the space provided. Some items may be correct.

1. *Pauls* reason was personal.

   _____

2. The future of *Americas* foreign policy is being debated.

   _____

3. *Teams* from all over the county have gathered at the stadium.

   _____

4. Luis isn't at all interested in *womens* issues.

   _____

5. The *girls* locker room is downstairs, but the *boys* is upstairs.

   _____

6. We are invited to the *Andersons* house for New *Years* Eve.

   _____

7. All of the *Rosses* are going out to eat.

   _____

8. Have you seen *Morris* iPod, which he left here yesterday?

   _____

9. Both of the *computers* keyboards need repair.

   _____

10. He'll be back in two *months* time.

    _____

Part B. Commas and semicolons

Directions: In the following sentences, insert or remove commas and semicolons as necessary. Some sentences may be correct.

1. While Bill was riding his bike got a flat tire.

2. The mail carrier did not leave the package for Valerie was not at home.

3. After doing his homework Mikey as you might expect talked on his cell phone for an hour.

4. His work criticized many commonly held beliefs however and it was strictly censored.

5. The car, that ran into mine at the intersection, was an SUV.

6. Dad went to the airport to pick up Dave Ellie went to the train station to meet Debbie.

7. The people who live by the water must be prepared for occasional flooding.

8. The boat, was seventy-five feet long and eighteen feet wide, its mast was about eighty feet tall.

9. To anyone interested in flying planes hold endless fascination.

10. Jeff and Steve left alone for the weekend invited all their friends to a party.

11. I need street maps of Boston; and Portland, Maine.

12. Some of the theories dealt with the political social and religious ideas of the time.

13. Students, who want to try out for the chorus, have been asked to report to room 330.

14. Doug for example is both a scholar and an athlete.

15. Monica refused to go, unless Phil went with her.

16. The hero of the book John Coffey rode his bike across the United States.

17. After all she did for him what she could.

18. Starting in Minnesota the Mississippi runs all the way to the Gulf of Mexico.

19. Harold Watkins who comes from Chicago won a full tuition scholarship to Duke.

20. Although the characters are stereotypes they were interesting to read about.

21. Yo-Yo Ma the famous cellist will perform a recital on Saturday night.

22. This test covers Spanish literature culture and history; and it lasts for three hours.

23. Michelle is pretty tall and dark but her older sister Norma is pretty short and light.

24. Sean the twin brother of Ian was struck by a falling tree limb.

25. The window washer dropped by last evening but he didn't bring his squeegee.

Answers are on page 112.

Capitalization

Capitalization isn't totally standardized, but it's not a free-for-all either. You won't go wrong following these guidelines:

1. Capitalize the first words of sentences, direct quotations, and lines of poetry (most of the time). This includes sentences that follow colons, as in:

He had all the symptoms of love: He could think of nothing but Cheryl all day long.

2. Capitalize proper nouns and adjectives derived from proper nouns: *Victoria, Victorian; Shakespeare, Shakespearean; France, French dressing* (but not *french fries*, which has become a generic term).

3. Capitalize place names: *North America, Lake Moosilauke, Yosemite National Park, Gobi Desert, Mount Rushmore, Panama Canal, the Arctic Ocean, Times Square, Route 66.* Don't capitalize north, east, south, and west unless you are referring to a particular region of the country, as in:

They went camping in the *West*.

Nor should you capitalize the common noun that is not part of the actual place name: the *canal across Panama, the city of Moline,* and *the plains of the Midwest.*

4. Capitalize languages, races, nationalities, and religions: *the Hungarian language, Inuit, Argentinian, Hispanic, Muslim.*

5. Capitalize organizations, institutions, and brand names: *United Nations, Pittsburgh Pirates, Library of Congress, Automobile Club of America, Amtrak, Southwest Airlines, the Internet, Toyota.* Don't, however, capitalize the common noun associated with the brand name, as in *Crest toothpaste or Starbuck's coffee.*

6. Capitalize titles of persons that indicate rank, office, profession, when they are used with the person's name: *Congressman Kelly, Doctor Dolittle, Coach McConnell, Judge Judy, Lieutenant Lawlor.* Also, the titles of high officials when they are used in place of the official's name, as in *the Secretary General, the Prime Minister, the Secretary of the Treasury.* Don't capitalize titles when referring generically to the position: *the superintendent of schools, the assistant librarian, the clerk of the highway department.*

7. Capitalize family relationships, but only when they are used with a person's name: *Uncle Wesley, Grandma Jones, Cousin Dave.*

8. Capitalize titles of books, plays, stories, articles, poems, songs, and other creative works: *The Grapes of Wrath, Hamlet,* "An Occurrence at Owl Creek Bridge," "Ode to a Grecian Urn," "Box of Rain." Note that articles, conjunctions and prepositions of less than five

letters are not capitalized unless they appear as the last or the first words in the title.

9. Capitalize references to the Deity and religious tracts: *God, the Gospel, the Torah, the Koran, the Lord, the Prophet.* Also capitalize pronouns referring to *Him* or *Her.*

10. Capitalize historical names, events, documents, and periods: *Battle of Gettysburg, Alien and Sedition Acts, War of 1812, Bill of Rights, Middle Ages.*

11. Capitalize days of the week, months, holidays: *Monday, May, Mothers' Day.* The seasons are not capitalized unless given an identity such as *Old Man Winter.*

12. Capitalize the names of specific courses and schools: *History 101, Forensic Science, Brookvale High School, Columbia College.* While course names are capitalized, subjects are not. Therefore, you study *history* in *American History 101* and learn *forensics* in *Forensic Science.* Similarly, you attend *high school* at *Brookvale High School* and go to *college* at *Columbia.*

Practice in Applying Capitalization

<u>Directions</u>: Add capital letters where they are needed in the following sentences.

1. on labor day bennington county's fire department plans to hold a turkey shoot on the field at miller's pond.

2. the judge gave district attorney lipman a book entitled *the rules of evidence* and instructed her to read it before she ever dared set foot in the court of appeals of the ninth circuit again.

3. the secretary of state greeted the president of austria at the ronald reagan airport in washington, d.c.

4. the shackleton expedition nearly met its doom on georgia island in antarctica.

5. for christmas he got a black & decker table saw from the sears store next to the old bedford courthouse.

6. according to georgetown's high school principal, eugene griffiths, georgetown high school attracts students from the whole west coast. at georgetown students may major in drawing and painting, design, graphics, or sculpture. mr. griffiths said, "i attended a similar high school in new england just after the vietnam war."

7. we expect to celebrate new year's eve again this year by renting a movie of an old broadway musical and by settling down in front of the dvd player with some pepsi and a box of oreos.

8. after traveling all the way to the pacific, the corps of discovery rode down the missouri river going east on their way back to st. louis.

9. This irish linen tablecloth was bought at k-mart in the emeryville mall off powell street.

10. yellowstone national park is located in the northwestern corner of the state of wyoming.

Answers are on page 112.

REVIEW

Here's the list of the twelve principles of good writing, reproduced to remind you once more that referring to them again and again will work to your advantage as you prepare for the SAT.

Pre-writing
Analyze the topic carefully.
Narrow the topic mercilessly.
Choose a main idea that matters.
Gather and arrange ideas purposefully.

Composing
Hook readers with a gripping introduction.
Develop paragraphs coherently.
Use plain and precise words.
Vary the sentence structure.
End the essay memorably.

Editing and Proofreading
Edit for clarity.
Edit for interest.
Check for standard usage and mechanics.

ANSWER KEY TO PRACTICE EXERCISES

Choosing a Main Idea, page 56

These are suggestions only. Your answers may be equally or more effective.

1. A. Henry Ford knew more about cars than about people, because talent, ability, and a little bit of luck are the most important ingredients of success.
   B. If Henry Ford's statement is correct, the world is filled with self-deluded people.
   C. From spelling bees to Nobel Prizes, nobody with a negative attitude has ever been a winner.
2. A. While rats may learn to run through a maze for a food pellet, children are different.
   B. Political history shows that if a dictator wants to control his people, he should scare the living daylights out of them.
   C. Knowing that acceptance to a good college waits for them, most students willingly go through hell, including the SAT, to get there.

3. A. Those who say "Money is the root of all evil" know what they are talking about.
   B. Dreaming of wealth is as American as apple pie—part of the great American dream.
   C. Only a ding-a-ling, or someone named Jay Gatsby, would truly believe that money can buy happiness.
4. A. Mandela is partly right and partly wrong because everything keeps changing.
   B. Going back to old places that haven't changed tells you more about what you were than about what you've become.
   C. After a recent visit to my old elementary school, I could not agree more with Mandela's observation.
5. A. Bryan is definitely on the right track. Nothing is as personally satisfying as achieving a goal through hard work.
   B. Which kind of success do I prefer? Frankly, I'll take it either way.
   C. I've heard that people make their own good luck by their decisions and choices. Therefore, it's simplistic to think that your destiny can be achieved without it.

Gathering and Arranging Ideas, pages 58–59

Answers will vary. The order of ideas is strictly a matter of personal preference.

A. Advantages:
   1. SUV's are comfortable to ride in and to drive.
   2. They are safer than ordinary cars.
   3. They can carry large loads of people or cargo.

   Disadvantages:
   1. SUV's are expensive.
   2. They guzzle gas, which adds to environmental pollution.
   3. Their size makes it hard to find a parking space.

B. Pro:
   1. Lotteries give everyone a chance to dream of being wealthy.
   2. They are fun to participate in.
   3. They help states raise money for good causes, such as education.

   Con:
   1. Lotteries raise and then dash people's hopes.
   2. They encourage addiction to gambling.
   3. They appeal mostly to people who can least afford to play.

C. For:
   1. Cheating is rampant and something should be done about it.
   2. A code will improve the moral climate in the school.
   3. Students must learn that there are consequences for cheating.

   Against:
   1. A code creates an atmosphere of fear and apprehension, like a police state.
   2. Students will be reluctant to rat on each other.
   3. It discourages students from helping each other learn.

D. Agree:
   1. War causes people and nations to abandon the qualities that make them human.
   2. Wars cause death, suffering, and destruction.
   3. Wars cost money that can and should be used for improving lives, not destroying them.

Disagree:
   1. War against terrorism provides security for the people.
   2. War to depose tyrants is of benefit to mankind.
   3. Wars on poverty, drugs, and other social evils improve the quality of life.

Writing an Appealing Opening, page 61

Answers will vary. Be confident that the essay openings you wrote may be no less effective than these samples.

1. Topic: The courage of one's convictions

   Most high school kids would rather be caught dead than be considered out of synch with the crowd. An exception to the rule is my best friend, Molly McBride. She would consider herself dead if she couldn't express her individuality and be different from everyone else.

2. Topic: Deadlines

   My dad recently bought me a Palm pilot. At first I thought it was a strange gift for a father to present to his son on his 17th birthday. After all, I'm not a business man or a lawyer or a high-powered boomer who needs to keep tabs on meetings and clients and overseas flights to catch. But Dad said that I'd need a Palm pilot very soon, and he was right! I'm applying to more than half a dozen colleges, each with its own deadlines to keep track of and meet, and without my Palm pilot my life would be even more chaotic than it is.

3. Topic: "Keep it! You may need it someday."

   If you've ever seen "The Antiques Road Show" on television, you'd never throw anything away, never hold a garage sale, never pass up an opportunity to buy an old toy, an ashtray from the World's Fair, a miniature Statue of Liberty, or any other piece of junk to fill your shelves and clutter up your closets. The reason is that all these things may be great investments and could someday be worth hundreds, even thousands, of times more than you paid for them.

4. Topic: The wrong time in the wrong place

   In 1939, almost a thousand Jews managed to escape from Hitler's Germany by boarding the SS *St. Louis*, an ocean liner bound for safety in Cuba. Once they arrived offshore in Havana, however, Cuban authorities would not let the ship dock. The United States also turned the *St. Louis* away, even though the passengers could see the lights of Miami in the distance. With no place to go, the ship sailed back to Europe. Many of the passengers settled in countries soon to be overrun by the Nazis and perished in the Holocaust.

5. Topic: Responsibility

 Why doesn't my mother trust me? Why do I get only $10 a week allowance? Why must I call home every two hours when I am out with my friends? Why won't my father ever let me borrow his car? How will I ever learn responsibility if I never have any?

Developing Topic Sentences, pages 63–67

Part A

1. Sentence 1
2. None. Implied topic sentence
3. Sentence 7
4. Sentence 10
5. Sentence 1
6. Sentence 1
7. Sentence 1
8. Sentence 3
9. Sentence 2
10. Sentence 6

Part B

Answers may vary.

1. Mother and Father are very different from each other.
2. In the past U.S. athletes dominated the Olympic Games.
3. Monopolies often destroy not only themselves but the incentive of businesses to change and make progress.
4. How little the aristocracy understood the needs of the masses.
5. Vera Simon wrote a gripping and realistic book.
6. Smoking in school is just not worth the trouble it can lead to.
7. But here are my requirements for the perfect roommate.
8. Age and experience have deprived me of courage and spirit.
9. No topic sentence is needed.
10. Although backward in some respects, a so-called primitive culture can be technologically sophisticated.

Part C

Answers will vary. The topic sentences you wrote may be as good as or even better than these examples.

a. Of all the equipment needed to traverse the inhuman land of Antarctica, nothing is more important than a team of well-trained sled dogs.
b. Antarctica takes your breath away.
c. This is not an idle comparison, because at every turn you are putting your health and safety in jeopardy.

Developing Paragraphs, pages 67–68

1.	2.	3.	4.	5.
a. 3	a. 3	a. 4	a. 5	a. 5
b. 5	b. 1	b. 2	b. 4	b. 3
c. 1	c. 4	c. 3	c. 1	c. 2
d. 2	d. 5	d. 1	d. 2	d. 1
e. 4	e. 2	e. 5	e. 3	e. 4

Identifying Paragraph Unity and Coherence, pages 68–70

1. Sentence 3 destroys the coherence of the paragraph. Delete it. There's no reason to save it, because the idea is reiterated in sentence 7.
2. The paragraph lacks unity. It starts by discussing consequences on young people of smoking marijuana and ends by explaining parents' problems. One way to overcome the paragraph's lack of unity is to divide it into two parts. Another is to expand the topic sentence to include parents, *e.g., Under present law, smoking marijuana can have serious consequences for both young people and their parents.* If this were done, however, the paragraph would need further development.
3. The paragraph is coherent except for sentence 5, which should be deleted. Sentence 2 strongly supports the topic sentence (1). The remaining sentences, except 5, support sentence 2, which is the major supporting sentence in the paragraph.
4. Although the entire paragraph discusses political parties, the discussion is not unified. Sentences 1–3 deal with the two-party system, while sentences 4–7 are about dictatorships. Either divide the paragraph, or add a topic sentence that justifies discussing both topics within a single paragraph.

5. Sentence 1 is the topic sentence. Sentence 4 is unrelated to the topic sentence. Delete it.

6. The paragraph is mostly unified and coherent, although the topic sentence would be more accurate if it mentioned the human qualities of porpoises.

7. Although the opening sentence leads the reader to think that what follows will be all about *Robinson Crusoe*, the paragraph is really about the author Daniel Defoe. To improve the coherence of the paragraph, delete or revise the misleading topic sentence.

8. Although the entire paragraph is about Greek philosophy, it is terribly disjointed. Only sentences 3 and 4 connect with each other. The others are independent thoughts, related in subject matter but not in style. For coherence, add a topic sentence, possibly using material in sentence 5. The fact that Socrates taught Plato, who taught Aristotle might serve as starting point in revising the paragraph.

9. The paragraph is coherent and unified until the last sentence. Delete sentence 6, but if the idea is too good to discard, save it for another place in the essay or revise sentence 1, the topic sentence.

10. The paragraph is unified and coherent. No revision needed.

Using Transitions, pages 71–72

These paragraphs only illustrate the use of transitions. Your answers will no doubt be different.

1. To get on the good side of a teacher takes practice, but the technique explained below almost never fails. <u>First</u> you must try to create the impression that you think, say, Ms. Douglas, is the best teacher in the world. You must <u>immediately</u> choose a seat that is near to her in the classroom. <u>Then</u> you must pretend to listen intently to her every word and nod your head as though you agree with everything she says. <u>Next</u>, smile at her, laugh at her jokes, and never leave the room right after class. <u>Soon after</u> the bell, ask her a question about the lesson and thank her profusely for taking the time to answer it. <u>After a while</u>, she'll think that you are an intelligent, highly-motivated student and with luck will reward you handsomely on your report card.

2. Some people are bored with their lives. <u>As a result</u>, they seek out dangerous situations in order to get a thrill. <u>Accordingly</u>, many movie stuntmen ache to put their lives in jeopardy. <u>As a result</u>, they volunteer to crash through windows, fall down stairs, jump from high places, drive cars into walls and into each other. <u>As a consequence</u>, they often get hurt, but their work is more important to them than their safety and well-being. <u>Hence</u>, it takes a sort of masochist to be a stuntman.

3. Because my father is an optimist and my mother a pessimist, they respond to life in different ways. <u>Unlike</u> my mother, my father is always pretty upbeat, even when he's worried about his job, about money, and about me and my sister. <u>On the other hand</u>, Mom frets about every little thing, from the weather (it's never quite right) to dirt on the living room rug (there's too much of it). <u>In spite of their differences</u>, Dad and Mom get along just fine. <u>Still</u>, I prefer Dad's way because it resembles mine. <u>Nevertheless</u>, I can see where Mom is coming from and love her all the same.

4. It's time to take another look at how the government squanders billions of dollars every year for what is called the International Space Station. Because money is <u>also</u> wasted on regular launches of the space shuttles, the shuttle program <u>also</u> should be re-evaluated. <u>In addition</u> to being a waste of taxpayers' dollars, neither program has been as fruitful as predicted. <u>Besides</u> failing to fulfill their promise, their successes have been either modest or irrelevant. <u>Moreover</u>, the public has lost interest in America's space program except when there are catastrophes such as the destruction of the *Challenger* in 1986 and the *Columbia* in 2003. <u>Besides</u>, the money spent on the space program is desperately needed to improve life right here on earth.

Using Precise Wording, pages 74–75

Answers will vary. The words in your sentences may be as precise as or even more precise than the words in these samples.

1. The barn's rotted walls bulged, its windows wouldn't open, and moss covered the sagging roof.

2. When accused of lying to the jury, the witness turned beet red, burst into tears, and, with eyes turned to heaven, asked, "What in the world is happening to me?"

3. After winning the election by a 3 to 1 margin, the senator grinned from ear to ear and told her supporters that she was ready to work in their behalf.

4. Molly's reward for six hours at her desk studying physics was a big fat F on the quiz.

5. The seniors celebrated their graduation but wept inside, realizing that tonight was the last time they would ever be together.

6. To make it on the swim team, the bowling team, or any other team, there are but three things to do: practice, practice, practice.

7. At the wake, Greg was startled by the joviality of the mourners, who rejoiced over Mr. O'Malley's life instead of lamenting his death.

8. In high school Linda rarely went to class, flunked English and math in summer school, and finally dropped out altogether.

9. Teddy and Joey, the family's twins, never went out at the same time because they shared the same pair of shoes.

10. Although the current had smashed the canoe against the rocks, Rod unhesitatingly leaped into the water to save the drowning child.

Writing Comparisons, page 77

The comparisons that you wrote may be as good as or even better than these examples.

A. 1. as comfortable as a baby in its mother's arms
    2. as tough as a wrecking ball
    3. as gorgeous as gold
    4. as silly as putty
    5. as serious as 9/11
    6. as perfect as a circle
    7. as wild as a leaping salmon
    8. as unpredictable as the lottery
    9. as impetuous as a flash of lightning
    10. as reliable as a sheepdog

B. School is like an airport, a place one passes through for the sole purpose of going somewhere else. Just as no one goes to the airport just to be at the airport, who would go to school in order to go to school. Instead, school is a step one takes while preparing for college

and for life. One spends a certain amount of time there, follows the rules, does the work, and then escapes like a traveler en route to Aruba, or Italy, or the Far East. Similarly, at the airport, you must obey the rules: check in at the counter, have your photo ID ready, go through security checks, stand in lines. If you fail to follow the prescribed procedure, trouble can follow, delaying your departure. In that sense, it's no different from school, where one must do what is expected in order to graduate on time.

Varying Sentences, pages 82–83

These are illustrative answers only. Many other variations are possible.

1. Mr. Finn is a good teacher but he runs the class like a dictatorship. Democracy and freedom have no place in his class. On the first day he announced his rules, among them no talking, no gum chewing, no hats in class, no lateness. If you arrive late, you should expect to find the door locked and to go to detention after school. All homework is compulsory. No one dares to come to class unprepared because a girl who once came to class without her homework turned colors and almost wept after Mr. Finn lowered the boom on her.

2. In the numerous science classes that I have taken, we talked about experiments instead of doing them because the equipment was obsolete and too costly to replace. We learned scientific theories but could not practice them in labs or see them demonstrated. To give students a better education, the science department needs money. About a million dollars would do.

3. By dumping garbage, sewage, and other hazardous waste products into the sea, many nations are polluting the world's oceans. They are making beaches and swimming dangerous. Toxic pollutants also taint all forms of sea life with materials that humans ingest when eating fish, lobsters, clams, and other seafood.

4. The earth has experienced a sharp increase in natural disasters, from about 100 per year in the 1960s to five times that number in the early part of the 21st century. Earthquakes, droughts, huge storms, and floods are not happening more frequently, however. Nor are they occur-

ring with greater intensity. Rather, the population of the world has increased. People in greater numbers now occupy areas that are prone to natural disasters, such as flood plains, coastal lands, and cities built on subterranean fault lines. The planet has not changed but humans have.

5. Although the American Dream is a popular concept, it means different things for different people. Most commonly, it means finding a good job, getting married, having a couple of kids and owning a home with a white picket fence and a two-car garage. Some people, thinking that dream shallow, say that the dream won't be complete without a good education, friends, a feeling of well-being, good health, and above all, the blessings of liberty, including the freedom of speech and religion and the freedom to choose to be 'part of an untraditional family made up of same-sex partners or any other combination of adults and children.

Writing Conclusions, page 85

Because every writer is different from every other, these answers are no more than possibilities for concluding three different essays.

1. In a generation or less, today's profanity may be no different from the everyday language in newspapers, on television, and even in essays like this one.
2. Some people succeed because they are lucky. Others succeed because they are more talented or smarter than the competition. But success comes to the vast majority because they have planned how to succeed. When a split second determines the winner in a race, is it fair to say that the second-place finisher is not as good as the winner? No, but it's a certainty that the winner planned his racing strategy better than the person who lost.
3. If by magic I happened to find myself in junior high again, I wouldn't rest until I'd made my escape.

Identifying Misplaced and Dangling Modifiers, pages 87–88

Your answers needn't be identical to these, but your sentences should be free of dangling and misplaced modifiers.

1. The pizza I ate after completing my chemistry homework tasted great.
2. Denise discovered her boyfriend sound asleep in the hammock.
3. Having been used all night to illuminate the steps, the flashlight needed new batteries.
4. While I drove down the mountain road, a rock smashed my windshield.
5. When I stopped to rest after a long hike, a grizzly bear stood in front of me.
6. Before the school bus picked me up, I ate a quick breakfast.
7. The police submitted a report about the bank robbery.
8. His family emigrated from Russia when Sasha was ten.
9. We gave the dog a bone we didn't want.
10. Left alone in the house, the child was terrified by every sound.

Identifying Parallel Structure, pages 89–90

These are suggested answers. Other answers may also be correct.

1. and inspirational
2. was accused not only of being a bigot but also of being too stupid
3. and gone to fewer parties
4. preparing reports, and making various types of telephone calls
5. and to get up early
6. and she had a habit of disappearing
7. or a commercial artist
8. felt both pride and satisfaction
9. Correct
10. plans to live simply
11. The kids had scattered their books not only all over the bus but also all over the sidewalk.
12. have a good location, have land around it, and enjoy a view
13. Joan's broken yellow pencil came from this box.
14. how to furnish and decorate the house simply

15. neither have a microwave in his room nor take a shower after 11:00 o'clock
16. and being miles from friends
17. The mouse will either find a quick way into the attic or gnaw at the siding for days.
18. and entertaining
19. and a job in the suburbs
20. that he'll defeat Tom in the sectionals, and that he'll emerge

Using Active Verbs, pages 92–93

Although your answers will differ from these, be sure that your sentences, like those here, are free of lifeless verbs.

1. The attack of 9/11 shocked most Americans.
2. Nearly three thousand people died in New York City.
3. Afterwards, a controversy raged over whom to blame for America's vulnerability to terrorism.
4. Efforts to strengthen homeland security began.
5. Some citizens agreed to give up their rights for the sake of security.
6. People struggle with the dilemma of how much freedom to give up for security.
7. The events of 9/11 led to a significant war in Afghanistan.
8. We dressed in sweatshirts and baggy pants whenever we went out.
9. The presence of an all-American high school player stirred up the crowd at the basketball game.
10. Obviously, the average college-bound student needs more training in math and science.

Revising Passive Sentences, page 94

Your sentences may differ from these, but be sure you've used the active voice.

1. Dead leaves covered the backyard.
2. We discussed the crisis in the Middle East.
3. I failed Friday's quiz because I had rehearsed for the play every night that week.
4. We began our weeklong vacation in Oregon by flying to Portland.
5. Captain Ahab and his crew pursued the great white whale.
6. Fido fetches the newspaper every morning.
7. The president and his advisors decided to go to war.

8. On Friday night, more than twenty customers took out dinners.
9. In three days, our group saw five Shakespearean plays.
10. Before you do something physical, the body normally calls on the brain.

Trimming Needless Words, pages 96–97

Part A

Answers will vary. Be sure that your version of each sentence approximates the meaning of the original.

1. Peter Jenkins wrote *A Walk Across America*, a book about his cross-country walk. To prepare for the trek, he walked twenty-five miles a day.
2. My suggestion for making meetings more productive and relevant to all students needn't offend the chairperson, Carolyn Welles.
3. In spite of low English grades and poor writing skills, Molly was elected to be the editor of the yearbook.
4. Some kinds of criticism help people cope with problems; other kinds tear people down instead of offering help.
5. By visiting historic places, Americans learn what is important to know about their country.

Part B

Avoiding discrimination is but one of many reasons for people to gain weight, according to Stanford University graduate Slim Snyder, who, at a recent conference on health, said "Lean people are victims of discrimination, just as obese people are." Fortunately, many up-to-date weight-gaining procedures are available to everyone. But they are ridiculed and kept well hidden because health experts agree that being lean is preferable to being obese.

Showing Instead of Telling, page 98

Answers will vary. Check your sentences for specific details that show rather than tell.

1. Whenever Mike enters a room, he ducks his head to avoid hitting the top of the doorway.
2. Her sense of accomplishment grew with every handshake and pat on the back. As her face ached from grinning so hard, she knew that she'd be back next year to win again.

3. On the sagging floor stood a rusted iron stove, a spinning wheel, and a broken rocking chair.

4. The smell of salt spray, seaweed, and sunblock filled Suzanne's nostrils.

5. During the lesson, four kids in the back played poker, another smoked pot in the corner, while the rest of the class either wisecracked with each other, applied make-up, or put their heads down and snoozed.

6. The pioneers left behind a trail of gravesites where dead children and adults had been hurriedly buried.

7. The cabin was everything that would give most people the creeps: dark, damp, chipped, rotting, full of holes, drafty, leaky and sagging—a celebration of neglect.

8. The air was filled with blue smoke that reddened our eyes and made some of us dizzy and gasping for air.

9. The end of the speech brought the crowd to its feet for fifteen minutes of applause and cheering.

10. Mary Jane's mother insists that visitors entering her house take off their shoes and be checked for fleas.

Using Punctuation, page 102

Part A. Possessives

1. Paul's
2. America's
3. Correct
4. women's
5. girls', boys'
6. Andersons', Year's
7. Correct
8. Morris's
9. computers'
10. months'

Part B. Commas and Semicolons, pages 102–103

1. While Bill was riding, his bike got a flat tire.
2. The mail carrier did not leave the package, for Valerie was not at home.
3. After doing his homework Mikey, as you might expect, talked on his cell phone for an hour.
4. His work criticized many commonly held beliefs, however, and it was strictly censored.

5. The car that ran into mine at the intersection was an SUV.
6. Dad went to the airport to pick up Dave; Ellie went to the train station to meet Debbie.
7. Correct
8. The boat was seventy-five feet long and eighteen feet wide; its mast was about eighty feet tall.
9. To anyone interested in flying, planes hold endless fascination.
10. Jeff and Steve, left alone for the weekend, invited all their friends to a party.
11. I need street maps of Boston and Portland, Maine.
12. Some of the theories dealt with the political, social, and religious ideas of the time.
13. Students who want to try out for the chorus have been asked to report to room 330.
14. Doug, for example, is both a scholar and an athlete.
15. Monica refused to go unless Phil went with her.
16. The hero of the book, John Coffey, rode his bike across the United States.
17. After all, she did for him what she could.
18. Starting in Minnesota, the Mississippi runs all the way to the Gulf of Mexico.
19. Harold Watkins, who comes from Chicago, won a full tuition scholarship to Duke.
20. Although the characters are stereotypes, they were interesting to read about.
21. Yo-Yo Ma, the famous cellist, will perform a recital on Saturday night.
22. This test covers Spanish literature, culture, and history, and it lasts for three hours.
23. Michelle is pretty, tall, and dark, but her older sister Norma is pretty, short, and light.
24. Sean, the twin brother of Ian, was struck by a falling tree limb.
25. The window washer dropped by last evening, but he didn't bring his squeegee.

Applying Capitalization, page 104

1. On Labor Day Bennington County's fire department plans to hold a turkey shoot on the field at Miller's Pond.
2. The judge gave District Attorney Lipman a book entitled *The Rules of Evidence* and instructed her to read it before she ever dared set foot in the Court of Appeals of the Ninth Circuit again.

3. The Secretary of State greeted the President of Austria at the Ronald Reagan Airport in Washington, D.C.

4. The Shackleton expedition nearly met its doom on Georgia Island in Antarctica.

5. For Christmas he got a Black & Decker table saw from the Sears store next to the old Bedford Courthouse.

6. According to Georgetown's high school principal, Eugene Griffiths, Georgetown High School attracts students from the whole west coast. At Georgetown students may major in drawing and painting, design, graphics, or sculpture. Mr. Griffiths said, "I attended a similar high school in New England just after the Vietnam War."

7. We expect to celebrate New Year's Eve again this year by renting a movie of an old Broadway musical and by settling down in front of the DVD player with some Pepsi and a box of Oreos.

8. After traveling all the way to the Pacific, the Corps of Discovery rode down the Missouri River going east on their way back to St. Louis.

9. This Irish linen tablecloth was bought at K-mart in the Emeryville Mall off Powell Street.

10. Yellowstone National Park is located in the northwest corner of Wyoming.

PART IV

ESSAYS FOR EVALUATION

How Essays Are Judged
  and Graded
Essay Topics for Practice

HOW ESSAYS ARE JUDGED AND GRADED

Your essay will be evaluated on a scale of 6 (best) to 1 (worst). Evaluators are trained to read the essays quickly, or *holistically*. That is, they'll avoid the "Gotcha! Syndrome"—hunting down every little error. Rather, they'll read for an overall impression of your writing. Recognizing that your essay has been composed in under half an hour, they won't hold minor mistakes against you and won't deduct a certain amount for every error in grammar, spelling, and punctuation.

Naturally, an essay overrun with flaws will leave a less favorable impression than one that's mostly correct. Like other readers, evaluators enjoy good writing and delight in thoughtful, neatly phrased ideas. They abhor empty platitudes and know in an instant when a writer is throwing the bull.

Evaluators will approach your essay with a positive mind set, prepared to reward you for what you've done well. When reading your essay, they'll compare it to other essays written on the same topic at the same time. Your essay, in other words, won't be competing against some ideal essay written by a professional author.

Handwriting is not supposed to count in the evaluation. But think about this: If readers have trouble deciphering your penmanship, several things can happen. Frustration may cause them to be unfavorably disposed toward the essay. They won't give you the benefit of the doubt about spelling or grammar if the letters are malformed or difficult to read. When readers are forced to stop regularly to puzzle out the words, your flow of ideas will be interrupted—with adverse effects. Unreadable essays will be given no credit at all. At this stage in your life, it may be difficult to change your penmanship. But if you know that teachers and others have a problem interpreting your script, try to slow down as you form the letters, or as a last resort, print clearly. For most people printing is slower than cursive writing, but with practice you can increase your speed.

GUIDELINES FOR EVALUATION

Essays are scored on a scale of 6 to 1.

Performance Categories	Score
Outstanding	6
Very Good	5
Good	4
Fair	3
Poor	2
Very Poor	1

Scores of 4, 5, and 6 reflect a level of proficiency in writing appropriate for first-year college students. Essays rated 1, 2, or 3 suggest a need for remediation. (A blank paper or a paper submitted on a topic unrelated to the prompt will be rated *zero*.)

No list of standards can include everything that SAT readers consider when they evaluate an essay, but the following descriptions list the main criteria. Readers are human. They try to be objective, but they must still make judgments. An essay assigned a score of 5 by one reader, therefore, may not be vastly superior than an essay given a 4 by another.

Outstanding. An *outstanding* essay is a well-conceived, orderly, and insightful treatment of the assigned task. The writer has fashioned a convincing main idea, amply supported by appropriate and specific details. The point of view, word choice, and use of sentences demonstrate an ability to control a wide range of elements of composition. Any errors that occur are inconsequential. Overall, the work is a model of clarity and sophistication.

Very Good. A *very good* essay demonstrates the writer's firm grasp of the assignment. It develops the main idea with purpose and conviction but may be somewhat less thorough and insightful than the best essays. It also may fall short of the mastery, sophistication, and control of composition exemplified by an outstanding essay. Nevertheless, its organization is sensible, its language and usage are appropriate, and its overall intent is clear and consistent.

Good. A *good* essay deals with the topic competently. It uses conventional language and sentence structure and provides some appropriate specific examples to support the main idea. It gives evidence of the writer's acquaintance with essay organization, coherence, and paragraph development. Some errors in word choice and awkward expression may exist, but no error seriously interferes with meaning.

Fair. A *fair* essay suggests mediocrity in writing. It may adequately respond to the prompt but gives evidence of an inconsistent control of the elements of composition. Although the essay has a recognizable structure, the organization may be confusing or not fully realized. Inaccuracies or lapses in logic may weaken the essay's overall effect. Occasional mechanical errors may detract from the essay's meaning although they don't necessarily obliterate communication.

Poor. A *poor* essay demonstrates a superficial or pedestrian understanding of the prompt. The essay's development is meager, and its treatment of the subject is imprecise and unconvincing. The point of the essay may be perceptible, but the presentation of ideas is characterized by faulty word choice, flawed sentences, and incoherent or confused organization.

Very Poor. A *very poor* essay reveals the writer's inability to make sense of the prompt. It may wander off the topic or include irrelevant or simplistic ideas. It may also be excessively brief or undeveloped. The prose may lack organization, coherence, and meaning. The writer shows little evidence of control of sentence structure or the rules of usage and grammar.

ESSAYS FOR EVALUATION

As you prepare to write an essay, read the following responses that other students wrote on SAT essay topics. Then review the explanations of how scores were determined.

The essays were completed in twenty-five minutes in a testing situation. They are unedited and typed exactly as written. Read them quickly, spending no more than three or four minutes on each, and then rate them using the SAT scale of 1 to 6. Write your best observations in the space provided for comments. Then compare your views with those of the SAT readers who actually scored the same essay. Because no two people are likely to agree on every detail, your evaluation will probably differ from those of the pros. Nevertheless, your observations may be equally valid and perceptive. What counts more than the similarity between your comments and those of SAT readers is the overall impression left by each piece and the score you gave it. If your scores differ greatly from the scores assigned by SAT readers, carefully examine what trained readers look for in an essay. Then keep those criteria in mind as you plan and write essays of your own.

Prompt for Essay #1

Think about the views expressed in the following passage:

"WANT TO GET AHEAD? TRY LYING" says a headline, with the idea that by always telling the truth, or by telling too much truth, we put ourselves at a disadvantage.

Stephen Lim tells the following story: "Working my way through school, I delivered special delivery mail for the U.S. Postal Service. Each morning the dispatcher handed drivers a pile of letters and packages. Before starting our route, we recorded the number of stops we had to make. While the other drivers padded their figures, I didn't. This made me look bad in comparison, lowering the supervisor's opinion of my performance."

Stephen paid a minor penalty for telling the truth. But others can suffer more serious consequences for being honest. Consider a few: Because they don't cheat on assignments and tests to boost their grades, some students fail to get into the college of their choice. Job applicants don't succeed in getting a coveted position because they refuse to pad their resumés.

"In a nutshell, it's harder and harder to be an honest person in today's society," says Stephen Lim. "After a while, you feel like a jerk when other people are getting ahead by taking shortcuts."

Adapted from Stephen Lim, "Telling the Truth—Does It Pay?" *Plain Truth*, May/June, 2001

Assignment: Does Stephen's statement describe the way things actually are, or is it a cynical distortion of the truth? Plan and write an essay that discusses your point of view on the issue. Support your position with evidence and reasoning drawn from your studies, reading, experience, or observation.

Wanda's Essay

Many people fall prey to lying mainly because it is so easy to do. It involves no physical labor, no strenuous activity, no expenses, and no special skills. All you have to do is open your mouth and let the words fall out.

Lying is a major part of getting a job you are not totally qualified for. You write up a nice little resumé with all the details of your life, most of which don't pertain to the job at all, such as, for instance, your marital status or that you won the Noble Serf Award in eleventh grade, an award that you invent right on the spot. Just in case you are asked during the interview what the award was for, you prepare a lie ahead of time, maybe something like it's an award for integrity, for being an extremely honest and trustworthy person. Also, you might not have quite enough experience for the job you are trying to get. So you fabricate a little more to show that you are used to hard work and responsibility. After all, what's the harm in shading the truth a little?

While it's true that your lies will have no immediate effect, what will happen if your employer checks on you, when he or she finds out that there is no such thing as the Noble Serf Award, and that you were not the assistant manager of the supermarket at all but just a lackey who retrieved shopping carts from the parking lot? This is when you must face the consequences of your "harmless" little lies. If you are caught lying, after your face goes back to its normal color, you will most likely be looking for another job.

Does that mean it's okay to lie as long as you don't get caught? Nothing could be farther from the truth because the effects of lying can be more serious. If you claim credit for something that is not yours and you hurt somebody, then you have crossed over the line. You have become not only a liar but a thief, and you have lost your integrity. Or even worse if someone causes pain to others because he or she believes in a lie you've told, the consequences can be very severe. Recently there was a male nurse who lied his way into jobs in several hospitals, and wherever he went the death rate of patients rose dramatically. For a long time no one noticed the correlation between him and the death rate, but by the time it was discovered, he had left a trail of dozens of innocent victims.

While this may be an extreme case, it still illustrates that lying, even though it may be as easy as breathing, can lead to very harmful results.

Your observations: _____

_____

_____

_____

_____

_____

The first reader commented: "*This essay combines a serious message with a bit of sophisticated humor. The light touch is a tribute to the writer's level of maturity. The examples she uses to support the thesis are well-written and sufficiently detailed. The overall presentation is lively, interesting, and virtually error-free.*"

   Score: 6

The second reader commented: "*A thoughtful and insightful piece of writing, this essay deserves the highest rating. The sequence of paragraphs is particularly apt: The first two paragraphs show that lying is prevalent because 'it is so easy.' Just how easy is wittily illustrated in the story of the fabricated resumé. The third paragraph discusses minor pitfalls of lying, but the fourth takes up its potential for disastrous, life-altering consequences. After presenting an example of compelling evidence—a homicidal nurse—in the last paragraph the writer draws the only possible conclusion: Lying 'can lead to very harmful results.'*

   "*Throughout the essay, the writer maintains a consistent tone, demonstrates skill in the use of interesting, lively language, and proves her mastery of the elements of composition.*"

   Score: 6

Vinnie's Essay

   I recently note a bumper sticker that stated, "Want to get ahead? Try Lying." I assumed this message was that people who always tell the truth are like handicapped because the truth is against them and they are doomed to fail. I pondered the idea for awhile and realized how ridiculous the statement is.

   While I think back on my own life, I realized that every time I have tried to lie I got caught. Once, one morning I was very young I told my parents that I was too sick to go to school when the truth was that I was afraid of a bully in the grade ahead of me who threatened to beat me up. I now realize that they knew I was lying. My father wanted me to go to the doctor to get checked, I told him that I better not go, or the doctor would catch my illness. My father and mother began to laugh and proceeded to dress me for school.

   Another time, I was in 8th grade I told my parents that I was going over to my friend Sam's house on a Friday night when I actually wanted to go bowling with some friends that my parents didn't approve of. Lying about it could enable me to stay out later. The next day my parents found out that I had lied, I think they met Sam's parents at the movies where they had a puzzled look about my being over at their house. When the truth came out, I was grounded for a month.

   There are many other times when my attempts at lying backfired in my face. It's not always possible to tell the whole truth, but whenever I tell little white lies or shade the truth, I think of that bumper sticker and wonder if the person who wrote it had ever lied in his life.

Your observations: _____

_____

_____

_____

_____

_____

_____

The first reader commented: *"This essay is lively and quite readable. Two examples that develop the main idea are pertinent but they don't prove the writer's assertion that he got caught 'every time' he told a lie. The piece is unified in theme and tone, and its reference to a bumper sticker at the end cleverly reminds the reader where the essay began. Lapses in verb tense and in expression keep the essay from earning a better rating."*
    Score: 4

The second reader commented: *"The writer of this adequate essay takes the position that it is 'ridiculous' to depend on lies to get ahead in life. Citing two personal experiences from his earlier life, he shows that lies 'backfired in my face,' a well-meant but awkwardly expressed image.*
    "The essay is organized into coherent paragraphs. Word choice is appropriate and the sentence structure is sufficiently varied, except for the first paragraph, in which every sentence begins with the same subject ('I'). A few sentence errors such as comma splices and run-ons detract from the overall quality of the essay. A few minor corrections might have lifted the score to a 4, but as is, the essay doesn't quite make it."
    Score: 3

Marylou's Essay

"Want to get ahead? Try lying" is described as a true statement in our society today. Usually good things happen when people don't lie, but today it is more likely that good things will happen to people who refrain from telling the truth.

For example, in our society insider trading tips in the stock market can make an investor pay off faster than another investor who is playing by the rules. Another example of how this statement is correct is when a person is applying for a job. He usually tries to exaggerate, in other words, lying, on their resumé so that he will be a more enticing employee. If he told the truth he might not be hired as readily.

Lying may get a person ahead, but they must also live with a conscious. Perhaps in the long run it isn't worth it because he will have to face the fact that the reason he is "ahead" is because he lied. He did not "get ahead" based on skills or knowledge but on the lie.

Severe lying is considered a psychological disease, like addiction, they even lie when here is no reason. Dependency on lying can be cured by therapy.

Your observations: _____

_____

_____

_____

_____

_____

The first reader commented: *"In this essay the main idea is developed somewhat haphazardly. In general, the writing is inept—crowded with usage errors. The third paragraph contradicts the earlier statement that 'good things happen to people who refrain from telling the truth.' Although the essay shows evidence of an ample vocabulary, its expression is awkward, and the last paragraph seems totally irrelevant."*
    Score: 2

The second reader commented: "This piece suggests only a limited mastery of composition. Starting with a puzzling and pointless assertion that the quotation 'is described as a true statement in our society' (by whom? one wonders), the writer generalizes that 'good things will happen to people' who lie. In support of this generalization, the writer offers two weak, underdeveloped examples of people whose lies paid off. Then, the third paragraph undercuts the essay's main idea with a brief discussion of liar's guilt. Still more of a puzzle is the last paragraph, which contains matters unrelated to anything that came before."

Score: 2

Prompt for Essay #2

Think carefully about the issue presented in the following statement:

> Fatalists believe that we must accept things as they are, that nothing can be done to change the world for the better. Martin Luther King had such people in mind when he remarked, "The hottest place in Hell is reserved for those who remain neutral in times of great moral conflict." Maya Angelou added, "If you don't like something, change it." And Phyllis Diller, putting it still another way, said, "Never go to bed mad. Stay up and fight."

Assignment: The first step in making things better is to recognize that a problem exists. Please plan and write an essay in which you identify a school, local, national, or world condition or flaw that, in your opinion, needs to be corrected, and explain why you chose it.

Max's Essay

A trend these days is to speak up about the world's mistreatment of the environment. I am not just a tree hugger by saying that without improvement in environmental conditions, my generation and the future generations will suffer in ways too awful to even imagine. At the end of the day you can say the survival of mankind is "hanging in the balance."

Many countries exploit the Earth's resources. In some countries, millions of acres of rainforest are being destroyed every year to make room for farmland or to cut lumber to export. Not only does this destroy the habitats of many animals, but kills species of trees and plants that may someday be found to cure cancer, AIDS, MS, or other diseases. In addition, rainforests produce the majority of the oxygen that we need to live. The bottom line is that by clear-cutting rainforests, we are beginning to suffocate ourselves to death.

Other nations exploit the oceans. By dumping garbage, sewage and other hazardous waste into the oceans, they pollute the water. Eventually, the garbage washes back on shore, making the beaches filthy and swimming dangerous. The pollutants also kill and taint the fish in the ocean with toxic materials. Then we end up eating these fish, and the toxins enter our bodies. Many people I know have given up eating tuna fish for the reason they don't want to put poisonous mercury into their bodies.

Another way the enviroment is abused is the treatment of the atmosphere. Until the famous Kyoto Treaty, most countries had no laws controlling the amount of harmful gases released by cars and trucks that causes global warming. Some countries still don't have such laws, and under the Bush administration, the United States withdrew from the Kyoto agreements. I think that governments around the world, including the US of A needs to force the corporations to reduce their burning of fossil fuels in order for less smoke to mix with clouds to form acid rain and to stop the trend to global warming.

These are just a few ways which the world abuses the environment. When all is said and done, all people must do their part to leave the world a better place for their children and grandchildren.

Your observations: _____

_____

_____

_____

_____

_____

_____

The first reader commented: *"Max's essay is very well focused, admirably organized, and clearly presented. He develops examples of environmental issues fully and appropriately. While not always gracefully expressed, Max's presentation is consistently informative and detailed. It reveals a high level of proficiency and solid control of the essay-writing process."*
 Score: 6

The second reader commented: *"Although this conventional five-paragraph 'formula' essay is competently written, it is not terribly inspired. The writer is well-informed on the subject, but he rarely transcends the environmental movement's customary talking points. Indeed, the impact of the essay is considerably diluted by the writer's reliance on clichés such as 'hanging in the balance,' 'at the end of the day,' 'the bottom line,' and others. Nevertheless, the essay is mostly error-free, and its organization and varied sentence structure demonstrate reasonably consistent mastery of the art of writing."*
 Score: 5

Tracy's Essay

The world is an imperfect place with many, many problems to solve. If I could help solve one of them, I would choose my high school. There are countless improvements to be made here because it is not one that meets the needs of everyone.

One thing wrong with this school is that there is not enough leeway for us to take all the classes that we want. For example, if someone is taking a music class and also wants to take art it is impossible without dropping a required course, such as Physical Education. Gym takes up so much of our school week. Physical exercise is important but there should be a better arrangement of classes so we can study the things we really want to.

Another criticism I have about this school is the way certain classes operate. There are many unnecessary rules, and many teachers treat students like infants which need basic instructions. They spend too much time on inane things like handing in homework on time, getting to class on time, a neat notebook, and a cover on your textbooks instead of concentrating on the more important issues such as making sure that students get the information and the experience they need for a good education and for college. If teachers could make the rules as a given, and trust the students, they might be able to get a better attitude back.

Your observations: _____

_____

_____

_____

_____

_____

_____

The first reader commented: *"The first paragraph clearly states the essay's purpose. The writer then chooses two excellent examples to illustrate problems at her high school. But these problems are only loosely tied to the main idea that the school fails to meet everyone's needs. The development of ideas is detailed, the highlight being Tracy's description in the third paragraph of teachers' preoccupation with 'inane' matters that waste instructional time. The last line of the essay refers to the students' attitude toward their teachers. Unfortunately, either because she ran out of time or forgot to explain, the reference leaves the reader in the lurch, wishing to know why Tracy mentioned it. Tracy's use of language is rarely interesting and almost consistently awkward. Minor lapses in grammar and usage weaken the effort. In all, the essay shows modest evidence of Tracy's promise as a writer.*
    Score: 4

The second reader commented: *"Although the writer claims that her school 'is not one that meets the needs of everyone,' the essay hardly deals with the school's failure to satisfy a diverse student population. Instead, the writer uses the essay to air gripes about her own experience. The second paragraph seems to grow out of disappointment over her choice of classes, and the third paragraph is used to complain about an overabundance of trivial rules in 'certain' unidentified classes. In effect, then, the bulk of the essay fails to live up to its promise."*
    Score: 3

Iiana's Essay

The way I would make things better is in divorce. Even though you can't taste, touch or smell divorce, you can still feel it. Divorce is a condition which many children have been made to understand by bitter experience, divorce has forced the progeny of broken marriages to suffer. "The hottest places in Hell" that Dr. King talks about should be reserved for parents who abandon their children so they can be divorced.

Why do people get married and repeat vows such as "until death us do part," if they end up ending their relationship? Where's the logic in this? not to mention their children suffering. While many of their friends are entering the three legged contest at family picnics, they end up sharing chicken pot pie with one of their parents. This may sound extreme for all divorces don't end up this way. However there are more that do.

Institutions such as churches and synogogues shouldn't allow people to be "joined in matrimony" If the people don't seem right for each other. Can't the Lord give the priest or rabii a sign? If it is against anti-religion to separate from your mate, why does the Lord allow such things? Doesn't the divine being know whether a man and a woman would remain married or not?

Divorce is almost as difficult as marriage. The fusion of two people may seem to be one of success, however when the "lawfully wedded" couple splints, the fission is one of disaster.

Your observations: _____

_____

_____

_____

_____

_____

The first reader commented: *"There's a good deal of passion in this essay, a quality that makes the essay quite readable, but the writer's deep feelings tend to interfere with the clarity of its message. The second paragraph, for instance, suffers from disjointedness, in particular it's allusion to a 'three-legged race.' The third paragraph includes questions about the nature of a supreme being that seem out of place in what is meant to be a discussion of problems related to divorce.*

   "The essay is soundly organized, and although the meaning of some ideas is fuzzy, a bit of the language—the fission/fusion dichotomy, for example—reveals a creative flair.

   Despite these merits, the flaws in the essay outweigh its strengths."
   Score: 3

The second reader commented: *"This piece demonstrates marginal mastery of the essay-writing process. Iliana opens with a direct, although somewhat awkward, statement of intent: 'The way I would make things better is in divorce,' but she fails to offer evidence in support of this idea. Instead, she uses the essay to lament the consequences of divorce, quite possibly stemming from her own experience as a child of divorce, although she doesn't say so.*

   Iliana raises worthwhile issues about marriage and divorce in the second paragraph, and in the third paragraph asks profound questions about the role of religion in marriage. But her progression of ideas lacks consistency. Instead, she employs a kind of stream of consciousness, apparently spilling ideas onto the page as they occur to her."
   Score: 3

Prompt for Essay #3

Think carefully about the issue presented in the following passage:

> *The moon belongs to everyone*
> *The best things in life are free,*
> *The stars belong to everyone*
> *They gleam there for you and me.*
> *The flowers in Spring,*
> *The robins that sing,*
> *The sunbeams that shine*
> *They're yours,*
> *They're mine!*
> *And love can come to everyone,*
> *The best things in life are free.*

"The Best Things in Life Are Free," song and lyrics by B. G. DeSylva,
Lew Brown, and Ray Henderson for the musical *Good News*.

Assignment. Please plan and write an essay in which you discuss the validity of the sentiment expressed by the lyrics of the song, "The Best Things in Life Are Free." Support your position with evidence and reasoning drawn from your studies, reading, experience, or observation.

Tucker's Essay

The idea that "the best things in life are free" is nothing except sentimental garbage, okay for a musical show but just a fantasy or a self-delusion in reality. Now almost everything costs money, and even if you don't have to take out your Visa card and pay for it then and there, there are hidden costs that can't really be calculated.

Take, for example, an ordinary walk in the park with a favorite girl, guy, or dog. Sure it's free to enter the park and stroll along. No out-of-pocket expenses there, but think of all that it costs to have that walk. For one thing, there is clothes and footgear. There is the need for transportation to the park and home again, and the need to be able to contact a friend by phone or email to arrange the walk. Just living in a place that has a park to walk in also costs money—in taxes, rent, mortgages, and the regular expenses of maintaining a decent lifestyle.

Okay, walking in the park may be a trivial example. How about something more profound? What most people value above all else is freedom—not just the freedoms granted in the Bill of Rights but the freedom to be what we can be, the freedom to love and associate with who we please, the freedom to live in a safe environment, free from violence and harm, freedom to go to school or go anyplace at any time without worrying about the government watching or breathing down your neck, and even the freedom to help others gain their freedom like the U.S. has done in Afghanistan and has been trying to do in Iraq at the cost of billions and billions of dollars, not to speak of the expense of death and human suffering.

It would be nice to believe that the best things in life are free, but only the blissfully ignorant could really believe it. Whoever said there's no such thing as a free lunch knew what they were talking about.

Your observations: _____

_____

_____

_____

_____

_____

The first reader commented: "Tucker's opening statement hooks the reader instantly and clearly articulates the essay's insight that everything has 'hidden costs that can't really be calculated.' The paragraphs that follow amplify and explain the costs, first of something mundane and ordinary like a walk in the park, and then something abstract, namely the price of freedom. The paragraph about freedom, however, fails to discuss the costs other than those incurred by helping other countries achieve a measure of freedom.

"In spite of this lapse, the progression of ideas testifies to a high level of critical thinking. Tucker also provides evidence of his mastery of writing with varied sentences, some colorful word choices, and a distinctive, natural style. The essay isn't perfect, but it creates the impression that Tucker is a highly gifted writer."
Score: 6

The second reader commented: "*This is an exemplary essay, not totally free of flaws, but close enough to rate as a first-rate piece of writing. The piece is extremely well focused on the issue, admirably organized, and very clearly presented in interesting and readable prose. The tone is slightly glib but nevertheless appealing and effective. All in all, the essay demonstrates not only the writer's maturity but also his control of written language.*"
   Score: 6

Emily's Essay

   I totally disagree with the statement "The best things in life are free" because hobbies of mine which I feel are "the best", are far from free.

   I enjoy vacationing in warm climates which is costly. First you must worry about transportation, air fare. Then once you get to your destination you will need a place to stay. Food and entertainment isn't free and if you literally have expensive taste, you must spend money, and lots of it.

   Shopping, which can be done almost anywhere, is often times expensive. If you need new bras and underwear, forget about clothes, you are talking a lot of money. Bathing suits can cost you about $150 a suit and everyone likes new suits, especially after the old ones become sun-bleached. If you need presents for special friends, jewelry will cost you especially if you want to buy sterling silver or 14K gold or precious and semi-precious stones.

   Scuba diving is probably one of the most incredible things I have ever done in my life time. The whole experience is phenominal. Image yourself in a giant room filled with water and you are just hanging out in the center of the room. You are suspended in water and you can breathe. This sport isn't cheap, its not like kicking a ball around a field.

   Materialistically the best things in life are not free. Its true that money doesn't buy happiness but some of the things that I think are great are expensive.

Your observations: _____

_____

_____

_____

_____

_____

_____

   The first reader commented: "*If one overlooks this essay's abundant sentence errors and errors in mechanics, the piece has considerable clout, created in large measure by the spirited voice of the writer. Inadvertently or not, Emily comes across as a strong, decisive character who knows what she likes and has no trouble articulating her beliefs.*

   "*The essay reveals that Emily is a relatively undisciplined writer. Yet, she has produced a standard five-paragraph essay with a clear introduction, three paragraphs of development, and a reasonable conclusion. To give the essay greater coherence, however, some transitional material might have linked the paragraphs more firmly.*

   "*In spite of its flaws, the essay demonstrates adequate mastery.*"
   Score: 4

The second reader commented: *"Demonstrating evidence of skill in critical thinking, the writer has chosen three 'hobbies' to argue against the views expressed in the song lyrics. She is aware of the freebies mentioned in the song, but she has little interest in sunbeams and love. As she observes in her final paragraph, 'Materialistically the best things in life are not free.'*

"The essay is generally well-organized, although the sequence of vacationing, shopping, and scuba-diving are not precisely parallel. Taking vacations is a more general activity than the other two, and although vacations are expensive, they merely provide Emily with opportunities to shop and scuba-dive. Also, the paragraph about scuba-diving deals mostly with the nature of the underwater experience rather than with the expense, which is the focus of the other paragraphs and of the essay as a whole."

Score: 4

Josephine's Essay

I agree with this sentiment that truly the best things in life are free. "To each his own" as they say, to me the best things in life are love, happiness, peace, and freedom. To obtain these things in ones life depends on the individual. You can find love with your parent, friend or even pet dog—this love can be unconditional, and costing only effort. Happiness you make, a smile, a laugh even a tear can make anyone happy. By doing a favor or even helping someone at your own expense can cost absolutely nothing except a cramp in your smile! Peace and freedom come along in life, it may be something you earn or deserve, it's like a stamp that's sealed in you at birth "I'm a free individual—in a free world, free to do what I want"! Peace comes from love and freedom you can give it or receive it, and it might not affect your bank account! To the individual it's opinionated as to what the "things" are in life that are free. It also depends what you want to buy in life these things that I stated before and materialist things that won't last forever!

Your observations: _____

_____

_____

_____

_____

_____

The first reader commented: *"After clearly stating the essay's purpose—to show why 'the best things in life are free,' the writer presents a series of related but largely incoherent reasons. The formlessness of the argument may spring from the writer's intent to discuss "love, happiness, peace, and freedom" in one short essay. This is a monumental undertaking even for a seasoned writer. In the hands of Josephine, the essay turns into a potpourri of generalizations, clichés, and miscellaneous observations that in the end prove nothing except that the writer's reach far exceeded her grasp."*

Score: 1

The second reader commented: *"This abbreviated essay demonstrates very little mastery of the art of writing. It proposes a main idea ('I agree with this sentiment that truly the best things in life are free'), but incoherent supporting material obscures meaning. Indeed, one idea ('helping someone at your own expense can cost absolutely nothing') seems to contradict not only itself but the essay's alleged purpose. Errors in sentence structure constitute but one of several writing problems in this writer's seriously flawed prose."*

Score: 1

ESSAY TOPICS FOR PRACTICE

In case you've just turned to this page without having read Parts III and IV, follow these directions for writing practice essays:

Time: 25 minutes

Plan and write an essay in response to the assigned topic. Use the essay as an opportunity to show how clearly and effectively you can express and develop ideas. Present your thoughts logically and precisely. Include specific evidence or examples to support your point of view. A plain, natural writing style is probably best. The number of words is up to you, but quantity is less important than quality.

Limit your essay to two sides of lined paper. You'll have enough space if you write on every line and avoid wide margins. Write or print legibly because handwriting that's hard or impossible to read will decrease your score.

If you finish in less than 25 minutes, check your work.

The ten prompts that follow are suggested for essay-writing practice. Because it's virtually impossible to write the same essay twice, try writing on the same prompt over and over, each time choosing another point of view. Then compare the results.

SAT prompts typically begin with a short passage or quotation followed by a related question, which you are to answer in your essay. Always support your answer with reasoning and examples taken from your observations, experience, studies, or reading.

1. The familiar admonition to "put your money where your mouth is" suggests that it's far easier to speak up for a principle than to live up to it. That's why most of us, whether we intend to or not, say one thing but often do another. It's just part of human nature.

Assignment: Is the common tendency to often say one thing but do another built into our nature, or is it something that experience teaches us to do?

2. "If you are like most people, your sadness over losing, say, $1,000, would be twice as great as your happiness at winning $1,000. That all-too-human tendency to feel pain of a loss more deeply than the joy of a gain is called 'loss aversion.'"

From an editorial in the *New York Times*, January 16, 2005

Assignment: Are negative emotions stronger than positive ones?

3. After rescuing a dozen men and women from a burning office building, Jim Smith, a New York City fire fighter, commented, "Courage is just a matter of luck—of being in the right place at the right time."

Assignment: Is courage a common human trait that most of us never have an opportunity to use or demonstrate, or is Jim Smith's courage unusual?

4. "While walking in her neighborhood, a friend saw a man who had tied a fishing line around a turtle's throat and was letting his kids drag it up and down the path. Feeling that a direct approach would lead to a confrontation, my friend said: 'I am a biologist with So-and-So University. Turtles are toxic; they secrete poison that may make your kids horribly sick.' The guy had his kids stop tormenting the turtle right away. Was this lie justified?"

From a letter by David Weinrich, published in "The Ethicist" by Randy Cohen, *New York Times Magazine*, January 16, 2005

Assignment: Is lying acceptable or even obligatory at times?

5. An old English proverb says, "What you don't know can't hurt you."

   Assignment: Can ignorance ever be better than knowledge?

6. "Destiny is not a matter of chance. It is a matter of choice. It is not a thing to be waited for, it is a thing to be achieved."

   William Jennings Bryan (1860–1925)

   Assignment: Do you believe that the choices we make, rather than our abilities and talents, show who we truly are?

7. "Suppose we were able to share meanings freely without a compulsive urge to impose our view or conform to those of others and without distortion and self-deception. Would this not constitute a real revolution in culture?"

   David Bohm

   Assignment: If we were to become completely open and honest with ourselves and with others, would society be better off?

8. "Every problem has a gift for you in its hands."

   Richard Bach

   Assignment: Is there always a gain from experiencing hardship?

9. "They may forget what you said, but they'll never forget how you made them feel."

   Carl W. Beuchner

   Assignment: Are human emotions more powerful, enduring, and meaningful than our intellect? Or to put it another way, does the heart matter more than the brain in our lives?

10. "I cannot believe the purpose of life is to be happy. I think that the purpose of life is to be useful, to be responsible, to be compassionate. It is, above all, to matter, to count, to stand for something, to have made a difference that you lived at all."

    Leo Rosten

    Assignment: Do happiness and contentment depend mainly on serving others and making a difference in their lives?

PART V

MULTIPLE-CHOICE QUESTIONS

INTRODUCTION

This chapter will prepare you to answer the three types of multiple-choice questions on the SAT Writing Test.

A solid grounding in basic English grammar will help you succeed. But if grammar mystifies you or your grammar skills are rusty, there is something you can do about it. For one thing, you can study!

To begin, read this chapter. Read it deliberately but slowly, absorbing a little bit at a time. Like any complex system of rules, grammar takes time to learn. Perseverance helps. But don't get bogged down trying to memorize every detail. Instead, save your energy for the exercises and practice tests.

You could also borrow a grammar book from your English teacher or from the library. Or go online (*www.webgrammar.com.* or *www.refdesk. com/factgram.html*) and spend many profitable hours browsing and reading. If time is short between now and test day, read and absorb as much of this chapter as you can. Learn the suggested strategies for answering the questions, do the exercises, and take the practice tests in Part VI. At the very least, become familiar with the format of the test questions.

IMPROVING SENTENCES QUESTIONS

More than half of the multiple-choice sections of the SAT Writing Test are Improving Sentences questions that ask you to recognize two types of errors:

1. Errors in standard English usage and grammar
2. Errors in style and expression

The Difference Between *Usage* and *Grammar*
Although the words are often used interchangeably, *usage* describes actual spoken and written language. "Standard" usage is the level of usage accepted by literate people who, in a general way, occupy positions of leadership and influence in society.

Grammar, on the other hand, is a set of rules that are followed when you speak and write "correctly."

All the sentence-improvement questions on the SAT begin with a sentence in which a part, or sometimes the entire sentence, is underlined. Then you are given five different ways of phrasing the underlined part. Your job is to choose the version that is expressed most clearly and concisely in standard English and is free of errors in grammar and usage.

The first choice of the five choices always repeats the original. If you think the original version is better than any of the alternatives, mark choice A on your answer sheet. Otherwise, choose the best version from the remaining choices, but steer clear of any sentence that changes the essential meaning of the original.

SAMPLE SENTENCE IMPROVEMENT QUESTIONS

Type 1: Sentences Containing Errors in Grammar or Usage

Because Lucy was furious, <u>she speaks</u> loudly.

(A) she speaks
(B) and speaking
(C) and she spoke
(D) as she spoke
(E) she spoke

The underlined segment of the sentence contains the subject of the sentence, *Lucy*, and the verb *speaks*. By using *speaks,* a verb in the present tense, rather than *spoke* (past tense), or *will speak* (future tense), or some other tense of the verb, the writer intends to convey the fact that the action is taking place at the present time.

A basic rule of English grammar is that the tense of verbs in a sentence must remain logically consistent. For example, it is nonsense, to say *Mike walked to school after he gets out of bed*, but it is perfectly acceptable to say *Mike walked to school after he got out of bed*.

Choice A uses *speaks*, a present tense verb. The sentence, however, begins in the past tense, saying that *Lucy was furious*. The shift from past to present tense makes the sentence incorrect. Choice A, therefore, is not a good answer.

In choice B, the phrase *and speaking* makes little sense because it has no grammatical connection to the words *Because Lucy was furious*.

Choice C has another kind of problem. The words *Because Lucy was furious* suggests that the rest of the sentence will explain what happened as a result of Lucy's anger. But the words *and she spoke* fail to do that.

Choice D is wrong because it has the same problem as choice C. In addition, *as she spoke* turns the construction into a sentence fragment—an incomplete sentence.

Choice E is the best answer because the verbs *was* and *spoke* are both in the past tense, and *she spoke loudly* accurately describes what happened when Lucy lost her cool.

(*For more details on the use of verb tenses, turn to pages 148–149.*)

Type 2: Sentences Containing Errors in Style or Expression

<u>Great enjoyment was experienced by me at the wedding of my sister</u>.

(A) Great enjoyment was experienced by me at the wedding of my sister
(B) The experience of my sister's wedding was greatly enjoyed
(C) Being at my sister's wedding was an experience of great enjoyment
(D) I greatly enjoyed my sister's wedding
(E) A greatly enjoyable experience for me was the wedding of my sister

Here the whole sentence is underlined. Because the original and all the choices are grammatically correct, you must analyze the writing style. Effective writing should be clear, brief, and bold, and of the five choices, only choice D has those qualities.

Choice A is a passive sentence, one in which the subject of the sentence is the receiver of the action. Because *enjoyment* is the subject of this sentence, it receives the primary emphasis, leaving *my sister* in a secondary, or passive, role.

Choice B leaves the reader uncertain about who had enjoyed the wedding.

Choice C includes the awkwardly-worded phrase *an experience of great enjoyment*.

Choice E contains many more words than are necessary. Compare it to the correct answer, choice D, which expresses the idea succinctly.

(*For help in making informed decisions about effective style and expression, read "Problems in Style and Expression," pages 136–139.*)

Type 3: Sentences Containing Errors in Standard English Usage

Cape Canaveral was renamed Cape Kennedy shortly after JFK <u>was assassinated, its original name was given back to it ten years later</u>.

(A) was assassinated, its original name was given back to it ten years later

(B) was assassinated and it got back its original name ten years later

(C) was assassinated; its original name was restored ten years later

(D) was assassinated, it was restored to its original name ten years later

(E) was assassinated; however, with the restoration of its original name ten years later

The underlined text of the original sentence has three problems. The first is punctuation. A comma improperly separates two individual sentences. To avoid this so-called *comma splice*, use (1) a semicolon, or (2) a period and a capital letter for the second sentence. A third option is to keep the comma and add an appropriate conjunction (*and, but, or, nor, for, yet*, or *so*).

The second problem is wordiness. The underlined text, which contains thirteen words, is less concise than any of the other choices.

And the third problem is awkwardness. The phrase *was given back to it* has a decidedly ungraceful sound.

Which, then, is the best choice?

Choice A repeats the original. Reject it.

Choice B adds the conjunction *and* but omits the comma ordinarily placed between the two parts of a compound sentence. In addition, *it got back its original name* is awkward, due in part to the use of *it* and *its* in the same phrase.

Choice C avoids the problems of the other choices. It is the best answer.

Choice D contains a comma splice. Also, like choice B, it awkwardly repeats the pronoun *it*.

Choice E contains a sentence fragment. That is, the construction beginning with *however* is an incomplete sentence.

It probably took you a few minutes to read the explanations of the three sample sentences. On the SAT, under the pressure of time, you are expected to do a similar but far quicker analysis. Some questions will have definite right and wrong answers; others require judgment. Sometimes two or more choices may be grammatically correct, but the best answer will be the most graceful and effectively expressed sentence. Some items may contain multiple errors, others just one. Some assess your knowledge of standard English usage. Others test your understanding of sentence structure and writing style.

In short, sentence-correction questions deal with dozens of writing problems. The majority, however, relate to one of the following:

Problems in Style and Expression
    Wordiness, page 136
    Awkwardness, page 137
    Faulty word choice, page 138
    Faulty idiom, page 138

Problems in Sentence Structure
    Sentence fragments, page 139
    Run-on sentences, page 141
    Semicolon errors, page 142
    Comma splices, page 142
    Mismatched sentence parts, page 143
        Faulty coordination and subordination, page 143
        Faulty parallelism, page 146
    Mixed construction, page 147
        Shifts in grammatical subject, page 148
        Shifts in verb tense, page 148
        Shifts from active to passive construction, page 150
        Misplaced modifiers, page 151
            Dangling modifiers, page 151

Problems in Standard English Usage
    Subject–verb agreement, page 152
    Faulty verb forms and tenses, page 156
    Use of pronouns
        Faulty pronoun case, page 157
        Shifts in pronoun person, page 159
        Pronoun–antecedent agreement, page 159
        Faulty pronoun reference, page 161
        Faulty comparisons, page 163

PROBLEMS IN STYLE AND EXPRESSION

Roughly 25% of the sentence-improvement questions on the SAT test your ability to pick out the best, clearest, and most cogently written sentences. To answer the questions you need to apply such basic principles of good writing as:

1. Omit needless words.
2. Avoid redundancies.
3. Choose precise words.
4. Use the natural order of English idiom.
5. Avoid awkward and clumsy expression.

In the pages that follow, common errors in style and expression are spelled out and illustrated. Read the material and answer the sample questions. And for more details turn to Part III, which fully discusses these and other principles of effective writing.

Wordiness

Sentences cluttered with unnecessary words are less effective than tightly written sentences in which every word matters. Some sentence-correction questions will contain words and phrases that needlessly repeat what has already been stated or implied. Look also for clauses that can be shortened to phrases and phrases that can be recast as single words.

Here are two examples:

1. During the months of July and August last summer, I had a wonderful summer vacation.

Because July and August are the names of months that occur in the summer, this sentence contains words to be deleted:

Last July and August I had a wonderful vacation.

2. As you continue down the road a little further, you will be pleased and delighted with the beautiful and gorgeous views of the scenery that you'll be seeing.

The sentence is overweight with redundancies. Revise it by reducing the initial clause to a phrase and eliminating the redundancies:

Continuing down this road, you'll be delighted with the beautiful scenery.

Sample Questions Containing Wordiness

1. <u>Among the many numerous threats in the contemporary world in which we live are both the threat of global warming and the threat of terrorism.</u>

   (A) Among the many numerous threats in the contemporary world in which we live are both the threat of global warming and the threat of terrorism
   (B) Among the many threats we face in the contemporary world in which we live are global warming and the threat of terrorism
   (C) Both global warming and terrorism are two of the many threats faced by today's world
   (D) Today's world faces, among many other threats, global warming and terrorism
   (E) We live in a contemporary world facing, among many other threats, the threats of global warming and terrorism

Choice A, in addition to repeating *threat*, contains two redundancies. The first is *many* and *numerous*; the second is *contemporary world* and *in which we live*. (After all, where else do we live except in the contemporary world?)

Choice B contains the redundant phrases *contemporary world* and *in which we live*. See choice A.

Choice C contains the redundant words *both* and *two*.

Choice D is free of excess words and redundancies. It is the best answer.

Choice E unnecessarily repeats *threat* and contains a variation of the redundancy in choice B.

2. <u>Because she was a girl was the reason why Emma felt she was deprived of a place playing on the varsity football team</u>.

(A) Because she was a girl was the reason why Emma felt she was deprived of a place playing on the varsity football team
(B) Emma felt that she was kept from playing on the varsity football team because she was a girl
(C) Because she was a girl, Emma gave as a reason why she was deprived of a place to play on the varsity football team
(D) Emma, a girl, feeling the reason why she was deprived of a place on the varsity football team
(E) A girl, Emma, felt that she could not play on the varsity football team

Choice A contains the redundancy *the reason why*. Use either *the reason* or *why*, not both. In addition, the phrase *place playing* is awkwardly expressed.

Choice B economically expresses the idea of the original sentence. It is the best answer.

Choice C contains the wordy phrase *of a place to play*. Delete *to play*.

Choice D contains the same redundancy as choice A. In addition, the construction is a sentence fragment.

Choice E, while economically written, significantly alters the meaning of the original sentence.

(*For more details and a practice exercise on trimming needless words, turn to page 94.*)

Awkwardness

Awkward and *clumsy* are vague words that cover a great many writing weaknesses, including poor grammar and flawed sentence structure. Most often, though, awkwardness occurs when the words sound peculiar, jarring, or out of tune. Awkwardness is difficult to define, but you know it when you hear it. Much of the time you must rely on your ear to detect odd and clumsily worded sentences because there are no specific rules that can explain their defects except that they fail to conform to standard English idiom.

Sample Questions Containing Awkward Construction

1. Inside the cave, Justin's eyes did not adjust to the dark as quickly as Ellie's <u>did, this is being why she found the skull and not he</u>.

(A) did, this is being why she found the skull and not he
(B) did, therefore Ellie and not him finded the skull
(C) did; therefore she found the skull and not he
(D) did, which being the reason why she found the skull and not him
(E) did, being the reason why she found the skull and not him

Choice A contains *this is being*, an awkward, nonstandard usage.

Choice B uses *him*, an object pronoun, instead of *he*, a subject pronoun. Also, the past tense of the verb *to find* is *found*, not *finded*.

Choice C is standard usage and is properly punctuated. It is the best answer.

Choice D contains *which being*, an awkward, nonstandard usage. It also uses the pronoun *him* instead of *he*.

Choice E contains the redundancy *the reason why*. Use either *the reason* or *why*, but not both. Also *him* should be *he*.

2. Vertical take-off and landing aircraft get their fixed-wing capability from high-speed air pumped from slots in the trailing edges of their <u>rotors, in which it increases the airflow</u> over them to create lift.

(A) rotors, in which it increases the airflow
(B) rotors, which increases the airflow
(C) rotors, therefore it increases the airflow
(D) rotors, the end result being it increases the airflow
(E) rotors, consequently which increases the airflow

Choice A is awkwardly worded, partly because the pronoun *it* fails to refer to a specific noun or other pronoun.

Choice B eliminates the awkwardness and is concise. It is the best answer.

Choice C is not awkward but it contains a comma splice.

Choice D contains the redundancy *end result* and leaves the pronoun *it* without a specific referent.

Choice E is awkward and ungrammatical.

Faulty Word Choice

Problems in word choice occur when writers ignore word connotations, fail to draw fine distinctions between synonyms, or simply don't know the precise meaning of words. For example:

The poem contains illusions to Greek mythology.

This sentence contains an error in diction because the writer meant *allusions*.

The boys ran a fowl of the law when they shoplifted the DVD.

Here the writer confused *a fowl* (a chicken or duck) with the word *afoul*.

Sample Questions Containing Faulty Word Choice

1. Marissa holded her father in disrespect by throwing a book at him during their argument over her curfew.

   (A) Marissa holded her father in disrespect by
   (B) Marissa showed disrespect for her father by
   (C) Marissa was disrespecting her father by
   (D) Disrespecting Marissa's father by
   (E) Having shown disrespect for her father by

Choice A uses the incorrect past tense of the verb *to hold*. Use *held* instead of *holded*.

Choice B uses the correct words in the correct order. It is the best answer.

Choice C uses faulty diction. The correct form of the verb is *has disrespected*.

Choices D and E are sentence fragments.

2. Another quality common to fire fighters is their reliability on their fellow fire fighters.

   (A) to fire fighters is their reliability on
   (B) of fire fighters is to depend on
   (C) to fire fighters is they must rely on
   (D) to fire fighters is their reliance on
   (E) to fire fighters is his reliability for

Choice A uses *reliability* instead of *reliance*, an example of faulty diction.

Choice B contains mismatched sentence parts; in standard usage a noun (*quality*) may not be defined with a verb (*to depend*) but only with another noun.

Choice C contains mismatched sentence parts; in standard usage a noun (*quality*) may not be defined by a clause (*they must rely . . .*) but only with another noun.

Choice D correctly conveys the meaning of the sentence. It is the best answer.

Choice E contains faulty idiom. The phrase *his reliability for* is not standard English.

Faulty Idiom

An idiom usually consists of a group of words that seems absurd if taken literally. When you "have a ball," the experience has nothing to do with a spherical object used on the basketball court or soccer field. The expression "that's cool" is not related to temperature, and so on. Such idioms often puzzle speakers of other languages, but to native speakers of English, they are as natural as breathing.

On the SAT, the word *idiom* refers not only to such expressions but also to idiomatic usage—that is, to the selection and sequence of words used to convey a meaning. The italicized words in the following sentence are examples of faulty idiom:

The general was unwilling to pay the *price for victory*.

Nancy has a negative *opinion towards* me.

As regards to her future, Tina said she'd go to college.

The meaning of each sentence is clear, but the italicized sections don't conform to standard English usage. Revised, the sentences would read:

The general was unwilling to pay the *price of victory*.

Nancy has a negative *opinion of* me.

With regard to her future, Tina said she'd go to college.

Sample Questions Containing Faulty Idiom

1. <u>Stopping at a dime is what the engineers were after when</u> they designed brakes for the high-speed train.

   (A) Stopping at a dime is what the engineers were after when
   (B) To stop at a dime is what the engineers were after when
   (C) Stopping at a dime is what the engineers sought
   (D) Stopping on a dime is what the engineers sought as
   (E) The engineers wanted to stop on a dime while

Choice A contains faulty idiom. The expression is *on a dime*, not *at a dime*.

Choices B and C use the same non-standard idiom.

Choice D uses the correct idiom. It is the best answer.

Choice E uses the correct idiom but changes the meaning by saying that the engineers, not the train, wanted to stop on a dime.

2. Einstein's theory of relativity is, for most of us, one that is <u>with difficult understanding</u>.

   (A) with difficult understanding
   (B) difficult for understanding
   (C) having difficulty being understood
   (D) understood only by difficultly
   (E) difficult to understand

Choices A, B, and D fail to adhere to standard English idiom.

Choice C is idiomatic but it fails to relate logically to the previous part of the sentence.

Choice E uses correct English idiom to convey the idea. It is the best answer.

For more details and a practice exercise in faulty idiom, turn to page 166.

For more details and a practice exercise in faulty idiom, turn to page 166.

PROBLEMS IN SENTENCE STRUCTURE

Sentence Fragments

Broadly speaking, a sentence is a group of words that begins with a capital letter and ends with an end mark of punctuation. It also conveys a more or less complete thought and is grammatically whole, which means that it has a subject and a verb.

Incomplete sentences, or sentence fragments, often look remarkably like complete sentences but are not because of one or more grammatical defects.

> The bike that Martha often borrowed.

This fragment seems to have all the characteristics of a sentence: It starts with a capital letter and ends with a period, it conveys a complete thought (*Martha often borrowed the bike* is a complete thought), and it appears to contain a subject and a verb. What makes it a fragment, though, is that the subject *bike* and the verb *borrowed* don't fit together. A bike, an inanimate object, can't do any borrowing—not in this world, anyway. Clearly, Martha did the borrowing, but the noun *Martha* cannot be the subject of the sentence because it is part of the subordinate clause, *that Martha borrowed*. Therefore, *bike* needs a verb of its own.

> The bike that Martha often borrowed was stolen.

With the addition of *was stolen*, the sentence is now complete.

Sentence fragments usually occur when writers fail to distinguish between dependent and independent clauses, when they confuse phrases and clauses, or when they attempt to use verbals as verbs. To determine whether a sentence is complete, uncover its bare bones. That is, deconstruct the sentence by eliminating dependent clauses, phrases, and verbals. If what remains does not have a subject and a verb, it's probably a fragment.

To identify the subject of long sentences may take some doing, but the "bare bones" strategy usually works. Using this approach, you'll strip away everything in a sentence but its subject and verb, a task that may be easier said than done. It's not very formidable, though, if you remember that the grammatical subject can never be in (a) a prepositional phrase, (b) a dependent clause, or (c) a phrase that interrupts the flow of the sentence.

To find the "bare bones" of a sentence:

Step 1: Look for prepositional phrases, such as *up the wall, around the corner, to the beach, over the counter,* and cross them out. For example, if you were to eliminate all the prepositional phrases in these sentences, only the subject and the verb—the "bare bones"—will remain.

Complete sentence:	In the middle of the night, Pricilla slept.
Bare bones:	Pricilla slept
Complete sentence:	Several of the sentences are in the book.
Bare bones:	Several are
Complete sentence:	One of Frida's friends is in need of help.
Bare bones:	One is

Step 2: Locate all the dependent clauses—those parts of sentences containing a noun and a verb but don't qualify as complete sentences because they begin with words and phrases like *although, as, as though, because, before, even though, if, in spite of, regardless of, since, so that, unless, whenever, whether,* and *while*. Another group of dependent clauses are statements (not questions) that start with *when, where, which, who,* and *what*.

After deleting the dependent clauses in the following sentences, only the main clause will remain. That's where to find the bare bones of each sentence.

Complete sentence:	Because she missed the bus, Marnie wept.
Bare bones:	Marnie wept
Complete sentence:	While Willie waited for the bus, he studied vocabulary
Bare bones:	he studied
Complete sentence:	Andy helps out whenever he has the time
Bare bones:	Andy helps out

Step 3: Look for and delete interrupters—those parts of sentences that impede the smooth flow of the main idea. Interrupters may be just one word, such as *however* and *nevertheless*, or dozens. They're often set off by commas.

Complete sentence:	Ellen, regardless of the look on her face, rejoiced.
Bare bones:	Ellen rejoiced
Complete sentence:	The boat, a sleek white catamaran, sank.
Bare bones:	boat sank
Complete sentence:	Marty, who got ticketed for doing 60 in a 30 MPH zone, paid the fine.
Bare bones:	Marty paid

Frankly, identifying the bare bones of a sentence is often a more complex process than that suggested by these examples. Sometimes the bare bones are buried in deep within long and complicated sentences. But by carefully peeling away sentence parts that cannot contain the subject or verb, you'll eventually find them.

Sample Questions Containing Sentence Fragments

1. During the night, the <u>stars that came</u> out like diamonds on black velvet.

    (A) stars that came
    (B) stars coming
    (C) stars, which are coming
    (D) stars came
    (E) stars, which came

Start your analysis of this sentence by deleting all the prepositional phrases, namely *During the night, like diamonds* and *on black velvet*. Now delete any dependent clauses; there is only one: *that came out*. The only words left are *the stars,* clearly not a complete sentence.

Choice A, therefore, is wrong because it is a sentence fragment.

Choice B is wrong because the *–ing* form of a verb may not be the main verb of a sentence unless it is accompanied by a helping verb, as in *is singing, has been raining, will be arriving*.

Choices C and E are also wrong because *which*, like *that*, introduces a dependent clause.

By the process of elimination, then, choice D is the best answer. *Stars* is the subject of the sentence, and *came* is the verb.

2. <u>A belief among superstitious people that</u> birth-marks are caused by influences on the mother before the child is born.

  (A) A belief among superstitious people that
  (B) Superstitious people believe that
  (C) Superstitious people believing that
  (D) Among superstitious people the belief that
  (E) Among beliefs of superstitious people are that

Analyze the sentence with the same technique used in question 1—by deleting all prepositional phrases and dependent clauses. Then search the reamining words for a subject and a verb.

Choice A has a grammatical subject, *belief*, but the construction is a fragment because it lacks a main verb. While *are caused* and *is born* are verbs, neither can be the main verb because they are in the dependent clause, *that birthmarks . . .*

Choice B contains both a subject, *people*, and a verb, *believe*. As a complete sentence, it is the best answer.

Choice C contains a subject, *people*, but no verb. The *–ing* form of a verb may not be the main verb of a sentence unless it is accompanied by a helping verb, as in *is singing, has been raining, will be arriving.*

Choice D has neither a subject nor a verb because the construction is made up only of phrases and a dependent clause.

Choice E has a verb, *are*, but no subject because all the nouns are either in phrases or in the dependent clause.

Run-on Sentences

A run-on sentence consists of two independent clauses separated by neither a conjunction (*and, but, or, nor, yet,* or *so*) nor an appropriate mark of punctuation, as in:

Birthstones are supposed to bring good luck mine has never brought me any.

A conjunction or a mark of punctuation is needed between *luck* and *mine*.

Birthstones are supposed to bring good luck, *but* mine has never brought me any.

Adding *but* solves the problem. A comma has also been added because sentences made up of two or more independent clauses joined by a conjunction usually require a comma. Another possibility is writing two separate sentences:

Birthstones are supposed to bring good luck. Mine has never brought me any.

Separating the sentences with a semicolon is also an acceptable alternative. In effect, the semicolon functions like a period. Note, however, that the initial letter of the second sentence is not capitalized:

Birthstones are supposed to bring good luck; mine has never brought me any.

Sample Questions Containing a Run-on Sentence

The campers hated the taste of powdered <u>milk they drank</u> water instead.

  (A) milk they drank
  (B) milk; preferring to drink
  (C) milk drinking
  (D) milk, so they drank
  (E) milk so they drank

Choice A is a run-on. A period or a semicolon is needed between *milk* and *they*.

Choice B is not a good alternative because a semicolon functions like a period, and the second clause is now a sentence fragment.

Choice C needs a comma and is awkwardly worded.

Choices D has a conjunction *so*, preceded by a comma. It is the best answer.

Choice E lacks the comma required before the conjunction *so*.

Semicolon Errors

Misuse of a semicolon is a common error in sentence-improvement questions. Remember that a semicolon is a substitute for a period, NOT for a comma. Correctly used, a semicolon must lie between two independent clauses.

> *Incorrect:*   On the test Lucy got a 90; which raised her final average.

The clause *which raised her final average* is not an independent clause.

> *Correct:*   On the test Lucy got a 90; this grade raised her final average.

Sample Questions Containing a Semicolon Error

Mending a fracture takes from four weeks to a <u>year; depending</u> on the size of the bone, the location, and the age of the person.

(A) year; depending
(B) year; all depending
(C) year depending
(D) year, it depends
(E) year, depending

Choices A and B consist of an independent clause and a sentence fragment—in this case a participial phrase—improperly separated by a semicolon.

Choice C needs a comma to be correct.

Choice D is a comma splice (see discussion that follows).

Choice E properly uses a comma to separate the two parts. The first part is an independent clause, the second a participial phrase.

Comma Splices

A form of run-on sentence is the comma splice, a construction in which a comma is used between two independent clauses instead of a period or a semicolon.

Sample Questions Containing a Comma Splice

Toni Morrison is one of America's outstanding <u>authors, she is known</u> for her critical essays, her novels, and her frequent appearances on television.

(A) authors, she is known
(B) authors; she is known
(C) authors famous
(D) authors since known
(E) authors being that she is known

Choice A is a comma splice. It uses a comma to join two independent clauses.

Choice B is correct because it uses a semicolon to separate two independent clauses. It is the best answer.

Choice C needs a comma to be correct.

Choices D and E are awkwardly expressed and ungrammatical.

Practice in Writing Correct Sentences

<u>Directions</u>: Some of the following are sentence fragments, others are run-ons, and still others contain comma splices. Use the spaces provided to write complete and correct sentences.

1. Although Elizabeth is stressed out about the SAT.

2. She asked the teacher for an extension on the assignment, the teacher agreed.

3. My grandmother is 86 years old therefore she walks very slowly.

4. Many other examples that I could choose to show who I am, many of them not vivid images of memorable moments, but everyday aspects of my life.

_____

_____

5. I woke up, having slept for the four shortest hours of my life, I force open my eyes and I crawl to the shower then my brain begins to function.

_____

_____

6. For me to believe that the crucial time has arrived when I will leave the protective world of high school and enter the world of college.

_____

_____

7. The large brown garage door creaks open slowly, out into the morning sunshine a rider on a road bike emerges.

_____

_____

8. What are the rules which we all must follow what might happen if we break them.

_____

_____

9. A biologist working in the field of genetic engineering and involved in the controversy surrounding cloning.

_____

_____

10. Using the space below, telling one story about yourself to provide the admissions committee, either directly or indirectly, with an insight into the kind of person you are.

_____

_____

Answers are on page 195.

Mismatched Sentence Parts

Sentences work best when their components fit harmoniously and grammatically together. But sometimes two clauses are incompatible, or a sentence begins in the active voice and ends in the passive. A breakdown in logic or clear thinking may also account for an error, as when two ideas expressed in a compound sentence are unrelated. The material that follows explains, first, the specific kinds of errors to watch for and, second, how to make corrections.

Faulty Coordination

In everyday conversation people often use lengthy compound sentences made up of several short sentences joined by *and*, *so*, or other conjunctions:

> In school on Tuesday the lights went out, *and* we were in the dark for more than an hour, *and* the electricity was off, *so* we couldn't use the computers, *and* we heard that a car had hit a utility pole, *and* the driver was killed, *and* they let us go home early.

This sentence tells a story without breaking a single rule of usage or grammar. Yet, it is stylistically flawed, not because it's monotonous but because each idea appears in an independent clause, suggesting that all the ideas are equally important. Clauses of equal rank in a sentence are called coordinate clauses and are usually joined by the conjunctions *and, but, or, nor, yet,* or *so*. Faulty coordination occurs (1) when it is illogical or inappropriate to assign equal importance to two or more coordinate clauses, or (2) when the connecting word fails to create a reasonable relationship between the clauses.

Tom was away at summer camp, and his parents decided to split up after twenty years of marriage.

The two coordinate clauses state seemingly unrelated ideas, obviously of unequal importance. In the following sentence, as well as in most other complex sentences, the contents of the independent clause are assumed to contain more important information than the contents of other clauses. In other words, making clauses dependent reduces the significance of the information they contain, thereby changing the effect of the sentence:

> While Tom was away at summer camp, his parents decided to split up after twenty years of marriage.

What follows is a sentence in which the conjunction *and* fails to convey a meaningful relationship between the ideas in the two clauses.

> Ms. Sheridan has become the new assistant principal, and she has never taught.

Making the second clause dependent by using *although* creates a more sensible connection between the ideas:

> Ms. Sheridan has become the new assistant principal, although she has never taught.

For the sake of unity and coherence, it is usually better not to shift from one grammatical subject to another between clauses. Maintaining the subject helps readers glide easily from one clause to the next without realigning their focus.

> *Faulty:* The plan will be a great success, or great failure will be the result.

Plan is the subject of the first clause; *failure* is the subject of the second.

> *Unified:* The plan will be a great success, or it will be a great failure.

The pronoun *it* keeps the subject in focus from one clause to the next.

Sample Questions Containing Faulty Coordination

1. Elizabeth hopes to attend Ohio Wesleyan, <u>and she has not yet sent in her application</u>.

    (A) and she has not yet sent in her application
    (B) and she hasn't sent her application in yet
    (C) but her application hasn't as yet been sent in by her
    (D) yet the sending of the application has not yet been done.
    (E) but she hasn't yet sent in her application

Choice A is incorrect because the conjunction *and* fails to express a reasonable relationship between the two coordinate clauses.

Choice B has the same problem as choice A.

Choice C expresses an apt relationship by using the conjunction *but*, but then it switches subjects and changes from active to passive construction.

Choice D switches subjects and is awkwardly worded.

Choice E conveys the relationship between the clauses and is consistent. It is the best answer.

2. <u>My weekend job at The GAP will help me as a marketing major, and I am learning about retail selling</u>.

    (A) My weekend job at The GAP will help me as a marketing major, and I am learning about retail selling
    (B) Learning about retail selling, my weekend job at The GAP will help me as a marketing major
    (C) My weekend job at The GAP, where I am learning about retail selling, will help me as a marketing major
    (D) Helping me as a marketing major is learning about retail selling in my weekend job at The GAP
    (E) My weekend job at The GAP will help me as a marketing major; I am learning about retail selling

Choice A is a sentence that gives equal weight to its two clauses even though the content of the first clause is probably more important than the content of the second.

Choice B properly changes the second clause into a phrase, but the change results in a dangling participle.

Choice C properly subordinates the second clause and embeds it in the independent clause. It is the best answer.

Choice D turns two clauses into one, but the subject *helping* and the predicate nominative *learning* make an awkwardly worded combination.

Choice E, despite the revision, fails to correct the original problem.

Faulty Subordination

By means of subordination, writers are able to convey not only the interrelationship of ideas but also the relative importance of one idea to another. Here, for instance, are two statements:

Joe rushed to school. He ate a tuna sandwich.

The relationship between the two ideas is not altogether transparent, but it can be clarified by subordinating one of the ideas.

While he rushed to school, Joe ate a tuna sandwich.
or
While he ate a tuna sandwich, Joe rushed to school.

In each sentence, the more important idea appears in the main clause instead of in the subordinate clause. The subordinate clause in both sentences begins with *while*, one of many common subordinating conjunctions. Others include *after, although, as if, as though, because, before, if, in order to, since, so that, that, though, unless, until, when, whenever, where, whereas, wherever,* and *whether*. The presence of one of these conjunctions in a sentence-improvement question should alert you to the possibility of faulty subordination. The sentences that follow illustrate typical problems:

While she is fifteen years old, she is afraid of the dark.

The subordinating conjunction *while* obscures both the meaning of the sentence and the relationship between the two statements.

Although she is fifteen years old, she is afraid of the dark.

A new subordinating conjunction clarifies the meaning.

I read in the paper *where* the fleet is coming back to Norfolk.

The meaning may be clear, but the context *where* is not standard usage.

I read in the paper *that* the fleet is coming back to Norfolk.

Another problem concerns the placement of emphasis. The conjunction *and* in the following sentence gives equal emphasis to unequal ideas.

I arrived home from school *and* I received my acceptance letter from Ohio State.

Stating the more significant event in the main clause places the emphasis where it belongs:

When I arrived home from school, I received my acceptance letter from Ohio State.

Sample Questions Containing Faulty Subordination

1. <u>Pedro is a new student in the school, and he comes from Portugal</u>.

   (A) Pedro is a new student in the school, and he comes from Portugal
   (B) Pedro, being from Portugal, is a new student in the school
   (C) Pedro, a new student in the school, comes from Portugal
   (D) Pedro, a new student in the school and a native of Portugal
   (E) Pedro is a new student from Portugal in the school

Choice A is grammatically correct, but it would be more effective if one clause were subordinated to the other.

Choice B subordinates a clause, but the use of *being* oddly suggests that Pedro's presence in the school is related to his nationality.

Choice C properly subordinates one idea and embeds it in the main clause. It is the best answer.

Choice D is a sentence fragment.

Choice E alters the meaning of the original sentence.

2.   <u>When he suddenly started to grin like an imbe-
     cile, I was walking with him in the park.</u>

     (A) When he suddenly started to grin like an
         imbecile, I was walking with him in the park
     (B) While I walked with him in the park, he
         suddenly started to grin like an imbecile
     (C) Suddenly starting to grin like an imbecile,
         he was walking in the park with me
     (D) He grinned suddenly like an imbecile and
         walked in the park with me
     (E) Walking in the park with me and suddenly
         grinning like an imbecile

Choice A is incorrect because it places the
more important idea in the subordinate clause.

Choice B places the main idea in the main
clause. It is the best answer.

Choice C is wrong because it puts the major
idea into a phrase.

Choice D is wrong because it changes the
meaning of the original sentence.

Choice E is a sentence fragment.

Faulty Parallelism

Faulty parallelism occurs most often when an item
in a series is not grammatically parallel to the others, when a sentence is constructed of mixed, or
unrelated parts, and when the subject or tense of a
verb changes from one part of a sentence to
another.

For example, a series of sentence elements—
clauses, phrases, verbs, and even nouns joined by
and, but, or, nor, or *for*—should be worded in parallel form. That is to say, their structure should be
repeated using the same parts of speech in the same
order. Parallel structure creates a sense of rhythm
and order. Without parallelism, you get jumbles
such as this:

Today a television newscaster must be attractive and a lot of charm.

The word *attractive* is an adjective modifying
newscaster; *charm* is a noun. Revise the sentence
by making both words nouns or both words adjectives that modify nouns, as in

Today a television newscaster must have good
looks and charm.
or
Today a television newscaster must be attractive and charming.

Another example:

Eighteen-year-olds are too young to sign contracts, but they may have been driving for
years.

The first clause states an idea in the present tense.
The second clause, however, takes an unexpected
and perplexing turn by changing the verb to the
past perfect. With the verbs in parallel form the
sentence is:

Eighteen-year-olds may drive, but they are too
young to sign contracts.

Or written more concisely:

Eighteen-year-olds are permitted to drive but
not to sign contracts.

Sample Questions Containing Faulty Parallelism

1.   Students lacking financial resources can still
     go to college because they can borrow money
     from banks, <u>hold part-time jobs, and scholar-
     ships are available</u>.

     (A) hold part-time jobs, and scholarships are
         available
     (B) jobs are available, and scholarships are
         available
     (C) hold part-time jobs, and win scholarships
     (D) holding part-time jobs and winning scholar-
         ships
     (E) holding part-time jobs and win scholarships

Choice A contains *scholarships are available*,
a construction that is not parallel to *borrow money
from banks* and *hold part-time jobs*.

Choice B contains constructions that are not
parallel to the structure of *borrow money from
banks*.

Choice C contains phrases parallel in form to
borrow money from banks. It is the best answer.

Choices D and E contains phrases that are not parallel to the structure of *borrow money from banks*.

2. When buying a piece of clothing, smart consumers consider how much the item costs, how good it looks, and <u>its durability</u>.

   (A) its durability
   (B) if it is durable
   (C) the durability of it
   (D) the ability of the item to last
   (E) how durable it is

The sentence contains three elements that must be in parallel form. Two of the three begin with *how*, followed by an adverb or adjective and then by a verb. Only choice E follows this pattern; therefore, choice E is the best answer.

For more details and a practice exercise in parallel structure, turn to page 88.

Mixed Construction

A variation of faulty parallelism is mixed construction, which occurs when the beginning of a sentence doesn't fit grammatically or logically with the end. Mixed sentence parts suggest that the writer, in finishing a sentence, ignored how it had begun:

> Maggie's goal is to be a nurse and is hoping to go to nursing school after graduation.

The grammatical subject *goal* appears to have been forgotten in the second half of the sentence because the verb *is hoping* lacks an appropriate subject.

> Maggie aspires to be a nurse, and she is hoping to go to nursing school after graduation.

With a compound sentence containing two subjects and two verbs, the problem is solved. But subordinating one of the clauses is an even better solution to the problem:

> Maggie, who aspires to be a nurse, hopes to go to nursing school after graduation.

Another example:

> When Lana came to school with a black eye was a signal that she is an abused child.

The verb *was* needs a subject.

> Lana's coming to school with a black eye was a signal that she is an abused child.

The problem has been solved by using *coming* as the grammatical subject.

Sample Questions Containing Mixed Construction

1. The next morning, after Christie's car was found abandoned, <u>there was a nationwide search for the missing author had started</u>.

   (A) there was a nationwide search for the missing author had started
   (B) there was the beginning of a nationwide search for the missing author
   (C) a nationwide search for the missing author will have began
   (D) there begun a nationwide search for the missing author
   (E) a nationwide search for the missing author began

Choice A is wrong because it contains a subject, *search*, with two verbs of different tenses, *was* and *had started*.

Choice B deletes one of the extra verbs in choice A but changes the grammatical subject to *beginning*, a weak alternative.

Choice C contains an error in verb form—*will have began* instead of *will have begun*.

Choice D contains an error in verb form—*begun* instead of *began*.

Choice E, a clause that grammatically and logically fits the previous part of the sentence, is the best answer.

2. The story is about how loyalty to a friend can create a moral <u>crisis, but where it challenges conventional values</u>.

    (A) crisis, but where it challenges conventional values
    (B) crisis, whereas conventional values are challenged
    (C) crisis in which conventional values are challenged
    (D) crisis, and the reason is that their challenge of conventional values
    (E) crisis because in it there are challenged conventional values

Choice A uses the conjunction *but*, which has no logical meaning in the context of the entire sentence.

Choice B uses *whereas*, a word that lacks a logical relationship with the rest of the sentence.

Choice C completes the sentence grammatically and logically. It is the best answer.

Choice D is a sentence fragment.

Choice E is an awkwardly worded and almost meaningless construction.

Shifts in Grammatical Subject

Still another type of faulty parallelism occurs when the grammatical subject of a sentence is changed from one clause to another. For example:

> To fix a flat tire, I jack up the car, and then the damaged tire is removed.

The subject of the first clause is *I*. In the second clause the subject is *tire*, a shift to the passive voice that weakens the effectiveness of the whole sentence.

> To fix a flat tire, I jack up the car and then remove the damaged tire.

When the grammatical subject is maintained, parallelism is restored, and the sentence is active and concise.

Sample Questions Containing a Shift in Grammatical Subject

The board recognizes the school's troubles and <u>now a giant fund-raising drive was being undertaken by them</u>.

    (A) now a giant fund-raising drive was being undertaken by them
    (B) it had undertaken a giant fund-raising drive now
    (C) has now undertaken a giant fund-raising drive
    (D) now they have taken a giant fund-raising drive
    (E) now, having undertaken a giant fund-raising drive

Choice A switches the grammatical subject from *board* in the first clause to *drive* in the second, resulting in a long-winded, passive sentence.

Choice B is wrong because sentence is cast in the present tense but shifts improperly to the past perfect.

Choice C maintains the subject and is concisely worded. It is the best answer.

Choice D contains the plural pronoun *they*, which fails to agree with its singular antecedent, *board*.

Choice E is a sentence fragment.

Shifts in Verb Tense

Sentences lose their effectiveness and sometimes their meaning when an inappropriate shift in the tense of verbs occurs from one part to another, as in

> Before it went out of business, the video store gives its DVDs away.

The sentence begins in the past tense, then shifts to the present. When cast in the past tense from start to finish, the sentence reads:

> Before it went out of business, the video store gave its DVDs away.

The English language offers writers and speakers six basic tenses that convey information about the time when an event or action took place:

Present:	I *eat* pasta every day.
Past:	She *ate* pasta every day.
Future:	Phil *will eat* pasta every day.
Present Perfect:	Monica *has eaten* pasta every day.
Past Perfect:	Enid *had eaten* pasta every day.
Future Perfect:	They all *will have eaten* pasta every day.

All verbs also have a progressive form, created by adding *–ing*, so that you can say things like:

They are swimming. (Present Progressive)

Rose was swimming. (Past Progressive)

The dog will be swimming. (Future Progressive)

I have been swimming. (Present Perfect)

Charles had been swimming. (Past Perfect)

They will have been swimming. (Future Perfect)

Each of these tenses permits you to indicate time sequence very precisely. Someone not attuned to the different meaning that each tense conveys may say something like this:

When her little brother was born, Sarah was toilet trained for six months.

Perhaps the meaning of the sentence is clear enough, but because precision is important, the sentence should read:

When her little brother was born, Sarah *had been* toilet trained for six months.

The revised version, using the past perfect verb *had been*, indicates that the action (Sarah's toilet training) had taken place prior to her brother's birth. The original sentence actually says that her brother's birth and Sarah's toilet training took place at the same time—a physical impossibility, since potty training usually takes weeks or even months.

Notice also the difference in meaning between these two sentences:

There was a condo where the park was.
There was a condo where the park had been.

The meaning of the first sentence may be clear, but it says that the condo and the park were in the same place at the same time. The revision more accu-

rately conveys the idea that the condo replaced the park.

These are subtle differences, perhaps explaining why the SAT frequently includes questions containing errors in verb tense. Such items help to separate students who use English precisely from those who don't.

Sample Questions Containing a Shift in Verb Tense

1. Jay had been working out in the weight room for months before the wrestling coach <u>invites him to try out</u> for the team.

    (A) invites him to try out
    (B) has invited him to try out
    (C) invited him to try out
    (D) had invited him to try out
    (E) inviting him for trying out

Choice A, with a verb in the present tense, is inconsistent with the past perfect tense of the verb *had been working*.

Choice B uses the present perfect tense instead of the past perfect tense.

Choice C correctly conveys the sequence of events. The use of the past tense (*invited*) indicates that Jay's workouts occurred not only prior to the coach's invitation but that they were in progress at the time the coach invited Jay to try out.

Choice D uses only the past perfect tense. Therefore, it fails to convey the precise sequence of events, as expressed by choice C.

Choice E uses faulty idiom.

2. The report said that years ago city planners had envisioned building a facility that turns salt water into fresh <u>water, and financial woes make that impossible</u>.

    (A) water, and financial woes make that impossible
    (B) water, and that is becoming impossible due to financial woes
    (C) water, but that it will have been made impossible by financial woes
    (D) water, but financial woes made that impossible
    (E) water, however, financial woes had made it impossible

Choices A and B contain coordinate clauses with an illogical sequence of verb tenses. Present financial woes are unrelated to plans made years in the past.

Choice C contains the pronoun *it* that fails to refer to specific antecedent

Choice D uses an appropriate and logical sequence of verb tenses. It is the best answer.

Choice E contains a comma splice between *water* and *however*.

For more details and a practice exercise in verb tenses, turn to page 180.

Shifts from Active to Passive Construction

Use active rather than passive construction except when: (1) the person or thing performing the action is unknown or insignificant, or (2) the sentence is meant to emphasize that the subject has been acted upon. For instance, in the following passive sentence, the action (scoring touchdowns) is given greater emphasis than the performer of the action (the team):

Three touchdowns were scored by the team.

Stated actively, the sentence emphasizes who performed the action:

The team scored three touchdowns.

On the SAT, sentences that shift from active to passive, and sometimes vice-versa, often need revision, as in:

After Dan worked all day in the hot sun, a shower was taken to cool off.

A shift from active to passive construction has occurred between the subordinate clause and the main clause.

After Dan worked all day in the hot sun, he took a shower to cool off.

Now both clauses are active; in addition, the grammatical subject has been maintained between the clauses.

Throughout the sentence-improvement sections of the SAT, stay alert for passive sentences. Consider them faulty unless you see a clear necessity for constructing them in the passive voice.

Sample Questions Containing a Shift from Active to Passive Construction

1. For the Thanksgiving weekend, Julie went to <u>Richmond; however, for Christmas a trip to Syracuse was made by her</u>.

   (A) Richmond; however, for Christmas a trip to Syracuse was made by her
   (B) Richmond, however, for Christmas a trip to Syracuse was made by her
   (C) Richmond but for Christmas a trip to Syracuse was made by her
   (D) Richmond, but however, she took a trip to Syracuse for Christmas
   (E) Richmond, but for Christmas she went to Syracuse

Choice A switches from active to passive construction for no logical reason.

Choice B is like A, but it also contains a comma splice between *Richmond* and *however*.

Choice C switches from active to passive construction for no logical reason.

Choice D maintains active construction but includes the redundancy *but however*.

Choice E is consistently active and is free of other errors. It is the best answer.

2. Because the factory owners and their employees worked together to improve efficiency, <u>a big profit was made</u>.

   (A) a big profit was made
   (B) the result were making a big profit
   (C) the factory owners had made big profits
   (D) making big profits were the result
   (E) resulting in a big profit

Choice A is a passive construction that appropriately emphasizes the result of an action rather than who performed it. It is the best answer.

Choice B is active but the plural verb *were* fails to agree with the singular subject *result*.

Choice C is active but contains an improper shift in verb tense.

Choice D is passive and contains a singular subject with a plural verb.

Choice E is a sentence fragment.

For more details and practice in changing sentences from passive to active, turn to page 93.

Misplaced Modifiers

For clarity, modifiers should be placed as close as possible to the word or words they are meant to modify. When they are far apart, sentences like this may result:

> The fellow in the blue SUV with the long hair must be on his way to the concert.

The prepositional phrase *with the long hair* is meant to modify *fellow*, but it modifies *SUV* instead. With the misplaced phrase in its proper place, the sentence reads:

> The fellow with the long hair in the blue SUV must be on his way to the concert.

For still further clarity, be sure that the word being modified is included in the sentence. Otherwise, you may have a dangling modifier on your hands, as in:

> Hurrying to chemistry lab, the bell rang.

According to this sentence, the bell rang as it hurried to chem lab—not a likely scenario. To fix this so-called dangling modifier, the object being modified (in this case, the person rushing to class) must be included in the main clause.

> Hurrying to his chemistry lab, Simon heard the bell ring.

The grammatical subject, *Simon*, is now properly modified by the participle *hurrying to his chemistry lab*.

Dangling Modifiers

The term *dangling modifier* refers to a clause or phrase that appears to modify a word in a sentence but doesn't. For example:

Dangling: Climbing the ladder, Pete's head knocked over the paint can.

At first, this sentence may not strike you as bizarre. But look again, and you'll notice that it says Pete's head climbed a ladder.

Revised: Climbing the ladder, Pete knocked over the paint can with his head.

Adding the noun *Pete* eliminates the dangling modifier.

Sample Questions Containing Misplaced and Dangling Modifiers

1. <u>The plaque was presented to the actor that was engraved with gold letters</u>

   (A) The plaque was presented to the actor that was engraved with gold letters
   (B) The plaque that was presented to the actor engraved with gold letters
   (C) The plaque was presented to the actor who was engraved with gold letters
   (D) The plaque, engraved with gold letters, and presented to the actor
   (E) The plaque presented to the actor was engraved with gold letters

Choice A is wrong because the clause *that was engraved with gold letters* modifies *actor* instead of *plaque*.

Choice B contains the same misplaced modifier as choice A and is also a sentence fragment.

Choice C is a variation of choice A.

Choice D is a sentence fragment.

Choice E has its modifiers in the right place and is a complete sentence. It is the best answer.

2. <u>Driving to Litchfield</u>, the freezing rain made the road slippery and hazardous.

   (A) Driving to Litchfield
   (B) While we drove to Litchfield
   (C) En route to Litchfield
   (D) To drive to Litchfield
   (E) We drove to Litchfield and

Choice A contains a dangling modifier. The phrase *Driving to Litchfield* modifies *rain* instead of the person who did the driving.

Choice B contains *we*, the subject who performed the action. It is the best answer.

Choice C contains the same dangling modifier as choice A.

Choice D makes no sense grammatically or logically.

Choice E is a sentence consisting of coordinate clauses that would be more effectively expressed if one clause were subordinated to the other.

For more details and a practice exercise in misplaced modifiers, turn to page 87.

Problems in Standard Usage

Subject–Verb Agreement

Sentence-improvement questions on the SAT always include items that test your command of the following rule: Subjects and verbs must agree in number. A singular subject must have a singular verb, and a plural subject must be accompanied by a plural verb. That's easy enough to remember, but in the following circumstances it is not so easy to apply.

1. When intervening words obscure the relationship between the subject and verb, as in:

   Delivery (singular subject) of today's newspapers and magazines *have been* (plural verb) delayed.

   The prepositional phrase *of today's newspapers and magazines* blurs the relationship between subject and verb. The plural noun *magazines* can mislead the writer into using a plural verb. With a singular subject and verb properly matched, the sentence reads:

   Delivery of today's newspapers and magazines *has been* delayed.

   Or with matched plural subject and verb:

   Deliveries of today's newspapers and magazines *have been* delayed.

   A writer can also err when words and phrases such as *including, in addition to, along with,* and *as well as* come between the subject and verb.

   One of his paintings, in addition to several photos, *is* on display at the library.
   The *bulk* of English poetry, including the plays of Shakespeare, *is* written in iambic pentameter.

2. When subjects are composed of more than one noun or pronoun. For example,

   a. Nouns, both singular and plural, when joined by *and*, are called compound subjects, which need plural verbs.

      The *picture and the text* (compound subject) *go* (plural verb) inside this box.
      Several *locust trees and a green mailbox stand* outside the house.

   b. Compound subjects thought of as a unit need singular verbs.

      Green *eggs and ham* (compound subject as a unit) *is* (singular verb) Sam's favorite breakfast.
      The parents' *pride and joy* over the birth of their baby *is* self-evident.

   c. Singular nouns joined by *or* or *nor* need singular verbs.

      A Coke *or* a Pepsi (two nouns joined by *or*) *is* (singular verb) what I thirst for.
      Neither my history teacher *nor* my economics teacher *plans* to discuss the crisis.

   d. When a subject consists of a singular noun and a plural noun joined by *or* or *nor*, the number of the verb is determined by the noun closer to the verb.

      Either a pineapple or some oranges are on the table.
      Neither the linemen nor the quarterback was aware of the tricky play.

   e. When a subject contains a pronoun that differs in person from a noun or another pronoun, the verb must agree with the closer subject word.

      Neither Meredith nor *you are* expected to finish the work today.
      Either he or *I am* planning to work late on Saturday.

f. When the subject is singular and the predicate noun is plural, or vice-versa, the number of the verb is determined by the subject.

The *bulk* of Wilkinson's work *is* two novels and a collection of stories.
Two *novels and a story are* the bulk of Wilkinson's work.

3. When singular subjects contain words that sound plural, use singular verbs. The names of books, countries, organizations, certain diseases, course titles, and other singular nouns may sound like plurals because they end in –*s*, but most of the time—although not always—they require a singular verb.

The *news is* good.
Measles is going around the school.

4. When the subject is sometimes singular and sometimes plural, the number of the verb depends on the context. Collective nouns sound singular but may be plural. A family, for example, is singular. But if you are referring to separate individuals, *family* takes a plural verb.

The *family* (members) *are* arriving for the wedding at different times.

Other collective nouns include *group, crowd, team, jury, soybeans, audience, herd, public, dozen, class, band, flock, majority, committee, heap,* and *lot*. Other words and expressions governed by the same rule are units of time, money, weight, measurement, and all fractions.

The *jury is* going to decide today.
The *jury are* returning to their homes tomorrow.

5. When the subject word is an indefinite pronoun. Subjects consisting of indefinite pronouns like *everyone, both,* and *any* pose a special problem. Some indefinite pronouns must be matched with singular verbs, some with plural verbs, and some with one or the other, depending on the sense of the sentence. There's no getting around the fact that you need to know which number applies to which pronoun.

a. These words, although they sound plural, get singular verbs: *each, either, neither,* the "ones" (*anyone, no one, everyone, someone*), and the "bodies" (*anybody, everybody, nobody, somebody*).

Each man and woman in the room *gets* only one vote.
Everyone who works hard *is* going to earn an "A."

b. These words get plural verbs: *both, many, few, several.*

In spite of rumors to the contrary, *both are* on the verge of a nervous breakdown.
Several in the band *are* not going on the trip to Boston.

c. The following words get singular verbs when they refer to singular nouns and plural verbs when they refer to plural nouns: *any, none, some, all, most.*

Some of the collection is valuable.

In this sentence, *some* is singular because it refers to *collection,* a singular noun.

Some of the bracelets are fake.

Here *some* is plural because it refers to *bracelets,* a plural noun.

6. When the subject comes after the verb. When the subject of a sentence follows the verb, the verb takes its number from the subject, as usual.

Behind the building *was* an *alley* (singular subject).
Behind the building *were* an *alley and a vacant lot* (compound subject).

Sample Questions Containing an Error in Subject–Verb Agreement

1. Thinking it over, <u>the solution to many people's problems with unwanted phone calls are</u> stricter laws and Caller ID.

   (A) the solution to many people's problems with unwanted phone calls are
   (B) people's problems with unwanted phone calls can be solved with
   (C) people's problems with unwanted phone calls are to be solved by
   (D) I believe that the solution to many people's problems with unwanted phone calls is
   (E) I think that the solution to many people's problems with unwanted phone calls are

   Choice A is incorrect because the subject *solution* is singular and the verb *are* is plural.
   Choices B and C are wrong because they contain dangling modifiers. In each sentence *Thinking it over* lacks an appropriate noun or pronoun to modify.
   Choice D contains a singular subject and verb and is grammatically correct. It is the best answer.
   Choice E has the same problem as choice A.

2. In some of the big state universities the problem <u>of giving scholarships and other rewards to good athletes have gotten out of hand</u>.

   (A) of giving scholarships and other rewards to good athletes have gotten out of hand
   (B) of giving scholarships and granting rewards for good athletic ability have gotten out of hand
   (C) of scholarships and other rewards for good athletes has gotten out of hand
   (D) has become out of hand when scholarships and rewards for good athletes
   (E) of rewarding good athletes with scholarships are out of hand

   Choice A is wrong because it uses a plural verb, *have*, that fails to agree with the singular subject, *problem*.
   Choice B is a variation of A.
   Choice C contains a verb that agrees in number with the subject. It is the best answer.
   Choice D is an incomplete construction.
   Choice E is wrong because it uses a plural verb, *are*, that doesn't agree in number with the singular subject, *problem*.

Practice in Establishing Noun–Verb Agreement

<u>Directions</u>: In some of the following sentences, nouns and verbs do not agree. Locate the error and write the corrected version in the space provided. Some sentences may be correct.

1. Tucker's talent in chess and weight lifting, two of our school's most popular teams, prove his mental and physical strength.

   _____
   _____

2. The book told stories of thirteen young heroes, each a member of a firefighting team, who dies fighting forest fires.

   _____
   _____

3. At the end of the season, the team, regardless of whether they win the championship, are splitting up.

   _____
   _____

4. Either Don or you is going to lead the class discussion on Tuesday.

   _____
   _____

5. Jane and Mark, who began their yard cleanup business last spring, have decided to hire two new helpers.

   _____
   _____

6. There is many levels on which a reader will be able to enjoy this book.

   _____
   _____

7. Admission proceeds from the concert is going toward rebuilding the gazebo, burned down by vandals during the summer.

_____

_____

8. The newspaper reports that a rescue team experienced in climbing rugged mountains are expected to arrive at the site of the crash tomorrow morning.

_____

_____

9. Before they were laid off by the company, neither the assistant managers nor Mr. McCallum were told that their jobs were in danger.

_____

_____

10. Many Democratic senators contend that reforms in the tax system has not brought about the economic growth that had been predicted.

_____

_____

11. Learning to read the daily box scores printed in the newspaper is a desirable thing to do by any fan who expect to develop a deep understanding of baseball.

_____

_____

12. Politics on both the national and local level have always been one of Dave's passions.

_____

_____

13. Charles Darwin, along with his contemporary, Abraham Lincoln, are among the most impressive figures in nineteenth-century history.

_____

_____

14. Katie Green, one of the hottest jazz pianists in town and known for something she calls "3-D playing," and her accompanist Lenny is planning to tour the South in May.

_____

_____

15. Nancy, along with her friend Sluggo, appear to be coming down the escalator.

_____

_____

16. The sale of computers in a market that has nearly a billion potential customers have created enormous hope for the company's future.

_____

_____

17. Here's the two statutes to which the defense lawyer referred during the trial.

_____

_____

18. The commissioner's insistence on high ethical standards are transforming the city's police force.

_____

_____

19. No one in the drum corps, in spite of how they all feel about the issue, want to participate in the rally.

_____

_____

20. According to school policy, there is to be two security guards stationed in the playground during recess to protect the children.

_____

_____

Answers are on page 196.

Faulty Verb Forms

Verb tenses convey information about when an action occurs. To express past action, add –*ed* to the present form: *walk/walked, cry/cried, type/typed.* To express future action, add *will* before the present tense: *will walk, will cry, will type.* For present perfect, past perfect, and future perfect forms, add *have, has, had,* or *will have,* as in *have walked, has cried, had typed,* and *will have arrived.*

A problem arises, however, with irregular verbs—those verbs that don't follow the usual pattern. The verb *to choose,* for example, is *choose* in the present, *chose* in the past, and *chosen* in its participle, or "perfect" form. Sentence errors occur when the wrong form is used.

Another error—usually a sentence fragment—occurs when a writer tries to use an *-ing* form of a verb as a sentence's main verb, as in:

> Julie, at the box office, *selling* movie tickets to the 7:00 show.

The problem is that the *–ing* form cannot be used as the main verb unless accompanied by a helping verb, as in:

> Julie, at the box office, *has been selling* movie tickets to the 7:00 show.

The addition of the helping verb *has been* corrects the error. Other helping verbs include *is, was, will be,* and other forms of the verb *to be.*

Sample Questions Containing Faulty Verb Forms

1. In spite of the cold and discomfort of making the journey, Max was glad <u>to have underwent the experience of seeing</u> the northern lights.

   (A) to have underwent the experience of seeing
   (B) having underwent the experience of seeing
   (C) to have undergone the experience of seeing
   (D) to see during the experience of
   (E) undergoing the experience of seeing

Choice A is wrong because it uses *have underwent,* a nonstandard form of the verb *to undergo.* Use *have undergone* instead.
Choice B is a variation of choice A.
Choice C uses the verb in its proper form. It is the best answer.
Choice D uses faulty idiom and makes little sense.
Choice E improperly uses an *–ing* form of a verb without a helping verb.

2. Brian Williams, the TV anchor man, <u>skillfully probing his guest's knowledge of the scandal, but showing</u> great tact because he didn't want to jeopardize his chance for a news scoop.

   (A) skillfully probing his guest's knowledge of the scandal, but showing
   (B) who skillfully probed his guest's knowledge of the scandal, but showing
   (C) skillfully probed his guest's knowledge of the scandal, showed
   (D) he was skilled in probing his guest's knowledge of the scandal, and showed
   (E) skillfully probing his guest's knowledge of the scandal, showed

Choices A and B are sentence fragments. Neither has a main verb.
Choice C is an incomplete construction. It lacks a conjunction before the verb *showed.*
Choice D is a mixed construction. The construction *he was skilled* lacks a grammatical relationship to the earlier part of the sentence.
Choice E is free of grammatical errors. It is the best answer.

Still other errors involving verbs occur when the writer uses the wrong tense. For details and a practice exercise, turn to page 180.

For more details and a practice exercise in verb forms, turn to page 181.

Use of Pronouns

A dozen common English pronouns—*I, me, he, she, him, her, it, they, them, we, us,* and *you*—cause more trouble than almost any other words in the language. Almost as troublesome—but not quite—are the possessive pronouns *my, mine, his, her, hers, your, yours, our, ours, their,* and *theirs*.

Faulty usage results most often:

- When pronouns in the wrong "case" are chosen
- When pronouns in the wrong "person" are chosen
- When pronouns fail to agree in number or gender with their antecedents
- When the pronoun reference is unclear or ambiguous

Faulty Pronoun Case

Most of the time you can probably depend on your ear to tell you what's right and wrong. For example, you'd never say to the bus driver, "Let *I* off at the corner." But when you can't depend on the sound of the words, it helps to know that those twelve pronouns fall into two groups.

Group 1	Group 2
I	me
he	him
she	her
it	it
they	them
we	us
you	you

In grammatical terms, the pronouns in Group 1 are in the **nominative case**; pronouns in Group 2 are in the **objective case**.

Remember that you mustn't mix pronouns from different cases in the same phrase. You may not, for example, use such pairs as *she and them* or *they and us*. Any time you need a pair of pronouns and you know that one of them is correct, you can easily pick the other from the same group. If you're not sure of either pronoun, though, substitute *I* or *me* for one of the pronouns. If *I* seems to fit, you're in Group 1; if *me* fits better, use Group 2.

Elvis asked that (he, him) and (she, her) practice handstands.

If you insert *me* in place of one of the pronouns, you'll get:

Elvis asked that *me* practice handstands.

Because no one would say that seriously, *I* must be the word that fits. So the pronouns you need come from Group 1, and the sentence should read:

Elvis asked that *he* and *she* practice handstands.

Now, if you can observe a few more rules, you'll be well prepared to deal with pronoun errors on the SAT.

1. Use nominative case pronouns for the subject of sentences and for predicate nominatives.

   Then he and I went home. (*he and I* = subject)
   The instructors in the course were Donald and he. (*instructors* = subject; *Donald and he* = predicate nominative)

   The term *predicate nominative* refers to words not in the subject of the sentence that identify, define, or mean the same as the subject.

2. Use objective case pronouns in phrases that begin with prepositions, as in:

   <u>between</u> *you* and *me*
   <u>to</u> Sherry and *her*
   <u>among</u> *us* women
   <u>at</u> *us*
   <u>from</u> *her* and *him*
   <u>with</u> *me* and *you*

3. Use objective case pronouns when the pronoun refers to a person to whom something is being done:

   Terry invited *him* to the prom.
   The waiter gave *her* and *me* a piece of cake.

4. To find the correct pronoun in a comparison, complete the comparison using the verb that would follow naturally:

   Jackie runs faster than *she* (runs).

   My brother has bigger feet than *I* (do).

   Carol is as tough as *he* (is).

   A woman such as *I* (am) could solve the problem.

5. When a pronoun appears side by side with a noun (*we* boys, *us* women), deleting the noun will help you pick the correct pronoun:

   (*We, Us*) seniors decided to take a day off from school in late May. (Deleting *seniors* leaves <u>*We decided to*</u> . . .).

   This award was presented to (*we, us*) students by the faculty. (Deleting *students* leaves *award was presented to <u>us</u> by the* . . .).

6. Use possessive pronouns (*my, our, your, his, her, their*) before a *gerund*, a noun that looks like a verb because of its –*ing* ending.

   Her asking the question shows that she is alert. (*Asking* is a gerund.)

   Mother was upset about *your* opening the presents too soon. (*Opening* is a gerund.)

What Is a Gerund?

A gerund is a verb form that ends in –*ing* and is used as a noun.

   Fishing is my grandpa's favorite pastime.

   He started *fishing* as a boy in North Carolina.

   As a result of all that *fishing*, he hates to eat fish.

In all three sentences the gerund is derived from the verb *to fish*. Don't confuse gerunds with the participle form of verbs, as in:

   Participle: *Fishing* from the bank of the river, my Grandpa caught a catfish.

   Gerund: *Fishing* from the bank of a river is my Grandpa's greatest pleasure.

Not every noun with an –*ing* ending is a gerund. Sometimes it's just a noun, as in *thing, ring, spring*. At other times, -*ing* words are verbs, in particular, they're participles that modify pronouns in the objective case.

   I hope you don't mind *my* intruding on your conversation. (Here *intruding* is a gerund.)

   I hope you don't mind *me* intruding on your conversation. (Here *intruding* is a participle.)

Sample Question Containing Faulty Pronoun Choice (Case)

The registration fee in New York is higher <u>than the amount paid by Rosemary and I</u> in Vermont.

  (A) than the amount paid by Rosemary and I

  (B) in comparison to the fee paid by Rosemary and I

  (C) than that which Rosemary and me pay

  (D) than the fee Rosemary and me paid

  (E) than the one Rosemary and I paid

Choices A and B are incorrect because each contains a phrase beginning with the preposition *by*, which calls for pronouns in the objective case. Use *me* instead of *I*.

Choice C and D call for pronouns in the nominative case. Use *I* instead of *me*.

Choice E uses the proper pronoun. It is the best answer.

Practice in Choosing the Case of Pronouns

<u>Directions</u>: Circle the correct pronoun in each of the following sentences.

1. Judith took my sister and (I, me) to the magic show last night.
2. We thought that Matilda and Jorge would be there, and sure enough, we saw (she, her) and (he, him) sitting in the front row.
3. During the intermission, Jorge came over and asked my sister and (I, me) to go out after the show.
4. Between you and (I, me) the magician was terrible.
5. It must also have been a bad evening for (he, him) and his assistant, Roxanne.
6. Trying to pull a rabbit out of a hat, Roxanne and (he, him) knocked over the table.
7. When he asked for audience participation, my sister and (I, me) volunteered to go on stage.

8. He said that in my pocket I would find $10 in change to split between (I, me) and my sister.
9. When the coins fell out of his sleeve, the audience laughed even harder than (we, us).
10. If I were (he, him), I'd practice for a long time before the next performance.

Answers are on page 196.

Shift in Pronoun Person

Pronouns are categorized by person:

> First-person pronouns: *I, we, me, us, mine, our, ours*
> Second-person pronouns: *you, your, yours*
> Third-person pronouns: *she, he, it, one, they, him, her, them, his, hers, its, their, theirs, ours*

Indefinite pronouns such as *all, any, anyone, each, none, nothing, one, several,* and *many* are also considered to be in the third person.

Pronouns must be in the same person as their **antecedents**—the words they refer to. When a sentence is cast in, say, the first person, it should stay in the first person throughout. Consistency is the key.

Inconsistent: When you (second person) walk your (second person) dog in that park, I (first person) must carry a pooper-scooper.

Consistent: When you (second person) walk your (second person) dog in that park, you (second person) must carry a pooper-scooper.

The need to be consistent applies also to the use of indefinite pronouns, particularly when a writer switches from singular to plural pronouns in mid-sentence:

Inconsistent: If *someone* tries to write a persuasive essay, *they* should at least include a convincing argument.

Consistent: If *one* tries to write a persuasive essay, *one* should at least include a convincing argument.

Sample Questions Containing Switch in Pronoun Person

<u>The more you travel around the country</u>, the more our horizons and outlook expand.

   (A) The more you travel around the country
   (B) The more we travel around the country
   (C) The more one travels around the country
   (D) As more traveling is done around the country
   (E) As they travel more around the country

Choice A is incorrect because the second-pronoun *you* shifts to the first-person pronoun *our* in the second clause.

Choice B consistently uses two plural pronouns in the first person. It is the best answer.

Choice C switches from the singular pronoun *one* to the plural pronoun *our* in the second clause.

Choice D uses the pronoun *our* that fails to refer to a specific noun or other pronoun.

Choice E improperly uses the first-person pronoun *our* to refer to the third-person pronoun *they*.

Pronoun–Antecedent Agreement

Singular pronouns must have singular antecedents; plural pronouns, plural antecedents. Errors occur when antecedents are indefinite, as in *each, neither, everyone* (also *no one, someone, anyone*), and *everybody* (also *nobody, somebody,* and *anybody*). Note the problem of pronoun-antecedent agreement in these sentences:

> Everybody is sticking to *their* side of the story.
> Anybody can pass this course if *they* study hard.
> Neither teacher plans to change *their* policy regarding late papers.

Properly stated, the sentences should read:

> Everybody is sticking to *his* side of the story.
> Anybody can pass this course if *she* studies hard.
> Neither teacher plans to change *his* policy regarding late papers.

Some people, objecting to the use of specific gender pronouns, prefer the cumbersome and tacky phrase "he or she," but most good writers avoid using it.

Still other words may sound singular but are plural in certain contexts:

The jury will render *its* verdict tomorrow.
The jury will return to *their* homes tomorrow.

The senior class posed for *its* picture.
The senior class had *their* portraits taken for the yearbook.

Sample Question Containing Faulty Pronoun–Antecedent Agreement

The Army, which paid soldiers large bonuses to re-enlist when their tours of duty were over, <u>changed this policy beginning when their budget was cut</u>.

(A) changed this policy beginning when their budget was cut
(B) begins to change this policy when their budget was cut
(C) began to change this policy when its budget was cut
(D) it changed this policy when their budget was cut
(E) beginning to change its policy, the budget was cut

Choice A is wrong because it uses the plural pronoun *their* to refer to the singular noun *Army*.

Choice B contains a shift in verb tense from past to present.

Choice C uses the singular pronoun *it* to refer to the singular noun *Army*. It is the best answer.

Choice D contains a comma splice.

Choice E contains two parts that lack both a grammatical and a logical relation to each other.

Practice in Recognizing Pronoun Shift and Pronoun Agreement

<u>Directions</u>: Some of the following sentences contain shifts in pronoun person or errors in agreement between pronouns and antecedents. Make all appropriate corrections in the spaces provided. Alter only those sentences that contain errors.

1. The English teacher announced that everyone in the class must turn in their term papers no later than Friday.

_____

_____

2. When you are fired from a job, a person collects unemployment.

_____

_____

3. The library put their collection of rare books on display.

_____

_____

4. Each of my sisters own their own car.

_____

_____

5. In that class, our teacher held conferences with us once a week.

_____

_____

6. In order to keep yourself in shape, one should work out every day.

_____

_____

7. The teacher dictates a sentence in French, and each of the students write it down in English and hand it in.

_____

_____

8. Each horse in the procession followed their riders down to the creek.

_____

_____

9. The school's chess team has just won their first match.

_____

_____

10. When one is visiting the park and you can't find a rest room, they should ask a park ranger.

_____

_____

Answers are on page 196.

Faulty Pronoun Reference

Sentences in which a pronoun fails to refer specifically to a noun or another pronoun, called an *antecedent*, can cause confusion or fail to convey the writer's intention. Some references are ambiguous because the pronoun seems to refer to one or more antecedents:

> The teacher, Ms. Taylor, told Karen that it was *her* responsibility to hand out composition paper.

Who is responsible? The teacher or Karen? It's impossible to tell because the pronoun *her* may refer to either of them. Revised, the sentence might read:

> Ms. Taylor told Karen that it was *her* responsibility as the teacher to hand out composition paper.

A sentence containing two or more pronouns with ambiguous references can be especially troublesome and unclear:

> Mike became a good friend of Mark's after *he* helped *him* repair *his* car.

Whose car needed fixing? Who helped whom? To answer these questions, the sentence needs to be rewritten:

> Mike and Mark became good friends after Mark helped Mike repair *his* car.

This version is better, but it's still uncertain who owned the car. One way to set the meaning straight is to use more than one sentence:

> When Mark needed to repair his car, Mike helped him do the job. Afterwards, Mike and Mark became good friends.

To be correct, a pronoun should refer directly and clearly to a specific noun or another pronoun, or it should refer by implication to an idea. Such implied references frequently involve the pronouns *it*, *they*, and *you*, and the relative pronouns *which*, *that*, and *this*, and cause trouble mostly when the pronoun is used to refer to rather general or ambiguous ideas, as in:

> Homeless people allege that the mayor is indifferent to their plight, *which* has been disproved.

What has been disproved? That an allegation was made? That the mayor is indifferent? The intended meaning is unclear because *which* has no distinct antecedent. To clear up the uncertainty, the sentence might read:

> Homeless people allege that the mayor is indifferent to their plight, but the allegation has been disproved.

Sample Question Containing an Ambiguous Pronoun Reference

Ricky, Marti, and Steve were driving non-stop from New York to Chicago <u>when, falling asleep at the wheel, he drove the car off the road</u>.

(A) when, falling asleep at the wheel, he drove the car off the road

(B) and then he drove the car off the road after falling asleep at the wheel

(C) when Ricky drove the car off the road after falling asleep at the wheel

(D) when Ricky drove the car off the road, since he fell asleep at the wheel

(E) and, since Ricky has fallen asleep at the wheel, he drove the car off the road

Choices A and B are incorrect because in each sentence the pronoun *he* fails to refer to a specific noun or other pronoun.

Choice C avoids the pronoun-reference problem by using the *Ricky* instead of *he*. It is the best answer.

Choice D contains an error in verb tense. Because Ricky had fallen asleep before he drove the car off the road, use *had fallen* instead of *fell*.

Choice E, a compound sentence, would be more effectively expressed with one independent clause and two subordinate clauses.

Practice in Identifying Faulty Pronoun Reference

Directions: Each of the following sentences suffers from a pronoun problem. Please eliminate the problem by revising each sentence. Use the blank spaces to write your answers.

1. When we teenagers loiter outside the theater on Friday night, they give you a hard time.

_____

_____

2. I answered the test questions, collected my pencils and pens, and handed them in.

_____

_____

3. Barbara told Ken that she wanted only a short wedding trip to Florida, which lies at the root of their problem.

_____

_____

4. His father let him know that he had only an hour to get to the airport.

_____

_____

5. During Dr. Rice's tenure in office, she traveled more than any other secretary of state.

_____

_____

6. Henry, an ambulance driver, disapproved of war but drove it to the front lines anyway.

_____

_____

7. After the campus tour, Mike told Todd that he thought he'd be happy going to Auburn.

_____

_____

8. Peggy's car hit a truck, but it wasn't even dented.

_____

_____

9. Within the last month, Andy's older brother Pete found a new job, broke his leg skiing, and got married to Felicia, which made their parents very happy.

_____

_____

10. Eddie grew fond of the novels of John Steinbeck because he had lived in California.

_____

_____

Answers are on page 196.

Faulty Comparisons

The sentence-improvement questions on the SAT will almost certainly test your understanding of the rules governing the use of comparisons. In addition to knowing about comparative degrees, you need to know that comparisons (1) need to be complete, (2) must be stated in parallel form, and (3) must pertain to things that may logically be compared.

Most comparisons are made by using different forms of adjectives or adverbs. The degree of comparison is indicated by the ending (usually *–er* and *–est*) or by the use of *more* or *most* (or *less* and *least*). The English language offers three degrees of comparison, called *positive*, *comparative*, and *superlative.*

Positive	Comparative	Superlative
tall	taller	tallest
dark	darker	darkest
handsome	handsomer *or* more handsome	handsomest *or* most handsome
graceful	more graceful	most graceful
prepared	less prepared	least prepared
happily	morc happily	most happily

Some words deviate from the usual pattern. For example:

good	better	best
well	better	best
bad	worse	worst
little	less	least
much	more	most
many	more	most

Use the following guidelines to hunt down errors in comparative degree:

1. To form the comparative and superlative degree of one-syllable words, add *–er* or *–est* to the positive form (*brave, braver, bravest; late, later, latest*).
2. To form the comparative and superlative degrees of most two-syllable words, use *more* or *most*, or *less* and *least* (*more famous, most nauseous, less skillful, least jagged*). Some two-syllable words follow the guidelines for words of one syllable (*pretty, prettier, prettiest*), although you wouldn't err by applying the rule for two-syllable words (*more pretty, most pretty*).

3. To form the comparative and superlative degree of three-syllable words and of all words ending in *–ly*, use *more* and *most*, or *less* and *least* (*beautiful, more beautiful, most beautiful; gladly, more gladly, most gladly*).
4. To compare two things use the comparative degree, but to compare three or more things use the superlative degree.

   My *younger* sister takes dancing lessons. (The writer has two sisters.)

   My *youngest* sister takes swimming lessons. (The writer has at least three sisters.)

5. Never create a double comparison by putting words like *more, most, less,* and *least* in the same phrase with words in the comparative or superlative degrees. For example, avoid *more friendlier, less prouder, most sweetest, least safest.* Such usages are both ungrammatical and redundant. Instead, use adjectives and adverbs in the positive degree: *more friendly, less proud, more sweet, least safe.*

Incomplete Comparisons

In everyday speech, people give emphasis to their opinions by saying things like "We had the best time" and "That was the worst accident!" Neither statement is complete, however, because technically the "best" time must be compared to other times, and the "worst" accident must be compared to other accidents.

An incomplete comparison made colloquially may suffer no loss of meaning, but standard written usage calls for unmistakable clarity. On the SAT you may find sentences that lack all the words needed to make a comparison clear:

Mimi visited her aged aunt longer than Kathy.

This could mean either that Mimi spent a longer time with her aunt than Kathy did, or that Mimi spent more time with her aunt than she spent with Kathy. To eliminate the ambiguity, simply complete the comparison:

Mimi visited her aged aunt longer than she visited Kathy.

A comparison using *as* usually requires a repetition of the word: as good *as* gold, as fast *as* a speeding bullet, as high *as* a kite.

Incomplete: On the exam, Nicole expects to do as well if not better than Nat.

Complete: On the exam, Nicole expects to do as well *as*, if not better than, Nat.

For the sake of completeness, when you compare one thing to a group of which it is a part, be sure to use *other* or *else*.

Lieutenant Henry was braver than any pilot in the squadron.

This suggests that Henry may not have been a member of the squadron. If he belonged to the squadron, however, add *other* to complete the comparison:

Lieutenant Henry was braver than any *other* pilot in the squadron.

Similarly, notice the difference between these two sentences:

Diana talks more nonsense than anyone in the class.

Diana talks more nonsense than anyone *else* in the class.

Only the second sentence makes clear that Diana is a member of the class.

Illogical Comparisons

Logic breaks down when two or more unlike things are compared.

Boston's harbor is reported to be more polluted than any city in the country.

This sentence is meant to compare pollution in the Boston harbor with pollution in the harbors of other cities. Instead, it compares Boston's harbor with a city, an illogical comparison. Properly expressed, it would read this way:

Boston's harbor is reported to be more polluted than the harbor of any other city in the country.

Similarly, note the difference between these two sentences.

Unlike most cars on the block, Ellie has her Toyota washed almost every week.

Ellie's Toyota, unlike most cars on the block, is washed almost every week.

The first sentence is intended to compare Ellie's car with the other cars on the block. But it nonsensically compares Ellie to the other cars.

Sample Questions Containing Faulty Comparisons

1. A more easier and direct route exist between Mt. Kisco and Pleasantville than the one we took.

   (A) A more easier and direct route exist
   (B) An easier and direct route exist
   (C) An easier and more direct route exists
   (D) Easier and directer routes exist
   (E) A both more easy and a more direct route exists

Choice A contains the phrase *more easier*, which is both a redundancy and an example of faulty diction.

Choice B contains an error in parallelism. *Easier*, an adjective in the comparative degree, is not parallel in form to *direct*. Use *more direct*.

Choice C accurately and grammatically conveys the meaning of the sentence. It is the best answer.

Choice D uses *directer*, not a standard English word, instead of *more direct*.

Choice E is wordy. *Both* and the repetition of *more* are unnecessary.

2. Elton John combines various techniques of singing and piano playing as effortlessly as any pop star ever has.

   (A) as effortlessly as any pop star ever has
   (B) as effortlessly as any other pop star ever has
   (C) effortlessly, as any pop star has
   (D) as effortlessly like any other pop star ever has
   (E) as effortlessly, if not more so, than any pop star ever has

Choice A is incorrect because it omits *other*, a word that must be used when comparing one thing with a group of which it is a member. Use *as any other*.

Choice B expresses the comparison correctly. It is the best answer.

Choice C uses awkward language that obscures the meaning of the sentence.

Choice D uses *like* instead of *as*. Use *like*, a preposition, to introduce a phrase; use *as* to introduce a clause.

Choice E fails to complete the comparison because it omits the second *as*. Use *as effortlessly as*.

For details and a practice exercise in parallelism, turn to page 89.

A Review

While looking for errors in sentence-improvement questions, use this checklist as a guide.

- **Verbs**. Check the tense (*page 156*), agreement with the subject (*page 152*), and parallelism (*page 146*).

- **Nouns**. Check the number (*page 152*), agreement with the verb (*page 152*), parallelism (*page 146*), and word choice (*page 138*).
- **Pronouns**. Check the case (*page 158*), number (*page 159*), agreement with antecedent (*page 159*), reference to a noun or another pronoun (*page 162*), agreement with verb (*page 154*), and parallel structure (*page 146*).
- **Adjectives.** Check the modification (*page 151*) and comparative degree (*page 163*).
- **Adverbs.** Check modification of verbs (*page 151*).
- **Phrases.** Check parallel structure (*page 146*) and sentence structure (*page 139*).
- **Clauses**. Check completeness (*page 139*), subordination and coordination (*pages 144, 145*).
- **Participles.** Check modification (*page 87*).
- **Punctuation**. Check use of commas and semicolons (*page 102*). Also sentence structure (*page 139*), including run-ons (*page 141*), fragments (*page 139*), and comma splices (*page 142*).

IDENTIFYING SENTENCE ERRORS

In this section of the SAT, you are given eighteen sentences, most of which contain an error in grammar, usage, or style. Your job is to identify which underlined portion of each sentence contains the error. Some sentences have no error.

Sample Question

<u>After reading</u> the two stories, the class <u>decided</u>
        A   B
that <u>the second one</u> was the <u>best</u>. <u>No error</u>.
            C   D   E

The sentence contains an error in comparison. When you compare two things, use words in the *comparative* degree, such as *better, lighter,* and *more able*. But when you compare more than two things, use words in the *superlative* degree, such as

best, lightest, and *most able*. In the sentence, two stories are being compared. Therefore use *better* instead of *best*. Choice D is the right answer.

Although Identifying Sentence Errors questions are shorter and less involved than those in the sentence-improvement sections of the exam, they deal with a wide range of grammar and usage problems.

The sentence errors you are most likely to meet in this section of the SAT are:

Errors in Expression and Style
    Faulty idiom, page 166
    Faulty diction, page 168
    Wordiness and redundancies, page 171
    Faulty parallelism, page 173
    Incomplete comparisons, page 174

Errors in Grammar and Usage
  Noun–verb agreement, page 176
  Pronoun–antecedent agreement, page 176
  Faulty pronoun reference, page 178
  Shift in pronoun person, page 179
  Faulty pronoun choice, page 179
  Faulty verb tense, page 180
  Faulty verb form, page 181

ERRORS IN EXPRESSION AND STYLE

Faulty Idiom

English is crammed with words, expressions, and phrases whose usage cannot be rationally explained. We say "three-foot ruler" when we mean "three-feet." A building "burns *down*," a piece of paper "burns *up*," and a pot of stew just "*burns*." Both *flammable* and *inflammable* mean the same thing—easily set afire. When you don't understand something, you might say it's "*over my head*," an expression that also means deep in debt. We accept these and many other linguistic quirks because they are simply part of our language. Likewise, native speakers of English say *go to the movies* and *arrive at the movies*. For someone just learning English, though, "arrive *to* the movies" would make perfect sense. But we don't say it because it's not idiomatic English.

On the SAT, you may find sentences containing faulty idiom. To identify errors in idiom you must, to a certain extent, follow your instincts and your ear for language. There are no specific guidelines to help untangle problems in idiom. An awkward-sounding word or phrase may be the only evidence.

The First Amendment is invoked *in those times* when journalists are asked to disclose their sources.

The phrase *in those times* is awkward. Replace *in* with *at*, a preposition that often refers to time—*at* four o'clock, *at* the turn of the century. Or better still, discard the phrase entirely:

The First Amendment is invoked when journalists are asked to disclose their sources.

Here is another example:

A knight was faithful to his king, to his church, and to his lady, and he would gladly die in the name of them.

The phrase *in the name of them* is grammatical but awkward.

A knight was faithful to his king, to his church, and to his lady, and he would gladly die in their name.

Although many errors in English idiom on the SAT involve the faulty use of prepositions, you're just as likely to find problematic verbs, adverbs, and other parts of speech.

Sample Questions Containing Faulty Idiom

1. <u>In appreciation</u> <u>about</u> her dedicated service to
        A   B
    the Safe Rides program, the local Lion's Club

    presented <u>her</u> with a scholarship <u>at graduation</u>.
                C   D
    <u>No error</u>.
      E

In standard English, the phrase *In appreciation about* should read *In appreciation for*. Choice B is the correct answer.

2. Mr. Andrews, the store manager, <u>feels</u> grateful
                                        A
    <u>that</u> every weekend this summer Phil and
      B
    George are ready <u>for working</u> at <u>a moment's</u>
                        C   D
    notice. <u>No error</u>.
              E

Faulty idiom results from the misuse of a verb. Instead of *for working*, use *to work*. Choice C is the correct answer.

3. <u>Speaking as</u> a member of the scholarly
        A

   panel, Dr. Muller <u>told</u> a story <u>filled up</u> with
                    B   C

   <u>allusions to</u> Norse mythology. <u>No error</u>.
   D   E

Faulty idiom results from the use of *up*, an unnecessary preposition. Use *filled* instead of *filled up*. Choice C is the correct answer.

Practice in Identifying Faulty English Idiom

<u>Directions</u>: Identify the errors in English idiom in the following sentences. Write revised versions in the spaces provided. Some sentences may contain no error.

1. It was an honor to die at battle for their religion.

2. After the ceremony, the newlyweds ascended up the stairs.

3. I hope that the admissions office will comply to my request for an extension.

4. Bronze was used by primitive people before either iron and tin.

5. Because of his preoccupation in classical music, Justin bought a subscription to Symphony Hall concerts.

6. Most rock climbers are lured by either danger and love of adventure.

7. When Lucy returned home, she felt as though she'd never been away.

8. The posse went in pursuit after the horse thieves.

9. The new security system uses electronic eye scans in the identifying of employees.

10. Work-study programs offer opportunities to both students and the business community.

11. No new plans were developed in respect to the environment.

12. Columbus sailed west in search for a way to the Indies.

13. The wounded marine could not endure that kind of a pain without passing out.

_____

_____

14. The children were waiting on the bus to arrive.

_____

_____

15. Generic drugs are not nearly as expensive than brand-name drugs.

_____

_____

16. Billy Collins is regarded to be one of the most popular contemporary American poets.

_____

_____

17. Artists must often make a choice between teaching or devoting their time to creating art.

_____

_____

18. Most people who travel at Thanksgiving prefer driving more than flying.

_____

_____

19. Because the boat's engine had failed, the sailor was never far away from harm during the storm.

_____

_____

20. Although Jackie's term paper was neither well written or fully researched, its grade was A+.

_____

_____

Answers are on page 196.

Faulty Diction

Faulty diction means faulty word choice. It occurs, say, when _good_ is used instead of _well_ after a certain verb, or when _where_ is used instead of _when_, as in "the time _where_ he took the bus to Jersey." The English language offers abundant opportunities to choose incorrect words, but on the SAT the range is limited to commonly misused words. For instance, use _who_ instead of _which_ when referring to people:

> Brian was one of several journalists _who_ were killed during the war in Iraq.

Use _which_ when referring to animals and nonliving things, as in:

> Foul language was bleeped out of the film's TV version, _which_ disturbed free-speech advocates.

That may be used to refer to people as well as to animals and nonliving things:

> Pedestrians _that_ jaywalk put their lives at risk.
> _Saving Private Ryan_ is the name of the film _that_ caused a great deal of controversy when it was shown on network television.

Sometimes, the choice of words is a toss-up. It's fine to say "Those are the geese _who_ are damaging the grass," but it's also acceptable to say "Those are the geese _that_ are damaging the grass." Because both usages are standard, the SAT won't ask you to make decisions about issues like that.

Sample Questions Containing Faulty Diction

1. Although <u>best known</u> for being a crooner
           A
   of old songs, Tony Bennett <u>also paints</u>
                              B
   watercolors, <u>whereas</u> <u>he has</u> enjoyed
                    C   D
   considerable success. <u>No error</u>.
                              E

The word *whereas*, meaning "although" or "considering that" is improperly used in the context. Because the writer probably meant to say *with which* or perhaps *whereby*, C is the correct answer.

2. Schoolteachers <u>which need</u> to keep themselves
                    A
   up-to-date <u>on</u> educational technology
              B
   <u>are being</u> encouraged <u>to attend</u> in-service
      C   D
   courses and workshops. <u>No error</u>.
                              E

The writer has improperly used *which* instead of *who* to refer to schoolteachers. Although some may regard schoolteachers as something other than human, on the SAT they should be considered people. Choice A is the correct answer.

3. A "fault" in tennis <u>is when</u> the ball <u>being served</u>
                          A   B
   to the opposing player lands outside the lines

   <u>that mark</u> the <u>boundary</u> of the service box.
      C   C
   <u>No error</u>.
      D

The construction *is when* is an error in diction because you can't define a noun with a clause but only with another noun. In standard English, the sentence might read something like "A 'fault' in tennis is a stroke that falls outside . . . ."

Another common error in diction occurs when an adjective is used where an adverb is needed. The reverse—using an adverb where an adjective belongs—also occurs, but less often. Part of your preparation for the SAT should include practice in using adjectives and adverbs properly.

To begin, identify the errors in these two sentences:

Children addicted to television often behave violent in the classroom.
I feel badly that Randy performed bad on the test.

If you spotted the errors, you should have no trouble with similar items on the SAT. And if you knew why *violent* should be *violently* and that *bad* and *badly* should switch places, you're probably up to par on adjective and adverb usage. But if you didn't notice or couldn't explain the errors, please read on.

Adjectives are words that describe, or modify, nouns and pronouns. *Good* is an example, as in *good* apple, *good* book, and *good* night. That's easy enough, but *good*, along with some other adjectives, sometimes causes trouble when used after a verb. *Good* should not be used after most verbs, so avoid *talks good, drives good, writes good*, and so on.

Here's the catch: *Good* may be used after some verbs, called linking verbs, among them *look, smell, taste, feel, appear, stay, seem, remain, grow, become*, and all forms of *to be*. Therefore, it's correct to say *sounds good, feels good*, and *is good*. (Notice that linking verbs often refer to the senses.)

And to complicate matters still more, linking verbs are sometimes used as active verbs. *Look* is a linking verb when it refers to the appearance of things, as in *The day looks good for jogging*. But it is an active verb when it refers to the act of looking, as in *Margie looked sadly at her sick dog*. If you're not sure whether a verb is used as a linking verb or as an active verb, substitute a form of the verb *to be*. If the sentence retains its basic meaning, the verb is probably a linking verb, as in *The juice tastes good/The juice is good*. If the meaning is lost, it is an active verb, as in *He feels badly about your loss*. Because you wouldn't say *He <u>is</u> badly about your loss, feels* is an active verb in that sentence.

Adverbs are words that describe, or modify, verbs, adjectives, or other adverbs, and can often be identified by their –*ly* endings. Most of the time they answer such questions as How? When? How much? Where? In what sequence? To what extent? In what manner? For example:

> How does the grass look? It looks *mostly* brown. (The adverb *mostly* modifies the adjective *brown*.)
>
> When does Roger run? He *usually* runs in the morning. (The adverb *usually* modifies the verb *runs*.)
>
> How much did it rain? It rained *enough* to flood the cellar. (The adverb *enough* modifies the verb *rained*.)

When you need to choose between an adjective and an adverb on the SAT, follow this procedure: Find the verb and determine whether it is a linking verb. If it is, use the adjective; if it isn't, use the adverb. More often than not, the verb is likely to be one of those that is sometimes active and sometimes linking. So, check it by substituting a form of *to be*, as described earlier. You can also check its modification. If it modifies an adjective or another adverb, use the adverb. If it modifies a noun or pronoun, use the adjective. If all this seems unduly complex, you'll catch on if you re-read this material two or three times and do the following practice exercise.

Sample Questions Regarding Adjective/Adverb Use

1. Alan, our trusty mechanic, studied

   the overheated engine careful and with
         A   B
   patience before declaring that he hadn't
                      C   D
   a clue what to do about it. No error.
                                     E

The word *careful* is an adjective. In the context of the sentence, it modifies the verb *studied*. Therefore, it should be *carefully*, an adverb. Choice B is the correct answer.

2. Results of the survey show a frightening pattern
    A   B   C
   of constant melting glaciers in the northern part
       D
   of Canada and the Arctic. No error.
                               E

The word *constant* is an adjective. Because it is used to modify the adjective *melting*, it should be an adverb—*constantly*. Choice D is the correct answer.

Practice in Using Adjectives and Adverbs

<u>Directions</u>: Check each sentence for faulty use of adjectives and adverbs. Write the correct words in the spaces provided. Some sentences are correct.

1. The nurse felt bitterly that she had contracted the flu from a patient.

   _____

2. There is simply no justification for the judge's ruling.

   _____

3. Meredith's bike is old, but it rides smooth.

   _____

4. In spite of her head cold, the soprano sang the aria beautiful.

   _____

5. The tenor's singing could only be described as horribly.

   _____

6. The black Mercedes drove slow up the gravel driveway.

   _____

7. Castro looked down cynical on the people assembled in the plaza.

   _____

8. Agnes played the part of the mother superficially.

   _____

9. No other basketball team blends as smooth as the Lakers.

10. Mark always feels good after a long run and a hot shower.

11. He walked down the hall completely obliviously to the train of papers he left behind.

12. Be sure the door is shut secure because it often swings open by itself.

13. The coach talked slow about the team's decline during the second half of the season.

14. The audience remained calmly, even when the hall began to fill rapidly with smoke.

15. No problem; I can do both jobs easy.

16. When the phone rang, Bob picked it up, optimistically that it was Sheila calling.

17. When they carried Terry off the field, everyone thought he was hurt bad.

18. Unfortunately, John never feels shyly about reading his poems aloud in public.

19. Amy spoke sincere when she promised to repay the money.

20. Jill looked mischievous at Jack as they secretly walked up the hill.

Answers are on page 197.

Wordiness and Redundancies

A sentence needs revision when it includes words and phrases that don't add meaning or that repeat or reiterate what has already been stated. For example:

> A necessary requirement for applying to most colleges is the SAT.
>
> An important essential ingredient of a hamburger is meat.
>
> You should read *Lust for Life*, the biography of the life of Vincent Van Gogh.

All three sentences contains a needless word or phrase. In the first sentence, omit *necessary* because *necessary* by definition implies *requirement*. Therefore, *necessary requirement* is redundant. In the next sentence, an ingredient described as *essential* must by definition be *important*, so delete the word *important*. And in the last sentence, the phrase *of the life* should be removed because a biography cannot be anything other than the story of someone's life.

Sample Questions Containing Wordiness and Redundancies

1. The commission's report <u>mentions</u> the
                       A
contributions made <u>by</u> both big corporations
                           B
<u>as well as</u> small <u>businesses</u> to the growth of
  C   D
the nation's economy. <u>No error</u>.
                      E

The word *both* and the phrase *as well as* are redundant. Substitute *and* for *as well as*. Choice C is the correct answer.

2. <u>For</u> <u>as many as</u> twenty years or more
　　A　　　B
Florence Nightingale fought <u>to bring about</u>
　　　　　　　　　　　　　　　　C
new standards <u>of</u> cleanliness in hospitals.
　　　　　　　　D
<u>No error</u>.
　E

The phrase *as many as* is unnecessary. Therefore, Choice A is the correct answer.

Practice in Detecting Wordiness

<u>Directions</u>: Revise the following sentences for economy of expression.

1. She constantly irritates and bothers me all the time.

2. He spoke to me concerning the matter of my future.

3. Is it a true fact that the ozone layer is being depleted?

4. I thought that if I didn't take chemistry that I couldn't go to a good college.

5. Consequently, as a result of the election, the state will have its first female governor.

6. My father's habitual custom is to watch the sun set in the West.

7. Harold picked up a brush at the age of ten years old and hasn't stopped painting since.

8. Research shows that avid sports fans not only suffer fewer depressions, but they are also generally healthier, too, than those not interested in sports.

9. His field of work is that of a chemist.

10. For the second time, the cough recurred again.

Answers are on page 197. For more details and more practice in trimming needless words, turn to page 94.

Faulty Parallelism

Orderly construction of a sentence keeps parallel ideas in the same grammatical form. For example, a sentence describing the contents of a school locker might read this way:

> The locker held a down jacket, aromatic sweatpants, three sneakers, two left-handed gloves, an unused tuna sandwich, a broken ski pole, a hockey puck, six overdue library books, a disposable camera, and a hiking boot.

Every item listed is an object, each expressed in the same grammatical form: a noun preceded by one or two adjectives. When the owner of the locker wrote a list of favorite pastimes, though, the sentence lost its balance:

> I like skiing, hiking, to take pictures, and running.

The message is clear, but the phrase "to take pictures" is not parallel with the other phrases. To revise it, write "taking pictures."

To recognize faulty parallelism in SAT sentences, you should know that:

1. Ideas in a series should be in the same grammatical form, even when the series consists of only two items:

> Her parents objected to the loud music she played and to the late hours she kept.

The parallel ideas are expressed as prepositional phrases, *to the loud music* and *to the late hours*, followed by the pronoun *she* and the past tense of each verb, *played* and *kept*.

> After graduation, she promised to turn the volume down and to come home earlier.

Each parallel idea consists of an infinitive followed by a noun and an adverb.

2. In comparisons, parallel ideas should be in the same grammatical form.

> Going out to eat no longer thrills me as much as to cook at home.

The gerund *going* may not be paired with the infinitive *to cook*.

> *Going* out to eat no longer thrills me as much as *cooking* at home.

The ideas are now stated in parallel form.

(For more details on comparisons, turn to "Making Comparisons," page 163. For a practice exercise on comparisons, see page 174.)

3. Parallel ideas are often signaled by pairs of words like *either/or, neither/nor, whether/or, both/and,* and *not only/but also.* A usage error to watch out for is the misuse of one word in the pair, as in:

> Alice will attend *neither* NYU *or* Columbia.

Revise by changing *neither* to *either*, or changing *or* to *nor*.
Still another error occurs when one of the words in the pair is situated too far from the parallel ideas, as in:

> Jake *both* started on the basketball and the volleyball teams.

The signal word *both* is too far removed from the parallel phrase, *basketball and volleyball teams.* Its placement misleads the reader into thinking that the verb *started* is one of the parallel ideas. Correctly worded, the sentence reads:

> Jake started on *both* the basketball and the volleyball teams.

Sample Questions Containing Faulty Parallel Structure

1. One of <u>the world's</u> greatest musicians, Leonard
               A
    Bernstein <u>was</u> a composer, <u>a conductor</u>, a
               B   C
    teacher, and <u>played the piano brilliantly</u>.
                  D
    <u>No error</u>.
     E

The phrase *played the piano brilliantly* should be *a brilliant pianist* in order to be parallel in form to the other items in the series. Choice D is the correct answer.

2. It is <u>far simpler</u> to swim the breast stroke
          A
    <u>than explaining</u> to a beginning swimmer
          B
    <u>in words</u> how to do <u>it</u>. <u>No error</u>.
     C   D   E

The phrase *than explaining* should be *to explain* in order to be parallel in form to the infinitive *to swim*. Choice B is the correct answer.

(For more details and a practice exercise in parallel structure, turn to page 88.)

Incomplete Comparisons

Sentences used to make comparisons usually follow a familiar pattern that requires the items being compared to be stated in parallel form. All words essential to completing the comparison must be present in order to avoid ungrammatical or illogical comparisons.

Sample Questions Containing Incomplete Comparisons

1. <u>According to</u> some historians, the quality of
        A
    FDR's presidency <u>was</u> on a par <u>with</u> or better
                      B   C
    <u>than Wilson</u> but not Lincoln's. <u>No error</u>.
         D   E

The sentence illogically compares *quality* with *Wilson* instead of with *Wilson's presidency*. Therefore, Choice D is the correct answer.

2. Jay Leno, the comedian, is <u>funnier</u> and
                                 A
    <u>more savage</u> than <u>any comedian</u> <u>on</u>
         B   C   D
    television. <u>No error</u>.
                  E

As written, the sentence compares Leno with all comedians on television, but Leno cannot be funnier than himself. Moreover, it remains unclear whether Leno is or is not a television comedian. To make a proper comparison, use "any *other* comedian." Choice C is the correct answer.

Practice in Completing Comparisons

<u>Directions</u>: Find the errors in comparison in the following sentences. Write the correct version of the sentence in the space provided. Some sentences may be correct.

1. Jane is more efficient than any member of the committee.

    _____

    _____

2. Andy looks more like his father than his brother.

    _____

    _____

3. In *The Great Gatsby*, I disliked Daisy as much as Tom.

    _____

    _____

4. Phil works faster than George does on most jobs.

    _____

    _____

5. Oscar was as tired if not more tired than Pete.

_____

_____

6. To do the research for my term paper, I read books more than searching the Web.

_____

_____

7. Although she's younger, Lillian looks as old if not older than Dorothy.

_____

_____

8. They talked more about Chekhov's stories than his plays.

_____

_____

9. Allen's canoe was destroyed in the rapids, just like his partner.

_____

_____

10. After reading *Siddhartha*, I admire Hesse more than any author.

_____

_____

11. I am more interested in rap music than Pete.

_____

_____

12. Experts say that walking is better for you than to jog the same distance.

_____

_____

13. Biology is more popular than any science.

_____

_____

14. The students respect Ms. Scotch's teaching style more than Mr. Green.

_____

_____

15. His ears were bigger than Dumbo.

_____

_____

16. It took us longer to reach Trenton than Camden.

_____

_____

17. Which is cheaper—flying to Washington or to take the train?

_____

_____

18. The lawyer insisted that her job took more hours than a teacher.

_____

_____

19. Carrying iPods is more common now among students than cell phones.

_____

_____

20. Cindy has applied to as many colleges if not more than Joanne.

_____

_____

Answers are on page 197.

ERRORS IN GRAMMAR AND USAGE

Noun–Verb Agreement

Nouns and verbs must agree in number. That is, singular nouns must have singular verbs; plural nouns must be accompanied by plural verbs.

The Identifying Sentence Errors section of the SAT almost always includes questions that expect you to recognize agreement errors. Sometimes the error occurs when the subject of the sentence fails to agree with its verb. Just as often, though, the error exists between some other noun and verb in the sentence. (*For a full discussion of subject-verb agreement, turn to page 152.*) Errors occur most often when:

1. Intervening words obscure the relationship between the noun and verb.
2. A singular noun sounds as though it is plural.
3. The noun is one that can be either singular or plural, depending on its use.
4. The noun comes after the verb in the sentence.

Sample Questions Containing Noun–Verb Agreement Errors

1. Ian's achievement <u>as a chef</u>, in addition to his
                              A
    <u>skills</u> as a speaker, <u>make</u> him a popular <u>figure</u>
      B   C   D
    on television cooking shows. <u>No error</u>.
                                        E

The subject of the sentence is the singular noun *achievement*. The verb *make* is plural. Because the noun and verb don't agree, Choice C is the correct answer. Note that words and phrases coming between a subject and a verb rarely affect the number of the verb.

2. Behind the house <u>there is</u> <u>just</u> one broken-down
                              A   B
    shed and one pile of rubble <u>that</u> need
                                        C
    <u>to be carted</u> to the town dump. <u>No error</u>.
        D   E

In this sentence, the subject words (*shed* and *pile*) come after the verb (*is*). Because the subject is a compound subject (two nouns joined by *and*), it is considered plural and must be accompanied by a plural verb. Instead of *is*, use *are*. Choice A is the correct answer.

3. <u>About</u> a million and a half dollars
      A
    <u>have been spent</u> on repairing the road, but
          B
    only recently <u>has</u> the shoddy construction
                        C
    methods <u>become</u> evident. <u>No error</u>.
                D   E

The plural noun *methods* fails to agree with the singular verb *has . . . become*. Because *has* should be *have*, Choice C is the correct answer.

Pronoun–Antecedent Agreement

Like nouns and verbs, pronouns and antecedents must also agree in number. Singular pronouns need singular antecedents; plural pronouns, plural antecedents. The Identifying Sentence Errors section on the SAT almost always includes one or more questions that test your ability to recognize errors in agreement between pronouns and their antecedents. (*For a full discussion of this topic, please turn to page 157.*)

Sample Questions Containing Errors in Pronoun–Antecedent Agreement

1. In some cultures a woman <u>is assigned</u> a role in
                                       A
   life and is <u>constantly</u> reminded of <u>their</u> duties
                        B   C
   <u>to</u> men. <u>No error</u>.
   D   E

The plural pronoun *their* refers to the singular antecedent *woman*. Use *her* instead of *their*. Because the pronoun and antecedent don't agree, Choice C is the correct answer.

2. The branches of the university, <u>which</u>
                                              A
   <u>long adhered to</u> a "no-layoff" policy, began
              B
   changing <u>its procedures</u> <u>under</u> the pressure
                    C   D
   of financial losses. <u>No error</u>.
                               E

The singular pronoun *its* fails to agree with its antecedent *branches*. Because *their* should be *its*, Choice C is the correct answer.

Practice in Recognizing Pronoun–Antecedent Agreement

<u>Directions</u>: Check the following sentences for errors in agreement between pronoun and antecedent. Use the space provided after each sentence to write your corrections. Some sentences contain no errors.

1. The coach said that everyone on the girls' basketball team will be required to get their physicals by the start of practice on Tuesday.

   _____

   _____

2. All of his male relatives live in their own condos.

   _____

   _____

3. Not one of us girls likes to have their schedule changed so late in the term.

   _____

   _____

4. By October the maple trees will be wearing its fall colors.

   _____

   _____

5. All those who want to go on the trip must bring his money tomorrow.

   _____

   _____

6. The library is again displaying their collection of rare books.

   _____

   _____

7. The senior class was proud of the way they conducted themselves at the graduation ceremonies.

   _____

   _____

8. Not a boy or a girl in the class was willing to donate their time and energy to such a frivolous undertaking.

   _____

   _____

9. When teachers retire, the yearbook is often dedicated to them.

   _____

   _____

10. These potter's wheels are relics of the past, but it still can be turned easily.

_____

_____

Answers are on page 197.

Faulty Pronoun Reference

Another common error occurs when pronouns fail to refer clearly to their antecedents. When the reference is unclear or ambiguous, the meaning of the sentence suffers. (*For a full discussion of this topic, please turn to page 157.*)

Sample Question Containing Pronoun Reference Errors

Sarah and her colleague, Kate, <u>received</u> equal
                                     A
bonuses from <u>their</u> boss last Christmas but <u>she</u> got
             B   C
a bigger one this year <u>because of</u> her outstanding
                       D
work. <u>No error</u>.
      E

Because the pronoun *she* may refer to Sarah or to Kate, the reference is ambiguous. To fix the problem, use *Sarah* or *Kate* in place of *she*. Choice C is the correct answer.

Practice in Identifying Faulty Pronoun Reference

<u>Directions</u>: The following sentences contain faulty pronoun references. Write a revised version of each sentence in the space provided.

1. Mrs. Parker loves to knit and spends most of her time doing it.

_____

_____

2. At the end, with all the questions on the test answered, I handed them in.

_____

_____

3. Peggy told Eileen that she was sure that she had handed in the homework.

_____

_____

4. Bill let his father know that he had only ten minutes left on the parking meter.

_____

_____

5. During Bush's administration, he sent troops to fight in Iraq.

_____

_____

6. Henry, a helicopter pilot, regularly flies it on rescue missions.

_____

_____

7. In Fitzgerald's *The Great Gatsby*, he wrote about the American Dream.

_____

_____

8. She decided to buy a plasma television, which is just what he wanted.

_____

_____

9. The agreement between Joan and Jane fell apart after she failed to show up for the meeting.

_____

_____

10. After the interview, Mike told Tom that he would probably like spending the next four years at Dartmouth.

_____

_____

Answers are on page 198.

Shift in Pronoun Person

Pronouns must also agree in person throughout a sentence. A sentence cast in first person, for example, should remain so from start to finish. On the SAT, you may find sentences containing improper shifts from one person to another. (*For a full discussion of this topic, please turn to page 159.*)

Sample Question Containing Shift in Pronoun Person

Although one <u>may hope</u> that <u>your education</u> is
         A   B
going to be excellent preparation for life, <u>what</u> one
                                   C
actually experiences does not always <u>live up to</u>
                                     D
expectations. <u>No error</u>.
            E

The sentence begins using *one*, a pronoun that should be followed by *one* or by such third-person pronouns as *he, she, himself*, and *herself*. Because the pronoun *your* is in the second person, an improper shift has occurred, making choice B the correct answer.

Faulty Pronoun Case

Pronouns must be in the proper case. Nominative case pronouns are reserved for grammatical subjects and predicate nominatives. Objective case pronouns are used everywhere else. Problems arise when writers fail to identify grammatical subjects or when they mix pronouns from different cases in the same phrase. (*For a full discussion of this topic, please turn to page 157.*)

Sample Questions Containing Errors in Pronoun Case

1. I learned <u>to my great regret</u> <u>that</u> the speeches
             A   B
given by <u>George and I</u> could <u>barely</u> be heard
          C   D
at the back of the auditorium. <u>No error</u>.
                               E

Because the construction *by George and I* is a prepositional phrase, the pronoun must be in the objective case. Use *me* instead of *I*. Choice C is the correct answer.

2. Having made <u>a most</u> persuasive proposal,
              A
<u>Carl, Mack, and him</u> <u>were awarded</u> the job of
       B   C
<u>redesigning</u> the school cafeteria. <u>No error</u>.
    D   E

Because the phrase *Carl, Mack, and him* is the subject of the sentence, the pronoun should be in the nominative case. Use *he* instead of *him*. Choice B is the correct answer.

Practice in Recognizing Shifts in Pronoun Person and Errors in Pronoun Case

<u>Directions</u>: Find the pronoun errors in the following sentences. Write the correct pronoun in the space provided. Some sentences contain no errors.

1. The biggest difference between her and I is our view on gun control.

_____

2. My aunt sent Sam and I a calendar for the new year.

_____

3. We're going to ask Gert and he to go to the movies on Saturday.

_____

4. When employees are laid off a job, you collect unemployment.

_____

5. Us women take sexual harassment very seriously.

_____

6. Are you expecting Jonathan and he to call tonight?

_____

7. If you are scheduled to deliver the speech to the class, one should expect to take your turn on Monday.

_____

8. Him and I plan to drive to Danbury tonight.

_____

9. If you really want to get better at the piano, one really needs to practice.

_____

10. Them singing at the top of their lungs disturbed the quiet neighborhood.

_____

11. Tim is more interested in applying to Oregon State than her.

_____

12. The group asked us guys to pitch in on the drive for canned goods.

_____

13. Most runners say they have to run every day in order to keep yourself in shape.

_____

14. The last time I saw him, he was as tall as me, if not taller.

_____

15. I never spoke with them, neither she nor her sister.

_____

Answers are on page 198.

Faulty Verb Tense

Verb tense indicates when an action takes place. When a sentence contains a verb in the wrong tense or when an improper shift in tense occurs from one part of the sentence to the other, the meaning of the sentence suffers. (*For a full discussion of this topic, please turn to page 148.*)

Sample Question Containing Faulty Verb Tense

1. The scene involves both Macbeth and Banquo

   on horses riding across the heath where they
   A   B
   encountered the three witches, often called the
   C   D
   three hags or three weird sisters. No error.
                                      E

The main verb of the sentence is *involves*, a verb in the present tense. Having been cast in the present tense, the sentence should remain so throughout, but the verb *encountered* is in the past tense. A shift has occurred, making choice C the correct answer.

2. When you drive the car on Sunday, please
   A   B
   remember to release the emergency brake
   C
   and fastened your seatbelt. No error.
   D   E

The sentence is cast in the present tense. The use of *fastened*, a verb in past tense, is not consistent with the other verbs. Therefore, choice D is the correct answer.

Practice in Identifying Faulty Verb Tenses

<u>Directions</u>: In these sentences, many of the underlined verbs are in the wrong tense. Write the revised verbs in the spaces provided. Some sentences contain no error.

1. They biked to the top of the mountain and then <u>come</u> back down in time to eat lunch.

_____

2. The garage mechanic thinks that Mrs. Murphy <u>has brought</u> her car in last night.

_____

3. For anyone with enough brains to have thought about the problem, now <u>is</u> the time to work out a solution.

_____

4. When Washington was sworn in as president, he <u>rode</u> to New York from his home in Virginia.

_____

5. If the wagon train <u>would have reached</u> Salt Creek in time, the massacre would have been prevented.

_____

6. The aircraft controller <u>expects</u> to have spotted the plane on radar before dusk last night.

_____

7. The family already <u>finished</u> dinner when the doorbell rang.

_____

8. First he built a fire, then dragged a log over to use as a seat, and finally <u>collected</u> enough wood to keep the fire going all night.

_____

9. Rose kept the promise she <u>has given</u> to Charles last year in India.

_____

10. When he talks with Horatio, Hamlet <u>began</u> to suspect foul play in the kingdom.

_____

11. As they drove to Vermont, they <u>had stopped</u> for lunch at Bucky's Bagel Shop.

_____

12. On Route 684, a trooper pulls him over and <u>gave</u> him a speeding ticket.

_____

13. <u>Working</u> all year to improve her writing, Debbie got a story published in the paper.

_____

14. That night at the show we met many people we <u>saw</u> that afternoon.

_____

15. Once the drought had hit eastern Africa, the Somalis <u>have suffered</u> terribly.

_____

Answers are on page 198.

Faulty Verb Form

Every verb has several forms, among them (1) the present, as in *laugh*; (2) the past, formed by adding *–ed* to the present, as in *laughed*; and 3) the participle, formed by adding *has, had,* or *have* to the verb's past tense, as in *has laughed* and *had laughed*. The vast majority of English verbs follow this pattern. But some verbs, called irregular verbs, don't follow it. Examples include *break (break, broke, has broken), begin (begin, began, has begun),* and *rise (rise, rose, has risen).*

On the SAT a question relating to a verb form, especially to an irregular verb form, appears occasionally.

Sample Question Containing Faulty Verb Form

1. <u>When</u> Dave went to dinner at the professor's
     A
   home, he combed his hair, <u>dressed himself</u>
                             B
   in a jacket and tie, and <u>brang</u> the hostess
                          C
   a bouquet <u>of flowers</u>. <u>No error</u>.
           D   E

Having begun in the past tense, the sentence requires other verbs to be in the past tense. The verbs *went, combed*, and *dressed* are in the proper form. The word *brang* is not. The past form of the verb *to bring* is *brought*. Therefore, choice C is the correct answer.

2. Ms. Barnes <u>suspected that</u> the paper may
                 A
   have been plagiarized, but Ray insisted that

   he <u>had wrote</u> it <u>himself</u> and <u>that</u> he could
       B   C   D
   prove it. <u>No error</u>.
          E

The sentence contains five verbs. Only one, *had wrote*, is not in the proper form. Because the past participle of the verb *to write* is *had written*, choice B is the correct answer.

Practice in Identifying Faulty Verb Forms

<u>Directions</u>: In these sentences, the underlined verbs may not be in the proper form. Write the correct form in the spaces provided. Some verbs may be correct.

1. Brian <u>use to arrive</u> late to class almost every day.

2. Conflicts between loggers and environmentalists have regularly <u>arose</u> in the Northwest and other areas of the country.

3. Given the choice of Monday, Wednesday, or Friday for her talk, Gwen stubbornly <u>demanded to speak</u> on Thursday.

4. After dinner, Sarah cleared the table and <u>blowed</u> out the candles.

5. They <u>had began</u> practice on their own before the coach arrived.

6. When the engine overheated, the radiator hose <u>had bursted</u>.

7. To get a front-row seat, you <u>should have went</u> to the play earlier than you did.

8. The chorus messed up that song because they <u>had never sang</u> it before.

9. Halfway to town I realized that the front tire of my bike <u>had sprang</u> a leak.

10. The novels of Judy Blume have managed <u>attracting</u> millions of adolescent readers.

Answers are on page 198.

A Review

While answering Identifying Sentence Error questions, use this checklist as a guide.

- If a verb is underscored, search for errors in tense (*page 180*), form (*page 181*), agreement with the subject or other noun (*page 152*), and parallel structure (*page 146*).
- If a noun is underscored, search for errors in number and agreement with a verb (*page 152*), parallelism (*page 146*), and word choice (*page 168*).
- If a pronoun is underscored, search for errors in case, number, gender, agreement with antecedent, reference to a noun or another pronoun, and agreement with verb (*pages 157–162*), and parallel structure (*page 146*).
- If an adjective or an adverb is underscored, search for errors in word choice (*page 168*), modification (*page 151*), and comparative degree (*page 173*).
- If a phrase or clause is underscored, search for errors in parallel structure (*page 146*) and sentence structure (*page 139*).
- If a participle is underscored, search for an error in modification (*page 87*).

IMPROVING PARAGRAPHS QUESTIONS

This section of the SAT asks six questions about how to revise a draft of a short essay. A question or two may ask about deleting or changing the location of a sentence. Another may ask which revision of a poorly written sentence is best. Still others may ask how to best combine a pair of sentences or to re-write a sentence in order to clarify the essay's main idea.

The wording of paragraph-improvement questions illustrates several of the matters you must deal with:

1. In context, which of the following revisions is necessary in sentence 3?
2. In context, which of the following phrases most logically replaces "them" in sentence 9?
3. The primary effect of sentence 11 is to . . .
4. Which of the following is best to add after sentence 13 as a concluding sentence?
5. Which of the following, if inserted before sentence 1, would make a good introduction to the essay?
6. In context, which is the best way to revise and combine sentences 4 and 5?

7. Which of the following sentences, if inserted before sentence 10, would best improve the fourth paragraph?
8. The best way to describe the relationship of sentence 4 to sentence 5 is that . . .
9. All of the following strategies are used by the writer of the essay EXCEPT . . .
10. In the second paragraph (sentences 5–9), the author tries to . . .

Improving Paragraphs questions occasionally concern grammar and usage, but most of them apply to broader issues of writing, such as the purpose of the essay, organization, unity, development of ideas, the relationship between sentences, and the writer's intentions. You may also be questioned on the structure and function of certain paragraphs as well as the role of individual sentences within paragraphs.

None of these concerns are unique to this section of the exam. In fact, they should sound familiar because they are related to matters of essay writing discussed earlier in this book. That's why you'll be referred repeatedly to previous pages to review and master selected skills of writing.

Reading the Essay

How well you answer the questions may depend in part on how you go about reading the essay. Try each of the following methods to find the one that produces the best results:

Method 1: Read the essay carefully from beginning to end. By having a firm grasp of the essay's meaning, you'll save time while answering the questions. Because you won't have to re-read the entire essay, you can focus only on those portions singled out by the questions.

Method 2: Read the essay quickly—faster than you normally would. A thorough reading at this point wastes time and may distract you from your goal—to answer six questions correctly. Ignoring its flaws, therefore, read the essay just carefully enough to catch its drift. Then turn to the questions.

Method 3: Skim the essay for its general meaning; then read it again, but more slowly. After two readings, one quick and one slow, you'll know the essay intimately. Then you can concentrate on the questions instead of worrying about what the essay says.

Which of the three methods works best for you can be determined only by experience. As you read the next pages and take the practice tests in Part VI, try each method. Stick to the one that works best for you and practice it over and over.

ANSWERING THE QUESTIONS

Improving Paragraphs questions follow the progress of the passage. Although it makes sense to answer them in sequence, don't be a slave to their order. If you're good at spotting sentence errors, then tackle those types of questions before concentrating on the others. Consider answering all the specific questions before coping with more general ones—those, say, that deal with the relationship between paragraphs or with the passage as a whole.

If you can't answer a question, don't stop. The last question may be a snap, even if you were stumped by a previous one.

Sample Essay and Questions

[1] On the water, sailboats and motorboats go faster than canoes. [2] They also go faster in stores. [3] People are buying them in greater numbers than ever before. [4] Not only are they more fashionable but they give status to their owners. [5] Yet, I'll take a canoe any time.

[6] For one thing, a canoe can last for more than thirty years. [7] Even if you get tired of it, you can sell it for a fairly large fraction of its original cost. [8] For example, a new aluminum canoe may cost about $600, but a used one costs about $500 or less. [9] In addition, a canoe has no moving parts to wear out. [10] Requiring almost no care at all, you only have to paint it every few years or bang out some dents if you ride it through rapids. [11] Some high-end canoes are made of canvas covering a sturdy wood frame, caned seats and copper and brass trim.

[12] Besides being economical, a canoe can be used in a variety of ways. [13] In the first place, you can use it in the ocean as well as on a tiny lake. [14] One can use it on rivers, too. [15] Marshes and small streams are fine for using a canoe. [16] As a result, wherever you go, there is bound to be a place for canoeing. [17] Not only can you take it anywhere, but you can go canoeing for a few hours or for weeks at a time. [18] In contrast to other boats, canoes don't depend on wind or fuel. [19] Furthermore, you don't have to waste time setting up or taking down a canoe. [20] Simply grab a paddle, and you're off on your own.

1. In the first paragraph the author is primarily

   (A) informing the reader about several kinds of boats
   (B) providing evidence that boating is a popular pastime
   (C) poking fun at those who prefer sailboats to canoes
   (D) telling a personal story about boating
   (E) preparing the reader for an unexpected disclosure

Choice A is not a good answer because the paragraph is more about boaters than about boats.

Eliminate choice B because the paragraph provides no real evidence that boating is a popular pastime. Neither choice C nor D is justified by the contents of the paragraph. Only choice E offers a reasonable answer. In fact, the paragraph deals favorably with sailboats and motorboats but ends with a slightly surprising statement—that the author prefers canoes. Choice E, therefore, is the best answer.

2. Sentence 2 differs from other sentences in the first paragraph because it

   (A) emphasizes a major point of the essay
   (B) changes the meaning of words taken from a previous sentence
   (C) presents the writer's personal opinion
   (D) changes the tone of the essay
   (E) provides an important transition between the sentences that precede and follow it

Eliminate choice A because the sentence is unrelated to the essay's main point. Choice C is wrong because sentence 2 states a fact that can be proved, not an opinion. Choice D is wrong because the tone of the essay has not yet been established, and choice E does not accurately describe the function of sentence 2. An analysis of the paragraph shows that the phrase *go faster* is used in both sentence 1 and sentence 2. In sentence 1, the phrase refers to the speed of boats on water. In sentence 2, it refers to the popularity of boats among consumers. Therefore, choice B is the best answer.

3. Of the following, which is the best version of the following underlined portion of sentence 10?

   Requiring almost no care at all, you only have to paint it every few years or bang out some dents if you ride it through rapids.

   (A) As it is now
   (B) Requiring little care, canoes need only to be painted
   (C) Requiring little care, paint is all it needs
   (D) Caring for it easily, you only have to paint it
   (E) Only paint it

The sentence needs revision because it contains an error in modification. Choice A is wrong because the phrase *Requiring almost no care at all* is a dangling participle that modifies *you* instead of

canoes. Choice C is a variation of A. Choices D and E, although grammatically correct, make little sense in the context. Choice B, the only remaining choice, is the best answer.

4. Which of the following should be done with sentence 11 (reproduced below)?

   Some high-end canoes are made of canvas covering a sturdy wood frame, caned seats and copper and brass trim.

   (A) Insert the phrase "Speaking of costs" at the beginning.
   (B) Delete it; the sentence is irrelevant.
   (C) Insert it between sentence 8 and sentence 9.
   (D) Combine it with sentence 4.
   (E) Move it to the end of paragraph 1 (after sentence 5).

Because the sentence contains information about the materials used to build canoes, it does not fit logically anywhere in the essay. The phrase suggested in choice A attempts to establish a link between the sentence and the second paragraph, but the writer is not discussing costs at that point in the essay. Therefore, choice B is the best answer.

5. In context, which is the best way to revise and combine sentences 14 and 15 (reproduced below)?

   One can use it on rivers, too. Marshes and small streams are fine for using a canoe.

   (A) One can use it on rivers, too, as well as marshes and small streams.
   (B) You can use it on rivers, too, and marshes and small streams are fine for using a canoe.
   (C) You can use it on rivers, marshes, and small streams.
   (D) Using it for rivers and paddling on marshes and small streams in a canoe.
   (E) One can use it on rivers and small streams and in marshes, which are fine for using a canoe.

Because the two sentences appear in a paragraph that uses the second-person pronoun (*you*), eliminate choices A and E. Choice D is a sentence fragment. Choice B is ineffective because its two coordinate clauses are not in the same grammatical form. Therefore, choice C, a concise and clear revision of the original sentences, is the best answer.

6. The primary effect of the final paragraph (sentences 12–20) is to

(A) summarize the ideas introduced in the previous paragraph
(B) reconsider a point made in the first paragraph
(C) support the validity of the essay's main idea
(D) explain a contradiction within the essay
(E) provide an additional example

Almost every sentence in the final paragraph adds another dimension to the writer's appreciation of canoes. Because the essay's intent is to prove that canoes excel other small vessels in several ways—cost, maintenance, versatility, ease of use—choice C is the best answer.

HOW TO ANSWER IMPROVING PARAGRAPHS QUESTIONS

Short of asking you to actually write an essay, Improving Paragraphs questions can test almost any aspect of your knowledge about writing, from grammar and usage to matters of style and expression.

Defining the Essay's Purpose

Once you've read the given essay, quickly jot down the essay's main idea in your test booklet. By keeping the main idea constantly in mind, you can more readily judge whether the essay has achieved its purpose.

Writers often have multiple purposes and complex attitudes toward their subject. The essay you'll be asked about on the SAT, however, will be short and simple. Don't look for subtleties, sophisticated techniques, or hidden meanings. The essay will have a purpose that can be easily and simply articulated. For example:

To inform readers about the progress of America's fight against terrorism.

To give an informed and entertaining account of the misadventures of a literary character.

To dispense helpful advice about how to use the Internet.

Such statements of purpose will establish the boundaries of the essay. Any material that oversteps the boundaries is fodder for Paragraph Improvement questions.

Organization of the Essay

If a question asks you about the organization of the essay, check the opening paragraph first. Be sure it introduces, limits, and makes clear the purpose of the essay. A good opening, often stated in a single sentence, points readers in a particular direction and names their destination. Subsequent paragraphs set up signposts along the way to remind readers where they've been and where they are headed. If readers lose sight of the goal, the essay's organization may be at fault.

Say, for example, that a writer wants to persuade readers to give up smoking. In outline, such an essay might look this way:

Introductory paragraph:	The ill effects of smoking
Second paragraph:	Effects on health
Third paragraph:	High monetary cost of smoking
Fourth paragraph:	Social costs of smoking
Concluding paragraph:	It's not worth it.

In the outline, each paragraph contains an antismoking argument. The organization is logical and clear. If, however, a paragraph had been devoted to the history of the tobacco industry or to smoking pot, it would violate the essay's clear and sensible organization.

Organizational breakdowns occur for all sorts of reasons, but usually because the writer has lost focus. An unfocused essay contains distractions and irrelevancies. Whole paragraphs may fail to contribute to the development of the main idea. Or worse, the essay's conclusion may undermine or contradict its introduction.

On the SAT, you may be asked to identify or revise sentences that don't fit the essay's organization. A question may ask you how to revise such a sentence or whether to move or delete it. As you answer the question, always keep the essay's purpose in mind.

Paragraph Structure, Unity, and Coherence

Knowing the qualities of well-written paragraphs and recognizing paragraphing weaknesses will help you answer some questions.

Structure of Paragraphs

Each paragraph of a well-written essay is, in effect, an essay in miniature. It has a purpose, an organizational plan, and a progression of ideas. By scrutinizing a paragraph in the same manner as you would a complete essay, you can discern its main idea and identify its development.

Topic Sentences and Supporting Sentences

Most paragraphs are made up of two kinds of sentences: A **topic sentence**, which states generally the contents of the paragraph, and **supporting sentences**, which provide the particulars that support and develop the topic sentence. Sometimes supporting sentences themselves need support, provided by minor, or secondary, supporting sentences. The paragraph that follows contains examples of each kind of sentence:

[1] Children with IQs well below average represent an almost insoluble problem for educators. [2] Such children often feel inadequate, rejected by teachers and peers in a school environment that values and rewards academic success. [3] Failure in school is the number one cause of poor behavior in school and of juvenile delinquency in general. [4] The best that schools can do for children with low IQs is to teach them how to get by in the world and to teach them a vocation. [5] But vocational training is very limited in many schools. [6] Those that provide such training usually do so only for older adolescents.

Sentence 1 is the topic sentence of the paragraph. To be convincing, it needs the support of sentences 2–5. Each supporting sentence adds a piece of evidence to prove the point of the paragraph—that children with low IQs create a problem for schools. Sentence 5 is a supporting sentence that requires additional support, provided by sentence 6.

Location of Topic Sentences. A topic sentence may be anywhere in a paragraph, but it usually appears at or close to the beginning. It isn't always a separate and independent sentence; it may be woven into a supporting sentence as a clause or phrase. (In the paragraph you are now reading, for example, the main idea is stated in the first clause of the initial sentence.) Writers vary the location of topic sentences to avoid monotony. They could, for example, save the topic sentence for the end, letting it stand out boldly as the climax of the paragraph. Or they might omit the topic sentence, letting an accumulation of telling details imply the paragraph's main idea.

Note the location of the topic sentence in each of the following paragraphs:

[1] It is pitch dark and very chilly. [2] No one in his right mind wants to pry open their eyes and leave the cozy warmth of bed and blanket. [3] No one wants to walk in bare feet across the frigid floor to peer out the window at the icy rain slanting down in the early morning gloom. [4] The thought of damp clothes and cold feet keeps you where you are, at least for a few more minutes. **[5] Isn't it hard to get up on a dark winter morning.**

The supporting details in sentences 1–4 lead inevitably to sentence 5, the topic sentence, which summarizes the meaning of the paragraph.

[1] For a long time about 50,000 people were killed annually in automobile accidents on the nation's roads. [2] Reduced speed limits, seatbelt requirements, and increased police patrols had almost no effect on changing the number of fatalities. **[3] The most promising way to reduce fatalities, however, proved to be making cars safer.** [4] Front and side airbags were installed in all new models. [5] Special seats and restraints were designed for children. [6] Stronger steel frames enabled people to survive crashes that would certainly have killed them before.

Sentence 3 is the topic sentence. It serves as the pivotal point between the description of the problem (sentences 1 and 2) and some effective solutions (sentences 4, 5, and 6).

The key to unlocking a paragraph's purpose lies in the topic sentence, and the effectiveness of a paragraph depends on how tightly the topic sentence is linked to its supporting details. On the SAT, you may be asked to improve a paragraph by tightening that link.

Or you may be asked to choose the best transition between ideas or paragraphs. A *transitional sentence* links the ideas in one paragraph with those in a previous or subsequent paragraph. In effect, it is a bridge between two different ideas. In short essays, it's rare to find full transitional sentences. Instead, bridges are usually built with transitional words and phrases, such as *in addition, in like manner, however, as a result,* and *finally.*

(For further details and practice exercises on topic sentences, turn to page 63. For details and a practice exercise on the use of transitions, turn to page 70.)

Unity and Coherence in Paragraphs

When a paragraph deals with more than one main idea, it lacks unity. When its sentences skip from topic to topic, it lacks coherence. The Paragraph Improvement questions often ask about sentences that undermine unity or weaken coherence. You may need to identify, for example, which of five sentences most effectively bridges the gap between unrelated ideas. Or you may be asked to pick a sentence that best restores continuity of thought within a paragraph. Notice, for instance, how sentence 4 has no business being between sentences 3 and 5:

[1] Like many other leaders throughout history, George Washington established his authority through the force of his personality. [2] Almost everyone who met him thought that he was charming, dignified, charismatic. [3] Some people of the time referred to him as a "superior being." [4] Yet the Father of Our Country had been soundly defeated in 1755, when he first sought elective office. [5] At six-feet two-inches in his stockings, he was taller and more impressive than most men of his time. [6] His frame was padded with well-developed muscles, indicating great strength, and his blue-grey eyes could sparkle with humor at one moment and grow hard and determined at the next. [7] John Adams described him as a "gentleman whose great talents and excellent universal character . . . would command the respect of all the Colonies."

The paragraph's purpose is to describe the power of Washington's personality. Because sentence 4 fails to contribute to this laudatory portrait of our first president, it should be deleted.

For more details and a practice exercise on paragraph unity and coherence, turn to page 62.

Coherence Through Sentence Combining

Disjointed paragraphs force readers to slow down or even stop dead at the end of each sentence. Instead of a smooth journey through a paragraph, readers experience mental bumps and jolts, often inflicted by a series of short, choppy sentences.

On the SAT, you may be asked to improve a paragraph's coherence by choosing a revision that effectively combines two or three disconnected or repetitive sentences. The following paragraph is an example:

[1] Colored balloons decorated the gym. [2] It was the annual spring dance. [3] Four men in black tuxedos stood on the stage. [4] Their shiny brass instruments were in their hands. [5] They provided the musical entertainment. [6] All the girls were dressed in pastel shades. [7] The girls talked in groups. [8] They were deciding which boys they would ask to dance. [9] Couples went onto the dance floor. [10] Soon it was full.

No doubt the paragraph is unified in thought—it's all about the annual spring dance. But it suffers from incoherence because each detail, no matter how important or trivial, is stated in a separate sentence. For the sake of greater coherence, the sentences need to be combined:

[1] For the annual spring dance, the gym had been decorated with colored balloons. [2] Four men in black tuxedos stood on the stage and provided the musical entertainment with their shiny brass instruments. [3] Dressed in pastel shades, the girls talked in groups deciding which boys they would ask to dance. [4] Soon the floor was filled with dancing couples.

Ten sentences have become four. Some words have been deleted or changed. Key ideas have been emphasized, secondary ideas played down. Overall, the revision exemplifies more skilled, more mature writing.

On the SAT, you may be asked to combine two or three short sentences within a longer paragraph. As you weigh the five choices given by a sentence-combining question, keep in mind that the most concise or cleverest revision may not always be the best one. Instead, the best revision is likely to be the one that fits most logically and stylistically into the context of the paragraph.

Practice in Combining Sentences

<u>Directions</u>: Use the spaces provided to combine the sentences in each of the following groups. Because any group can be combined in numerous ways, write at least two versions. If necessary, add, delete, and alter words. Try alternatives; that's the best way to discover the possibilities and to improve your skill

1. She is only thirteen. She is an expert gymnast. She has won recognition.

_____

_____

_____

2. An accident occurred. The accident was a hit and run. Broken glass lay on the street.

_____

_____

_____

3. Aunt Ellen went to the grocery store. She bought tomato juice. The tomato juice was in a glass bottle. The bottle was in the grocery bag. Aunt Ellen dropped the grocery bag. The bottle broke. Aunt Ellen had a mess. The mess was on her hands.

_____

_____

_____

4. The baseball hit the picture window. The picture window belonged to Mr. Strickman. The glass shattered. The glass shattered in a thousand pieces.

_____

_____

_____

5. There was a storm. The snow fell. Snow fell on the roads. It was two feet deep. I could not go out. I had nothing to do. I watched TV. I worked on a jigsaw puzzle. Time passed slowly.

_____

_____

_____

6. The Earth revolves around the sun. It takes about 365 days for a revolution. The Earth rotates on its axis. One rotation occurs every 24 hours. The revolution determines the length of the year. The rotation determines the duration of a day.

_____

_____

_____

7. Euripides lived more than 2,000 years ago. He lived in ancient Greece. He wrote plays. The plays were tragedies. The plays are still performed.

_____

_____

_____

8. Music has a unique power. Music often transports people's minds. People dream and think while listening to music. People often feel refreshed after listening to music.

_____

_____

_____

9. Human beings have skulls. Skulls are made up of bones. The skull has twenty-two bones. Eight bones make up the cranium. The cranium protects the brain. Fourteen bones are used to form the face and jaw.

_____

_____

_____

10. The Hopi Indians value peace and contentment. The word "Hopi" means peaceful and happy. The name reflects the culture. The culture lacks tension. The people lack competitiveness. Material possessions are unimportant. Self-discipline is important. So is restraint. So is concern for the welfare of others. The family is the highest value. The family is the whole Hopi tribe.

_____

_____

_____

Answers are on page 198. For details and a practice exercise in varying sentences, turn to page 77.

Paragraph Development

Like an essay, each paragraph should have a recognizable plan. A paragraph may consist of little more than a collection of facts that support the topic sentence. Or it may take the form of a brief narrative, its events spelled out in the order they occurred. Another paragraph may be organized to compare and contrast two people or conditions, still another to define a term or explain a process.

Depending on the paragraph's purpose, details that support the main idea may be arranged spatially, chronologically, in order of importance, from general to specific or vice-versa—or in any arrangement that develops the topic.

On the SAT, you may be asked to identify a paragraph's organizational plan. Therefore, you should know the most common patterns of paragraph development. Don't bother memorizing them for the exam, but your ability to recognize each pattern when you see it could be helpful.

1. **Argument and proof.** In this organizational plan, a paragraph's supporting sentences consist of arguments or examples meant to prove the validity of the topic sentence.

> In wartime, the military develops a way of speaking that disguises meaning and makes the horrors of battle less dirty and gruesome. Euphemisms enable both soldiers and civilians to keep a psychological distance and turn war into an antiseptic, clinical abstraction. In Vietnam, for example, when our own troops were shelled by mistake, the event was called an "accidental delivery of ordnance equipment." In the Gulf War and Iraqi campaign, "friendly fire" became the phrase of choice. Similarly, when wayward bombs killed innocent civilians, "incontinent ordnance" was responsible for causing "collateral damage." Arms and legs are not blown off in combat; they are severed in a "traumatic amputation." Such euphemisms, according to language experts, can be protective, but at the same time, they put us in danger of losing the real sense of war's ghastliness.

The first sentence is the topic sentence. The rest of the paragraph consists of examples that illustrate the "way of speaking."

2. **Definition.** Paragraphs of definition do more than simply offer a dictionary meaning of a word or idea. Broad, abstract concepts such as loyalty, beauty, evil, success, and countless others are better defined by *example*, by *analogy*, or by *comparison and contrast*. For instance, the following defines the word *utopia* by describing a utopian society and explaining the word's origin.

Utopia is the name often given to a society in which everything is thought to be perfect. Everything in the society, from its economic policies to its social practices, is designed to keep the society functioning without difficulty. In Utopia all people are happy, wise, equal, prosperous, and well-educated. Utopia is an appropriate name. It comes from the Greek word meaning "no place."

3. **Definition by analogy.** The qualities of a spider web are defined in the following paragraph by comparing a web and a fine musical instrument.

A spider's web is an exquisite musical instrument. It is constructed of many strings of different lengths under various degrees of tension. It is played upon by the rain and the wind, by other insects, and by the master musician herself, the spider. So sensitive is the spider's sense of touch that from one corner of the web she can locate a struggling victim, determine its size, and, by the rhythms and tempo of vibrations, judge it to be a moth, a hapless mosquito, housefly, or other insect.

4. **Comparison and contrast.** In the paragraph that follows the personalities of two men—one real and one fictional—are defined by comparing and contrasting some of their traits.

Albert Perry may have been the model for Hal Roet in Thayer's new novel. Thayer calls Roet an "unpredictable farmer." The real-life Perry was a tobacco farmer for years and was known throughout Piedmont County as Peripatetic Perry. At 30, he unexpectedly left his wife and went to New York to become a rock and roll singer. Roet, too, left his farm in the hands of his wife and traveled around the country with a rodeo. But the similarity ends there. Perry was compulsively self-revealing; Roet was quiet and unassuming. Perry was indifferent to his family, while Roet was torn, anguished, and guilt-ridden about abandoning Marion and the three children. Finally, Perry craved fame. Roet, in contrast, didn't care a nickel about becoming a famous bronco rider. He was in it for the thrill of doing something dangerous.

5. **Cause and effect.** The details of a cause-and-effect paragraph explain or demonstrate how one event or set of circumstances leads to, or causes, another event or set of circumstances. The following passage describes the consequences of one-sixth gravity.

Because the moon has only one-sixth the gravity of the Earth, people on the lunar surface weigh only a fraction of their normal poundage. They walk easily, each step evolving into a rhythmic, bounding motion that feels like a stroll on a trampoline. At the same time, starting and stopping require unusual bursts of energy. To stop forward motion, they must dig their heels into the ground and lean backward. If they fall, they descend in slow motion, and the impact is no stronger than falling onto a feather bed. Getting up again is difficult and enervating, however.

6. **Process analysis.** A paragraph analyzing a process explains how to perform the steps of a process or procedure.

When repainting a room, it's best to remove as much furniture and carpeting as possible. Be sure to cover everything left behind with a tarpaulin or plastic sheet. Using a roller, paint the ceiling first. While the ceiling dries, paint windows, doors, and trim, except for baseboards. Then paint the walls. Try to avoid changing paint cans in the middle of a wall because the paint color from two different cans may not match exactly. If you expect to finish a can before you finish a wall, pour the paint from two cans into a large bucket and mix well. One coat of paint is usually not enough, so be prepared to apply a second coat to all surfaces. Paint the baseboards last.

7. **Classification.** A paragraph of classification breaks a general category into its component parts.

Vegetables can be classified according to climate and growing requirements. Early vegetables like leaf lettuce, spinach, radishes, and peas grow best in cool weather and are planted shortly before the last frost. Moderately hardy vegetables, including potatoes and onions, should also be grown before the intense heat of summer. Late spring is the time to start hardy vegetables like carrots, beets, cabbage, and cauliflower because they easily endure the summer sun's heat. Some vegetables are extremely sensitive to cold and, therefore, can be planted only weeks after the last frost. These include soybeans, cucumbers, summer squash, and watermelons. Such plants as tomatoes, peppers, and eggplant are usually started indoors and transplanted outside in late spring or early summer.

Because purpose dictates structure, an effective paragraph can be developed in more than one way. To prove a point or make a persuasive argument, for instance, a writer may combine facts with definition and the analysis of a process. Although writers rarely follow a formula to develop paragraphs, most abide by a rule of thumb that says a paragraph of one or two sentences is too skimpy. To develop an idea thoroughly often takes several sentences. Since the overall effectiveness of a paragraph may depend on its organization, SAT questions may ask you to add a sentence to a paragraph, delete a sentence, or even relocate an existing sentence by moving it within a paragraph or to a different paragraph.

Most sentences contain clues that assign them to a place—and only one place—in a paragraph. Meaning is the primary clue, but such words and phrases as *for example, also, but,* and *on the other hand* also serve to put sentences into a particular order. In the following, for instance, observe how the italicized words and phrases determine the sequence of sentences:

[1] Part-time jobs for high school students are a mixed blessing. [2] *They* help young people learn the value of money. [3] It is *also* satisfying for young people to help with their family's finances. [4] *On the other hand,* jobs often distract students from their schoolwork. [5] *Moreover,* many jobs are so boring that students get the idea that work and boredom go hand in hand.

Sentence 1 expresses the most general idea in the paragraph and serves as the topic sentence. The pronoun *they,* which begins sentence 2, refers to *jobs,* a noun in the first sentence. Sentence 3 contains the connecting word *also,* indicating that a new thought is being added to one expressed in the

previous sentence. Sentence 4 begins with *On the other hand,* a common transitional phrase used to indicate that a contrasting idea will follow. The last sentence begins with *Moreover,* another common transition that signals the addition of still another idea in the same vein. Because of these linking elements, these five sentences cannot be arranged in any other sequence without destroying the paragraph's coherence.

(For more details and a practice exercise on transitions, turn to page 70.)

Practice in Arranging Sentences

<u>Directions</u>: The sentences in each group make up a paragraph. But they are not in the proper order. In the blank spaces write the number that represents the proper place of each sentence in the paragraph.

1. ____ a. In the end, morale got so low that members started quitting the team.

   ____ b. Whether you were a polevaulter, a sprinter, or a distance runner, practices were the same for everyone.

   ____ c. He was forcing the team to work out the same way every day.

   ____ d. Mr. Reese, the track coach, had been acting like a tyrant.

2. ____ a. First, put in the large, firm, and heavy items that won't be crushed or damaged by putting something on top of them.

   ____ b. Meanwhile, think of all the items that can be easily bruised, crushed, or broken, such as eggs, packages of bread, fruit, and light bulbs.

   ____ c. To fill up a paper bag with groceries usually takes about fifteen seconds if you do it right.

   ____ d. Immediately after that, put in light but firm items such as crackers, cereal, and butter.

   ____ e. Canned goods and bottles fit the bill perfectly.

   ____ f. Those should be saved for last.

3. ____ a. Then, too, I started feeling comfortable talking with adults.

____ b. Most people think of "maturity" in terms of responsibility, but I think it has more to do with learning to control one's actions.

____ c. I could actually talk to them instead of shutting up like a clam and just standing there like a dummy.

____ d. For example, I knew that I was more mature than others when I didn't laugh out loud in science class when the teacher talked about reproduction.

4. ____ a. As blood circulates, it cleans out body waste, like the collector who cruises the neighborhood picking up trash.

____ b. In return, it deposits oxygen and food in every body part, from the top of the head to the little toe.

____ c. Yet human life depends on those four quarts of blood that are pumped from the heart, flow to every cell in the body, and return to the heart to be pumped again.

____ d. If you drained the blood from the body of a girl weighing about 125 pounds, you would fill little more than a gallon milk container.

5. ____ a. The essay was to be handed in on Monday morning.

____ b. The first part of the exam was a take-home essay in which we were to answer one of three questions.

____ c. On Friday night I settled myself down with my textbook and took exceptionally detailed notes.

____ d. Four weeks ago, I, like many other eleventh graders, worked hard to prepare for an American History midterm exam.

____ e. The next day, determined to have more information than I could use when I began to write the essay, I went to the public library to do further research.

6. ____ a. His mistake was corrected fifty years later by Carl Blegen of the University of Chicago.

____ b. He figured out that every few centuries a new city had been built upon the ruins of the old.

____ c. In the 1870s, the archeologist Heinrich Schliemann dug in the correct spot and discovered nine ancient cities of Troy, one lying on top of the other.

____ d. But without realizing it, Schliemann had dug right past the layer he had been seeking, the layer containing the ruins of the famous city of the Trojan Horse.

____ e. By then, it was too late for Schliemann, who had been dead for fifty years.

7. ____ a. For months at a time Jerry's fans would devotedly follow his group around the country wherever it played in concert.

____ b. Just two years after its debut, Jerry and his band left an indelible mark on millions of young fans.

____ c. In spite of his family, who told him that he would never be a successful professional singer, Jerry decided to take up guitar and form a musical group.

____ d. He not only created a whole new subculture but developed a following.

8. ____ a. He felt terribly anxious about his wounded leg.

____ b. The slightest movement of his knee caused a sudden and intense pain, unlike anything he had ever felt before.

____ c. He could not sleep, in spite of the sedative administered to him by the British nurse.

____ d. In Milan, the lieutenant lay in a hospital bed.

____ e. It was even worse than the pain he recalled when, as a child, he had pulled a pot of steaming water over on himself.

9. ____ a. Each layer is another page that tells the story of volcanic eruptions, massive floods, and the advance and retreat of the Ice Age.

____ b. Unfortunately, it also tells of the present day's pollution of the earth's air and lands.

____ c. If you can read its language, the sediments contain a record of all the dramatic and catastrophic events that have occurred through the earth's history.

____ d. The ocean floor is a diary of the earth.

10. ____ a. He became blind in 1652 and used his daughter as an instrument to write some of his finest poems.

____ b. His daughter, with her quill pen in hand, sat with her father to record his thoughts, to read them back, to make revisions in whatever way Milton wanted.

____ c. The first poet to use a word processor was John Milton.

____ d. The actual processing of words went on in Milton's head.

11. ____ a. After winning two Critics' Circle awards and the Pulitzer Prize for drama, Tennessee Williams earned fame and lots of money.

____ b. Usually, he's named with Eugene O'Neill and Arthur Miller as one of the leading American dramatists of the 20th century.

____ c. They flocked to Broadway to see his plays and later swarmed to the movies to see filmed versions of his works.

____ d. All of a sudden, the public began to view him as one of the best of the modern playwrights.

Answers are on page 199. For more details and a practice exercise on paragraph development, see page 62.

Functions of Paragraphs

A paragraph-improvement question may single out a paragraph or one of its parts and ask you to identify its role in the essay. To answer the questions, you should understand how paragraphs function in an essay. Part III, on essay writing, offers a thorough discussion of this topic, but here is a brief overview.

The First Paragraph. An effective opening paragraph introduces the essay and makes the intent of the essay clear to the reader. Because the essay you'll scrutinize on the SAT won't be more than three or four paragraphs long, its introduction will be succinct and straightforward. SAT questions often refer to sentences in the first paragraph that are irrelevant to the essay's main idea.

The Last Paragraph. The final paragraph should give the reader a sense of completion. A weak or irrelevant conclusion may dilute or even obliterate the effect of the essay. No ending is as effective and emphatic as one that grows logically out of a thoughtful arrangement of the writer's ideas. A good last paragraph, for example may suggest a solution to a problem discussed in the essay. Or it may call on the reader to think about an issue or perform an action. On the SAT any concluding paragraph that seems to end the essay very abruptly, that dissolves into irrelevancy, or that fits the essay too loosely is fair game for a multiple-choice question.

Developmental Paragraphs. Paragraphs usually perform more than one function in an essay's development. For example, a paragraph may carry forward the main point of the essay by contributing a solution to the problem being discussed. At the same time, it may reinforce an idea proposed earlier and also supply background information for the next paragraph.

On the SAT, you may be asked to identify the main function of a particular paragraph. Function has little to do with meaning. Rather, it pertains to the role the paragraph plays in the journey from the beginning to the end of the essay. Developmental paragraphs can perform myriad functions, among them:

- Reinforce an idea with a telling example
- Evaluate an opinion stated earlier

- Add new ideas
- Cast doubt on a common misconception
- Tell a brief anecdote that illustrates a point
- Continue the discussion begun in an earlier paragraph
- Provide a contrasting point of view
- Explain or define a term
- Persuade readers to change their opinions
- Summarize the argument made thus far
- Turn the essay in a new direction
- Describe the relationship between ideas presented earlier
- Provide background material
- Justify or explain contradictions within the essay
- Ask a hypothetical or rhetorical question about the topic

A common question on the SAT may be worded something like this: *"Which of the following sentences, if inserted after sentence 6, would best improve the third paragraph?"* Knowing how paragraphs function in an essay will give you a leg up in finding the correct answer.

A Review

While looking for errors in Improving Paragraph questions, use this checklist as a guide. Always keep in mind:

- The strategies used to answer both the Sentence Improvement and Identifying Sentence Error questions (*page 133* and *page 165*).
- How topic sentences signal the purpose and organization of each paragraph and of the essay as a whole (*page 63*).
- Potential contradictions, breakdowns in logic, and shifts in emphasis throughout the essay (*page 55*).
- The unity and coherence of each paragraph and of the whole essay (*page 62*).
- The relationship of each sentence to those that precede and follow it (*page 70*).
- Transitional words and phrases (*page 70*).
- The functions of opening, closing, and developmental paragraphs (*pages 59, 83,* and *62*).

ANSWER KEY TO PRACTICE EXERCISES

Writing Correct Sentences, page 142

Answers will vary. No doubt some of your sentences will be better than these.

1. Although Elizabeth is stressed out about the SAT, she won't let it get her down.
2. The teacher agreed to her request for an extension on the assignment.
3. At eighty-six years old, my grandmother walks very slowly.
4. I could choose many other examples to show who I am, not all of them vivid images of memorable moments but rather everyday aspects of my life.
5. I woke up, having slept for the four shortest hours of my life. I force my eyes open and crawl to the shower. Only then my brain begins to function.
6. I can't believe that I'll soon leave the protective world of high school and enter the world of college.
7. The large brown garage door creaks open slowly. Out into the morning sunshine emerges a rider on a road bike.
8. What are the rules? What happens if we break them?
9. Phyllis, a biologist in the field of genetic engineering, is involved in the cloning controversy.
10. Use the space below to tell one personal story to provide the admissions committee, either directly or indirectly, an insight into the kind of person you are.

Establishing Noun–Verb Agreement, page 154

1. talent . . . proves
2. heroes . . . die
3. team . . . is
4. Correct
5. Correct
6. are . . . levels
7. proceeds . . . are
8. team . . . is
9. neither . . . was
10. reforms . . . have
11. fan . . . expects
12. Politics . . . has
13. Darwin . . . is
14. Katie Green . . . and accompanist . . . are
15. Nancy . . . appears
16. sale . . . has
17. Here are . . . statutes
18. insistence . . . is
19. No one . . . wants
20. are . . . guards

Choosing the Case of Pronouns, page 158

1. me
2. her, him
3. me
4. me
5. him
6. he
7. I
8. me
9. we
10. he

Recognizing Pronoun Shift and Pronoun Agreement, page 160

Answers may vary.

1. The English teacher announced that everyone in the class must turn in his term paper no later than Friday.
2. When fired from a job, one collects unemployment.
3. The library put its collection of rare books on display.
4. Each of my sisters owns her own car.
5. Correct

6. In order to stay in shape, you should work out every day.
7. The teacher dictates a sentence in French. Then each student writes it down in English and hands it in.
8. Each horse in the procession followed its rider down to the creek.
9. The school's chess team has just won its first match.
10. When you visit the park, ask a park ranger if you can't find a rest room.

Identifying Pronoun Reference, page 162

These are suggested answers. Yours may be different but equally valid.

1. When teenagers loiter outside the theater on Friday night, the police give them a hard time.
2. Before collecting my pencils and pens, I handed in the test questions I had answered.
3. At the root of Barbara and Ken's problem is that she wanted only a short wedding trip to Florida.
4. With only an hour to get to the airport, his father was in a rush and told him so.
5. During her tenure in office, Dr. Rice traveled more than any other secretary of state.
6. Although he disapproved of the war, Henry drove his ambulance to the front lines.
7. After the campus tour, Mike told Todd, "I'd be happy going to Auburn."
8. Peggy's car wasn't even dented after it hit a truck.
9. Within the last month, Andy's older brother Pete broke his leg skiing and got a new job. He also married Felicia, which made his parents very happy.
10. Because he had lived in California, Eddie grew fond of John Steinbeck's novels.

Identifying Faulty English Idiom, page 167

1. in battle
2. ascended the stairs
3. comply with
4. either iron or tin
5. preoccupation with
6. either danger or love
7. Correct
8. in pursuit of
9. to identify employees

10. Correct
11. with respect to
12. in search of a way
13. that kind of pain
14. for the bus
15. as expensive as
16. regarded as
17. between teaching and devoting
18. driving to flying
19. far from harm
20. neither well-written nor fully researched

Using Adjectives and Adverbs, page 170

1. bitter
2. No error
3. smoothly
4. beautifully
5. horrible
6. slowly
7. cynically
8. No error
9. smoothly
10. No error
11. oblivious
12. securely
13. slowly
14. calm
15. easily
16. optimistic
17. badly
18. shy
19. sincerely
20. mischievously

Detecting Wordiness, page 172

Answers may vary.

1. She constantly bothers me.
2. He spoke to me about my future.
3. Is it true that the ozone layer is being depleted?
4. I thought that without chemistry I couldn't go to a good college.
5. As a result of the election, the state will have its first female governor.
6. My father habitually watches the sun set.
7. Harold hasn't stopped painting since picking up a brush at age ten.
8. Research shows that avid sports fans suffer fewer depressions and are generally healthier than those not interested in sports.

9. He is a chemist.
10. The cough recurred twice.

Completing Comparisons, page 174

These are suggested answers. Other answers may also be correct.

1. Jane is more efficient than any other member of the committee.
2. Andy looks more like his father than his brother does.
3. In *The Great Gatsby*, I disliked Daisy as much as I disliked Tom.
4. Correct
5. Oscar was as tired as, if not more tired than, Pete.
6. To do the research for my term paper, I read books more than I searched the Web.
7. Although she's younger, Lillian looks as old as, if not older than, Dorothy.
8. They talked more about Chekhov's stories than about his plays.
9. Allen's canoe was destroyed in the rapids, just like his partner's was.
10. After reading *Siddhartha*, I admire Hesse more than any other author.
11. I am more interested in rap music than Pete is.
12. Experts say that walking is better for you than jogging the same distance.
13. Biology is more popular than any other science.
14. The students respect Ms. Scotch's teaching style more than Mr. Green's.
15. His ears were bigger than Dumbo's.
16. It took us longer to reach Trenton than to reach Camden.
17. Which is cheaper—flying to Washington or taking the train?
18. The lawyer insisted that her job took more hours than a teacher's job.
19. Carrying iPods is more common now among students than carrying cell phones.
20. Cindy has applied to as many colleges as, if not more than, Joanne.

Recognizing Pronoun–Antecedent Agreement, page 177

1. . . . her physical
2. No error
3. . . . her schedule

4. . . . their fall colors
5. . . . their money
6. . . . its collection
7. . . . it conducted itself
8. . . . donate his or her time
9. No error
10. . . . they can

Identifying Faulty Pronoun Reference, page 178

These are suggested answers. Other answers may also be correct.

1. Doing what she loves, Mrs. Parker spends most of her time knitting.
2. At the end, having answered all the questions, I handed the test in.
3. Peggy was sure she had handed in the homework and told Eileen.
4. Bill had only ten minutes left on the parking meter and told his father.
5. During his administration, Bush sent troops to fight in Iraq.
6. Henry, a pilot, regularly flies a helicopter on rescue missions.
7. In *The Great Gatsby*, Fitzgerald wrote about the American Dream.
8. Because he wanted a plasma television, she decided to buy him one.
9. The agreement between Joan and Jane fell apart after Joan failed to show up for the meeting.
10. After his interview, Mike thought he would probably like spending the next four years at Dartmouth and told Tom.

Recognizing Shifts in Pronoun Person and Errors in Pronoun Case, page 179

1. between her and me
2. Sam and me
3. Gert and him
4. they collect
5. We women
6. Jonathan and him
7. you should expect
8. He and I
9. you really need
10. Their singing
11. than she
12. No error

13. keep themselves
14. as I
15. her nor her sister

Identifying Faulty Verb Tense, page 181

1. came
2. brought
3. No error
4. had ridden
5. had reached
6. expected
7. had finished
8. No error
9. gave
10. begins
11. stopped
12. gives
13. Having worked
14. had seen
15. suffered

Identifying Faulty Verb Form, page 182

1. used to arrive
2. arisen
3. Correct
4. blew
5. had begun
6. had burst
7. should have gone
8. had never sung
9. had sprung
10. to attract

Combining Sentences, page 189

Because many different answers are possible, these are suggestions only. As you compare your answers to these, be sure that you have included all the information from each group of sentences.

1. At 13, she has already won recognition as an expert gymnast.
2. After the hit and run accident, broken glass lay on the street.
3. Aunt Ellen had a mess on her hands after she dropped a bag containing a glass bottle of tomato juice that she had bought at the grocery store.
4. The baseball hit Mr. Strickman's picture window, shattering it into a thousand pieces.

5. Since the storm dumped two feet of snow on the roads, I could not go out. I had nothing to do but watch TV and assemble a jigsaw puzzle. The time passed slowly.

6. The Earth revolves around the sun every 365 days. At the same time, it rotates on its axis every 24 hours. The Earth's revolution around the sun determines the length of a year just as its rotation determines the duration of a day.

7. The 2,000-year-old tragedies of Euripides, an ancient Greek playwright, are still performed today.

8. Music has the unique power to transport people's minds. While listening, people often dream and think, and afterwards feel refreshed.

9. The skulls of humans consist of twenty-two bones: eight in the cranium, which protects the brain, and fourteen in the face and jaw.

10. The culture of the Hopi Indians, whose name means "peaceful and happy," exemplifies peace and contentment. Lacking competitiveness, Hopis rarely feel tense. What they value instead are self-discipline, restraint, and the welfare of others. But the highest value is the family, consisting of the entire Hopi tribe.

Arranging Sentences, page 192

1. a. 4   b. 3   c. 2   d. 1
2. a. 2   b. 5   c. 1   d. 4   e. 3   f. 6
3. a. 3   b. 1   c. 4   d. 2
4. a. 3   b. 4   c. 2   d. 1
5. a. 3   b. 2   c. 4   d. 1   e. 5
6. a. 4   b. 2   c. 1   d. 3   e. 5
7. a. 4   b. 2   c. 1   d. 3
8. a. 3   b. 4   c. 2   d. 1   e. 5
9. a. 3   b. 4   c. 2   d. 1
10. a. 2   b. 4   c. 1   d. 3
11. a. 1   b. 4   c. 3   d. 2

PART **VI**

TESTS FOR PRACTICE

PRACTICE TEST A

Section 1
Essay

TIME—25 MINUTES

> Directions: Plan and write an essay in response to the assigned topic. Use the essay as an opportunity to show how clearly and effectively you can express and develop ideas. Present your thoughts logically and precisely. Include specific evidence or examples to support your point of view. A plain, natural writing style is probably best. The number of words is up to you, but quantity is less important than quality.
>
> Limit your essay to two sides of the lined paper provided. You'll have enough space if you write on every line and avoid wide margins. Write or print legibly because handwriting that's hard or impossible to read will decrease your score.
>
> BE SURE TO WRITE ONLY ON THE ASSIGNED TOPIC. AN ESSAY WRITTEN ON ANOTHER TOPIC WILL BE SCORED "ZERO."
>
> If you finish in less than 25 minutes, check your work. Do not turn to another section of the test.

Think carefully about the following passage and the assignment below.

> Describing his vision for the world's future, President Franklin D. Roosevelt told Congress in 1941 that " . . .we look forward to a world founded upon four essential human freedoms. The first is freedom of speech and expression. . . . The second is freedom of every person to worship God in his own way. . . . The third is freedom from want. . . . The fourth is freedom from fear."

Assignment: All four freedoms are crucial in a free society. Yet, Roosevelt may be faulted for not adding a fifth, a sixth, or even more freedoms to the list. Given the opportunity to add another freedom, what would you choose? Feel free to invent a new freedom or simply pick one that already exists in the Bill of Rights or elsewhere. Support your position with reasoning and examples taken from your observations, experience, studies, or reading.

Section 1

ESSAY
Time allowed: 25 minutes
Limit your essay to two pages. Do not skip lines. Write only inside the box.

Essay (continued)

ANSWER SHEET FOR MULTIPLE-CHOICE QUESTIONS

Section 2
Improving Sentences

1. Ⓐ Ⓑ Ⓒ Ⓓ Ⓔ
2. Ⓐ Ⓑ Ⓒ Ⓓ Ⓔ
3. Ⓐ Ⓑ Ⓒ Ⓓ Ⓔ
4. Ⓐ Ⓑ Ⓒ Ⓓ Ⓔ
5. Ⓐ Ⓑ Ⓒ Ⓓ Ⓔ
6. Ⓐ Ⓑ Ⓒ Ⓓ Ⓔ
7. Ⓐ Ⓑ Ⓒ Ⓓ Ⓔ
8. Ⓐ Ⓑ Ⓒ Ⓓ Ⓔ
9. Ⓐ Ⓑ Ⓒ Ⓓ Ⓔ
10. Ⓐ Ⓑ Ⓒ Ⓓ Ⓔ
11. Ⓐ Ⓑ Ⓒ Ⓓ Ⓔ

Identifying
Sentence Errors

12. Ⓐ Ⓑ Ⓒ Ⓓ Ⓔ
13. Ⓐ Ⓑ Ⓒ Ⓓ Ⓔ
14. Ⓐ Ⓑ Ⓒ Ⓓ Ⓔ
15. Ⓐ Ⓑ Ⓒ Ⓓ Ⓔ
16. Ⓐ Ⓑ Ⓒ Ⓓ Ⓔ
17. Ⓐ Ⓑ Ⓒ Ⓓ Ⓔ
18. Ⓐ Ⓑ Ⓒ Ⓓ Ⓔ
19. Ⓐ Ⓑ Ⓒ Ⓓ Ⓔ
20. Ⓐ Ⓑ Ⓒ Ⓓ Ⓔ
21. Ⓐ Ⓑ Ⓒ Ⓓ Ⓔ
22. Ⓐ Ⓑ Ⓒ Ⓓ Ⓔ
23. Ⓐ Ⓑ Ⓒ Ⓓ Ⓔ
24. Ⓐ Ⓑ Ⓒ Ⓓ Ⓔ
25. Ⓐ Ⓑ Ⓒ Ⓓ Ⓔ
26. Ⓐ Ⓑ Ⓒ Ⓓ Ⓔ
27. Ⓐ Ⓑ Ⓒ Ⓓ Ⓔ
28. Ⓐ Ⓑ Ⓒ Ⓓ Ⓔ
29. Ⓐ Ⓑ Ⓒ Ⓓ Ⓔ

Improving Paragraphs

30. Ⓐ Ⓑ Ⓒ Ⓓ Ⓔ
31. Ⓐ Ⓑ Ⓒ Ⓓ Ⓔ
32. Ⓐ Ⓑ Ⓒ Ⓓ Ⓔ
33. Ⓐ Ⓑ Ⓒ Ⓓ Ⓔ
34. Ⓐ Ⓑ Ⓒ Ⓓ Ⓔ
35. Ⓐ Ⓑ Ⓒ Ⓓ Ⓔ

Section 3
Improving Sentences

1. Ⓐ Ⓑ Ⓒ Ⓓ Ⓔ
2. Ⓐ Ⓑ Ⓒ Ⓓ Ⓔ
3. Ⓐ Ⓑ Ⓒ Ⓓ Ⓔ
4. Ⓐ Ⓑ Ⓒ Ⓓ Ⓔ
5. Ⓐ Ⓑ Ⓒ Ⓓ Ⓔ
6. Ⓐ Ⓑ Ⓒ Ⓓ Ⓔ
7. Ⓐ Ⓑ Ⓒ Ⓓ Ⓔ
8. Ⓐ Ⓑ Ⓒ Ⓓ Ⓔ
9. Ⓐ Ⓑ Ⓒ Ⓓ Ⓔ
10. Ⓐ Ⓑ Ⓒ Ⓓ Ⓔ
11. Ⓐ Ⓑ Ⓒ Ⓓ Ⓔ
12. Ⓐ Ⓑ Ⓒ Ⓓ Ⓔ
13. Ⓐ Ⓑ Ⓒ Ⓓ Ⓔ
14. Ⓐ Ⓑ Ⓒ Ⓓ Ⓔ

Remove answer sheet by cutting on dotted line.

Section 2
Multiple-Choice Questions

TIME—25 MINUTES

IMPROVING SENTENCES

Directions: The underlined sentences and sentence parts below may contain errors in standard English, including awkward or ambiguous expression, poor word choice (diction), incorrect sentence structure, or faulty grammar, usage, and punctuation. Read each sentence carefully and identify which of the five alternative versions most effectively and correctly expresses the meaning of the underlined material. Indicate your choice by filling in the corresponding space on the answer sheet. Choice A always repeats the original. Choose A if none of the other choices improves the original sentence.

EXAMPLE   ANSWER

The campers slept <u>more poorer</u> on   Ⓐ Ⓑ Ⓒ ● Ⓔ
the first night than on the second

(A) more poorer
(B) less poorer
(C) poorest
(D) more poorly
(E) more poorest

1. <u>The captain standing on the bridge of the ship,</u> <u>he</u> had never seen such a strong wind in all his years at sea.

    (A) The captain standing on the bridge of the ship, he
    (B) Standing on the bridge of the ship, the captain he
    (C) Standing on the bridge of the ship, the captain
    (D) To stand on the bridge of the ship, the captain
    (E) The captain stood on the bridge of the ship, and he

2. What can beat the thrill <u>of kicking a soccer ball</u> <u>past the goalie for a score and to hear applause</u> <u>from the crowd</u>?

    (A) of kicking a soccer ball past the goalie for a score and to hear applause from the crowd
    (B) of kicking a soccer ball past the goalie for a score and to hear applause by the crowd
    (C) of kicking a soccer ball past the goalie for a score and hearing the crowd applaud
    (D) to kick a soccer ball past the goalie scoring a goal, and to hear the crowd applaud
    (E) of hearing the crowd applaud after having kicked a soccer ball past the goalie for a score

3. The White House Chief of Staff, in addition to the First Lady, <u>increasingly influence the administration's policies</u>.

   (A) increasingly influence the administration's policies

   (B) are being more and more influential in the administration's policies

   (C) are increasing their influence on the administration's policies

   (D) is becoming increasingly more influential in determining the administration's policies

   (E) increasingly influences the administration's policies

4. To celebrate the 100th anniversary of the college, <u>honoring those alumni who had graduated fifty years ago</u>.

   (A) honoring those alumni who had graduated fifty years ago

   (B) ceremonies for graduates of fifty years ago were held in honor of these alumni

   (C) alumni graduating fifty years ago received honors

   (D) alumni who had graduated fifty years ago were honored

   (E) graduating alumni of fifty years ago were honored

5. Professor <u>Bromley, the first historian to reveal the story of the Mandan tribe, doing it</u> appropriately in conjunction with the bicentennial of the Lewis and Clark expedition.

   (A) Bromley, the first historian to reveal the story of the Mandan tribe, doing it

   (B) Bromley was the first historian to reveal the story of the Mandan tribe, and who did so

   (C) Bromley was the first historian to have revealed the story of the Mandan tribe and does it

   (D) Bromley was the first historian to reveal the story of the Mandan tribe, telling the tale

   (E) Bromley, the first historian revealing the story of the Mandan tribe, the tale was told

6. Dede and Michelle were among the players chosen for the all-county field hockey <u>team, their performance in this having been exceptional</u>.

   (A) team, their performance in this having been exceptional

   (B) team; they have performed exceptionally in this

   (C) team, for they have performed exceptionally in this

   (D) team; their performance having been exceptional

   (E) team, for their performance has been exceptional

7. The film's special effects and gripping story <u>give audiences a thrill</u>.

   (A) give audiences a thrill

   (B) thrills the people who are watching

   (C) give a thrill to the people in the audience watching it

   (D) give thrills in the watching of it to the audience

   (E) gives people thrills in watching it

8. Some of the trees looked on the verge of dying, or <u>as if already they had died</u>.

   (A) as if already they had died

   (B) if they had already

   (C) whether they had died already

   (D) as though they had already died

   (E) like they had died already

9. <u>Although the speakers never having reached their audience, they couldn't</u> express themselves plainly or in a down-to-earth manner.

   (A) Although the speakers never having reached their audience, they couldn't

   (B) The speakers never reached their audience, they couldn't

   (C) Never having reached their audience, the speakers couldn't

   (D) The speakers never reached their audience; however, they couldn't

   (E) The speakers never reached their audience because they couldn't

10. <u>If we agree to purchase the house today</u>, we would have saved $,5000.

    (A) If we agree to purchase the house today
    (B) Had we agreed to purchase the house today
    (C) If we would of agreed to purchase the house today
    (D) If the purchasing of the house was agreed today
    (E) If today we will agree to purchase the house

11. Manned flights to Mars will not be planned until the far-distant <u>future because it requires</u> costly technology that is yet to be developed.

    (A) future because it requires
    (B) future because it would require
    (C) future because they require
    (D) future, each requires
    (E) future since they are requiring

IDENTIFYING SENTENCE ERRORS

<u>Directions</u>: The underlined and lettered parts of each sentence below may contain an error in grammar, usage, word choice (diction), or expression (idiom). Read each sentence carefully and identify which item, if any, contains an error. Indicate your choice by filling in the corresponding space on the answer sheet. No sentence contains more than one error. Some sentences may contain no error. In that case, the correct choice will always be E (No error).

EXAMPLE

Jill went <u>speedily</u> to the <u>crest</u> of the
        A   B
hill in a <u>more</u> faster time <u>than</u> her
         C   D
friend, Jack. <u>No error</u>.
        E

ANSWER

Ⓐ Ⓑ ● Ⓓ Ⓔ

12. Written by William Golding, the novel

    Lord of the Flies <u>tells</u> <u>what happens</u> when
                A   B
    a group of schoolboys <u>get stranded</u> <u>on</u> an
                       C   D
    uninhabited island. <u>No error</u>.
               E

13. Using special lighting techniques, food stores

    <u>subtly enhance</u> the color of produce on <u>their</u>
         A   B
    shelves, <u>thereby</u> attracting consumers,
            C
    encouraging impulse buying, and most

    important, <u>it creates</u> the appearance of
                D
    freshness and wholesomeness. <u>No error</u>.
                               E

14. While looking around the infirmary, I observed

    many <u>other</u> patients <u>which</u> happened to be
           A   B

    suffering <u>from</u> the same upper respiratory
             C

    infection as <u>I</u>. <u>No error</u>.
           D   E

15. <u>There's</u> no doubt that the safe-driving
     A

    campaign scheduled to begin next week

    <u>would have been</u> postponed for another week
           B

    <u>because</u> we lack the time to plan it <u>well</u>.
       C   D

    <u>No error</u>.
     E

16. Experts in marine life say that <u>there is</u> a
                             A

    closer relationship between barracudas <u>with</u>
                                 B

    man-eating sharks <u>than</u> <u>had been</u> previously
                 C   D

    thought. <u>No error</u>.
         E

17. The threat <u>to suspend</u> students <u>caught</u> using
             A   B

    cell phones during class without permission

    seems <u>like</u> an over-reaction to the problem
         C

    <u>because</u> the principal is ordinarily sensitive
     D

    and level-headed. <u>No error</u>.
               E

18. Ray Bradbury and Isaac Asimov stand

    <u>side by side</u> as two of America's greatest
      A

    science fiction writers, but the latter,

    <u>having written</u> more <u>than</u> 500 books, is
        B   C

    by far the <u>most</u> prolific. <u>No error</u>.
           D   E

19. <u>Behind</u> almost all successful candidates for
     A

    public office <u>stands</u> a staff, a team of
              B

    volunteers, a group of fund raisers, and,

    <u>of course</u>, a platform that convinced the
     C

    electorate to choose <u>them</u>. <u>No error</u>.
                    C   E

20. Although a sales tax may seem like an efficient

    way for cities <u>to raise</u> revenues, <u>they are</u> more
                A   B

    harmful to low-income consumers <u>than to</u>
                              C

    wealthy <u>ones</u>. <u>No error</u>.
           D   E

21. <u>Being</u> lost in the mountains of Colorado for
     A

    two days <u>as a boy</u>, Dave is <u>always careful</u> to
           B   C

    take a detailed map with him <u>when</u> he sets out
                         D

    for a backpacking adventure in the wilderness.

    <u>No error</u>.
     E

22. Many students <u>who</u> successfully use computers
            A

    <u>in the bettering of</u> vocabulary for the SATs
           B

    <u>find that</u> a computer <u>provides</u> limited help in
       C   D

    the improvement of writing skills. <u>No error</u>.
                              E

23. The FBI agents chose <u>not</u> to arrest the suspect
                   A

    <u>in the bank</u> that afternoon, <u>but instead</u> arrested
        B   C

    him at the airport before he <u>is boarding</u> a flight
                           D

    to Atlanta. <u>No error</u>.
           E

24. <u>Although</u> it appears cold and forbidding on
    A

<u>its</u> surface, the Caspian Sea, the <u>greatest of all</u>
B   C

inland seas, teems with aquatic life <u>in its depths</u>.
                               D

<u>No error</u>.
E

25. The names Leno and Letterman <u>may be</u>
                            A

alphabetically close together, <u>but</u> Leno is
                       B

<u>the funnier</u> comedian and Letterman
C

<u>the quickest</u>. <u>No error</u>.
D   E

26. The in-class activity <u>consisted of</u> forming <u>into</u>
               A   B

groups, discussing the questions about the

book, and <u>give</u> a presentation <u>in front of</u> the
      C   D

class. <u>No error</u>.
      E

27. <u>Reflecting on</u> the size of our national debt,
    A

one might <u>well</u> ask <u>yourself</u> how the most
       B   C

powerful nation on earth <u>could have gotten</u>
                           D

itself into such a mess. <u>No error</u>.
                 E

28. At Burger King, the hamburgers are very

<u>similar to McDonald's</u>, <u>except</u> they are
A   B

<u>slightly smaller</u> and contain <u>less</u> fat.
C   D

<u>No error</u>.
E

29. The achievements as well as the failures of

the space program <u>has been</u> <u>a matter</u> of
           A   B

contention for many years <u>as</u> many interest
                    C

groups compete <u>for</u> a share of the federal
           D

budget. <u>No error</u>.
      E

IMPROVING PARAGRAPHS

Directions: The passage below is the draft of a student's essay. Some parts of the passage need improvement. Read the passage and answer the questions that follow. The questions are about revisions that might improve all or part of the passage's organization, development, sentence structure, or choice of words. Choose the answer that best follows the requirements of standard written English.

Questions 30–35 refer to the following passage.

[1] It is difficult to deny that modern technology has changed human behavior. [2] The style, sound, and recording techniques of pop music, for example, have been altered greatly. [3] Thousands of unknown musicians, aiming to become famous, have turned to the Internet to distribute their music digitally.

[4] For next to nothing, young musicians can put their music on the Web. [5] In the past, it would cost many thousands of dollars to put out a sample record or tape. [6] The members of a high school rock band rent a recording studio for hundreds of dollars an hour. [7] They might not do their best work in a rush to save money. [8] And they would incur huge expenses to record just one song. [9] It is expensive to distribute tapes or CDs to agents, radio stations, disk jockeys, clubs, or any other place where someone might give a listen. [10] Getting a tape or CD into record stores is almost impossible for musicians without a huge following or reputation. [11] Now, however, tens of thousands of musicians can bypass the usual route to stardom and record whatever they want, using the lyrics and sounds they like, and post their songs on Web sites. [12] Recording at their own pace, the songs won't be ready until the musicians are satisfied that it represents their best work. [13] Some musicians have released full-length albums on the Web. [14] A new award category has been added to the Video Music Awards. [15] MTV presents the awards annually. [16] The new award is called "Best Band Web Site."

[17] Using the Internet is no guarantee of success. [18] A group called the Bossa Nova Beatniks put a collection of their songs on the Web. [19] Within three months, over 4,000 listeners had downloaded their music.

30. The sentence that best states the main idea of the essay is

(A) sentence 1
(B) sentence 3
(C) sentence 4
(D) sentence 11
(E) sentence 17

31. To best connect sentence 6 to the rest of the second paragraph, which is the best word or phrase to insert after "rock band" in sentence 6 (reproduced below)?

The members of a high school rock band rent a recording studio for hundreds of dollars an hour.

(A) can
(B) will
(C) might
(D) shall
(E) decided to

32. Which of the following is the best way to revise and combine the underlined portions of sentences 7 and 8 (reproduced below)?

They might not do their best work <u>in a rush to save money. And they would incur huge expenses</u> to record just one song.

(A) in a rush to save money they would incur huge expenses.
(B) rushing to save money, incur huge expenses
(C) incurring huge expenses in their rush to save money
(D) and rushing to save money, huge expenses would be incurred
(E) in a rush to save money and would incur huge expenses

33. Which of the following is the best revision of the underlined portion of sentence 12 (reproduced below)?

Recording at their own pace, the songs won't be published until the musicians are satisfied that it represents their best work.

(A) the work won't be published until the musicians are satisfied that the songs they have recorded represent their best work

(B) musicians won't be satisfied publishing songs unless it represents their best work

(C) musicians won't publish or be satisfied with any song that represents less than their best work

(D) musicians know that their songs won't be ready for publication and they won't be satisfied until they represent their best work

(E) the songs won't be published or satisfy the musicians until they represent their best work

34. In the context of the essay, which of the following is the best combination of sentences 14, 15, and 16 (reproduced below)?

A new award category has been added to the Video Music Awards. MTV presents the awards annually. The new award is called "Best Band Web Site."

(A) A new award, called "Best Band Web Site," has been added to MTV's annual Video Music Awards.

(B) The "Best Band Web Site," added as a category to the Video Music Awards, is presented by MTV annually.

(C) Annually MTV presents Video Music Awards, and the category of "Best Band Web Site" has been added.

(D) Having added the category "Best Band Web Site" to its Video Music Awards, MTV presents the awards annually.

(E) The Video Music Awards presented annually has added "Best Band Web Site" to its awards, which is presented by MTV.

35. In the context of the last paragraph, which sentence would be most appropriate to follow sentence 19?

(A) Consequently, the sound of the Bossa Nova Beatniks has great appeal.

(B) The group's music, by the way, is an eclectic mix of ska, calypso, and rockabilly.

(C) The Beatniks' leader, Tom Gould, says he doesn't want to be the next Bon Jovi or Pearl Jam.

(D) The experience of the Bossa Nova Beatniks, however, is a rare exception to the rule.

(E) In fact, it has been predicted that many musicians will start using the Web as a mode of distribution.

End of Section 2.
Do not return to Section 1. Do not proceed to Section 3 until the allotted time for Section 2 has passed.

Section 3
Multiple-Choice Questions

TIME—10 MINUTES

IMPROVING SENTENCES

Directions: The underlined sentences and sentence parts below may contain errors in standard English, including awkward or ambiguous expression, poor word choice (diction), incorrect sentence structure, or faulty grammar, usage, and punctuation. Read each sentence carefully and identify which of the five alternative versions most effectively and correctly expresses the meaning of the underlined material. Indicate your choice by filling in the corresponding space on the answer sheet. Choice A always repeats the original. Choose A if none of the other choices improves the original sentence.

1. After the book was published, the author has been criticized for plagiarizing passages from other books.

   (A) author has been criticized for plagiarizing
   (B) author was criticized for plagiarizing
   (C) author will be criticized for plagiarizing
   (D) author would have been criticized for plagiarizing
   (E) author, being criticized for plagiarizing

2. The new nuclear desalinization plant, being built on the river bank, and is costing far more than expected.

   (A) plant, being built on the river bank, and is costing far more than expected
   (B) plant is costing far more than expected, it is being built on the river bank
   (C) plant being built on the river bank is costing far more than expected
   (D) plant is costing far more than expected being built on the river bank
   (E) plant to be built on the river bank and to cost far more than expected

3. At five years old, my father took me to get a haircut for the very first time.

   (A) At five years old, my father took me to get a haircut for the very first time
   (B) At five years old, my father took me to get my first haircut
   (C) My father took me at five years old to get a haircut for the very first time
   (D) When I was five, my father took me for my first haircut
   (E) At age five I was taken by my father to get my first haircut, something I had never had before

4. Not three weeks following Lance Armstrong's victory in the Tour de France bicycle race but the doctors diagnosed him with cancer.

   (A) but the doctors diagnosed him with cancer
   (B) but the doctors had him diagnosed with cancer
   (C) than he has been diagnosed by the doctors that he had cancer
   (D) but cancer had been diagnosed in him by doctors
   (E) than doctors diagnosed his cancer

5. Claude Monet studied the light and color of the French countryside, and <u>these are the impressions that he incorporated</u> in many of his paintings.

   (A) these are the impressions that he incorporated
   (B) the incorporation of these impressions were
   (C) these impressions having been incorporated
   (D) his incorporation of these impressions
   (E) incorporated his impressions

6. <u>In this article it characterizes Collins as being brilliant, ruthless, and likely to resign soon</u>.

   (A) In this article it characterizes Collins as being brilliant, ruthless, and likely to resign soon
   (B) Collins, characterized in this article as being brilliant, ruthless, and likely to resign soon
   (C) In this article, Collins is characterized as brilliant, ruthless, and he is likely to resign soon
   (D) This article, which characterizes Collins as brilliant and ruthless, says that he is likely to resign soon
   (E) This article, in which Collins is characterized as being brilliant, ruthless and likely to resign soon

7. Therefore, I admire any organization that speaks up for democratic principles, <u>even when they are for selfish aims</u>.

   (A) even when they are for selfish aims
   (B) even if its motive is selfish
   (C) even if their motive is to be for its own selfish aims
   (D) whether or not it is for their own selfish aims
   (E) even whether or not their motive is for their own selfish aims

8. The book is filled with color <u>photographs that offer vivid reminders to both veterans and</u> civilians of the horrors of the Vietnam War.

   (A) photographs that offer vivid reminders to both veterans and
   (B) photographs, which offers vivid reminders to both veterans and
   (C) photographs, which offer both vivid reminders to veterans plus
   (D) photographs; it offers vivid reminders to both veterans as well as
   (E) photographs; this offers vivid reminders both to veterans and

9. One of the great literary figures of the 20th century, <u>Maxwell Perkins, an editor at Scribners, helping</u> Hemingway, Fitzgerald, and Thomas Wolfe break into print.

   (A) Maxwell Perkins, an editor at Scribners, helping
   (B) Maxwell Perkins who worked as an editor and helped
   (C) Maxwell Perkins edited at Scribners who helped
   (D) Maxwell Perkins, an editor at Scribners, helped
   (E) the editor, Maxwell Perkins, helped at Scribners

10. <u>Still being bought for its</u> appearance and charm, teddy bears rank among the most popular toys ever invented.

    (A) Still being bought for its
    (B) Still having been bought for its
    (C) They are consistently bought for their
    (D) Because they were bought for their
    (E) Consistently bought for their

11. Twenty years ago Peterson took a job with the federal Bureau of Land Management, <u>and he has been responsible for maintaining public lands ever since</u>.

   (A) and he has been responsible for maintaining public lands ever since
   (B) since then his responsibility has been maintaining public lands
   (C) wherever since he is responsible for maintaining public land
   (D) he has been responsible for maintaining public lands since then
   (E) and since then is responsible for maintaining public lands

12. Flowing through sand, rocks, and silt, <u>variations in the speed of underground water are many</u>.

   (A) variations in the speed of underground water are many
   (B) underground water travels at various speeds
   (C) the speed of underground water varies
   (D) underground water speeds vary
   (E) running underground water vary in speed

13. <u>They not only spoke enthusiastically about the new fertilizer but also praised</u> the farmers who tried it.

   (A) They not only spoke enthusiastically about the new fertilizer but also praised
   (B) They not only spoke enthusiastically about the new fertilizer but also praising
   (C) They not only spoke enthusiastically about the new fertilizer but also to praise
   (D) They spoke enthusiastically not only about new fertilizer but also praising
   (E) They spoke both enthusiastically about the new fertilizer, but they also praised

14. In his zeal to make a realistic movie, the director studied the language of the street <u>gang, and the dialogue was made to sound authentic</u>.

   (A) gang, and the dialogue was made to sound authentic
   (B) gang and making the dialogue sound authentic
   (C) gang and made the dialogue sound authentic
   (D) gang, with the result being that the dialogue is authentic-sounding
   (E) gang in where the dialogue sounds authentic

End of Section 3.
Do not return to Sections 1 or 2.

END OF WRITING TEST.

ANSWER KEY

SECTION 1—THE ESSAY

Guide for Scoring Your Essay

Using this guide, rate yourself in each of these six categories. Enter your scores in the spaces provided, and calculate the average of the six ratings to determine your final score.

On the SAT itself, two readers will score your essay on a scale of 6 (high) to 1 (low), or *zero* if you fail to write on the assigned topic. The score will be reported to you as the sum of the two ratings, from 12 to 0.

Remember that SAT essays are judged in relation to other essays written on the same topic. Therefore, this scoring guide may not yield a totally accurate prediction of the score you can expect on the exam. Because it is difficult to read your own essay with total objectivity, you might improve the validity of your score by getting a second opinion about your essay from an informed friend or a teacher.

Overall Impression

6   Consistently outstanding in clarity and competence; very insightful; few, if any, errors

5   Reasonably consistent in clarity and competence; occasional errors or lapses in quality; contains some insight

4   Adequate competence; some lapses in quality; fairly clear and with evidence of insight

3   Generally inadequate but demonstrates potential competence; contains some confusing aspects

2   Seriously limited; significant weaknesses in quality; generally unclear or incoherent

1   Demonstrates fundamental incompetence; contains serious flaws; significantly undeveloped or confusing

Score ☐

Development of Point of View

6   Fully developed with clear and appropriate supporting material; demonstrates high level of critical thinking

5   Generally well developed with appropriate examples, reasons, and other evidence to support a main idea; demonstrates strong critical thinking

4   Partly develops a main idea with relatively appropriate examples and reasons; shows some evidence of critical thinking

3   Weak development of main idea and little evidence of critical thinking; barely appropriate examples or other supporting material

2   Lacks a focus on a main idea; weak critical thinking; inappropriate or insufficient evidence

1   Fails to articulate a viable point of view; provides virtually no evidence of understanding the prompt

Score ☐

Organization of Ideas

6   Extremely well organized and focused on a main idea; supporting evidence presented in an effective, logical sequence

5   Generally well organized and reasonably focused on a main idea; mostly coherent and logical presentation of supporting material

4   Reasonably organized; shows some evidence of thoughtful sequence and progression of ideas

3   Limited organization and vague focus on main idea; contains some confusion in the sequence of ideas

2   Barely recognizable organization; little coherence; serious problems with sequence of ideas

1   No discernable organization; incoherent sequence of ideas

Score ☐

Language and Word Choice

6   Highly effective and skillful use of language; varied, appropriate, and accurate vocabulary

5   Demonstrates competence in use of language; appropriate and correct vocabulary

4   Adequate but inconsistent use of effective language; conventional but mostly correct use of vocabulary

3   Some minor errors in expression; generally weak or limited vocabulary; occasionally inappropriate word choice

2   Frequent errors in expression; very limited vocabulary; incorrect word choice interferes with meaning

1   Seriously deficient in use of language; meaning obscured by word choice

Score ☐

Sentence Structure

6   Varied and engaging sentence structure

5   Sufficiently varied sentence structure

4   Some sentence variation

3   Little sentence variation; minor sentence errors

2   Frequent sentence errors

1   Severe sentence errors; meaning obscured

Score ☐

Grammar, Usage, and Mechanics

6	Virtually or entirely error-free
5	Contains some minor errors
4	Some minor errors; one or two major errors
3	Accumulated minor and major errors
2	Contains frequent major errors that interfere with meaning
1	Contains severe errors that obscure meaning

Score ☐

<u>For rating yourself</u>

Total of six scores _____

Divide total by 6 to get score: _____ (A)
(Round to the nearest whole number.)

<u>For a second opinion</u>

Total of six scores _____

Divide total by 6 to get score: _____ (B)
(Round to the nearest whole number.)

(A) + (B) = ESSAY SUBSCORE _____
                              (0–12)

ANSWERS TO MULTIPLE-CHOICE QUESTIONS

Section 2

1. C	11. C	21. A	31. C
2. C	12. C	22. B	32. E
3. E	13. D	23. D	33. C
4. D	14. B	24. E	34. A
5. D	15. B	25. D	35. D
6. E	16. B	26. C	
7. A	17. E	27. C	
8. D	18. D	28. A	
9. E	19. B	29. A	
10. B	20. B	30. B	

Section 3

1. B	11. A
2. C	12. B
3. D	13. A
4. E	14. C
5. E	
6. D	
7. B	
8. A	
9. D	
10. E	

PERFORMANCE EVALUATION CHART

I. Self-Rating Chart

Section 2

Improving Sentences, questions 1–11   Number correct _____

Identifying Sentence Errors, questions 12–29   Number correct _____

Improving Paragraphs, questions 30–35   Number correct _____

Section 3

Improving Sentences, questions 1–14   Number correct _____

Subtotal _____ (A)

Wrong answers (Do not count unanswered questions)

Section 2   Number wrong _____

Section 3   Number wrong _____

Subtotal _____ (B)

Subtract ¼ point (0.25) from (B) for each wrong answer   _____ (C)

(A) minus (C) = _____ (D)

Round (D) to the nearest whole number for your MULTIPLE-CHOICE RAW SCORE   _____

ESSAY SUBSCORE   _____

CONVERSION TABLE

This table will give you an approximation of what your score would be if this practice test had been an actual SAT Writing Test. The essay counts for roughly 30% of the final score; the multiple-choice questions, for roughly 70%.

For example, if your Multiple-Choice Raw Score was 35 and your Essay Subscore was 6, the table indicates that your final score on the test would be approximately halfway between 500 and 710, or 600.

Multiple-Choice Raw Score	Essay Subscore						
	0	2	4	6	8	10	12
40–49	520–690	530–720	550–740	580–770	620–800	650–800	680–800
30–39	430–630	450–660	470–680	500–710	530–740	560–770	590–800
20–29	360–540	370–570	390–590	420–620	460–650	490–690	520–710
10–19	270–460	280–490	300–510	330–540	370–580	400–610	430–630
0–9	200–380	200–410	210–430	240–450	270–490	300–520	330–560
–12– –1	200–280	200–310	200–330	200–350	240–390	270–420	300–450

ANSWER EXPLANATIONS

Note: Although many choices contain multiple errors, only a single error is listed for each incorrect answer.

SECTION 2—IMPROVING SENTENCES

1. **C**   A. Mixed construction. The construction that begins with *The captain standing* has no grammatical relationship with the main clause.
B. Redundancy. Use either *he* or *the captain*, not both.
D. Mixed construction. The infinitive phrase that begins *To stand* is not logically related to the main clause.
E. Faulty coordination. This compound sentence contains two ideas that would be more effectively stated in a complex sentence.

2. **C**   A. Faulty parallelism. Coordinate elements in a sentence should be in parallel grammatical form. The phrases *of kicking* and *to hear* are not parallel.
B. Idiom error. In context, the preposition *by* is not standard usage. Use *of* or *from*.
D. Idiom error. In context the phrase *to kick* is not standard English usage.
E. Misplaced modifier. The phrase *after having kicked a soccer ball* should not refer to crowd but to the scorer of the goal. Use *after I have kicked*.

3. **E**   A. Subject–verb agreement. *Chief of Staff* is singular; *influence* is plural.
B. Subject–verb agreement. *Chief of Staff* is singular; *are being* is plural.
C. Subject–verb agreement. *Chief of Staff* is singular; *are increasing* is plural.
D. Wordiness. The words *increasingly* and *more* are redundant.

4. **D**   A. Sentence fragment. The construction lacks a subject and a verb.
B. Wordiness and redundancy. The phrase *graduates of fifty years ago* and the word *alumni* are redundant.
C. Verb tense. The verb *graduating* implies present action, but the sentence refers to events in the past.
E. Diction error. *Alumni* do not graduate from college; *students* do.

5. **D**   A. Sentence fragment. The construction lacks a main clause.
B. Mixed construction. The clause beginning *and who did so* is grammatically unrelated to the first clause.
C. Shift in verb tense. Cast in the past tense, the sentence shifts to the present.
E. Shift in grammatical subject. The subject shifts from *Bromley* to *the tale*.

6. **E**   A. Pronoun reference. The pronoun *this* fails to refer to a specific noun or other pronoun.
B. Same as A.
C. Same as A.
D. Sentence fragment. Semicolons separate complete sentences. The construction that starts *their performance* lacks a verb and is, therefore, incomplete.

7. **A**   B. Subject–verb agreement. The compound subject, *special effects and gripping story*, requires a plural verb. Use *thrill*.
C. Wordiness. The construction is needlessly wordy.
D. Clumsy construction.
E. Pronoun reference. The pronoun *it* fails to refer specifically to a noun or other pronoun.

8. **D**   A. Syntax error. The placement of *already* makes the phrase nonstandard.
B. Incomplete construction. The verb should be *had died*.
C. Diction error. The use of the word *whether* makes no sense in the context.
E. Diction error. *Like* introduces a phrase; *as* introduces a clause. Use *as* here.

9. **E**   A. Faulty subordination. The first clause lacks both a grammatical and a logical relationship with the second.
B. Comma splice. A comma may not be used to separate two independent clauses.
C. Sentence shift. The phrase beginning *Never having* lacks a logical relationship with the remainder of the sentence.
D. Diction error. The word *however* makes little sense in the context.

10. **B**   A. Shift in verb tense. In context, the verb *agree* indicates future action and is inconsistent with the main verb of the sentence *would have saved*, which indicates action already completed.
C. Faulty diction. *Would of* is nonstandard. Use *would have*.
D. Clumsy construction. The phrase *the purchasing of the house* is awkwardly expressed.
E. Shift in verb tense. The future action indicated by the verb *will agree* is inconsistent with the main verb *would have saved*, which indicates action already completed.

11. **C**   A. Pronoun–antecedent agreement. *Flights* is plural; *it* is singular. Use *they*.
B. Same as A.
D. Comma splice. A comma may not be used to separate two independent sentences.
E. Verb tense. The sentence refers to events that won't occur until the future. The verb *are requiring* pertains to the present.

Section 2—Identifying Sentence Errors

12. **C**   Noun–verb agreement. The word *group* is singular, the verb *get* is plural. Use *gets*.

13. **D**   Faulty parallelism. The phrase *it creates* is not parallel to the other verbs. Use *creating*.

14. **B**   Pronoun choice. Use *who* instead of *which* when referring to people.

15. **B**   Verb tense error. Use the future tense to describe events taking place in the future. Use *will have to be*.

16. **B**   Idiom error. Use *and* instead of *with*.

17. **E**   No error.

18. **D**   Faulty comparison. Use *more* when comparing two entities; use *most* for comparing three or more.

19. **B**   Subject–verb agreement. A compound subject requires a plural verb. Use *stand*.

20. **B**   Pronoun–antecedent agreement. The antecedent *tax* is singular. The pronoun–verb phrase *they are* is plural. Use *it is*.

21. **A**   Verb tense. The participle *being* should be used only to describe an action occurring at the same time as the action described by the main verb. Use *having been*.

22. **B**   Idiom error. The phrase *in the bettering of* is nonstandard. Use *to improve*.

23. **D**   Tense shift. The sentence is cast in the past tense. Use *boarded*.

24. **E**   No error.

25. **D**   Faulty comparison. Add *–er* to the positive form when comparing two entities. Add *–est* when comparing three or more. Use *quicker*.

26. **C**   Faulty parallelism. The verb is not parallel to the other verbs in the series. Use *giving*.

27. **C**   Pronoun shift. The sentence, cast in third person, shifts to second person. Use *oneself*.

28. **A**   Faulty comparison. *Hamburgers* may not be compared to *McDonald's*. Use *similar to those at McDonald's*.

29. **A**   Subject–verb agreement. The subject *achievements* is plural; the verb *has been* is singular. Use *have been*.

SECTION 2—IMPROVING PARAGRAPHS

30. **B**   Choice A seems like the main idea but it is far too broad and sweeping for the limited subject matter of this essay. Ideally, it ought to be eliminated.
Choice B contains the essay's main point. It is the best answer.
Choice C develops the idea introduced at the end of the first paragraph.
Choice D specifies one consequence of the change brought about by the Internet.
Choice E alters the direction of the essay and is too limited to qualify as the main idea.

31. **C** Choice A, a verb in the present tense, does not fit the context.
Choice B, a verb in the future tense, does not fit the context.
Choice C explains a situation that illustrates an idea introduced by the preceding sentence. It is the best answer.
Choice D expresses a future condition that, in context, is irrelevant.
Choice E, a verb in the past tense, is unrelated to the conditional *would*, used in sentences 5 and 8, and to *might*, used in sentence 7.

32. **E** Choice A is a run-on sentence. It needs punctuation between *money* and *they*.
Choice B contains mixed sentence construction that leaves the verb *incur* without a grammatical subject.
Choice C represents the work of a writer who has taken leave of his senses.
Choice D contains a problem in modification; the phrase *rushing to save money* must modify the performer of the action (*they*), not *expenses*.
Choice E is a direct and economical version of the original. It is the best answer.

33. **C** Choice A contains a dangling modifier. The phrase *Recording at their own pace* should modify *musicians*, not *work*.
Choice B contains pronoun–antecedent disagreement. *Songs* is plural, *it* is singular.
Choice C corrects the dangling modifier that marred the original sentence and clearly states the author's intent.
Choice D, besides being wordy, contains two pronouns with ambiguous antecedents.
Choice E contains a dangling modifier. The phrase *Recording at their own pace* should modify *musicians*, not *songs*. In addition, the references of the pronouns *they* and *their* are ambiguous, if not downright confusing.

34. **A** Choice A combines all the important ideas in a clear statement. It supports the author's intent to illustrate the coming-of-age of Web-based music. It is the best answer.
Choice B includes all the important ideas but ignores the author's intent by emphasizing the frequency of the MTV presentation rather than the addition of an award recognizing achievement in Web-site publication of music.
Choice C is a compound sentence that includes two clauses—one in active voice, the other in passive voice.
Choice D stresses the frequency of the award presentation, a distortion of the author's intended meaning.
Choice E, among other things, contains an ambiguous pronoun reference and noun–verb disagreement.

35. **D** Choices A, B, C, and E fail to develop the paragraph's main idea—that using the Internet is no guarantee of success—stated in sentence 17. Because Choice D alludes to that point, it is the best answer.

SECTION 3—IMPROVING SENTENCES

1. **B**   A. Shift in verb tense. The verb *has been criticized* shifts the sentence, cast in the past tense, to the present perfect tense.
    C. Shift in verb tense. The verb *will be criticized* shifts the sentence, cast in the past tense, to the future tense.
    D. Shift in verb tense. The verb *would have been criticized* shifts the sentence, cast in the past tense, to the future perfect tense.
    E. Sentence fragment. The construction lacks a main verb.

2. **C**   A. Mixed construction. The use of *and* introduces a construction grammatically and logically unrelated to the earlier part of the sentence.
    B. Comma splice. A comma (between *expected* and *it*) may not be used to separate two independent clauses.
    D. Syntax error. The word order is not standard English.
    E. Sentence fragment. The grammatical subject *plant* lacks a main verb.

3. **D**   A. Misplaced modifier. *At five years old* should modify *I* (the speaker), not *my father*.
    B. Misplaced modifier. *At five years old* should modify *I* (the speaker), not *my father*.
    C. Wordiness. Substitute *my first haircut* for *a haircut for the very first time* to make the sentence more cogent.
    E. Redundancy. *First* and *never had before* are redundant.

4. **E**   A. Diction error. In the context, the use of *but* is not standard English.
    B. Diction error. In the context, the use of *but* is not standard English.
    C. Shift in tense. The use of *has been*, a verb in the present perfect tense, is inconsistent with use of *had*, a verb in the past tense.
    D. Awkwardness. The use of passive voice leads to an awkwardly worded construction.

5. **E**   A. Faulty coordination. This compound sentence contains ideas that would be more effectively expressed by subordinating one clause to the other.
    B. Subject–verb agreement. The singular subject *incorporation* requires a singular verb. Use *was* instead of *were*.
    C. Sentence fragment. The second clause lacks a main verb.
    D. Sentence fragment. The second clause lacks a verb.

6. **D**   A. Faulty pronoun reference. The pronoun *it* lacks a specific referent.
    B. Sentence fragment. The construction lacks a main verb.
    C. Faulty coordination. The two coordinate clauses state seemingly unrelated information and contain ideas of unequal importance.
    E. Sentence fragment. The grammatical subject, *article*, lacks a verb.

7. **B**   A. Pronoun–antecedent agreement. The noun *organization* is singular; the pronoun *they* is plural. Use *it*.
    C. Shift in pronoun number. The pronoun shifts plural to singular.
    D. Pronoun reference. The pronoun *it* lacks a specific referent.
    E. Wordy. The phrase *their own selfish aims* is redundant. By definition *selfish aims* are for one-self.

8. **A**   B. Noun–verb agreement. The plural noun *photographs* requires a plural verb. Use *offer*.
     C. Misplaced modifier. The word *both* should modify *veterans*, not *vivid reminders*.
     D. Wordy. *Both* and *as well as* are redundant. Use one or the other.
     E. Pronoun reference. The pronoun *this* lacks a specific referent.

9. **D**   A. Faulty verb form. The *–ing* form of a verb may not serve as the main verb of a sentence without a helping verb.
     B. Sentence fragment. The construction lacks a main verb.
     C. Incorrect pronoun reference. The pronoun *who* refers to *Scribners* instead of *Perkins*.
     E. Idiom error. The construction *helped at Scribners Hemingway, etc.* . . . is not standard English.

10. **E**   A. Pronoun–antecedent agreement. The noun *teddy bears* is plural; the pronoun *its* is singular. Use *their*.
     B. Shift in tense. In the context of a sentence cast in the present tense, using the past perfect verb *having been* is incorrect.
     C. Comma splice. A comma may not be used to separate two independent clauses.
     D. Faulty subordination. The subordinating conjunction *because* fails to establish a logical relationship between clauses.

11. **A**   B. Comma splice. A comma may not be used to separate two independent clauses.
     C. Idiom error. The phrase *wherever since* is not standard English.
     D. Comma splice. A comma may not be used to separate two independent clauses.
     E. Verb tense. The use of *is*, a verb in the present tense, may not be used to describe past and continuing action. Use *has been*.

12. **B**   A. Dangling participle. The participial phrase that begins *Flowing through* should modify *water* instead of *variations*.
     C. Dangling participle. The participial phrase that begins *Flowing through* should modify *water* instead of *speed.*
     D. Dangling participle. The participial phrase that begins *Flowing through* should modify *water* instead of *speeds.*
     E. Subject–verb agreement. *Water* is singular; *vary* is plural. Use *varies*.

13. **A**   B. Faulty parallelism. The verb *spoke* is not parallel in form to *praising*.
     C. Faulty parallelism. The verb *spoke* is not parallel in form to the infinitive *to praise*.
     D. Faulty parallelism. The phrase *about the new fertilizer spoke* is not parallel to the verb *praising*.
     E. Incomplete construction. The use of *both* indicates the need for a second adverb paired with *enthusiastically*.

14. **C**   A. Mixed construction. The first clause of the compound sentence is in the active voice, the second in the passive voice.
     B. Faulty verb form. The *–ing* form of a verb may not serve as the main verb of a sentence without a helping verb.
     D. Wordy. The construction contains too many unnecessary words.
     E. Idiom. The phrase *gang in where* is not standard English.

PRACTICE TEST B

Section 1
Essay

TIME—25 MINUTES

Directions: Plan and write an essay in response to the assigned topic. Use the essay as an opportunity to show how clearly and effectively you can express and develop ideas. Present your thoughts logically and precisely. Include specific evidence or examples to support your point of view. A plain, natural writing style is probably best. The number of words is up to you, but quantity is less important than quality.

Limit your essay to two sides of the lined paper provided. You'll have enough space if you write on every line and avoid wide margins. Write or print legibly because handwriting that's hard or impossible to read will decrease your score.

BE SURE TO WRITE ONLY ON THE ASSIGNED TOPIC. AN ESSAY WRITTEN ON ANOTHER TOPIC WILL BE SCORED "ZERO."

If you finish in less than 25 minutes, check your work. Do not turn to another section of the test.

Think carefully about the following passage and the assignment below.

Passage 1

Educators recognize that academic growth is the highest priority of a school. To assure that academic growth is not impeded by participation in athletics and other activities, certain restrictions must be placed on student participation. These restrictions are intended for the students' guidance and assistance and are meant to contribute to the achievement of the goals set by schools in carrying out their mission.

Passage 2

- There are nearly 1 million high school football players and about 550,000 basketball players. Of that number, about 250 make it to the NFL and about 50 make an NBA team.
- Less than 3% of college seniors will play one year in professional basketball.
- The odds of a high-school football player making it to the pros at all—let alone having a career—are about 6,000 to 1; the odds for a high school basketball player—10,000 to 1.

Adapted from a letter to students written by Cedric W. Dempsey,
President of the National Collegiate Athletic Association

Assignment: In many high schools, students who fail a certain number of academic courses are ineligible to participate in varsity athletics and other time-consuming extracurricular activities. Do you believe it is proper to link participation in school sports and activities to classroom performance? Plan and write an essay that explains your point of view. Support your opinion with evidence and examples drawn from your studies, reading, observation, or experience.

Section 1

ESSAY
Time allowed: 25 minutes
Limit your essay to two pages. Do not skip lines. Write only inside the box.

Essay (continued)

ANSWER SHEET FOR MULTIPLE-CHOICE QUESTIONS

Section 2
Improving Sentences

1. Ⓐ Ⓑ Ⓒ Ⓓ Ⓔ
2. Ⓐ Ⓑ Ⓒ Ⓓ Ⓔ
3. Ⓐ Ⓑ Ⓒ Ⓓ Ⓔ
4. Ⓐ Ⓑ Ⓒ Ⓓ Ⓔ
5. Ⓐ Ⓑ Ⓒ Ⓓ Ⓔ
6. Ⓐ Ⓑ Ⓒ Ⓓ Ⓔ
7. Ⓐ Ⓑ Ⓒ Ⓓ Ⓔ
8. Ⓐ Ⓑ Ⓒ Ⓓ Ⓔ
9. Ⓐ Ⓑ Ⓒ Ⓓ Ⓔ
10. Ⓐ Ⓑ Ⓒ Ⓓ Ⓔ
11. Ⓐ Ⓑ Ⓒ Ⓓ Ⓔ

Identifying
Sentence Errors

12. Ⓐ Ⓑ Ⓒ Ⓓ Ⓔ
13. Ⓐ Ⓑ Ⓒ Ⓓ Ⓔ
14. Ⓐ Ⓑ Ⓒ Ⓓ Ⓔ
15. Ⓐ Ⓑ Ⓒ Ⓓ Ⓔ
16. Ⓐ Ⓑ Ⓒ Ⓓ Ⓔ
17. Ⓐ Ⓑ Ⓒ Ⓓ Ⓔ
18. Ⓐ Ⓑ Ⓒ Ⓓ Ⓔ
19. Ⓐ Ⓑ Ⓒ Ⓓ Ⓔ
20. Ⓐ Ⓑ Ⓒ Ⓓ Ⓔ
21. Ⓐ Ⓑ Ⓒ Ⓓ Ⓔ
22. Ⓐ Ⓑ Ⓒ Ⓓ Ⓔ
23. Ⓐ Ⓑ Ⓒ Ⓓ Ⓔ
24. Ⓐ Ⓑ Ⓒ Ⓓ Ⓔ
25. Ⓐ Ⓑ Ⓒ Ⓓ Ⓔ
26. Ⓐ Ⓑ Ⓒ Ⓓ Ⓔ
27. Ⓐ Ⓑ Ⓒ Ⓓ Ⓔ
28. Ⓐ Ⓑ Ⓒ Ⓓ Ⓔ
29. Ⓐ Ⓑ Ⓒ Ⓓ Ⓔ

Improving Paragraphs

30. Ⓐ Ⓑ Ⓒ Ⓓ Ⓔ
31. Ⓐ Ⓑ Ⓒ Ⓓ Ⓔ
32. Ⓐ Ⓑ Ⓒ Ⓓ Ⓔ
33. Ⓐ Ⓑ Ⓒ Ⓓ Ⓔ
34. Ⓐ Ⓑ Ⓒ Ⓓ Ⓔ
35. Ⓐ Ⓑ Ⓒ Ⓓ Ⓔ

Section 3
Improving Sentences

1. Ⓐ Ⓑ Ⓒ Ⓓ Ⓔ
2. Ⓐ Ⓑ Ⓒ Ⓓ Ⓔ
3. Ⓐ Ⓑ Ⓒ Ⓓ Ⓔ
4. Ⓐ Ⓑ Ⓒ Ⓓ Ⓔ
5. Ⓐ Ⓑ Ⓒ Ⓓ Ⓔ
6. Ⓐ Ⓑ Ⓒ Ⓓ Ⓔ
7. Ⓐ Ⓑ Ⓒ Ⓓ Ⓔ
8. Ⓐ Ⓑ Ⓒ Ⓓ Ⓔ
9. Ⓐ Ⓑ Ⓒ Ⓓ Ⓔ
10. Ⓐ Ⓑ Ⓒ Ⓓ Ⓔ
11. Ⓐ Ⓑ Ⓒ Ⓓ Ⓔ
12. Ⓐ Ⓑ Ⓒ Ⓓ Ⓔ
13. Ⓐ Ⓑ Ⓒ Ⓓ Ⓔ
14. Ⓐ Ⓑ Ⓒ Ⓓ Ⓔ

Section 2
Multiple-Choice Questions

IMPROVING SENTENCES

Directions: The underlined sentences and sentence parts below may contain errors in standard English, including awkward or ambiguous expression, poor word choice (diction), incorrect sentence structure, or faulty grammar, usage, and punctuation. Read each sentence carefully and identify which of the five alternative versions most effectively and correctly expresses the meaning of the underlined material. Indicate your choice by filling in the corresponding space on the answer sheet. Choice A always repeats the original. Choose A if none of the other choices improves the original sentence.

EXAMPLE

My old Aunt Maud loves to cook, and eating also.

ANSWER

Ⓐ ● Ⓒ Ⓓ Ⓔ

(A) cook, and eating also
(B) cook and to eat
(C) cook, and to eat also
(D) cook and eat besides
(E) cook and, in addition, eat

1. While walking down Market Street, that was when Clarissa sighted her old guitar in the pawn shop window.

   (A) that was when Clarissa sighted her old guitar in the pawn shop window
   (B) Clarissa sighted her old guitar in the pawn shop window
   (C) then the sighting of Clarissa's old guitar took place
   (D) Clarissa's old guitar was sighted in the pawn shop window
   (E) in the window of the pawn shop her old guitar was sighted by Clarissa

2. As a student at Penn State, where Julie grew to love history with a passion, ultimately leading to a job as a historian at the United States Library of Congress.

   (A) where Julie grew to love history with a passion, ultimately leading
   (B) Julie grew to love history with a passion that ultimately led
   (C) where she grew to love history with a passion, as a result leading Julie ultimately
   (D) Julie's love for history grew with a passion and it ultimately led her
   (E) where Julie grew to passionately love history, ultimately leading her

3. The letter was intended for <u>Betsy and him, but the actual recipients of the bad news were Peter and I</u>.

   (A) Betsy and him, but the actual recipients of the bad news were Peter and I
   (B) Betsy and I, but the actual recipients of the bad news were Peter and I
   (C) Betsy and him, but Peter and me actually received the bad news.
   (D) Betsy and he, but the actual recipients of the bad news turned out to be Peter and me
   (E) Betsy and I, but the bad news was actually received by Peter and I

4. <u>Funds that are earned as tips is</u> one of the most difficult sources of income for the Internal Revenue Service to monitor.

   (A) Funds that are earned as tips is
   (B) How money that gets earned as tips is
   (C) Earning tips are
   (D) Tips are
   (E) The funds earned by tipping is

5. The fictional characters in the novel *War and Peace* <u>are as similar as</u> the friends and acquaintances that the author, Leo Tolstoy, actually had.

   (A) are as similar as
   (B) is similar to
   (C) resembling
   (D) is the same as
   (E) are similar to

6. Today there is more violence <u>than</u> the 1950s and 1960s, when guns were more difficult to obtain.

   (A) than
   (B) then there was in
   (C) than in
   (D) than around
   (E) compared to

7. All along the road in Pennsylvania, one sees wonderful old horse barns, <u>each with its unique decorations</u>.

   (A) each with its unique decorations
   (B) each having their own unique decorations
   (C) and each of them have unique decorations of their own
   (D) which has its own unique decorations
   (E) they all have their own unique decorations

8. The consultant, Dr. Smart, agreed to study the school's schedule <u>and she would meet with students, teachers, and administrators to discuss it</u>.

   (A) and she would meet with students, teachers, and administrators to discuss it
   (B) and meeting with students, teachers, and administrators for discussing it
   (C) in holding discussions at meetings with students, teachers, and administrators about it
   (D) meeting for discussing about it with students, teachers, and administrators
   (E) by discussing it with students, teachers, and administrators.

9. <u>Because dinosaurs were the hugest creatures ever to roam the Earth is the reason why</u> they are fascinating to us.

   (A) Because dinosaurs were the hugest creatures ever to roam the Earth is the reason why
   (B) Because dinosaurs were the hugest creatures ever to roam the Earth,
   (C) Dinosaurs were the hugest creatures that ever roamed the Earth and is the reason why
   (D) As a result of dinosaurs, the hugest creatures ever to roam the Earth,
   (E) Dinosaurs are the hugest creatures ever to roam the Earth,

10. Reciting poems, one of the earliest forms of <u>entertainment, it increased in complexity as well as sophistication</u> as time went on.

   (A) entertainment, it increased in complexity as well as sophistication
   (B) entertainment, they increased in both complexity and sophistication
   (C) entertainment which both increased in complexity as well as sophistication
   (D) entertainment, and they increased in their complexity as well as growing more sophisticated
   (E) entertainment, increased in complexity and sophistication

11. Thomas Wolfe, the early 20th-century American <u>writer often confused with the contemporary novelist Tom Wolfe, grew up in Asheville, North Carolina</u>.

   (A) writer often confused with the contemporary novelist Tom Wolfe, grew up in Asheville, North Carolina
   (B) writer, having grown up in Asheville, North Carolina, is often mistaken with the contemporary novelist Tom Wolfe
   (C) writer, grew up in Asheville, North Carolina, but is often confused with the contemporary novelist Tom Wolfe
   (D) writer has often been confused with Tom Wolfe, the contemporary novelist, growing up in Asheville, North Carolina
   (E) writer, while growing up in Asheville, North Carolina, was often confused with the contemporary novelist Tom Wolfe

IDENTIFYING SENTENCE ERRORS

<u>Directions</u>: The underlined and lettered parts of each sentence below may contain an error in grammar, usage, word choice (diction), or expression (idiom). Read each sentence carefully and identify which item, if any, contains an error. Indicate your choice by filling in the corresponding space on the answer sheet. No sentence contains more than one error. Some sentences may contain no error. In that case, the correct choice will always be E (No error).

EXAMPLE

Jill went <u>speedily</u> to the <u>crest</u> of the
        A   B
hill in a <u>more</u> faster time <u>than</u> her
        C   D
friend, Jack. <u>No error</u>.
         E

ANSWER

Ⓐ Ⓑ ● Ⓓ Ⓔ

12. If Toby McGuire <u>was</u> alive <u>during</u> the heyday
               A   B
of Hollywood's debonair leading actors, he

probably would have been considered

<u>too naïve</u> and boyish <u>to succeed</u> as a big star.
    C   D
<u>No error</u>.
  E

13. <u>Of</u> the two Hemingway novels I have read,
  A
I like *A Farewell to Arms* <u>the best</u>, not only
                       B
because of its structure but also <u>because</u> of
                           C
<u>its</u> fascinating story. <u>No error</u>.
 D   E

14. Telemarketers are finding <u>greater</u> success
                                                A
    making sales <u>when</u> they <u>phoned</u> customers
                      B   C
    in the morning <u>rather than</u> late in the day.
                          D
    <u>No error</u>.
        E

15. Child psychologists <u>will tell you that</u> young
                                      A
    children <u>which</u> are pushed <u>into</u> activities
                  B   C
    prematurely <u>may suffer</u> the pain of failure
                          D
    and frustration. <u>No error</u>.
                          E

16. <u>Although</u> Martin Luther King's birthday <u>is</u>
        A   B
    January 15th, <u>it is celebrated</u> on the third
                          C
    Monday of January, <u>regardless</u> of the date.
                                D
    <u>No error</u>.
        E

17. Work in specialized fields <u>such as</u> bacteriology,
                                      A
    public health, and physics <u>require</u> at least a
                                      B
    bachelor's degree, and for a career in

    management or research, a master's degree

    <u>or even</u> a doctorate <u>is</u> required. <u>No error</u>.
        C   D   E

18. The governor <u>has often proposed</u> reductions
                          A
    in the sales tax <u>because</u> consumers can benefit
                          B
    from <u>this</u> <u>whenever</u> they go to the store.
            C   D
    <u>No error</u>.
        E

19. <u>In his memoir</u>, Baker tells stories <u>about the time</u>
        A   B
    before he entered high school, when he

    <u>is having to</u> deliver newspapers to the huge
        C
    estates and mansions <u>that lined</u> the riverfront.
                                D
    <u>No error</u>.
        E

20. <u>Even</u> after Elvis died <u>it was rumored</u> that
        A   B
    he was seen roaming the land, driving his car,

    showing up <u>unexpectedly</u> at rock-n-roll
                      C
    concerts, and <u>he made</u> his countless fans very
                        D
    excited. <u>No error</u>.
                  E

21. <u>To</u> the disappointment of the crowd, <u>neither</u>
        A   B
    the president nor <u>any</u> of his aides <u>were</u> able to
                          C   D
    attend the ceremony. <u>No error</u>.
                              E

22. Melissa was taught early in life <u>that,</u>
                                          A
    <u>regardless about</u> her feelings, she should
        B
    <u>always</u> wear a smile, try to be cheerful and
        C
    upbeat, and never say anything bad about

    <u>someone else</u>. <u>No error</u>.
        D   E

23. As a freshman becomes <u>adjusted to</u> the
                                  A
    routines and demands of college life, <u>one</u> may
                                                B
    <u>realize that</u> the rigors of high school <u>were</u>
        C   D
    good preparation. <u>No error</u>.
                            E

24. The collective thoughts, reflections, memories,

    and opinions <u>expressed by</u> the seniors in the
                      A
    pages of the <u>student</u> magazine <u>reveal</u> the
                      B   C
    diversity and uniqueness that <u>characterizes</u>
                                         D
    Brookdale High School. <u>No error</u>.
                                  E

25. Many teachers advocate <u>changing</u> the way
                                  A
    young children learn <u>to read</u>, <u>theorizing</u> that
                              B   C
    <u>they</u> will be more successful in the long run.
     D
    <u>No error</u>.
     E

26. <u>No matter</u> how <u>careful</u> passengers are
     A   B
    screened <u>at the airport</u>, a determined terrorist
              C
    will inevitably find a way to board <u>an</u>
                                          D
    airplane. <u>No error</u>.
                    E

27. <u>At</u> the start of the hockey season, the coach
     A
    <u>paid a visit</u> to my <u>parents and I</u> to explain
         B   C
    <u>why</u> he cut me from the varsity. <u>No error</u>.
     D   E

28. When Annie <u>set out</u> to buy an affordable
                    A
    automobile, she decided to look <u>for</u> a car
                                          B
    <u>different than</u> <u>those</u> that her friends were
         C   D
    driving. <u>No error</u>.
                   E

29. The award-winning *Sound of Music*

    <u>has been seen</u> by more moviegoers <u>than</u>
         A   B
    <u>any musical</u> film <u>in</u> the history of the movies.
         C   D
    <u>No error</u>.
     E

IMPROVING PARAGRAPHS

Directions: The passage below is the draft of a student's essay. Some parts of the passage need improvement. Read the passage and answer the questions that follow. The questions are about revisions that might improve all or part of the passage's organization, development, sentence structure, or choice of words. Choose the answer that best follows the requirements of standard written English.

Questions 30–35 refer to the following passage.

[1] Much of Russia lies under a cover of snow and ice for most of the year. [2] Permafrost covers the tundra. [3] Ports in northern Russia are not navigable for most of the year because they are frozen in. [4] In the south, the Black Sea gives Russia access to warm water ports. [5] The reason that the Black Sea is important is because it gives them the ability to export timber, furs, coal, oil, and other raw materials that are traded for food and manufactured goods. [6] The Black Sea will continue to help their economic growth.

[7] The English Channel has served as a barrier between Great Britain and the rest of Europe. [8] It has prevented attacks on Great Britain for hundreds of years. [9] Except for the Norman invasion more than 900 years ago. [10] This allowed the nation to develop economically and remain politically stable. [11] The isolation of Great Britain allowed the industrial revolution to begin in England.

[12] Much of Egypt is covered by desert. [13] The desert is irrigated by the Nile River. [14] It is longer than any river in the world. [15] The land along the river has historically been the site of farms and other settlements. [16] For centuries, the river had deposited rich particles of soil for growing crops along its banks. [17] Since building the Aswan High Dam in 1968, the farmers downstream from the dam have been using artificial fertilizer. [18] The banks of the Nile and the river's delta are among the most productive farming areas in the world. [19] Therefore, Egypt's people depend on the Nile.

[20] Russia, Great Britain, and Egypt are only three countries that have been shaped and developed by bodies of water.

30. Which is the best revision of the underlined segment of sentence 5 (reproduced below?

    The reason that the Black Sea is important is because it gives them the ability to export timber, furs, coal, oil, and other raw materials that are traded for food and manufactured goods.

    (A) that it enables Russia to export
    (B) its ability to allow exports of
    (C) the ability of Russia to export
    (D) because of exporting opportunities of
    (E) for Russian exports of

31. In the context of the second paragraph, which is the best revision of sentences 8 and 9 (reproduced below)?

    It has prevented attacks on Great Britain for hundreds of years. Except for the Norman invasion more than 900 years ago.

    (A) The English channel has prevented Great Britain's being attacked for hundreds of years; except for the Norman invasion of 1066.
    (B) It has prevented attacks, except for the Norman invasion in 1066, on Great Britain for hundreds of years.
    (C) Except for not preventing the Norman invasion more than 900 years ago, the English Channel has prevented attacks on Great Britain for hundreds of years.
    (D) It has prevented attacking Great Britain for 900 years, except the Normans.
    (E) For hundreds of years it has prevented attacks on Great Britain, except for the Norman invasion of 1066.

32. Which is the best way to combine sentences 12, 13, and 14 (reproduced below)?

    Much of Egypt is covered by desert. The desert is irrigated by the Nile River. It is longer than any river in the world.

    (A) The Nile, the longest river in the world, irrigates the desert that covers much of Egypt.
    (B) Egypt, which is covered by desert, is irrigated by the Nile, which is longer than any river in the world.
    (C) The desert, which covers much of Egypt is irrigated by the Nile, which is longer than any river in the world.
    (D) The longest river in the world, the Nile River, irrigates the Egyptian desert, which means that the river irrigates most of the country.
    (E) Much of the desert covering much of Egypt lies alongside the Nile, the longest river in the world, and much of it is irrigated by it.

33. To improve the coherence of paragraph 3, which of the following sentences would be best to delete?

    (A) Sentence 15
    (B) Sentence 16
    (C) Sentence 17
    (D) Sentence 18
    (E) Sentence 19

34. Which of the following sentences is most in need of further support and development?

    (A) Sentence 1
    (B) Sentence 2
    (C) Sentence 5
    (D) Sentence 11
    (E) Sentence 14

35. Considering the essay as a whole, which one of the following least accurately describes the function of sentence 20?

    (A) It summarizes the essay's main idea.
    (B) It serves to unify the essay.
    (C) It proves the validity of the essay's main idea.
    (D) It defines the purpose of the essay.
    (E) It gives the essay a sense of completion.

End of Section 2.
Do not return to Section 1. Do not proceed to Section 3 until the
allotted time for Section 2 has passed.

Section 3
Multiple-Choice Questions

TIME—10 MINUTES

IMPROVING SENTENCES

Directions: The underlined sentences and sentence parts below may contain errors in standard English, including awkward or ambiguous expression, poor word choice (diction), incorrect sentence structure, or faulty grammar, usage, and punctuation. Read each sentence carefully and identify which of the five alternative versions most effectively and correctly expresses the meaning of the underlined material. Indicate your choice by filling in the corresponding space on the answer sheet. Choice A always repeats the original. Choose A if none of the other choices improves the original sentence.

1. A teacher's job is to set a good example for children <u>as well as teaching them</u> the material they need to know.

   (A) as well as teaching them
   (B) as well as to teach them
   (C) and they also teach them
   (D) and as well, teach them also
   (E) also teaching them

2. The strength and appearance of denim fabric <u>account for its popularity</u> among campers, hikers, and other outdoor enthusiasts.

   (A) account for its popularity
   (B) accounts for its popularity
   (C) account for their popularity
   (D) explains why it is popular
   (E) are the reasons for their popularity

3. In his speech, the candidate <u>made a comment of spending</u> sleepless nights worrying over the large number of people without health insurance.

   (A) made a comment of spending
   (B) commented on the spending of his
   (C) gave a comment that he spent
   (D) commented on his spending
   (E) made a comment stating about spending

4. As the sales of SUVs continue to rise, automakers <u>asserting that it is working on the improvement of gas mileage by</u> spending profits on research and development.

   (A) asserting that it is working on the improvement of gas mileage by
   (B) asserting that work on improving gas mileage by
   (C) assert that they will improve gas mileage and
   (D) asserts that improving gas mileage by
   (E) assert that they will improve gas mileage by

5. During Andy's freshman year in college, his academic advisor suggested that he consider majoring in music, English, creative writing, <u>or studying medicine</u>.

   (A) or studying medicine
   (B) or working in the field of medicine
   (C) or a medical field
   (D) or a profession in medicine
   (E) and to think about attending medical school

6. The game warden believes that <u>bow-hunting is safer than a rifle</u>.

   (A) bow-hunting is safer than a rifle
   (B) hunting with a bow is safer than hunting with a rifle
   (C) bows is more safe than rifles in hunting
   (D) bow-hunting is more safe than hunting with a rifle
   (E) a bow in hunting is safer than a rifle in hunting.

7. Convinced that her all-night study sessions on Thursdays enabled her to pass math tests on Friday, <u>Susan is shocked to learn that last week she got an F</u>.

   (A) Susan is shocked to learn that last week she got an F.
   (B) Susan was shocked to learn that she got an F last week
   (C) shock is what Susan had when learning that last week she got an F
   (D) it is a shock for Susan to learn that last week she receives an F
   (E) last week's F shocked Susan

8. When someone works as a ranger in a national park, <u>you will be employed by</u> the U.S. Department of the Interior, a branch of the federal government.

   (A) you will be employed by
   (B) it is being employed by
   (C) you would be an employee of
   (D) he or she is employed by
   (E) the employment is being by

9. Having ordered a cup of black coffee at the Starbucks counter, <u>the fumes smelled pleasing to Howard</u>.

   (A) the fumes smelled pleasing to Howard
   (B) the fumes' smell pleased Howard
   (C) smells from the fumes pleased Howard
   (D) Howard smelled the fumes pleasingly
   (E) Howard was pleased by the smell of the fumes

10. When Charlotte arrived at school on Tuesday morning, her friend <u>Thalia told her that her first period class had been cancelled</u>.

    (A) Thalia told her that her first period class had been cancelled
    (B) from Thalia she learned that her first period class had been cancelled
    (C) Charlotte was told by Thalia that her first period class had been cancelled
    (D) Thalia said that Charlotte's first period class had been cancelled
    (E) hearing from Thalia about the cancellation of her first period class

11. When you plan a plane trip, you choose a flight, <u>make a reservation, and then that reservation entitles you to a seat</u> on the aircraft.

    (A) make a reservation, and then that reservation entitles you to a seat
    (B) and make a reservation that entitles you to a seat
    (C) and make a reservation, then you are entitled to a seat
    (D) and make a reservation, then entitling you to a seat
    (E) and make a reservation, you are entitled to a seat then

12. Better military equipment, such as stronger bullet-proof vests, has been <u>valuable so that it helps</u> soldiers feel more secure when they go into battle.

    (A) valuable so that it helps
    (B) valuable because it helps
    (C) valuable, even though it will help
    (D) valuable in order that they help
    (E) valuable for it to help

13. The president of the <u>company grew up in poverty, he gradually</u> turned his life around.

   (A) company grew up in poverty, he gradually

   (B) company, having his growing up in poverty, gradually

   (C) company grew up in poverty, but he gradually

   (D) company, having grown up poor, but he gradually

   (E) company, poverty stricken while he grew up, he gradually

14. This book shows readers not only what might happen if they try to deal with the problem by themselves <u>but it's all right to seek help</u>.

   (A) but it's all right to seek help

   (B) but explains that help is all right to seek

   (C) explaining that it's all right to seek help

   (D) and also explains that it's all right to seek help

   (E) but also explains that it's all right to seek help

End of Section 3.
Do not return to Sections 1 or 2.

END OF WRITING TEST.

ANSWER KEY

Guide for Scoring Your Essay

Using this guide, rate yourself in each of these six categories. Enter your scores in the spaces provided, and calculate the average of the six ratings to determine your final score.

On the SAT itself, two readers will score your essay on a scale of 6 (high) to 1 (low), or *zero* if you fail to write on the assigned topic. The score will be reported to you as the sum of the two ratings, from 12 to 0.

Remember that SAT essays are judged in relation to other essays written on the same topic. Therefore, this scoring guide may not yield a totally accurate prediction of the score you can expect on the exam. Because it is difficult to read your own essay with total objectivity, you might improve the validity of your score by getting a second opinion about your essay from an informed friend or a teacher.

Overall Impression

6   Consistently outstanding in clarity and competence; very insightful; few, if any, errors

5   Reasonably consistent in clarity and competence; occasional errors or lapses in quality; contains some insight

4   Adequate competence; some lapses in quality; fairly clear and with evidence of insight

3   Generally inadequate but demonstrates potential competence; contains some confusing aspects

2   Seriously limited; significant weaknesses in quality; generally unclear or incoherent

1   Demonstrates fundamental incompetence; contains serious flaws; significantly undeveloped or confusing

Score ☐

Development of Point of View

6   Fully developed with clear and appropriate supporting material; demonstrates high level of critical thinking

5   Generally well developed with appropriate examples, reasons, and other evidence to support a main idea; demonstrates strong critical thinking

4   Partly develops a main idea with relatively appropriate examples and reasons; shows some evidence of critical thinking

3   Weak development of main idea and little evidence of critical thinking; barely appropriate examples or other supporting material

2   Lacks a focus on a main idea; weak critical thinking; inappropriate or insufficient evidence

1   Fails to articulate a viable point of view; provides virtually no evidence of understanding the prompt

Score ☐

Organization of Ideas

6   Extremely well organized and focused on a main idea; supporting evidence presented in an effective, logical sequence

5   Generally well organized and reasonably focused on a main idea; mostly coherent and logical presentation of supporting material

4   Reasonably organized; shows some evidence of thoughtful sequence and progression of ideas

3   Limited organization and vague focus on main idea; contains some confusion in the sequence of ideas

2   Barely recognizable organization; little coherence; serious problems with sequence of ideas

1   No discernable organization; incoherent sequence of ideas

Score ☐

Language and Word Choice

6   Highly effective and skillful use of language; varied, appropriate, and accurate vocabulary

5   Demonstrates competence in use of language; appropriate and correct vocabulary

4   Adequate but inconsistent use of effective language; conventional but mostly correct use of vocabulary

3   Some minor errors in expression; generally weak or limited vocabulary; occasionally inappropriate word choice

2   Frequent errors in expression; very limited vocabulary; incorrect word choice interferes with meaning

1   Seriously deficient in use of language; meaning obscured by word choice

Score ☐

Sentence Structure

6   Varied and engaging sentence structure

5   Sufficiently varied sentence structure

4   Some sentence variation

3   Little sentence variation; minor sentence errors

2   Frequent sentence errors

1   Severe sentence errors; meaning obscured

Score ☐

Grammar, Usage, and Mechanics

6   Virtually or entirely error-free
5   Contains some minor errors
4   Some minor errors; one or two major errors
3   Accumulated minor and major errors
2   Contains frequent major errors that interfere with meaning
1   Contains severe errors that obscure meaning

Score ☐

For rating yourself

Total of six scores _____

Divide total by 6 to get score: _____ (A)
(Round to the nearest whole number.)

(A) + (B) = ESSAY SUBSCORE _____
                          (0–12)

For a second opinion

Total of six scores _____

Divide total by 6 to get score: _____ (B)
(Round to the nearest whole number.)

ANSWERS TO MULTIPLE-CHOICE QUESTIONS

Section 2

1. B	11. A	21. D	31. E
2. B	12. A	22. B	32. A
3. A	13. B	23. B	33. C
4. D	14. C	24. D	34. D
5. E	15. B	25. D	35. C
6. C	16. E	26. B	
7. A	17. B	27. C	
8. E	18. C	28. C	
9. B	19. C	29. C	
10. E	20. D	30. A	

Section 3

1. B	11. B
2. A	12. B
3. D	13. C
4. E	14. E
5. C	
6. B	
7. B	
8. D	
9. E	
10. D	

PERFORMANCE EVALUATION CHART

I. Self-Rating Chart

Section 2

Improving Sentences, questions 1–11   Number correct _____

Identifying Sentence Errors, questions 12–29   Number correct _____

Improving Paragraphs, questions 30–35   Number correct _____

Section 3

Improving Sentences, questions 1–14   Number correct _____

                                                                    Subtotal _____ (A)

Wrong answers (Do not count unanswered questions)

Section 2   Number wrong _____

Section 3   Number wrong _____

                                                                    Subtotal _____ (B)

Subtract ¼ point (0.25) from (B) for each wrong answer   _____ (C)

(A) minus (C) = _____ (D)

Round (D) to the nearest whole number for your MULTIPLE-CHOICE RAW SCORE   _____

ESSAY SUBSCORE   _____

CONVERSION TABLE

This table will give you an approximation of what your score would be if this practice test had been an actual SAT Writing Test. The essay counts for roughly 30% of the final score; the multiple-choice questions, for roughly 70%.

For example, if your Multiple-Choice Raw Score was 35 and your Essay Subscore was 6, the table indicates that your final score on the test would be approximately halfway between 500 and 710, or 600.

Multiple-Choice Raw Score	Essay Subscore						
	0	2	4	6	8	10	12
40–49	520–690	530–720	550–740	580–770	620–800	650–800	680–800
30–39	430–630	450–660	470–680	500–710	530–740	560–770	590–800
20–29	360–540	370–570	390–590	420–620	460–650	490–690	520–710
10–19	270–460	280–490	300–510	330–540	370–580	400–610	430–630
0–9	200–380	200–410	210–430	240–450	270–490	300–520	330–560
–12––1	200–280	200–310	200–330	200–350	240–390	270–420	300–450

ANSWER EXPLANATIONS

Note: Although many choices contain multiple errors, only a single error is listed for each incorrect answer.

1. **B**   A. Wordiness. The use of both *While* and *that was when* creates a redundancy.
C. Mixed construction. The clause that starts with *then* is grammatically unrelated to the previous part of the sentence.
D. Dangling participle. The construction *While walking down Market Street* modifies *guitar* instead of *Clarissa*.
E. Passive construction. Using *guitar* instead of *Clarissa* as the grammatical subject leads to a passive, awkwardly worded construction.

2. **B**   A. Sentence fragment. The construction consists only of subordinate clauses and lacks a main verb.
C. Mixed construction. The phrase *as a result* is not grammatically related to the earlier part of the sentence
D. Misplaced modifier. The phrase *As a student at Penn State* modifies *love* instead of *Julie*.
E. Sentence fragment. The construction lacks a main verb.

3. **A**   B. Pronoun error. The pronoun in *Betsy and I* is an object of a preposition, and, therefore, should be *me*.
C. Pronoun error. The pronoun in *Peter and me* is in the nominative case and, therefore, should be *I*.
D. Pronoun error. *He* should be *him*. See B.
E. Pronoun error. In both instances, *I* should be *me*. See B.

4. **D**   A. Subject–verb agreement. *Funds* is plural; *is* is singular.
B. Mixed construction. Choice B is not grammatically or logically related to the rest of the sentence.
C. Subject–verb agreement. *Earning* is singular; *are* is plural.
E. Idiom error. In standard English, the phrase is *earned from tips*.

5. **E**   A. Faulty idiom. In this context, the phrase *are as similar as* is not standard English.
B. Subject–verb agreement. *Characters* is plural; *is* is singular.
C. Sentence fragment. The construction lacks a main verb.
D. Subject–verb agreement. *Characters* is plural; *is* is singular.

6. **C**   A. Faulty comparison. *Violence* is compared to *the 1950s and 1960s*, an illogical comparison.
B. Faulty diction. In making comparisons, use *than* instead of *then*.
D. Faulty idiom. In this context, *than around* is not standard English.
E. Faulty comparison. *Violence* is compared to *the 1950s and 1960s*, an illogical comparison.

7. **A** B. Pronoun–antecedent agreement. *Each* is singular; *their* is plural.
C. Wordiness. The construction *each of them have unique decorations* and the phrase *of their own* are redundant.
D. Pronoun–antecedent agreement. *Barns* is plural; *its* is singular.
E. Comma splice. A comma may not be used to separate two independent clauses.

8. **E** A. Wordiness. The two coordinate clauses of this compound sentence contain related ideas that could be more concisely expressed by replacing *and she would meet with* with *by meeting*.
B. Awkwardness. The phrase *meeting . . . for discussing it* is awkwardly expressed.
C. Faulty idiom. The construction *to study the school's schedule in holding discussions* is not expressed in standard English.
D. Faulty idiom. The phrase *discussing about it* is not standard English.

9. **B** A. Wordiness. *Because* and *the reason why* are redundant.
C. Subject–verb agreement. *Dinosaurs* is plural; *is* is singular.
D. Mixed construction. *As a result of dinosaurs* fails to relate grammatically to *they are fascinating to us*.
E. Comma splice. A comma may not be used to separate independent clauses.

10. **E** A. Mixed construction. The construction that begins with *it* is grammatically unrelated to the previous part of the sentence.
B. Pronoun reference. The pronoun *they* fails to refer to a specific plural noun or other pronoun.
C. Sentence fragment. The construction lacks a main verb.
D. Faulty parallelism. The coordinate phrases *in their complexity* and *growing more sophisticated* are not in parallel form.

11. **A** B. Faulty idiom. The phrase *mistaken with* is not standard English.
C. Faulty coordination. The conjunction *but* fails to create a logical relationship between the two clauses in the sentence.
D. Misplaced modifier. *Growing up in Asheville . . .* modifies the contemporary Tom Wolfe instead of the earlier writer Thomas Wolfe.
E. Verb tense error. The use of *while growing* and *was often confused* creates a logical impossibility because Thomas Wolfe grew up long before Tom Wolfe made a name for himself.

SECTION 2—IDENTIFYING SENTENCE ERRORS

12. **A** Tense shift. Because this sentence calls for use of the past perfect tense, use *had been* instead of *was*.

13. **B** Faulty comparison. For comparing two objects, use the comparative degree instead of the superlative. Use *better* instead of *the best*.

14. **C** Tense shift. The sentence is cast in the present tense. Use *phone* instead of *phoned*.

15. **B** Pronoun choice. Use *who* instead of *which* when referring to people.

16. **E**   No error.

17. **B**   Subject–verb agreement. The subject *work* is singular; the verb *require* is plural. Use *requires*.

18. **C**   Pronoun–antecedent agreement. The antecedent *reductions* is plural; the pronoun *this* is singular.

19. **C**   Tense shift. Although the sentence is cast in the present tense (*tells*), it recalls past events. Use *had to* instead of *is having to*.

20. **D**   Faulty parallelism. Verbs in a series should be in parallel form. Use *making* instead of *he made*.

21. **D**   Subject–verb agreement. The subject *neither* is singular; the verb *were* is plural. Use *was*.

22. **B**   Idiom error. The construction is not in standard English. Use *regardless of*.

23. **B**   Shift in pronoun person. The antecedent *freshman* should be followed by a personal pronoun (*he/she*), not by the impersonal pronoun *one*.

24. **D**   Noun–verb agreement. The nouns *diversity and uniqueness* should have a plural verb. Use *characterize* instead of *characterizes*.

25. **D**   Ambiguous pronoun reference. Pronouns should refer to specific nouns or other pronouns. Here, the pronoun *they* could refer to *teachers* or to *children*.

26. **B**   Diction error. An adjective may not be used where an adverb is needed. Use *carefully*.

27. **C**   Pronoun case. The phrase *parents and I* is the object of the preposition *to*. Use the objective case pronoun *me*.

28. **C**   Idiom error. In standard English, the phrase is *different from* instead of *different than*.

29. **C**   Faulty comparison. The word *other* must be included in a comparison of one thing with a group of which it is a member. Use *any other musical film*.

SECTION 2—IMPROVING PARAGRAPHS

30. **A**   Only Choice A is concisely expressed in standard English. The language of the other choices is awkward or nonstandard.

31. **E**   Choice A contains a sentence fragment after the semicolon.
Choice B divides the main clause awkwardly.
Choice C is wordy and repetitious. It unnecessarily repeats *the English Channel*, the subject of sentence 7.
Choice D is an unclear, awkwardly constructed sentence.

32. **A**   Choice B contains a faulty comparison. The Nile cannot be longer than itself.
Choice C is similar to B.
Choice D is accurate but also wordy and repetitious.
Choice E is awkwardly expressed.

33. **C**   Although it is related to the topic of the paragraph, sentence 17 steers the discussion away from the paragraph's main topic, Egypt's dependence on the Nile. Therefore, choice C is the best answer.

34. **D**   Sentence 11 states a complex idea that needs further explanation. The other sentences are facts that stand on their own.

35. **C**   Choice C does not describe the function of the last paragraph. The essay's main idea is validated by the contents of the essay's three main paragraphs, not by the final paragraph.

SECTION 3—IMPROVING SENTENCES

1. **B**   A. Faulty parallelism. Coordinate elements in a sentence must be in parallel form. *To set a good example* and *as well as teaching* are not in parallel form.
C. Faulty pronoun reference. The pronoun *they* fails to refer to any specific noun or other pronoun.
D. Redundancy. *As well as* and *also* are redundant.
E. Faulty parallelism. See A.

2. **A**   B. Subject–verb agreement. *Strength and appearance* is plural; *accounts* is singular.
C. Pronoun reference. The pronoun *their* should refer to *fabric*, but because *their* is plural, it seems to refer to *strength and appearance*.
D. Subject–verb agreement. *Strength and appearance* is plural; *explains* is singular.
E. Pronoun reference. The pronoun *their* should refer to *fabric*, but because *their* is plural, it seems to refer to *strength and appearance*.

3. **D**   A. Idiom error. The construction *made a comment of spending* is not standard English.
B. Clumsy construction. *Commenting on the spending of his* is awkwardly expressed.
C. Diction. In context the verb *gave* is not standard English.
E. Wordiness. *Made a comment* and *stating* are redundant.

4. **E**   A. Pronoun–antecedent agreement. The antecedent *automakers* is plural; the pronoun *it* is singular.
B. Sentence fragment. The construction lacks a main verb.
C. Faulty parallelism. Verbs in a series should be in parallel form. *Will improve* is not parallel to *spending*.
D. Subject–verb agreement. The subject *automakers* is plural; the verb *asserts* is singular.

5. **C**   A. Faulty parallelism. Items in a series should be in parallel form. *Studying medicine* is not parallel to *music, English*, and *creative writing*.
B. Faulty parallelism. Items in a series should be in parallel form. *Working in the field of medicine* is not parallel to *music, English*, and *creative writing*.
D. Faulty parallelism. Items in a series should be in parallel form. *A profession in medicine* is not parallel to *music, English*, and *creative writing*.
E. Mixed construction. The phrase that begins *and to think* is not grammatically related to the earlier portion of the sentence.

6. **B**   A. Faulty comparison. *Hunting* is compared to *rifle*, an illogical comparison.
        C. Noun–verb agreement. *Bows* is plural; *is* is singular. Use *are*.
        D. Comparative degree. Add *–er* to one-syllable adjectives to indicate a higher degree. Use *safer*.
        E. Clumsy construction. In this context, the phrase *in hunting* is awkward.

7. **B**   A. Tense shift. The sentence, cast in the past tense, shifts to the present.
        C. Misplaced modifier. The phrase that starts with *Convinced that* modifies *shock* instead of *Susan*.
        D. Tense shift. The sentence, cast in the past tense, shifts to the present.
        E. Misplaced modifier. The phrase that starts with *Convinced that* modifies *last week's F* instead of *Susan*.

8. **D**   A. Tense shift. The sentence, cast in the present tense, shifts to the future tense.
        B. Pronoun reference. The pronoun *it* fails to refer to a specific noun or other pronoun.
        C. Pronoun shift. The sentence begins with the impersonal pronoun *someone* but improperly shifts to the second person pronoun *you*.
        E. Idiom error. The construction is not in standard English.

9. **E**   A. Dangling participle. The construction that begins *Having ordered . . .* should modify *Howard* instead of *the fumes*.
        B. Dangling participle. The construction that begins *Having ordered . . .* should modify *Howard* instead of *smell*.
        C. Dangling participle. The construction that begins *Having ordered . . .* should modify *Howard* instead of *smells*.
        D. Diction error. In the context, *pleasingly* fails to convey the intended meaning because it is not a synonym for *with pleasure*.

10. **D**   A. Ambiguous pronoun reference. The second *her* may refer either to Charlotte or to Thalia.
        B. Ambiguous pronoun reference. The second *her* may refer either to Charlotte or to Thalia.
        C. Ambiguous pronoun reference. The pronoun *her* may refer either to Charlotte or to Thalia.
        E. Sentence fragment. The construction lacks a main verb.

11. **B**   A. Wordiness. The sentence contains unnecessary repetition.
        C. Comma splice. A comma may not be used to separate two independent clauses.
        D. Mixed construction. The construction that begins with *then entitling you* fails to relate grammatically with the previous part of the sentence.
        E. Idiom error. The word *then* is misplaced. Put it after *are*.

12. **B**   A. Faulty idiom. The construction does not accurately convey the intended meaning. Instead of expressing the idea that better equipment *has the effect* of helping soldiers, it says that better equipment has been valuable *in order to* help soldiers.
        C. Faulty idiom. The phrase *even though* conveys just the opposite of the intended meaning.
        D. Pronoun reference. The pronoun *they* fails to refer to a specific noun or other pronoun.
        E. Faulty idiom. The construction is not in standard English and fails to convey a logical meaning.

13. **C**   A. Comma splice. A comma may not be used to separate two independent clauses.
B. Idiom error. The phrase *having his growing up* is not standard English.
D. Subordination error. The clause beginning with *but* fails to relate logically to the earlier part of the sentence.
E. Mismatched sentence parts. The construction beginning with *he* is not grammatically related to the earlier part of the sentence.

14. **E**   A. Faulty parallelism. The verb *shows* lacks a grammatical parallel, namely a verb in the same form.
B. Clumsy construction. The construction *help is all right to seek* is awkward.
C. Faulty parallelism. The verb *explaining* is not parallel in form to *shows*.
D. Idiom error. Most parallel ideas introduced by *not only* must be completed with <u>*but*</u> *also*.

PRACTICE TEST C

Section 1
Essay

TIME—25 MINUTES

Directions: Plan and write an essay in response to the assigned topic. Use the essay as an opportunity to show how clearly and effectively you can express and develop ideas. Present your thoughts logically and precisely. Include specific evidence or examples to support your point of view. A plain, natural writing style is probably best. The number of words is up to you, but quantity is less important than quality.

Limit your essay to two sides of the lined paper provided. You'll have enough space if you write on every line and avoid wide margins. Write or print legibly because handwriting that's hard or impossible to read will decrease your score.

BE SURE TO WRITE ONLY ON THE ASSIGNED TOPIC. AN ESSAY WRITTEN ON ANOTHER TOPIC WILL BE SCORED "ZERO."

If you finish in less than 25 minutes, check your work. Do not turn to another section of the test.

Think carefully about the following passage and the assignment below.

We thought that he was everything
To make us wish that we were in his place

These words from Edwin Arlington Robinson's famous poem "Richard Cory" describe what people often feel when they see others who apparently lead happier, richer, more content lives than they do.

Assignment: The kind of envy to which Robinson refers may serve as a strong motivating force for some people to improve their condition and place in life. On the other hand, envy may be a self-defeating and ultimately frustrating emotion because it may lead people to strive in vain for unattainable goals. In your view, is envy generally a positive or a negative force in people's lives? To support your position, use reasoning and examples taken from your studies, reading, or personal observation and experience.

Section 1

ESSAY
Time allowed: 25 minutes
Limit your essay to two pages. Do not skip lines. Write only inside the box.

Essay (continued)

ANSWER SHEET FOR MULTIPLE-CHOICE QUESTIONS

Section 2
Improving Sentences

1. (A) (B) (C) (D) (E)
2. (A) (B) (C) (D) (E)
3. (A) (B) (C) (D) (E)
4. (A) (B) (C) (D) (E)
5. (A) (B) (C) (D) (E)
6. (A) (B) (C) (D) (E)
7. (A) (B) (C) (D) (E)
8. (A) (B) (C) (D) (E)
9. (A) (B) (C) (D) (E)
10. (A) (B) (C) (D) (E)
11. (A) (B) (C) (D) (E)

Identifying
Sentence Errors

12. (A) (B) (C) (D) (E)
13. (A) (B) (C) (D) (E)
14. (A) (B) (C) (D) (E)
15. (A) (B) (C) (D) (E)
16. (A) (B) (C) (D) (E)
17. (A) (B) (C) (D) (E)
18. (A) (B) (C) (D) (E)
19. (A) (B) (C) (D) (E)
20. (A) (B) (C) (D) (E)
21. (A) (B) (C) (D) (E)
22. (A) (B) (C) (D) (E)
23. (A) (B) (C) (D) (E)
24. (A) (B) (C) (D) (E)
25. (A) (B) (C) (D) (E)
26. (A) (B) (C) (D) (E)
27. (A) (B) (C) (D) (E)
28. (A) (B) (C) (D) (E)
29. (A) (B) (C) (D) (E)

Improving Paragraphs

30. (A) (B) (C) (D) (E)
31. (A) (B) (C) (D) (E)
32. (A) (B) (C) (D) (E)
33. (A) (B) (C) (D) (E)
34. (A) (B) (C) (D) (E)
35. (A) (B) (C) (D) (E)

Section 3
Improving Sentences

1. (A) (B) (C) (D) (E)
2. (A) (B) (C) (D) (E)
3. (A) (B) (C) (D) (E)
4. (A) (B) (C) (D) (E)
5. (A) (B) (C) (D) (E)
6. (A) (B) (C) (D) (E)
7. (A) (B) (C) (D) (E)
8. (A) (B) (C) (D) (E)
9. (A) (B) (C) (D) (E)
10. (A) (B) (C) (D) (E)
11. (A) (B) (C) (D) (E)
12. (A) (B) (C) (D) (E)
13. (A) (B) (C) (D) (E)
14. (A) (B) (C) (D) (E)

Section 2
Multiple-Choice Questions

TIME—25 MINUTES

IMPROVING SENTENCES

Directions: The underlined sentences and sentence parts below may contain errors in standard English, including awkward or ambiguous expression, poor word choice (diction), incorrect sentence structure, or faulty grammar, usage, and punctuation. Read each sentence carefully and identify which of the five alternative versions most effectively and correctly expresses the meaning of the underlined material. Indicate your choice by filling in the corresponding space on the answer sheet. Choice A always repeats the original. Choose A if none of the other choices improves the original sentence.

EXAMPLE   ANSWER

My old Aunt Maud loves   Ⓐ ● Ⓒ Ⓓ Ⓔ
to cook, and eating also.

(A) cook, and eating also
(B) cook and to eat
(C) cook, and to eat also
(D) cook and eat besides
(E) cook and, in addition, eat

1. The book's descriptions of the country and the town, in addition to its recent release as a movie, explains why sales of the book have suddenly boomed in stores and online.

   (A) explains why sales of the book have suddenly boomed
   (B) explain the sudden boom in its sales
   (C) are the reason why the book's sales having boomed suddenly
   (D) explain why it has suddenly boomed it's sales
   (E) is the explanation for the sudden boom in sales

2. Jogging a mile consumes the same number of calories as if you walk two miles.

   (A) as if you walk
   (B) as to walk
   (C) than to walk
   (D) as walking
   (E) as it does when walking

3. Because Lisa expected not to go to college, <u>she is taking little interest in school and doing poorly</u>.

   (A) she is taking little interest in school and doing poorly
   (B) she took little interest in school and did poorly
   (C) she takes little interest in school and does poorly
   (D) school interested her little and did poorly
   (E) she would take little interest in school and does poorly

4. No one was <u>more happier than me</u> that you won a college scholarship.

   (A) more happier than me
   (B) happier but me
   (C) more happy like myself
   (D) as happy like I am
   (E) happier than I

5. After 9/11, some people questioned the government's authority to <u>determine about more thorough screening of passengers</u> at the airport.

   (A) determine about more thorough screening of passengers
   (B) determine whether passengers should be more thoroughly screened
   (C) determine whether or not the screening of passengers more thoroughly
   (D) determine about the screening of passengers more thoroughly
   (E) determine if more thorough passenger screening

6. <u>The pollution of the municipal well having been discovered,</u> the town posted notices urging people to boil their water.

   (A) The pollution of the municipal well having been discovered,
   (B) The municipal well's pollution being discovered,
   (C) When having made the discovery of the pollution of the water in the municipal well;
   (D) After discovering pollution in the municipal well,
   (E) Pollution was discovered in the municipal well,

7. <u>Whether Charles in fact sent the e-mail or did not</u> to Rose is unclear, but the letter would definitely have given her morale a boost.

   (A) Whether Charles in fact sent the e-mail or did not
   (B) Whether in reality Charles sent the e-mail or did not
   (C) The actuality of the sending of the e-mail by Charles
   (D) That Charles in fact sent the e-mail
   (E) Charles, whether or not he sent the e-mail

8. Two years ago, Ohio State University defeated all of its rivals in <u>football, nevertheless, they</u> did not win the honorary title of National Champion.

   (A) football, nevertheless, they
   (B) football, they nevertheless
   (C) football, they
   (D) football; consequently, it
   (E) football, but it

9. Because it is blessed with a mild and pleasant climate, southern <u>California has become more popular than</u> Florida as a place to retire.

   (A) California has become more popular than
   (B) California had been as popular as
   (C) California having become more popular than
   (D) California's popularity is more than
   (E) California has greater popularity as

10. <u>Wandering through the town that he had once called home, everything</u> had changed: the barbershop was gone, the deli was now a laundromat, and his old house had been turned into a condo.

   (A) Wandering through the town that he had once called home, everything

   (B) He wandered through the town that had once been called home, everything

   (C) As he, wandering though the town that had once called home, saw that everything

   (D) While wandering through his ex-hometown, everything

   (E) Wandering though the town that had once been home, he saw that everything

11. An event in Richard's life story that moved me greatly was <u>when he was separated from the family</u>.

   (A) when he was separated from the family

   (B) when he and the family were separated

   (C) his separation from the family

   (D) the separating from the family

   (E) the separation between he and the family

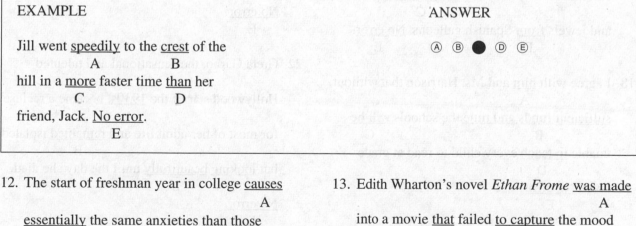

IDENTIFYING SENTENCE ERRORS

Directions: The underlined and lettered parts of each sentence below may contain an error in grammar, usage, word choice (diction), or expression (idiom). Read each sentence carefully and identify which item, if any, contains an error. Indicate your choice by filling in the corresponding space on the answer sheet. No sentence contains more than one error. Some sentences may contain no error. In that case, the correct choice will always be E (No error).

EXAMPLE

Jill went <u>speedily</u> to the <u>crest</u> of the
        A   B

hill in a <u>more</u> faster time <u>than</u> her
        C   D

friend, Jack. <u>No error</u>.
          E

ANSWER

Ⓐ Ⓑ ● Ⓓ Ⓔ

12. The start of freshman year in college <u>causes</u>
                        A

<u>essentially</u> the same anxieties <u>than</u> <u>those</u>
  B   C   D

experienced by ninth graders entering high

school. <u>No error</u>.
      E

13. Edith Wharton's novel *Ethan Frome* <u>was made</u>
                           A

into a movie <u>that</u> failed <u>to capture</u> the mood
         B   C

and meaning of the <u>original story</u>. <u>No error</u>.
               D   E

14. The <u>present</u> senior class has a <u>greater</u> <u>number</u>
       A   B   C
    of scholarship winners than last <u>year</u>. <u>No error</u>.
                                              D   E

15. <u>A disruptive student</u> will <u>get no pity</u> from the
         A   B
    dean of discipline and <u>will be deprived</u> of
                                          C
    privileges after being told that they <u>betrayed</u>
                                                           D
    a trust that they had been given. <u>No error</u>.
                                                      E

16. My parents instilled their moral values <u>for</u> my
                                                          A
    sister and <u>me</u>, <u>enabling us</u>, by the time we
                    B   C
    reached <u>our</u> teen years, to know right from
                 D
    wrong. <u>No error</u>.
                  E

17. The earliest pirates, <u>who resided</u> on Caribbean
                                    A
    islands, rustled cattle, smoked the meat and
    sold <u>it</u> to passing ships, attacked and burned
          B
    colonial settlements, and <u>were stealing</u> gold
                                          C
    and jewels <u>from</u> Spanish galleons. <u>No error</u>.
                     D   E

18. I agree with <u>him</u> and Ms. Harrison that without
                       A
    <u>sufficient funds and time</u> the schools <u>will be</u>
                 B   C
    unable <u>to teach</u> every child to read at grade
                D
    level. <u>No error</u>.
                  E

19. <u>As</u> Katie opened the refrigerator, she instantly
       A
    noticed that a huge chunk of chocolate icing
    had been <u>bit</u> <u>off</u> the birthday cake and
                  B   C
    immediately suspected that Mark <u>was</u>
                                               D
    responsible. <u>No error</u>.
                        E

20. Gilbert W. Davis is a first-rate trial lawyer
    who, <u>like</u> a wary predator on the prowl,
              A
    <u>has mastered</u> the art of capitalizing
          B
    <u>on the mistakes</u> and weaknesses of <u>their</u>
              C   D
    opponents in the courtroom. <u>No error</u>.
                                             E

21. If <u>you'd</u> been willing to take him <u>for</u> face
          A   B
    value <u>and had not</u> tried to search for hidden
              C
    motives, I'm sure you <u>would have found him</u>
                                         D
    a cooperative and hard-working employee.

    <u>No error</u>.
        E

22. Greta Garbo, the sensational and talented
    Hollywood star of the <u>1930s</u>, became a recluse
                                A
    for most of her adult life and <u>remained</u> isolated
                                               B
    but <u>looking</u> <u>beautifully</u> until the day she died.
             C   D
    <u>No error</u>.
        E

23. An incident that <u>further</u> embittered the
                A

colonists occurred <u>on</u> a Boston street when
            B

British troops <u>fired into</u> a group of protesters,
               C

<u>killing five and</u> wounding six of them.
     D

<u>No error</u>.
  E

24. <u>Prior to</u> her presidency, an attitude of cockiness
   A

and carelessness <u>were</u> common, and safety
            B

rules were <u>rarely</u> <u>taken</u> seriously. <u>No error</u>.
       C   D   E

25. The experience of taking a car on the road

with a driving teacher <u>fosters</u> learning far
               A

more useful than <u>that which</u> results <u>as</u> students
           B   C

<u>sit through</u> a dull lecture. <u>No error</u>.
  D   E

26. <u>Following</u> traditional family values <u>have</u>
   A   B

become one of the distinct differences

<u>between</u> my parents and <u>me</u>. <u>No error</u>.
  C   D   E

27. Mr. Donahue made <u>it</u> perfectly clear that he
           A

did not intend <u>to drive</u> all the way to North
         B

Carolina <u>again</u> without <u>Rose and I</u> to keep
        C   D

him company. <u>No error</u>.
           E

28. Helene hopes <u>to convince</u> Chuckie that she
          A

neither is interested in going out with <u>other</u>
                          B

boys <u>or</u> that she ever loved <u>anyone else</u> in
     C   D

a romantic way. <u>No error</u>.
            E

29. Foremost <u>among</u> the voters' concerns <u>is</u> the
         A   B

problem of what to do <u>about</u> waste disposal
               C

and the issues <u>surrounding</u> the construction of
           D

low-income housing. <u>No error</u>.
              E

IMPROVING PARAGRAPHS

Directions: The passage below is the draft of a student's essay. Some parts of the passage need improvement. Read the passage and answer the questions that follow. The questions are about revisions that might improve all or part of the passage's organization, development, sentence structure, or choice of words. Choose the answer that best follows the requirements of standard written English.

Questions 30–35 refer to the following passage.

[1] Back in 1900, who could have predicted the amazing technological achievements that would be made during the next hundred years? [2] By the year 2000, advances in communications, nuclear energy, and medicine transformed people's lives in many unexpected ways.

[3] One of the most important developments was the invention of communication satellites that allow images and messages to be sent wirelessly around the world. [4] One advantage of this technology is that current events can be sent worldwide instantly. [5] News used to travel overseas by boat and would take weeks or months to spread. [6] When disaster struck the World Trade Center on 9/11, most of the world saw it immediately. [7] To achieve this technological marvel, many satellites have been very costly, however. [8] As a result, many poor countries have been left behind and can barely participate in so-called "globalization."

[9] The invention and use of nuclear energy is another important technological development. [10] One positive feature of nuclear energy is that energy is cheaper and can be made easy. [11] France, for one, depends almost entirely on electricity generated by nuclear power. [12] But the dangers of nuclear energy dampen the world's enthusiasm. [13] Watch out for human error and careless workmanship. [14] They can cause huge disasters such as the one in Chernobyl in 1986, which killed countless people and radiated half the Earth.

[15] There have also been many significant technological advances in medicine. [16] One such development was the CAT scan. [17] The CAT scan permits doctors to take pictures of your brain to see if there is a growth on it. [18] One positive effect of the CAT scan is that doctors can diagnose brain tumors and brain cancer at an early stage. [19] Many lives have been saved. [20] But CAT scans are expensive, so uninsured Americans and the poor of all countries have been deprived of this modern medical marvel.

30. Considering the main idea of the essay, which of the following is the best revision of sentence 1 (reproduced below)?

Back in 1900, who could have predicted the amazing technological achievements that would be made during the next hundred years?

(A) Back in 1900 who would anticipate the technological developments in the twentieth century?

(B) Recent technological achievements would blow the mind of people in 1900.

(C) The twentieth century saw remarkable technological achievements, but has it improved the lives of all people?

(D) Nobody has known whether the twenty-first century will produce as much technological progress as the twentieth century.

(E) Technological progress in communications, nuclear energy, and medicine is wonderful, but in the process we are destroying ourselves and our environment.

31. Which is the best revision of the underlined segment of sentence 10 (reproduced below)?

One positive feature of nuclear energy is that <u>energy is cheaper and can be made easy</u>.

(A) energy is cheaper and can be made easily
(B) energy is made cheaper and more easily made
(C) it is cheap and easy to make
(D) it is both cheap as well as made easily
(E) it's more cheaper and easier to make

32. To improve the coherence of paragraph 2, which of the following is the best sentence to delete?

(A) Sentence 4
(B) Sentence 5
(C) Sentence 6
(D) Sentence 7
(E) Sentence 8

33. In the context of the sentences that precede and follow sentence 13, which is the best revision of sentence 13 (reproduced below)?

Watch out for human error and careless workmanship.

(A) Human error and careless workmanship are almost unavoidable
(B) Especially human error and careless workmanship.
(C) There's hardly no foolproof way to prevent human error and careless workmanship.
(D) You must never put down your guard against human error and careless workmanship.
(E) Accidents can happen accidentally by human error and careless workmanship.

34. With regard to the entire essay, which of the following best explains the writer's intention in paragraphs 2, 3, and 4?

(A) To compare and contrast three technological achievements
(B) To provide examples of the pros and cons of technological progress
(C) To analyze the steps needed for achievement in three areas
(D) To convince readers to be open to technological change
(E) To advocate more funds for technological research and development

35. Assume that sentences 15 and 16 were combined as follows: *A significant advance in medicine has been the invention of the CAT scan.* Which of the following is the best way to continue the paragraph?

(A) The CAT scan allows your doctors to make pictures of a brain to see if it has a growth on it, a cancer is growing, or tumors at an early stage.
(B) The CAT scan permits your doctors to make a picture and see if your brain has a growth on it, or whether or not you have brain tumors or brain cancer at an early stage.
(C) Taking pictures with a CAT scan, your brain is studied by doctors for growths, brain tumors, and cancer at an early stage.
(D) Doctors may make pictures of your brain to see if there is a growth, a tumor, or cancer at an early stage of it.
(E) With this device a doctor may look into a patient's brain to check for growths and to detect cancerous tumors at an early stage.

End of Section 2.
Do not return to Section 1. Do not proceed to Section 3 until the
allotted time for Section 2 has passed.

Section 3
Multiple-Choice Questions

TIME—10 MINUTES

IMPROVING SENTENCES

Directions: The underlined sentences and sentence parts below may contain errors in standard English, including awkward or ambiguous expression, poor word choice (diction), incorrect sentence structure, or faulty grammar, usage, and punctuation. Read each sentence carefully and identify which of the five alternative versions most effectively and correctly expresses the meaning of the underlined material. Indicate your choice by filling in the corresponding space on the answer sheet. Choice A always repeats the original. Choose A if none of the other choices improves the original sentence.

1. During this decade, paying for a college education is more difficult for the average family than it was in the past.

 (A) than it was in the past
 (B) than for past families
 (C) than the past
 (D) than families in the past
 (E) than it used to be in the past

2. Gwen Harper, one of the most popular students in the school, winning the election for class president three years in a row.

 (A) school, winning the election for class president three years in a row
 (B) school, winning the election for class president, which she won three years in a row
 (C) school, and she won the election for class president three years in a row
 (D) school, won the election for class president three years in a row
 (E) school, three years in a row she won the election for class president.

3. The novel as we know it today came into being early in the 17th century with *Don Quixote* by Miguel Cervantes, and Cervantes was clearly ahead of his time.

 (A) Cervantes, and Cervantes was clearly ahead of his time
 (B) Cervantes, who was clearly ahead of his time
 (C) Cervantes, being clearly ahead of his time
 (D) Cervantes, which novel was clearly ahead of its time
 (E) Cervantes, Cervantes was clearly ahead of his time

4. Not all athletes who have high motivation or are significantly talented in a sport can be assured of a place on an Olympic team.

 (A) have high motivation or are significantly talented
 (B) have either high motivation or else talent in significant amounts
 (C) are highly motivated or who have significant talent instead
 (D) are highly motivated or significantly talented
 (E) have high motivation or else significant amounts of talent

5. Although she dislikes city living and has never been east of the Mississippi, Sarah intends to move to New York or Boston after she graduates from college.

   (A) she dislikes city living and has never been east of the Mississippi
   (B) she is without liking for city living nor having been east of the Mississippi
   (C) she dislikes city living nor has she visited there
   (D) she does not like city living and has never been a visitor
   (E) it is without a liking for city living nor having visited there

6. When you visit a foreign country, we can almost always find someone who speaks English.

   (A) When you visit a foreign country, we can
   (B) When visiting a foreign country, one can
   (C) When we visit a foreign country, one can
   (D) While you are on a visit to a foreign country, one can
   (E) During our visiting of a foreign country, we

7. Having Kelly Collins as our talented coordinator and the enthusiastic support of the community and the Chamber of Commerce helped to make the town's Octoberfest a rousing success.

   (A) Having Kelly Collins as our talented coordinator
   (B) The having of the coordinating talent of Kelly Collins
   (C) Kelly Collins as our talented coordinator
   (D) To be coordinated by talented Kelly Collins
   (E) The coordination talents of Kelly Collins

8. When Beethoven's music was introduced to the public for the first time, they found it difficult to understand and unpleasant to listen to.

   (A) When Beethoven's music was introduced to the public for the first time, they found it
   (B) When it was introduced to the public for the first time, they found Beethoven's music
   (C) When the music of Beethoven was introduced, the public found it
   (D) When they were introduced to Beethoven's music, the public had found it
   (E) Introducing Beethoven's music for the first time, the public found it

9. Two Coast Guard crews were dispatched to check an anonymous informant's warning, and he had observed a boatload of illegal immigrants approaching Florida's west coast.

   (A) an anonymous informant's warning, and he
   (B) the warning of an anonymous informant that he
   (C) that an anonymous warning of an informant he
   (D) the anonymous informant's warning saying he
   (E) information anonymously warning that he

10. Therefore, I admire organizations that speak up for fairness and democratic principles, even if it is motivated by selfishness.

   (A) even if it is motivated by selfishness
   (B) even when their motives are selfish
   (C) even when the motive is to be for its own selfish aims
   (D) whether or not it's for their own selfish aims
   (E) whether their motive is for selfish aims or not for selfish aims

11. If you wish to study transcendental meditation, <u>which is when a person completely relaxes their mind and body</u>, you will find several relevant books on the shelf.

   (A) which is when a person completely relaxes their mind and body
   (B) which is when a person completely relaxes his mind and body
   (C) which is when someone completely relax their mind and body
   (D) the complete relaxation of the mind and body
   (E) which completely relaxes their mind and body

12. Women in a hunter-gatherer society led demanding <u>lives, the reason was that they collected plant food for the family while protecting herself and her children</u> from wild beasts.

   (A) lives, the reason was that they collected plant food for the family while protecting herself and her children
   (B) lives, it was that she had to collect plant food for the family while also protecting herself and her children
   (C) lives; collecting plant food for the family while protecting herself and her children
   (D) lives because its responsibilities included collecting plant food for the family while protecting themselves and their children
   (E) lives because they not only collected plant food for the family but also protected themselves and their children

13. Nursing homes that violate regulations have become <u>an important statewide problem, and it has become</u> a hot political issue.

   (A) an important statewide problem, and it has become
   (B) a problem of statewide importance, that is
   (C) a problem of statewide importance; it was, therefore
   (D) an important statewide problem that is
   (E) an important statewide problem, which they have become

14. Of all the roads making up America's Interstate Highway System, <u>more people drive on I-95 than any highway</u>.

   (A) more people drive on I-95 than any highway
   (B) travelers are driving on I-95 in the largest amount
   (C) the largest amount of drivers are on I-95
   (D) I-95 is the more heavily traveled
   (E) I-95 is the most heavily traveled

End of Section 3.
Do not return to Sections 1 or 2.

END OF WRITING TEST.

ANSWER KEY

Guide for Scoring Your Essay

Using this guide, rate yourself in each of these six categories. Enter your scores in the spaces provided, and calculate the average of the six ratings to determine your final score.

On the SAT itself, two readers will score your essay on a scale of 6 (high) to 1 (low), or *zero* if you fail to write on the assigned topic. The score will be reported to you as the sum of the two ratings, from 12 to 0.

Remember that SAT essays are judged in relation to other essays written on the same topic. Therefore, this scoring guide may not yield a totally accurate prediction of the score you can expect on the exam. Because it is difficult to read your own essay with total objectivity, you might improve the validity of your score by getting a second opinion about your essay from an informed friend or a teacher.

Overall Impression

6   Consistently outstanding in clarity and competence; very insightful; few, if any, errors

5   Reasonably consistent in clarity and competence; occasional errors or lapses in quality; contains some insight

4   Adequate competence; some lapses in quality; fairly clear and with evidence of insight

3   Generally inadequate but demonstrates potential competence; contains some confusing aspects

2   Seriously limited; significant weaknesses in quality; generally unclear or incoherent

1   Demonstrates fundamental incompetence; contains serious flaws; significantly undeveloped or confusing

Score ☐

Development of Point of View

6   Fully developed with clear and appropriate supporting material; demonstrates high level of critical thinking

5   Generally well developed with appropriate examples, reasons, and other evidence to support a main idea; demonstrates strong critical thinking

4   Partly develops a main idea with relatively appropriate examples and reasons; shows some evidence of critical thinking

3   Weak development of main idea and little evidence of critical thinking; barely appropriate examples or other supporting material

2   Lacks a focus on a main idea; weak critical thinking; inappropriate or insufficient evidence

1   Fails to articulate a viable point of view; provides virtually no evidence of understanding the prompt

Score ☐

Organization of Ideas

6   Extremely well organized and focused on a main idea; supporting evidence presented in an effective, logical sequence

5   Generally well organized and reasonably focused on a main idea; mostly coherent and logical presentation of supporting material

4   Reasonably organized; shows some evidence of thoughtful sequence and progression of ideas

3   Limited organization and vague focus on main idea; contains some confusion in the sequence of ideas

2   Barely recognizable organization; little coherence; serious problems with sequence of ideas

1   No discernable organization; incoherent sequence of ideas

Score ☐

Language and Word Choice

6   Highly effective and skillful use of language; varied, appropriate, and accurate vocabulary

5   Demonstrates competence in use of language; appropriate and correct vocabulary

4   Adequate but inconsistent use of effective language; conventional but mostly correct use of vocabulary

3   Some minor errors in expression; generally weak or limited vocabulary; occasionally inappropriate word choice

2   Frequent errors in expression; very limited vocabulary; incorrect word choice interferes with meaning

1   Seriously deficient in use of language; meaning obscured by word choice

Score ☐

Sentence Structure

6   Varied and engaging sentence structure

5   Sufficiently varied sentence structure

4   Some sentence variation

3   Little sentence variation; minor sentence errors

2   Frequent sentence errors

1   Severe sentence errors; meaning obscured

Score ☐

Grammar, Usage, and Mechanics

6	Virtually or entirely error-free
5	Contains some minor errors
4	Some minor errors; one or two major errors
3	Accumulated minor and major errors
2	Contains frequent major errors that interfere with meaning
1	Contains severe errors that obscure meaning

Score ☐

<u>For rating yourself</u>

Total of six scores _____

Divide total by 6 to get score: _____ (A)
(Round to the nearest whole number.)

<u>For a second opinion</u>

Total of six scores _____

Divide total by 6 to get score: _____ (B)
(Round to the nearest whole number.)

(A) + (B) = ESSAY SUBSCORE _____
                              (0–12)

ANSWERS TO MULTIPLE-CHOICE QUESTIONS

Section 2

1. B	11. C	21. B	31. C
2. D	12. C	22. D	32. B
3. B	13. E	23. E	33. A
4. E	14. D	24. B	34. B
5. B	15. A	25. C	35. E
6. D	16. A	26. B	
7. D	17. C	27. D	
8. E	18. E	28. C	
9. A	19. B	29. B	
10. E	20. D	30. C	

Section 3

1. A	11. D
2. D	12. E
3. B	13. D
4. D	14. E
5. A	
6. B	
7. E	
8. C	
9. B	
10. B	

PERFORMANCE EVALUATION CHART

I. Self-Rating Chart

Section 2

Improving Sentences, questions 1–11   Number correct _____

Identifying Sentence Errors, questions 12–29   Number correct _____

Improving Paragraphs, questions 30–35   Number correct _____

Section 3

Improving Sentences, questions 1–14   Number correct _____

Subtotal _____ (A)

Wrong answers (Do not count unanswered questions)

Section 2   Number wrong _____

Section 3   Number wrong _____

Subtotal _____ (B)

Subtract ¼ point (0.25) from (B) for each wrong answer   _____ (C)

(A) minus (C) = _____ (D)

Round (D) to the nearest whole number for your MULTIPLE-CHOICE RAW SCORE   _____

ESSAY SUBSCORE   _____

CONVERSION TABLE

This table will give you an approximation of what your score would be if this practice test had been an actual SAT Writing Test. The essay counts for roughly 30% of the final score; the multiple-choice questions, for roughly 70%.

For example, if your Multiple-Choice Raw Score was 35 and your Essay Subscore was 6, the table indicates that your final score on the test would be approximately halfway between 500 and 710, or 600.

Multiple-Choice Raw Score	Essay Subscore						
	0	2	4	6	8	10	12
40–49	520–690	530–720	550–740	580–770	620–800	650–800	680–800
30–39	430–630	450–660	470–680	500–710	530–740	560–770	590–800
20–29	360–540	370–570	390–590	420–620	460–650	490–690	520–710
10–19	270–460	280–490	300–510	330–540	370–580	400–610	430–630
0–9	200–380	200–410	210–430	240–450	270–490	300–520	330–560
–12––1	200–280	200–310	200–330	200–350	240–390	270–420	300–450

ANSWER EXPLANATIONS

Note: Although many choices contain multiple errors, only a single error is listed for each incorrect answer.

SECTION 2—IMPROVING SENTENCES

1. **B**   A. Subject–verb agreement. The singular verb *explains* fails to agree with the plural subject *descriptions*.
   C. Verb tense. The participle *having boomed* is used instead of the present perfect *have boomed*.
   D. Word choice. The contraction *it's* is used instead of the possessive *its*.
   E. Subject–verb agreement. The singular verb *is* fails to agree with the plural subject *descriptions*.

2. **D**   A. Faulty parallelism. Elements being compared in a sentence must be in the same grammatical form. *Jogging* differs in form from *as if you walk*.
   B. Faulty parallelism. See A.
   C. Faulty comparison. *Jogging*, a gerund, may not be compared to a phrase, *than to walk*.
   E. Faulty pronoun reference. The pronoun *it* fails to refer to a specific noun or other pronoun.

3. **B**   A. Tense shift. The verb tense improperly shifts from the past to the present progressive in the second clause.
   C. Tense shift. The verb tense improperly shifts from the past to the present in the second clause.
   D. Incomplete construction. The absence of the pronoun *she* causes meaning to be distorted.
   E. Tense shift. The verb tense improperly shifts from the past to other tenses in the second clause.

4. **E**   A. Faulty comparison. The phrase *more happier* is redundant. Use *happier* or *more happy*.
   B. Idiom error. In context the construction *happier but me* is not standard English.
   C. Idiom error. In context the construction *more happy like myself* is not standard English.
   D. Tense shift. The verb tense improperly shifts from the past to the present.

5. **B**   A. Idiom error. The phrase *determine about* is not standard English.
   C. Incomplete construction. Lacking a verb, the clause is a sentence fragment.
   D. Idiom error. The phrase *determine about* is not standard English.
   E. Incomplete construction. Lacking a verb, the clause is a sentence fragment.

6. **D**   A. Comma splice. A comma may not be used to separate two independent clauses.
   B. Mixed construction. The first and second clauses are grammatically unrelated.
   C. Wordy. The entire clause, containing a string of prepositional phrases, is excessively wordy.
   E. Comma splice. A comma may not be used to separate two independent clauses.

7. **D**   A. Incomplete construction. The phrase *or did not* is both misplaced and incomplete. Insert *did or did not send* after *in fact*.
B. Incomplete construction. The phrase *or did not* is both misplaced and incomplete. Insert *did or did not send* after *Charles*.
C. Clumsy construction. The phrase *sending of the e-mail by Charles to Rose* is awkwardly worded.
E. Clumsy construction. The use of *Charles* as the grammatical subject makes the sentence non-sensical.

8. **E**   A. Comma splice. A comma may not be used to separate two independent clauses.
B. Pronoun–antecedent agreement. *Ohio State University* is singular; *they* is plural. Use *it*.
C. Comma splice. A comma may not be used to separate two independent clauses.
D. Word choice. In context the use of *consequently* makes no sense.

9. **A**   B. Tense shift. The sentence, cast in the present tense, shifts to the past.
C. Sentence fragment. The construction lacks a main verb.
D. Faulty comparison. *Popularity* is compared to *Florida*, an illogical comparison.
E. Idiom error. The phrase *has greater popularity as* is nonstandard English.

10. **E**   A. Dangling participle. The phrase that begins *Wandering through* should modify *he* instead of *everything*.
B. Comma splice. A comma may not be used to separate independent clauses.
C. Awkwardness. The construction awkwardly separates the subject and the verb.
D. Dangling participle. The phrase that begins *While wandering through* should modify *he* instead of *everything*.

11. **C**   A. Idiom error. *Event* is a noun that must be defined by another noun, not by a subordinate clause.
B. Idiom error. See A.
D. Clumsy construction. The wording of *the separating* is awkward.
E. Pronoun choice. Pronouns in prepositional phrases should be in the objective case. Use *him*.

SECTION 2—IDENTIFYING SENTENCE ERRORS

12. **C**   Diction error. Use *as* instead of *than* when pointing out likenesses.

13. **E**   No error.

14. **D**   Faulty comparison. *Winners* is being compared to *last year*, an illogical comparison. Use *last year's* (senior class).

15. **A**   Pronoun–antecedent agreement. The antecedent *A disruptive student* is singular. The pronoun *they* is plural. Use *Disruptive students*.

16. **A**   Idiom error. Use *in* instead of *for*.

17. **C**   Faulty parallelism. Items in a series should be in grammatically parallel form. Use *stole* instead of *were stealing*.

18. **E**   No error.

19. **B**   Verb form. The past perfect form of *to bite* is *bitten*. Use *had been bitten*.

20. **D**   Pronoun–antecedent agreement. The antecedent *Gilbert W. Davis* is singular; the pronoun *their* is plural. Use *his*.

21. **B**   Idiom error. Use *at* instead of *for*.

22. **D**   Diction error. Adjectives are used with linking verbs to modify verbs. Use *beautiful*.

23. **E**   No error.

24. **B**   Subject–verb agreement. *Attitude* is singular; *were* is plural. Use *was*.

25. **C**   Diction error. Use *when* or *while* instead of *as*.

26. **B**   Subject–verb agreement. The subject *following* is singular; the verb *have* is plural. Use *has*.

27. **D**   Pronoun case. A pronoun that serves as the object of a preposition (*without*) must be in the objective case. Use *me*.

28. **C**   Idiom error. In standard English *neither* is paired with *nor*, not with *or*.

29. **B**   Subject–verb agreement. The compound subject *problem* and *issues* is plural; the verb *is* is singular. Use *are*.

SECTION 2—IMPROVING PARAGRAPHS

30. **C**   Choice A implies that the essay's purpose is to point out technological marvels of the twentieth century. But the purpose is deeper—to show that technological progress in the twentieth century failed to benefit all people.
Choice B is similar to choice A and also contains an inappropriate colloquialism.
Choice D incorrectly suggests that the essay is meant to discuss the prospects for continued technological progress.
Choice E summarizes the three areas discussed in the essay but indicates that we would be better off without technological progress, an idea neither stated nor implied by the essay.

31. **C**   Choice A repeats *energy* unnecessarily and contains an incomplete comparison. Cheaper than what?
Choice B contains an incomplete comparison. Energy is cheaper than what? It also contains an error in parallel construction.
Choice D is wordy. The word *both* and the phrase *as well as* are redundant.
Choice E contains *more cheaper*, a nonstandard construction. Use *cheaper*.

32. **B**   Although related to communications, the information contained in sentence 5 is not relevant to the discussion of modern communications satellites.

33. **A**   Choice B is a sentence fragment.
Choice C contains the double negative *hardly no*.
Choice D improperly shifts to the second person.
Choice E is needlessly repetitious.

34. **B**   Choices A, C, and D accurately describe neither the paragraph structure nor the point of the essay.
Choice E is a remote possibility but is not justified by evidence in the essay.

35. **E**   Choice A unnecessarily repeats *CAT scan* and contains faulty parallelism.
Choice B is wordy, and it unnecessarily repeats *CAT scan*.
Choice C contains a dangling participle. The phrase that begins *Taking pictures* should modify *doctors*, not *brains*.
Choice D has no discernible connection with the previous sentence.

Section 3—Improving Sentences

1. **A**   B. Faulty comparison. *Paying* is compared to *families*, an illogical comparison.
C. Faulty comparison. *Paying* is compared to *past*, an illogical comparison.
D. Faulty comparison. *Paying* is compared to *families*, an illogical comparison.
E. Redundancy. The phrases *used to be* and *in the past* are redundant.

2. **D**   A. Sentence fragment. *Gwen Harper*, the grammatical subject of the sentence, lacks a verb.
B. Sentence fragment. *Gwen Harper*, the grammatical subject of the sentence, lacks a verb.
C. Faulty coordination. The conjunction *and* fails to create a grammatical relation between the independent clause and the phrase with which the sentence begins.
E. The clause that begins *three years in a row* lacks a grammatical relationship with the rest of the sentence.

3. **B**   A. Faulty coordination. The two coordinate clauses are not of equal importance. The second clause should be a subordinate clause.
C. Mismatched sentence parts. The word *being* has no grammatical relationship with the rest of the sentence.
D. Word choice. *Which* has no logical meaning. In the context *whose* would be a better choice.
E. Comma splice. A comma may not be used to separate two independent clauses.

4. **D**   A. Faulty parallelism. *High motivation* is a noun phrase; *significantly talented* is an adjective phrase. Were these constructions in parallel grammatical form, the sentence would be more effective.
B. Redundancy. The word *either* and the phrase *or else* are redundant. Omit *else*.
C. Wordiness. The use of two successive subordinate clauses each beginning with *who* is wordy.
E. Faulty parallelism. The phrase *high motivation* consists of an adjective and a noun. The phrase *significant amounts of talent* consists of an adjective, a noun, and a prepositional phrase. Were these constructions in parallel grammatical form, the sentence would be more effective.

5. **A**   B. Idiom. The construction is extremely awkward and is not in standard English.
C. Syntax error. The word *there* doesn't refer to a specific place. Where is it that Sarah has not visited?
D. Incomplete construction. The place(s) that Sarah has not visited has been left out of the sentence.
E. Idiom. The construction fails to conform to standard English idiom.

6. **B**   A. Shift in pronoun person. The sentence shifts from second to third person—from *you* to *we*.
C. Shift in pronoun number. The sentence shifts from plural to singular—from *we* to *one*.
D. Shift in pronoun person. The pronouns shift from second person (*you*) to the impersonal *one*.
E. Awkwardness. The construction *our visiting* is awkwardly worded.

7. **E**   A. Faulty parallelism. Coordinate elements in a series should be parallel in form. *Having Kelly Collins* . . . is not parallel to *the enthusiastic support* . . . .
B. Awkwardness. *The having of the coordinating talent* . . . is awkwardly expressed and is not standard English.
C. Faulty parallelism. Coordinate elements in a series should be parallel in form. *Kelly Collins as our* . . . is not parallel to *the enthusiastic support* . . . .
D. Mismatched sentence parts. The phrase *To be coordinated* . . . has no grammatical relation to the rest of the sentence.

8. **C**   A. Redundancy. The construction *introduced . . . for the first time* is redundant.
B. Faulty pronoun reference. The pronoun *they* is meant to refer to *public*, but being in a prepositional phrase, *public* may not be the antecedent.
D. Tense shift. The sentence, cast in the past tense, shifts to the past perfect.
E. Dangling modifier. Because it wasn't the public that introduced Beethoven's music, the construction is illogical.

9. **B**   A. Mismatched sentence parts. The first clause of the sentence is grammatically and logically unrelated to the second clause.
C. Idiom. The construction fails to use standard English.
D. Awkwardness. The construction is clumsily worded.
E. Pronoun reference. The pronoun *he* does not refer to a specific noun or other pronoun.

10. **B**   A. Pronoun reference. The pronoun *it* lacks a specific referent.
C. Tense shift. The sentence, cast in the present tense (*admire*) shifts to the future tense (*is to be*).
D. Diction error. The word *it's* is a contraction of *it is*. Nor would *its* be correct because it is a singular pronoun that fails to agree with its plural antecedent *organizations*.
E. Wordy. The construction is repetitious and long-winded.

11. **D**   A. Pronoun–antecedent agreement. The pronoun *their* is plural; the antecedent *person* is singular. Use *his* or *her*.
B. Idiom error. In standard usage, nouns are defined by other nouns, not by clauses. Because *meditation* is a noun, *is when* is nonstandard.
C. Noun–verb agreement. *Someone* is singular; *relax* is plural.
E. Pronoun reference. The pronoun *their* doesn't refer to any specific noun or pronoun.

12. **E**   A. Comma splice. Commas may not be used to separate two independent clauses.
B. Pronoun reference. The pronoun *it* fails to refer to a specific noun or other pronoun.
C. Sentence fragment. Because the construction after the semicolon lacks a verb, it is not a complete sentence.
D. Pronoun–antecedent agreement. The pronoun *its* is singular; the antecedent *lives* is plural.

13. **D**   A. Pronoun reference. The pronoun *it* fails to refer to a specific noun or pronoun.
   B. Comma splice. Commas may not be used to separate two independent clauses.
   C. Tense shift. The sentence, cast in the present tense, improperly shifts to the past tense.
   E. Idiom. The construction is in nonstandard English.

14. **E**   A. Faulty comparison. *Other* should be used when comparing one thing with a group of which it is a member. Use *any other highway*.
   B. Misplaced modifier. The phrase that begins *Of all the roads . . .* should modify *I-95*, not *travelers*.
   C. Diction error. Use *amount* to refer to mass quantities; use *number* to refer to anything that can be individually counted.
   D. Faulty comparison. When comparing three or more things, use *most* instead of *more*.

PRACTICE TEST D

Section 1
Essay

TIME—25 MINUTES

<u>Directions</u>: Plan and write an essay in response to the assigned topic. Use the essay as an opportunity to show how clearly and effectively you can express and develop ideas. Present your thoughts logically and precisely. Include specific evidence or examples to support your point of view. A plain, natural writing style is probably best. The number of words is up to you, but quantity is less important than quality.

Limit your essay to two sides of the lined paper provided. You'll have enough space if you write on every line and avoid wide margins. Write or print legibly because handwriting that's hard or impossible to read will decrease your score.

BE SURE TO WRITE ONLY ON THE ASSIGNED TOPIC. AN ESSAY WRITTEN ON ANOTHER TOPIC WILL BE SCORED "ZERO."

If you finish in less than 25 minutes, check your work. Do not turn to another section of the test.

Think carefully about the following passage and the assignment below.

The passion for change almost always leads to tension between those who want change and those who don't. Most advocates of change equate change with progress, an improvement of some kind. Those supporting the status quo perceive change as a threat—a threat to their well being, a threat to their traditions and values, even a threat to their basic rights. As of yet, no one has devised a way to bring about change without conflict.

Assignment: Plan and write an essay that comments on the validity of this description of change. Support your position with reasoning and examples taken from your studies, experience, observation, or reading.

Section 1

ESSAY

Time allowed: 25 minutes

Limit your essay to two pages. Do not skip lines. Write only inside the box.

Essay (continued)

End of essay.
Do not proceed to Section 2 until the allotted time for Section 1 has passed.

ANSWER SHEET FOR MULTIPLE-CHOICE QUESTIONS

Section 2
Improving Sentences

1. Ⓐ Ⓑ Ⓒ Ⓓ Ⓔ
2. Ⓐ Ⓑ Ⓒ Ⓓ Ⓔ
3. Ⓐ Ⓑ Ⓒ Ⓓ Ⓔ
4. Ⓐ Ⓑ Ⓒ Ⓓ Ⓔ
5. Ⓐ Ⓑ Ⓒ Ⓓ Ⓔ
6. Ⓐ Ⓑ Ⓒ Ⓓ Ⓔ
7. Ⓐ Ⓑ Ⓒ Ⓓ Ⓔ
8. Ⓐ Ⓑ Ⓒ Ⓓ Ⓔ
9. Ⓐ Ⓑ Ⓒ Ⓓ Ⓔ
10. Ⓐ Ⓑ Ⓒ Ⓓ Ⓔ
11. Ⓐ Ⓑ Ⓒ Ⓓ Ⓔ

Identifying
Sentence Errors

12. Ⓐ Ⓑ Ⓒ Ⓓ Ⓔ
13. Ⓐ Ⓑ Ⓒ Ⓓ Ⓔ
14. Ⓐ Ⓑ Ⓒ Ⓓ Ⓔ
15. Ⓐ Ⓑ Ⓒ Ⓓ Ⓔ
16. Ⓐ Ⓑ Ⓒ Ⓓ Ⓔ
17. Ⓐ Ⓑ Ⓒ Ⓓ Ⓔ
18. Ⓐ Ⓑ Ⓒ Ⓓ Ⓔ
19. Ⓐ Ⓑ Ⓒ Ⓓ Ⓔ
20. Ⓐ Ⓑ Ⓒ Ⓓ Ⓔ
21. Ⓐ Ⓑ Ⓒ Ⓓ Ⓔ
22. Ⓐ Ⓑ Ⓒ Ⓓ Ⓔ
23. Ⓐ Ⓑ Ⓒ Ⓓ Ⓔ
24. Ⓐ Ⓑ Ⓒ Ⓓ Ⓔ
25. Ⓐ Ⓑ Ⓒ Ⓓ Ⓔ
26. Ⓐ Ⓑ Ⓒ Ⓓ Ⓔ
27. Ⓐ Ⓑ Ⓒ Ⓓ Ⓔ
28. Ⓐ Ⓑ Ⓒ Ⓓ Ⓔ
29. Ⓐ Ⓑ Ⓒ Ⓓ Ⓔ

Improving Paragraphs

30. Ⓐ Ⓑ Ⓒ Ⓓ Ⓔ
31. Ⓐ Ⓑ Ⓒ Ⓓ Ⓔ
32. Ⓐ Ⓑ Ⓒ Ⓓ Ⓔ
33. Ⓐ Ⓑ Ⓒ Ⓓ Ⓔ
34. Ⓐ Ⓑ Ⓒ Ⓓ Ⓔ
35. Ⓐ Ⓑ Ⓒ Ⓓ Ⓔ

Section 3
Improving Sentences

1. Ⓐ Ⓑ Ⓒ Ⓓ Ⓔ
2. Ⓐ Ⓑ Ⓒ Ⓓ Ⓔ
3. Ⓐ Ⓑ Ⓒ Ⓓ Ⓔ
4. Ⓐ Ⓑ Ⓒ Ⓓ Ⓔ
5. Ⓐ Ⓑ Ⓒ Ⓓ Ⓔ
6. Ⓐ Ⓑ Ⓒ Ⓓ Ⓔ
7. Ⓐ Ⓑ Ⓒ Ⓓ Ⓔ
8. Ⓐ Ⓑ Ⓒ Ⓓ Ⓔ
9. Ⓐ Ⓑ Ⓒ Ⓓ Ⓔ
10. Ⓐ Ⓑ Ⓒ Ⓓ Ⓔ
11. Ⓐ Ⓑ Ⓒ Ⓓ Ⓔ
12. Ⓐ Ⓑ Ⓒ Ⓓ Ⓔ
13. Ⓐ Ⓑ Ⓒ Ⓓ Ⓔ
14. Ⓐ Ⓑ Ⓒ Ⓓ Ⓔ

Section 2
Multiple-Choice Questions

Time—25 minutes

IMPROVING SENTENCES

Directions: The underlined sentences and sentence parts below may contain errors in standard English, including awkward or ambiguous expression, poor word choice (diction), incorrect sentence structure, or faulty grammar, usage, and punctuation. Read each sentence carefully and identify which of the five alternative versions most effectively and correctly expresses the meaning of the underlined material. Indicate your choice by filling in the corresponding space on the answer sheet. Choice A always repeats the original. Choose A if none of the other choices improves the original sentence.

EXAMPLE

My old Aunt Maud loves
to cook, and eating also.

(A) cook, and eating also
(B) cook and to eat
(C) cook, and to eat also
(D) cook and eat besides
(E) cook and, in addition, eat

ANSWER

Ⓐ ● Ⓒ Ⓓ Ⓔ

1. If you wish to truly understand Jefferson's notion of "the pursuit of happiness," the letters Jefferson wrote to his son should be read.

(A) the letters Jefferson wrote to his son should be read
(B) Jefferson's letters to his son should be read
(C) you should read the letters Jefferson wrote to his son
(D) you should read his letters to his son
(E) a person should read his letters to his son

2. Yellowstone, an extremely popular national park, has been described as the noisiest park and also the most tranquil of them.

(A) the noisiest park and also the most tranquil of them
(B) not only the noisiest park, but also more tranquil than any
(C) the noisiest park, at the same time it is the most tranquil park
(D) at once the noisiest and also the most tranquil of them
(E) the noisiest and yet the most tranquil of parks

3. The country's most important city for the arts and entertainment, <u>tourists by the millions visit New York each year</u>.

   (A) tourists by the millions visit New York each year
   (B) millions of tourists visit New York annually
   (C) each year millions of tourists visit New York
   (D) tourists by the millions are attracted to New York every year
   (E) New York attracts millions of tourists each year

4. <u>There is plenty of Thoreau's practical advice about life, which every reader can benefit from in his *Walden*.</u>

   (A) There is plenty of Thoreau's practical advice about life, which every reader can benefit from in his *Walden*.
   (B) In Thoreau's *Walden*, they give the reader plenty of practical and beneficial advice about life.
   (C) Reading Thoreau's *Walden*, plenty of practical and beneficial advice about life is offered.
   (D) In *Walden*, Thoreau offers readers plenty of practical and beneficial advice about life.
   (E) Because of offering plenty of practical and beneficial advice about life in Thoreau's *Walden*.

5. Nuclear waste disposal is a growing problem <u>considering that no state permits radioactive material transported on its roads or to bury it inside its borders</u>.

   (A) considering that no state permits radioactive material transported on its roads or to bury it inside its borders
   (B) considering that no state permits neither radioactive material transported on its roads or buried inside its borders
   (C) because no state permits radioactive material transported on its roads or buried inside its borders
   (D) because no state will permit radioactive material not only to be carried on its roads but in addition also buried inside its borders
   (E) being that no state had permitted radioactive material to be carried on its roads or buried inside its borders

6. Although many young painters learned to paint from Rembrandt himself, when the master died, <u>no immediate successors have come into being</u>.

   (A) no immediate successors have come into being
   (B) he had no immediate successors
   (C) the coming of immediate successors were not to be
   (D) there was not a coming of an immediate successor
   (E) there were not immediate successors

7. <u>Newspaper editorials across the country argue brilliantly against the Supreme Court's decision on affirmative action</u>.

   (A) Newspaper editorials across the country argue brilliantly against the Supreme Court's decision on affirmative action
   (B) Newspaper editorials across the country that brilliantly argue against the Supreme Court's decision on affirmative action
   (C) The Supreme Court's decision on affirmative action, brilliantly opposed by newspaper editorials across the country
   (D) The Supreme Court's decision on affirmative action being brilliantly opposed across the country by newspaper editorials
   (E) Brilliant arguments against the Supreme Court's decision on affirmative action that have appeared in newspapers across the country

8. Allan asked Sadie to go to the prom with <u>him, this surprised Sadie</u> because she thought Allan would ask Marnie.

   (A) him, this surprised Sadie
   (B) him, therefore Sadie was surprised
   (C) him, surprising Sadie
   (D) him, which surprises Sadie
   (E) him, that was surprising to Sadie

9. Just as the number of applications to Stanford and Yale has grown annually since 1998, <u>so has Columbia's applicant pool risen steadily</u>.

(A) so has Columbia's applicant pool risen steadily
(B) Columbia attracted applicants in steadily rising numbers
(C) Columbia is steadily gaining applicants in its pool
(D) and so then, for Columbia, a rising applicant pool has grown steadily
(E) and like them Columbia's steadily rising pool of applicants

10. The city of Oakland, California, <u>suffers from a high crime rate, while it is</u> a very desirable place to live.

(A) suffers from a high crime rate, while it is
(B) although suffering from a high crime rate, is
(C) suffering from a high crime rate made it
(D) which suffers from a high crime rate, although it is
(E) whose rate of crime is high, makes it

11. Drivers in Washington, D.C., say that the city is at once frustrating because of its numerous traffic circles <u>but they have designed it beautifully</u>.

(A) but they have designed it beautifully
(B) although it is beautifully designed
(C) yet it is beautiful in its design
(D) while being designed so beautifully
(E) and pleasing because of its beautiful design

IDENTIFYING SENTENCE ERRORS

Directions: The underlined and lettered parts of each sentence below may contain an error in grammar, usage, word choice (diction), or expression (idiom). Read each sentence carefully and identify which item, if any, contains an error. Indicate your choice by filling in the corresponding space on the answer sheet. No sentence contains more than one error. Some sentences may contain no error. In that case, the correct choice will always be E (No error).

EXAMPLE

Jill went <u>speedily</u> to the <u>crest</u> of the
        A   B

hill in a <u>more</u> faster time <u>than</u> her
        C   D

friend, Jack. <u>No error</u>.
           E

ANSWER

Ⓐ Ⓑ ● Ⓓ Ⓔ

12. The plight of immigrants, <u>vividly depicted</u> in
                             A

Sinclair's novel, *The Jungle*, <u>are</u> <u>no less</u>
                        B   C

heartbreaking <u>than</u> the suffering of the migrant
             D

workers in Steinbeck's *Grapes of Wrath*.

<u>No error</u>.
  E

13. The orchestra played <u>so</u> <u>loud</u> throughout the
                    A B

wedding reception, that <u>it was</u> barely possible
                      C

<u>to hold</u> a conversation without shouting.
  D
<u>No error</u>.
  E

14. A number of the athletes <u>which</u> were
                    A

participating in the Olympics <u>were found</u> to
                      B

have used steroids and other muscle-building

substances <u>to enhance</u> <u>their</u> performance.
          C   D
<u>No error</u>.
  E

15. <u>Throughout</u> the year, the park attracts visitors
    A

who come <u>for</u> hiking in the wilderness,
         B

climbing the mountains, <u>water sports</u>, and
                   C

catching trout and <u>other</u> prized game fish.
            D
<u>No error</u>.
  E

16. Carolyn's mother <u>was</u> born and raised in
             A

Baltimore, where she <u>attended</u> high school
              B

and college, got <u>married</u>, and <u>gave</u> birth to
          C   D
Carolyn on October 20, 1993. <u>No error</u>.
                      E

17. Mike read a novel <u>where</u> the author,
              A

<u>experimenting with</u> a new structure, <u>devoted</u> a
  B   C
separate chapter <u>to each</u> character. <u>No error</u>.
          D   E

18. His <u>lifelong</u> career as a drug dealer and <u>his</u>
      A   B

    murder of three FBI agents <u>proves</u> that he
                                  C

    is one of the <u>most notorious</u> criminals in
                     D

    American history. <u>No error</u>.
                    E

19. <u>As</u> the lovers row across the lake in a small
    A

    boat, Catherine fears the approaching storm,

    but <u>when</u> they arrive on the opposite shore
        B

    she <u>said</u> that she <u>had not been frightened</u>
        C   D

    during the trip. <u>No error</u>.
                 E

20. <u>Notice</u> that this cereal not only <u>costs</u>
    A   B

    more <u>than</u> the other one, <u>plus being</u> packed
         C   D

    in a smaller container. <u>No error</u>.
                     E

21. If you expect to be absent <u>when</u> senior papers
                       A

    are due, <u>one</u> should <u>submit</u> the paper early or,
         B   C

    <u>if necessary</u>, arrange for an extension.
       D

    <u>No error</u>.
      E

22. The large beech trees in our <u>neighbors'</u> yards
                      A

    always shed <u>their</u> dark red leaves late <u>in the fall</u>
             B   C

    <u>when</u> the other trees are bare. <u>No error</u>.
    D   E

23. <u>Although</u> I can't concur <u>in</u> the speaker's
    A   B

    opinions, I am grateful for the opportunity

    <u>to have heard</u> <u>them</u> expressed so eloquently.
        C   D

    <u>No error</u>.
      E

24. <u>After all</u>, Elizabeth is the strongest candidate
    A

    for the job <u>because</u> her looks, experience, and
           B

    natural intelligence <u>invites</u> voters <u>to cast</u> their
                      C   D

    ballots for her. <u>No error</u>.
               E

25. <u>Although</u> Roxanne, the valedictorian, <u>has</u> the
    A   B

    highest grade-point average in the class, her

    score on the SAT was far lower <u>than</u> <u>Charles</u>.
                           C   D

    <u>No error</u>.
    E

26. That Naomi, the <u>book's main character</u> and
                  A

    possibly <u>its</u> hero, is <u>a mere child</u> during the
          B   C

    Revolution makes the story <u>even more</u>
                         D

    appealing to young readers. <u>No error</u>.
                       E

27. High school jocks who wish to <u>become</u>
                           A

    <u>a professional athlete</u> should remember that
            B

    the odds <u>against</u> being successful <u>are simply</u>
            C   D

    staggering. <u>No error</u>.
              E

28. The <u>fact is</u> that one is often faced <u>with a choice</u>
       A   B

    between <u>doing</u> the ethical thing <u>or</u> acting in
           C   D

    one's own self-interest. <u>No error</u>.
                    E

29. The false alarm <u>frightened</u> everyone in the
                 A

    condo, and <u>she</u> <u>more than</u> the other residents
             B   C

    because she <u>had once lived</u> in a building that
                D

    burned down. <u>No error</u>.
               E

IMPROVING PARAGRAPHS

Directions: The passage below is the draft of a student's essay. Some parts of the passage need improvement. Read the passage and answer the questions that follow. The questions are about revisions that might improve all or part of the passage's organization, development, sentence structure, or choice of words. Choose the answer that best follows the requirements of standard written English.

Questions 30–35 refer to the following passage.

[1] Many reasons are used to justify the cruel practice of keeping animals penned up in zoos. [2] Parents bring their kids to gawk at the caged creatures. [3] Then, thinking they are being kind to the poor creatures, they drop quarters into food dispensers and toss a few pellets to the monkeys or elephants. [4] There must be better reasons, imprisoning wild animals is simply barbaric.

[5] Some people argue that a zoo is educational by allowing visitors to see what animals look like. [6] If someone is so dumb that they don't know what a zebra looks like, they should look it up online. [7] But humans have no right to pull animals from their natural environment and to seal their fate forever behind a set of cold metal bars. [8] Animals need to run free and live, but by putting them in zoos we are disrupting and disturbing nature.

[9] Then there is the issue of sanitary conditions for animals at the zoo. [10] When the animals have been at the zoo for a while they adopt a particular lifestyle. [11] They lounge around all day, and they're fed at a particular time. [12] They get used to that. [13] That means that they would never again be able to be placed back in their natural environment. [14] They would never survive. [15] And if they reproduce while in captivity, they are born into an artificial lifestyle. [16] After a few generations the animals become totally different from their wild and free ancestors, and visitors to the zoo see animals hardly resembling those living in their natural habitat.

30. In context, which of the following is the best phrase to insert at the beginning of sentence 2 (reproduced below)?

    Parents bring their kids to gawk at the caged creatures.

    (A) In any case, one would be
    (B) For one thing,
    (C) However, this is that
    (D) That is to say,
    (E) An excellent choice would be that

31. In context, which of the following revisions would most improve sentence 4 (reproduced below)?

    There must be better reasons, imprisoning wild animals is simply barbaric.

    (A) Begin with "I disagree because."
    (B) Change "There must" to "There's got to."
    (C) Delete the comma and add "because" in its place.
    (D) Substitute "terribly" for "simply."
    (E) Change "imprisoning" to "to imprison."

32. Taking sentence 5 into account, which of the following is the most effective revision of sentence 6?

   (A) Reading about animals online rather than studying them firsthand.
   (B) A book or a website can give you more information about zebras and other animals.
   (C) They claim that viewing a live animal is much more informative than looking at its picture.
   (D) Doesn't everyone know what a zebra looks like, even little children?
   (E) But if someone is so dumb that they don't know what a zebra looks like, they should look it up online.

33. Which of the following reasons most accurately describes the author's purpose in choosing the words underlined in sentence 7 (reproduced below)?

   But humans have no right to pull animals from their natural environment <u>and to seal their fate forever behind a set of cold metal bars</u>.

   (A) to inform the reader that animals in the zoo live in cages
   (B) to propose a solution to the plight of animals in the zoo
   (C) to arouse in the reader an emotional response to the problem
   (D) to appeal to the reader to weigh both sides of the issue
   (E) to prove that animals don't enjoy being in the zoo

34. Which of the following revisions of sentence 9 is the best topic sentence for the third paragraph?

   (A) Captivity alters the basic nature of animals.
   (B) No one favors zoos that deliberately try to change the lifestyle of animals in captivity.
   (C) Living conditions for animals in the zoo are ordinarily harsh and cruel.
   (D) Living in the zoo, conditions of animals affect them permanently.
   (E) Life in the zoo for animals is not a bowl of cherries.

35. Which revision most effectively combines sentences 12, 13, and 14?

   (A) Because they would never be able to survive again back in their natural environment, they grow used to being fed.
   (B) Having grown used to regular feedings, the animals would be unable to survive back in their native environment.
   (C) Growing accustomed to that, placing them back in their native habitat and being unable to survive on their own.
   (D) They, having gotten used to being fed regularly, in their natural environment would never survive.
   (E) Being unable to survive back in their natural environment, the animals have grown accustomed to regular feedings.

End of Section 2.
Do not return to Section 1. Do not proceed to Section 3 until the
allotted time for Section 2 has passed.

Section 3
Multiple-Choice Questions

TIME—10 MINUTES

IMPROVING SENTENCES

Directions: The underlined sentences and sentence parts below may contain errors in standard English, including awkward or ambiguous expression, poor word choice (diction), incorrect sentence structure, or faulty grammar, usage, and punctuation. Read each sentence carefully and identify which of the five alternative versions most effectively and correctly expresses the meaning of the underlined material. Indicate your choice by filling in the corresponding space on the answer sheet. Choice A always repeats the original. Choose A if none of the other choices improves the original sentence.

1. Having a mother who plays in a symphony orchestra and a father who teaches music in high school, the violin and the piano are two of the instruments that Rosie learned at an early age.

   (A) the violin and the piano are two of the instruments that Rosie learned at an early age
   (B) violin and piano were taught to Rosie at an early age
   (C) two instruments, the violin and the piano, Rosie learned to play at an early age
   (D) at an early age Rosie learned to play both the violin and the piano
   (E) Rosie learned the playing of both violin and piano at an early age

2. When children change from little boys and girls to young men and women, ordinarily causing them to become more self-sufficient and independent.

   (A) ordinarily causing them to become
   (B) and ordinarily causing them to become
   (C) they ordinarily become
   (D) and as a result they ordinarily become
   (E) causing them to become ordinarily

3. Susan does not have absolute free will because what she does would have to be determined by the culture and the environment.

   (A) free will because what she does would have to be determined
   (B) free will because what she does is determined
   (C) free will because it has to be determined
   (D) free will, and the reason is that her actions being determined
   (E) free will, her actions are determined

4. The students' final Social Studies exam has been stolen from the teacher's desk; this situation causing them to take a make-up test on Saturday.

   (A) desk; this situation causing them to take a make-up
   (B) desk, which was the cause of their taking a make-up
   (C) desk, this causing them to take a make-up
   (D) desk, a situation that will cause the class to take a make-up
   (E) desk, with it they are caused to take a make-up

5. The atmosphere in the classroom changed when the snow started to fall <u>outside and the teacher could not get them to pay attention to the lesson after that</u>.

(A) outside and the teacher could not get them to pay attention to the lesson after that

(B) outside, the teacher was unable to bring the class's attention back to the lesson after that

(C) outside, and the teacher could no longer get the children to pay attention to the lesson

(D) outside, causing them to lose attention to the lesson, despite the teacher's effort

(E) outside, in spite of the teacher's effort was unable to get them to pay attention to the lesson after that

6. Of the four seasons in New England, Granny most loves the <u>autumn, of which she finds the mild days and cool nights especially appealing</u>.

(A) autumn, of which she finds the mild days and cool nights especially appealing

(B) autumn; she finds the mild days and cool nights especially appealing

(C) autumn, and it is especially the mild days and cool nights that are of appeal

(D) autumn; the appeal of the mild days and cool nights especially

(E) autumn, especially appealing to Granny are the mild days and cool nights

7. Today's newspaper says that mathematics is far more popular among Japanese high school students <u>than among American students</u>.

(A) than among American students

(B) than students in America

(C) compared to American high school students

(D) than mathematics is among high school students in America

(E) than its popularity among American students

8. In the 19th century, immigrants entered the United States with few limitations and <u>restrictions, but they have multiplied since then</u>.

(A) restrictions, but they have multiplied since then

(B) restrictions, but they have now multiplied

(C) restrictions, and have since multiplied

(D) restrictions, which, since then, have multiplied

(E) restrictions, since multiplied

9. In Moscow, <u>famous composers, artists, and writers are buried in a special cemetery, and they only must be Russian</u>.

(A) famous composers, artists, and writers are buried in a special cemetery, and they only must be Russian

(B) there had been buried in a special cemetery famous composers, artists, and writers who have been only Russian

(C) being buried in a special cemetery only for famous composers, artists, and writers who are Russian

(D) a special cemetery for burying only famous Russian composers, artists, and writers

(E) famous Russian composers, artists, and writers are buried in a special cemetery

10. The Boston Tea Party was a minor historical <u>event with which the colonists either intended to challenge or abolish</u> the king's unfair tax on imports.

(A) event with which the colonists either intended to challenge or abolish

(B) event, about which either the colonists intended to challenge or to abolish

(C) event that had the intention of either challenging or to abolish

(D) event, the use of which was either a challenge or it abolished

(E) event that the colonists used to challenge or abolish

11. <u>Should a college application essay be required,</u> one ought to set aside a large block of time and avoid writing it at the last minute.

   (A) Should a college application essay be required
   (B) Should you need to write a college application essay
   (C) If you need to write a college application essay
   (D) In any event that one needs to write a college application essay
   (E) If a college application essay is necessary for anyone to write

12. <u>Waste products from cutting lumber, such as wood chips and sawdust, are some of the ingredients</u> of waferboard panels used in residential construction.

   (A) Waste products from cutting lumber, such as wood chips and sawdust, are some of the ingredients
   (B) Waste products from cutting lumber, such as wood chips and sawdust, is some of the ingredients
   (C) Waste products from cutting lumber, such as wood chips and sawdust, makes one of the ingredients
   (D) Lumber cutting waste products, which include wood chips and sawdust, making them the ingredients
   (E) Lumber cutting waste products that includes not only wood chips but sawdust is an ingredient of

13. <u>If you compare the number of NY Yankee pennants with the Boston Red Sox, you'll see that the Yankees</u> are traditional winners.

   (A) If you compare the number of NY Yankee pennants with the Boston Red Sox, you'll see that the Yankees
   (B) Comparing the number of NY Yankee pennants and the Boston Red Sox, you'll see that the Yankees
   (C) In comparison with the Boston Red Sox, the number of NY Yankee pennants shows that the Yankees
   (D) Making a comparison between the number of NY Yankee pennants with the Boston Red Sox pennants show that the Yankees
   (E) A comparison of the number of NY Yankee pennants and Boston Red Sox pennants shows that the Yankees

14. <u>Many countries punish citizens who speak out against the government, keeping the U.N. Commission on Human Rights very busy, mostly using torture and imprisonment.</u>

   (A) Many countries punish citizens who speak out against the government, keeping the U.N. Commission on Human Rights very busy, mostly using torture and imprisonment
   (B) Many countries, punishing citizens mostly using torture and imprisonment for speaking out against the government, keep the U.N. Commission on Human Rights very busy
   (C) In many countries punishing citizens who speak out against the government, U.N. Commission on Human Rights is kept very busy, mostly using torture and imprisonment
   (D) Using torture and imprisonment, many countries punish citizens who speak out against the government, a situation that keeps the U.N. Commission on Human Rights very busy
   (E) Punishing citizens who speak out against the government using torture and imprisonment in many countries, the U.N. Commission on Human Rights is kept very busy

End of Section 3.
Do not return to Sections 1 or 2.

END OF WRITING TEST.

ANSWER KEY

Guide for Scoring Your Essay

Using this guide, rate yourself in each of these six categories. Enter your scores in the spaces provided, and calculate the average of the six ratings to determine your final score.

On the SAT itself, two readers will score your essay on a scale of 6 (high) to 1 (low), or *zero* if you fail to write on the assigned topic. The score will be reported to you as the sum of the two ratings, from 12 to 0.

Remember that SAT essays are judged in relation to other essays written on the same topic. Therefore, this scoring guide may not yield a totally accurate prediction of the score you can expect on the exam. Because it is difficult to read your own essay with total objectivity, you might improve the validity of your score by getting a second opinion about your essay from an informed friend or a teacher.

Overall Impression

6   Consistently outstanding in clarity and competence; very insightful; few, if any, errors

5   Reasonably consistent in clarity and competence; occasional errors or lapses in quality; contains some insight

4   Adequate competence; some lapses in quality; fairly clear and with evidence of insight

3   Generally inadequate but demonstrates potential competence; contains some confusing aspects

2   Seriously limited; significant weaknesses in quality; generally unclear or incoherent

1   Demonstrates fundamental incompetence; contains serious flaws; significantly undeveloped or confusing

Score ☐

Development of Point of View

6   Fully developed with clear and appropriate supporting material; demonstrates high level of critical thinking

5   Generally well developed with appropriate examples, reasons, and other evidence to support a main idea; demonstrates strong critical thinking

4   Partly develops a main idea with relatively appropriate examples and reasons; shows some evidence of critical thinking

3   Weak development of main idea and little evidence of critical thinking; barely appropriate examples or other supporting material

2   Lacks a focus on a main idea; weak critical thinking; inappropriate or insufficient evidence

1   Fails to articulate a viable point of view; provides virtually no evidence of understanding the prompt

Score ☐

Organization of Ideas

6   Extremely well organized and focused on a main idea; supporting evidence presented in an effective, logical sequence

5   Generally well organized and reasonably focused on a main idea; mostly coherent and logical presentation of supporting material

4   Reasonably organized; shows some evidence of thoughtful sequence and progression of ideas

3   Limited organization and vague focus on main idea; contains some confusion in the sequence of ideas

2   Barely recognizable organization; little coherence; serious problems with sequence of ideas

1   No discernable organization; incoherent sequence of ideas

Score ☐

Language and Word Choice

6   Highly effective and skillful use of language; varied, appropriate, and accurate vocabulary

5   Demonstrates competence in use of language; appropriate and correct vocabulary

4   Adequate but inconsistent use of effective language; conventional but mostly correct use of vocabulary

3   Some minor errors in expression; generally weak or limited vocabulary; occasionally inappropriate word choice

2   Frequent errors in expression; very limited vocabulary; incorrect word choice interferes with meaning

1   Seriously deficient in use of language; meaning obscured by word choice

Score ☐

Sentence Structure

6   Varied and engaging sentence structure

5   Sufficiently varied sentence structure

4   Some sentence variation

3   Little sentence variation; minor sentence errors

2   Frequent sentence errors

1   Severe sentence errors; meaning obscured

Score ☐

Grammar, Usage, and Mechanics

6	Virtually or entirely error-free
5	Contains some minor errors
4	Some minor errors; one or two major errors
3	Accumulated minor and major errors
2	Contains frequent major errors that interfere with meaning
1	Contains severe errors that obscure meaning

Score ☐

<u>For rating yourself</u>

Total of six scores _____

Divide total by 6 to get score: _____ (A)
(Round to the nearest whole number.)

<u>For a second opinion</u>

Total of six scores _____

Divide total by 6 to get score: _____ (B)
(Round to the nearest whole number.)

(A) + (B) = ESSAY SUBSCORE _____
_____ (0–12)

ANSWERS TO MULTIPLE-CHOICE QUESTIONS

Section 2

1. C	11. E	21. B	31. C
2. E	12. B	22. E	32. C
3. E	13. B	23. B	33. C
4. D	14. A	24. C	34. A
5. C	15. C	25. D	35. B
6. B	16. E	26. E	
7. A	17. A	27. B	
8. C	18. C	28. D	
9. A	19. C	29. B	
10. B	20. D	30. B	

Section 3

1. D	11. A
2. C	12. A
3. B	13. E
4. D	14. D
5. C	
6. B	
7. A	
8. D	
9. E	
10. E	

PERFORMANCE EVALUATION CHART

I. Self-Rating Chart
   Section 2
   Improving Sentences, questions 1–11   Number correct _____

   Identifying Sentence Errors, questions 12–29   Number correct _____

   Improving Paragraphs, questions 30–35   Number correct _____

   Section 3
   Improving Sentences, questions 1–14   Number correct _____

                                                        Subtotal _____ (A)

Wrong answers (Do not count unanswered questions)
   Section 2   Number wrong _____

   Section 3   Number wrong _____

                                                        Subtotal _____ (B)

Subtract ¼ point (0.25) from (B) for each wrong answer   _____ (C)

   (A) minus (C) = _____ (D)

Round (D) to the nearest whole number for your MULTIPLE-CHOICE RAW SCORE   _____

ESSAY SUBSCORE   _____

CONVERSION TABLE

This table will give you an approximation of what your score would be if this practice test had been an actual SAT Writing Test. The essay counts for roughly 30% of the final score; the multiple-choice questions, for roughly 70%.

For example, if your Multiple-Choice Raw Score was 35 and your Essay Subscore was 6, the table indicates that your final score on the test would be approximately halfway between 500 and 710, or 600.

Multiple-Choice Raw Score	Essay Subscore						
	0	2	4	6	8	10	12
40–49	520–690	530–720	550–740	580–770	620–800	650–800	680–800
30–39	430–630	450–660	470–680	500–710	530–740	560–770	590–800
20–29	360–540	370–570	390–590	420–620	460–650	490–690	520–710
10–19	270–460	280–490	300–510	330–540	370–580	400–610	430–630
0–9	200–380	200–410	210–430	240–450	270–490	300–520	330–560
−12−−1	200–280	200–310	200–330	200–350	240–390	270–420	300–450

ANSWER EXPLANATIONS

Note: Although many choices contain multiple errors, only a single error is listed for each incorrect answer.

SECTION 2—IMPROVING SENTENCES

1. **C** A. Sentence shift. By switching the grammatical subject *you* in the first clause to *letters* in the second, the sentence shifts from the active to the passive voice.
   B. Mixed construction. The first clause begins in the second person (*you*). The second clause eliminates the pronoun and becomes impersonal.
   D. Pronoun reference. The pronoun in *his letters* lacks a specific referent.
   E. Pronoun reference. The pronoun his refers to *person* instead of to *Jefferson*.

2. **E** A. Pronoun reference. The pronoun *them* doesn't refer to a specific plural noun or other pronoun.
   B. Faulty parallelism. The adjective *noisiest* and the phrase *more tranquil than any* should be in parallel form. Use *the most tranquil*.
   C. Comma splice. Commas may not be used to separate two independent clauses.
   D. Pronoun reference. The pronoun *them* doesn't refer to a specific plural noun or other pronoun.

3. **E** A. Misplaced modifier. The phrase *most important city* should modify *New York* instead of *tourists*.
   B. Misplaced modifier. The phrase *most important city* should modify *New York* instead of *millions*.
   C. Misplaced modifier. The phrase *most important city* should modify *New York* instead of *year*.
   D. Misplaced modifier. The phrase *most important city* should modify *New York* instead of *tourists*.

4. **D** A. Pronoun reference. The pronoun *his* refers to *reader* instead of to *Thoreau*.
   B. Pronoun reference. The pronoun *they* lacks an antecedent.
   C. Dangling participle. The phrase *Reading Thoreau's <u>Walden</u>* should modify *reader* instead of *plenty*.
   E. Sentence fragment. The construction is a subordinate clause, not a complete sentence.

5. **C** A. Faulty parallelism. Coordinate elements in a sentence should be in parallel form. The verb phrase *transported on its roads* is not parallel to *to bury it inside its borders*
   B. Idiom error. The construction *neither . . . or* is not standard English. Use *neither . . . nor.*
   D. Redundancy. The phrases *not only* and *but in addition also* are redundant.
   E. Shift in verb tense. The sentence, cast in the present tense, shifts to the past perfect.

6. **B**   A. Shift in verb tense. The sentence, cast in the past tense, shifts to the present perfect.
C. Subject–verb agreement. The subject *coming* is singular. The verb *were* is plural. Use *was*.
D. Idiom error. The phrase *not a coming* is not standard English.
E. Idiom error. The phrase *not immediate successors* is not standard English.

7. **A**   B. Sentence fragment. The grammatical subject (*editorials*) lacks a verb. The verb *argue* cannot be the verb because it is in a subordinate clause.
C. Sentence fragment. The grammatical subject (*decision*) lacks a verb. The verb *opposed* cannot be the verb because it is in a clause whose sole function is to modify a noun.
D. Sentence fragment. The construction lacks a main verb. The *–ing* form of a verb (*being*) may not be used as the main verb without a helping verb, as in *is being*.
E. Sentence fragment. The grammatical subject (*arguments*) lacks a verb. The verb *appeared* cannot be the verb because it is in a subordinate clause.

8. **C**   A. Comma splice. A comma may not be used to separate two independent clauses.
B. Comma splice. A comma may not be used to separate two independent clauses.
D. Tense shift. The sentence, cast in the past tense, shifts to the present.
E. Comma splice. A comma may not be used to separate two independent clauses.

9. **A**   B. Shift in verb tense. The sentence, cast in present perfect tense (*has grown*), shifts to the past tense (*attracted*).
C. Faulty comparison. The noun *number* is being compared to *Columbia*, an illogical comparison.
D. Awkwardness. The construction is not in standard English.
E. Sentence fragment. The construction lacks a main verb.

10. **B**   A. Faulty subordination. The conjunction *while* fails to create a logical relationship between the two clauses in the sentence.
C. Mixed construction. The verb *made* has no logical relationship with the subject of the sentence.
D. Faulty subordination. The conjunction *although* fails to create a logical relationship between the two clauses in the sentence.
E. Mixed construction. The verb *makes* has no logical relationship with the subject of the sentence.

11. **E**   A. Pronoun reference. The pronoun *they* fails to refer to a specific noun or other pronoun.
B. Faulty parallelism. Coordinate elements in a sentence should be in parallel form. The phrase *at once frustrating* is not parallel to *although it is beautifully designed*.
C. Faulty parallelism. Coordinate elements in a sentence should be in parallel form. The phrase *at once frustrating* is not parallel to *yet it is beautiful in its design*.
D. Faulty parallelism. Coordinate elements in a sentence should be in parallel form. The phrase *at once frustrating* is not parallel to *while being designed so beautifully*.

SECTION 2—IDENTIFYING SENTENCE ERRORS

12. **B**   Subject–verb agreement. The subject *plight* is singular. The verb *are* is plural. Use *is*.

13. **B**.   Diction error. An adverb is needed to modify the verb *played*. Use *loudly*.

14. **A**   Pronoun choice. Standard usage requires the use of *who* rather than *which* to refer to people.

15. **C** Faulty parallelism. Coordinate elements in a sentence should be in parallel form. *Water sports* is not parallel to *hiking . . . climbing . . . and catching*.

16. **E** No error.

17. **A.** Idiom error. Use *in which* instead of *where*.

18. **C.** Subject–verb agreement. The compound subject *career . . . and . . . murder* requires a plural verb. Use *prove*.

19. **C** Verb tense. The sentence is cast in the present tense. The verb *said* is in the past tense. Use *says*.

20. **D** Idiom error. In context, the phrase *plus being* may not be used in place of *but is also*. In addition, *being* may not be used as a main verb without a helping verb, as in *is being*.

21. **B** Shift in pronoun person. The second person pronoun (*you*) improperly switches to the impersonal pronoun (*one*).

22. **E** No error.

23. **B** Idiom error. In standard usage, the phrase is *concur with*.

24. **C** Noun–verb agreement. Nouns in a series require plural verbs. Use *invite*.

25. **D** Faulty comparison. *Score* cannot be compared to *Charles*. Use *Charles's* or *Charles's score*.

26. **E** No error.

27. **B** Shift in number. Because the noun *jocks* is plural, *athlete* should also be plural. Use *athletes*.

28. **D** Idiom error. In standard English, the objects of the preposition *between* should be joined by *and* instead of *or*.

29. **B** Pronoun choice. Pronouns in the objective case are used to refer to persons who receive an action. In this sentence, use "the alarm frightened . . . *her*."

SECTION 2—IMPROVING PARAGRAPHS

30. **B** A. Not a good choice because the purpose of the sentence is to cite one of the reasons used to justify keeping animals in zoos.
B. The phrase is used to introduce an illustration of an idea stated in the previous sentence. It is the best answer.
C. In context, the phrase makes no sense.
D. Not a good choice because it suggests that sentence 2 will rephrase an idea stated in sentence 1.
E. In context, the phrase is irrelevant.

31. **C**   A. In context, *disagree* is a poor word choice. If anything, the writer *disapproves* of the parents' actions described in sentence 3.
B. This revision makes the plural subject of the sentence (*reasons*) disagree with the singular verb *is*, found in the contraction *There's*.
C. This choice eliminates the comma splice, retains the basic meaning of the sentence, and subordinates one idea to another. It is the best answer.
D. Because the sentence contains a comma splice, this revision fails to improve the sentence appreciably.
E. Because the sentence contains a comma splice, this revision fails to improve the sentence appreciably.

32. **C**   A. This is a sentence fragment. It lacks a main verb.
B. This sentence contradicts the idea stated in sentence 5.
C. This choice develops the point stated in sentence 5. It is the best answer.
D. This choice is irrelevant to the idea in sentence 5.
E. This sentence is written in a hostile and inappropriate tone.

33. **C**   A. This is not a good answer because it contains information that readers already know, and highly charged language is not a good vehicle for passing along information.
B. This is unrelated to the words in question.
C. This is the best answer because the words are meant to shock and disturb the reader.
D. This suggests that the author is trying to be objective, but the words in question are anything but objective.
E. This describes the purpose of the whole essay, not the particular words in question.

34. **A**   A. This introduces the main idea of the paragraph. It is the best answer.
B. Because this choice raises an issue not mentioned in the remainder of the paragraph, it is not a good topic sentence.
C. This contains an idea not discussed in the paragraph, which focuses on how animals behave in captivity, not on living conditions at the zoo.
D. This contains a dangling modifier. The phrase *Living in the zoo* should modify *animals* instead of *conditions*.
E. This contains a frivolous cliché that is inconsistent with the tone of the essay.

35. **B**   A. Although grammatical, this choice reverses the cause-effect relationship stated by the original sentences.
B. This accurately and economically conveys the ideas of the original sentences.
C. Lacking a main verb, this choice is a sentence fragment. The *–ing* forms of verbs (*growing, placing, being*) may not be used as the main verb without a helping verb, as in *was growing, is placing*, and so on.
D. This is grammatically correct but stylistically awkward because the subject *They* is too far removed from the verb *would . . . survive*.
E. This is virtually meaningless because the cause-effect relationship has been reversed.

SECTION 3—IMPROVING SENTENCES

1. **D**   A. Dangling participle. The phrase that begins *Having a mother* should modify *Rosie* instead of the *violin and the piano*.
   B. Dangling participle. The phrase that begins *Having a mother* should modify *Rosie* instead of *violin and piano*.
   C. Dangling participle. The phrase that begins *Having a mother* should modify *Rosie* instead of *two instruments*.
   E. Awkwardness. The phrase *learned the playing of* is awkwardly expressed.

2. **C**   A Sentence fragment. The *–ing* form of a verb (*causing*) may not be used as the main verb or a clause or sentence without a helping verb, as in *is causing, will be causing*, and so on.
   B. Same as A.
   D. Mixed construction. The second clause is not grammatically related to the first clause.
   E. Idiom error. The phrase *to become ordinarily* is not standard English.

3. **B**   A. Tense shift. The sentence, cast in the present tense (*does not have*), shifts to the future conditional tense (*would have to be*).
   C. Pronoun reference. The pronoun *it* does not refer to any specific noun or other pronoun.
   D. Sentence fragment. The second clause of the compound sentence lacks a main verb. The *–ing* form of a verb (*being*) may not be used as the main verb without a helping verb (*is being, was being*, etc.).
   E. Comma splice. A comma may not be used to separate two independent clauses.

4. **D**   A. Sentence fragment. The construction beginning with *this*, if meant to be a complete sentence, lacks a main verb. The *–ing* form of a verb (*causing*) may not be used as the main verb without a helping verb (*is causing, will be causing*, etc.).
   B. Tense shift. The sentence, cast in the present perfect tense (*has been*) shifts to the past tense.
   C. Faulty verb form. The *–ing* form of a verb (*causing*) may not be used as the main verb without a helping verb (*is causing, will be causing*, etc.).
   E. Pronoun reference. The pronoun *it* fails to refer to a specific noun or other pronoun.

5. **C**   A. Pronoun reference. The pronoun *them* fails to refer to any specific noun or other pronoun.
   B. Comma splice. A comma may not be used to separate two independent clauses.
   D. Pronoun reference. The pronoun *them* fails to refer to any specific noun or other pronoun.
   E. Incomplete construction. The construction lacks a noun to go with the verb *was*.

6. **B**   A. Idiom. The phrase *of which* is nonstandard usage when referring to a singular noun.
   C. Awkwardness. The construction *are of appeal* is awkwardly worded.
   D. Sentence fragment. The construction beginning with *the appeal of* lacks a verb.
   E. Comma splice. A comma may not be used to separate two independent clauses.

7. **A**   B. Faulty comparison. Illogically, *mathematics* is compared to *American students*.
   C. Faulty parallelism. Coordinate elements in a comparison must be in parallel form.
   D. Wordiness. Although grammatically correct, the construction is wordy.
   E. Mixed construction. The construction is not grammatically related to the earlier part of the sentence.

8. **D**   A. Pronoun reference. The pronoun *they* refers to *immigrants* when it is meant to refer to *restrictions*.
B. Pronoun reference. The pronoun *they* refers to *immigrants* when it is meant to refer to *restrictions*.
C. Incomplete construction. The construction lacks a noun to go with the verb *have . . . multiplied*.
E. Mixed construction. The phrase *since multiplied* has no grammatical connection with the previous part of the sentence.

9. **E**   A. Faulty coordination. To make the sentence more effective, the second clause, because it contains information of secondary importance, should be subordinated to the first clause.
B. Misplaced modifier. *Only* should modify *famous composers . . .* instead of *Russian*.
C. Sentence fragment. The construction lacks a main verb.
D. Sentence fragment. The construction lacks a main verb.

10. **E**   A. Misplaced modifier. Move *either* to follow *intended*. Then add *to* before *abolish*.
B. Idiom. In context, the phrase *about which* is not standard English.
C. Parallelism error. Coordinate elements must be in parallel form. *Challenging* is not in the same form as *to abolish*. Use *or abolishing*.
D. Parallelism error. Coordinate elements must be in parallel form. *A challenge* is not in the same form as *or it abolished*. Use *an attempt to abolish*.

11. **A**   B. Pronoun shift. Because the sentence is cast with the impersonal pronoun (*one*), the second person pronoun *you* should not be used.
C. Pronoun shift. Because the sentence is cast with the impersonal pronoun (*one*), the second person pronoun *you* should not be used.
D. Idiom error. The standard idiom is *in the event*.
E. Awkwardness. The construction *necessary for anyone to write* is clumsily worded.

12. **A**   B. Subject–verb agreement. *Products* is plural; *is* is singular.
C. Subject–verb agreement. *Products* is plural; *makes* is singular.
D. Sentence fragment. The construction lacks a main verb.
E. Noun–verb agreement. *Products* is plural; *includes* is singular.

13. **E**   A. Faulty comparison. The *number of . . . pennants* is being compared to the *Boston Red Sox*, an illogical comparison.
B. Faulty comparison. The *number of . . . pennants* is being compared to the *Boston Red Sox*, an illogical comparison.
C. Faulty comparison. The *Boston Red Sox* team is being compared to the *number of Yankee pennants,* an illogical comparison.
D. Subject–verb agreement. The subject *Making* is singular; the verb *show* is plural.

14. **D**   A. Misplaced modifier. The phrase that begins *mostly using torture* should modify *countries*, not *U.N. Commission*.
B. Misplaced modifier. The phrase that begins *mostly using torture* should modify *countries*, not *citizens*.
C. Dangling modifier. The construction beginning *Punishing citizens* should modify *countries*, not *U.N. Commission*.
E. Dangling modifier. The construction beginning *Punishing citizens* should modify *countries*, not *U.N. Commission*.

INDEX